Elements of Language

Introductory Course

HOLT
Literacy
HANDBOOK

Lee Odell • Richard Vacca • Renée Hobbs • Judith L. Irvin

HOLT, RINEHART AND WINSTON
A Harcourt Education Company

Orlando • Austin • New York • San Diego • Toronto • London

STAFF CREDITS

EDITORIAL

Executive Editor
Kristine E. Marshall

Program Editor
Kathryn Rogers

Project Editors
Gail Coupland
Randy Dickson
Ann Michelle Gibson

Copyediting
Michael Neibergall, *Copyediting Manager;* Mary Malone, *Copyediting Supervisor;* Elizabeth Dickson, *Senior Copyeditor;* Christine Altgelt, Emily Force, Julia Thomas Hu, *Copyeditors*

Project Administration
Marie Price, *Managing Editor;* Christine Degollado, Janet Jenkins, *Editorial Coordinators*

DESIGN

Book Design
Joe Melomo, *Design Director*

Image Acquisitions
Curtis Riker, *Director;* Jeannie Taylor, *Photo Research Supervisor;* Sam Dudgeon, *Senior Staff Photographer;* Victoria Smith, *Staff Photographer*

Media Design
Richard Metzger, *Design Director*

Cover Design
Betty Mintz

EDITORIAL PERMISSIONS
Susan Lowrance

PRODUCTION
Carol Trammel, *Production Manager;* Belinda Barbosa Lopez, Michael Roche, *Senior Production Coordinators*

MANUFACTURING
Shirley Cantrell, *Senior Manufacturing Supervisor;* Mark McDonald, *Inventory Analyst;* Amy Borseth, *Manufacturing Coordinator*

Copyright © 2004 by Holt, Rinehart and Winston

All rights reserved. No part of this publication may be reproduced or transmitted in any form or by any means, electronic or mechanical, including photocopy, recording, or any information storage and retrieval system, without permission in writing from the publisher.

Requests for permission to make copies of any part of the work should be mailed to the following address: Permissions Department, Holt, Rinehart and Winston, 10801 N. MoPac Expressway, Building 3, Austin, Texas 78759.

Acknowledgments and other credits appear on pages 369–370, which are extensions of the copyright page.

Printed in the United States of America

ISBN 0-03-035306-8

1 2 3 4 5   048   05 04 03

PROGRAM AUTHORS

▶ **LEE ODELL** helped establish the pedagogical framework for the composition strand of the *Elements of Language Holt Literacy Handbook*. In addition, he guided the development of the scope and sequence and pedagogical design of the Writing Workshops. Dr. Odell is Professor of Composition Theory and Research and, since 1996, Director of the Writing Program at Rensselaer Polytechnic Institute. He began his career teaching English in middle and high schools. More recently he has worked with teachers in grades K–12 to establish a program that involves students from all disciplines in writing across the curriculum and for communities outside their classrooms. Dr. Odell's most recent book (with Charles R. Cooper) is *Evaluating Writing: The Role of Teachers' Knowledge about Text, Learning, and Culture* (1999). He is Past Chair of the Conference on College Composition and Communication and of NCTE's Assembly for Research.

▶ **RICHARD VACCA** helped establish the conceptual basis for the reading strand of the *Elements of Language Holt Literacy Handbook*. In addition, he guided the development of the pedagogical design and the scope and sequence of skills in the Reading Workshops. Dr. Vacca is Professor of Education at Kent State University. He recently completed a term as the forty-second President of the International Reading Association. Originally a middle school and high school teacher, Dr. Vacca served as the project director of the Cleveland Writing Demonstration Project for several years. He is the co-author of *Content Area Reading; Reading and Learning to Read;* and articles and chapters related to adolescents' literacy development. In 1989, Dr. Vacca received the College Reading Association's A. B. Herr Award for Outstanding Contributions to Reading Education. Currently, he is co-chair of the IRA's Commission on Adolescent Literacy.

▶ **RENÉE HOBBS** helped develop the theoretical framework for the viewing and representing strand of the *Elements of Language Holt Literacy Handbook*. She guided the development of the scope and sequence; served as the authority on terminology, definitions, and pedagogy; and directed the planning for the video series. Dr. Hobbs is Associate Professor of Communication at Babson College in Wellesley, Massachusetts, and Director of the Media Literacy Project. Active in the field of media education, Dr. Hobbs has served as Director of the Institute on Media Education, Harvard Graduate School of Education; Director of the "Know TV" Project, Discovery Networks and Time Warner Cable; and Board Member, The New York Times Newspaper in Education Program. She works actively in staff development in school districts nationwide. Dr. Hobbs has contributed articles and chapters on media, technology, and education to many publications.

▶ **JUDITH L. IRVIN** also helped establish the conceptual basis for the reading strand of the *Elements of Language Holt Literacy Handbook*. Dr. Irvin taught middle school for several years before pursuing graduate studies in Reading-Language Arts. She now teaches courses in curriculum, middle school education, and educational leadership at Florida State University. She chaired the Research Committee of the National Middle School Association and was the editor of *Research in Middle Level Education Quarterly* for six years. Dr. Irvin writes a column, "What Research Says to the Middle Level Practitioner," for the *Middle School Journal*. Her many publications include *What Research Says to the Middle Level Practitioner* and *Reading and the Middle School Student: Strategies to Enhance Literacy*.

PROGRAM CONSULTANTS

The program consultants reviewed instructional materials to ensure consistency with current research, classroom appropriateness, and alignment with curriculum guidelines.

Ann Bagley
Senior Administrator for Secondary English
Wake County Public Schools
Raleigh, North Carolina

Vicki R. Brown
Professor of Education, Grambling State University
Principal, Grambling Middle School
Grambling, Louisiana

Max Hutto
Supervisor of Middle School Language Arts
Hillsborough County Schools
Tampa, Florida

Beth Johnson
Supervisor of Language Arts
Polk District Schools
Bartow, Florida

Kathleen Jongsma
Associate Professor, Department of Education Chair
Texas Lutheran University
Seguin, Texas

Kaye Price-Hawkins
Language Arts Consultant
Abilene, Texas

Lanny van Allen
Consultant, Texas Center for Reading and Language Arts
The University of Texas at Austin
Austin, Texas

CRITICAL REVIEWERS

The critical reviewers read and evaluated pre-publication materials for this book.

Judy Champney
Science Hill High School
Johnson City, Tennessee

Mary M. Goodson
Pershing Middle School
Houston, Texas

Katherine Grace
Labay Junior High School
Houston, Texas

Dorothy Harrington
Marshall Middle School
Beaumont, Texas

Gail Hayes
South Florence High School
Florence, South Carolina

Nancy Levi
Oakland High School
Murfreesboro, Tennessee

Mary Alice Madden
Lathrop Intermediate School
Santa Ana, California

Mary Ann Norwood
Ligon Middle School
Raleigh, North Carolina

LeeAnn W. Packer
Adele C. Young Intermediate School
Brigham City, Utah

Elizabeth G. Pope
Memorial Middle School
Sioux Falls, South Dakota

Judith Shane
Carr Intermediate School
Santa Ana, California

Belinda Small
Davidson Middle School
Crestview, Florida

Betty Templeton
Riverside High School
Greer, South Carolina

Michael J. Wallpe
Metropolitan School District
Indianapolis, Indiana

Janice Woo
Union Middle School
San Jose, California

TEACHER/STUDENT CONTRIBUTORS

The following teachers and students worked with HRW's editorial staff to provide models of student writing for the book.

Teachers

Jane Anderson
Garfield Elementary School
Sand Springs, Oklahoma

Peter J. Caron
Cumberland Middle School
Cumberland, Rhode Island

Dorothy Harrington
Marshall Middle School
Beaumont, Texas

Debra Hester
Richbourg Middle School
Crestview, Florida

Dana Humphrey
North Middle School
O'Fallon, Missouri

Students

Natalie Banta and Amy Tidwell
Olympus Junior High School
Salt Lake City, Utah

Diana DeGarmo
Garfield Elementary School
Sand Springs, Oklahoma

Tyler Duckworth
Liberty Middle School
Morganton, North Carolina

Matthew Hester
Richbourg Middle School
Crestview, Florida

Genna Offerman
Marshall Middle School
Beaumont, Texas

Anthony C. Rodrigues
Cumberland Middle School
Cumberland, Rhode Island

Stephanie Thompson
North Middle School
O'Fallon, Missouri

FIELD TEST PARTICIPANTS

The following teachers participated in the pre-publication field test or review of prototype materials for the *Elements of Language* series.

Nadene Adams
Robert Gray Middle School
Portland, Oregon

Carol Alves
Apopka High School
Apopka, Florida

Susan Atkinson
O. P. Norman Junior High School
Kaufman, Texas

Sheryl L. Babione
Fremont Ross High School
Fremont, Ohio

Jane Baker
Elkins High School
Missouri City, Texas

Martha Barnard
Scarborough High School
Houston, Texas

Jennifer S. Barr
James Bowie High School
Austin, Texas

Leslie Benefield
Reed Middle School
Duncanville, Texas

Gina Birdsall
Irving High School
Irving, Texas

Sara J. Brennan
Murchison Middle School
Austin, Texas

Janelle Brinck
Leander Middle School
Leander, Texas

Geraldine K. Brooks
William B. Travis High School
Austin, Texas

Peter J. Caron
Cumberland Middle School
Cumberland, Rhode Island

Patty Cave
O. P. Norman Junior High School
Kaufman, Texas

Mary Cathyrne Coe
Pocatello High School
Pocatello, Idaho

Continued

Geri-Lee DeGennaro
Tarpon Springs High School
Tarpon Springs, Florida

Karen Dendy
Stephen F. Austin Middle School
Irving, Texas

Dianne Franz
Tarpon Springs Middle School
Tarpon Springs, Florida

Doris F. Frazier
East Millbrook Magnet Middle School
Raleigh, North Carolina

Shayne G. Goodrum
C. E. Jordan High School
Durham, North Carolina

Bonnie L. Hall
St. Ann School
Lansing, Illinois

Doris Ann Hall
Forest Meadow Junior High School
Dallas, Texas

James M. Harris
Mayfield High School
Mayfield Village, Ohio

Lynne Hoover
Fremont Ross High School
Fremont, Ohio

Patricia A. Humphreys
James Bowie High School
Austin, Texas

Jennifer L. Jones
Oliver Wendell Holmes Middle School
Dallas, Texas

Kathryn R. Jones
Murchison Middle School
Austin, Texas

Bonnie Just
Narbonne High School
Harbor City, California

Vincent Kimball
Patterson High School #405
Baltimore, Maryland

Nancy C. Long
MacArthur High School
Houston, Texas

Carol M. Mackey
Ft. Lauderdale Christian School
Ft. Lauderdale, Florida

Jan Jennings McCown
Johnston High School
Austin, Texas

Alice Kelly McCurdy
Rusk Middle School
Dallas, Texas

Elizabeth Morris
Northshore High School
Slidell, Louisiana

Victoria Reis
Western High School
Ft. Lauderdale, Florida

Dean Richardson
Scarborough High School
Houston, Texas

Susan M. Rogers
Freedom High School
Morganton, North Carolina

Sammy Rusk
North Mesquite High School
Mesquite, Texas

Carole B. San Miguel
James Bowie High School
Austin, Texas

Jane Saunders
William B. Travis High School
Austin, Texas

Gina Sawyer
Reed Middle School
Duncanville, Texas

Laura R. Schauermann
MacArthur High School
Houston, Texas

Stephen Shearer
MacArthur High School
Houston, Texas

Elizabeth Curry Smith
Tarpon Springs High School
Tarpon Springs, Florida

Jeannette M. Spain
Stephen F. Austin High School
Sugar Land, Texas

Carrie Speer
Northshore High School
Slidell, Louisiana

Trina Steffes
MacArthur High School
Houston, Texas

Andrea G. Freirich Stewart
Freedom High School
Morganton, North Carolina

Diana O. Torres
Johnston High School
Austin, Texas

Jan Voorhees
Whitesboro High School
Marcy, New York

Ann E. Walsh
Bedichek Middle School
Austin, Texas

Mary Jane Warden
Onahan School
Chicago, Illinois

Beth Westbrook
Covington Middle School
Austin, Texas

Char-Lene Wilkins
Morenci Area High School
Morenci, Michigan

CONTENTS IN BRIEF

PART 1 **Communications** 1
      Taking Tests: Strategies and Practice 2
  1 **Narration/Description:** Sharing Our Stories 16
  2 **Exposition:** Reporting the News 48
  3 **Exposition:** Explaining How 84
  4 **Exposition:** Comparing and Contrasting 118
  5 **Exposition:** Responding to a Novel 152
  6 **Exposition:** Sharing Your Research 186
  7 **Persuasion:** Making a Difference 226

PART 2 **Quick Reference Handbook** 261
    The Dictionary 262
    Document Design 264
    The History of English 272
    The Library/Media Center 276
    Reading and Vocabulary 286
    Speaking and Listening 301
    Studying and Test Taking 315
    Viewing and Representing 325
    Writing 337

CONTENTS

PART 1 **Communications** 1

Taking Tests: Strategies and Practice 2
Taking Reading Tests 3
Taking Writing Tests 11

CHAPTER 1

Sharing Our Stories 16

Narration/Description

Connecting Reading and Writing 17

READING WORKSHOP: *An Autobiographical Incident* 18
Preparing to Read 18
READING SKILL ■ Making Inferences: Forming Generalizations
READING FOCUS ■ Chronological Order

Reading Selection: from *Rosa Parks: My Story,* Rosa Parks
with Jim Haskins 19
Vocabulary Mini-Lesson: *Context Clues* 25
Test-Taking Mini-Lesson: *Making Inferences* 26

WRITING WORKSHOP: *A Life Experience* 27
Prewriting 27
Critical-Thinking Mini-Lesson: *Arranging Ideas*

Writing 32
Framework for an Autobiographical Incident
A Writer's Model: "A Night to Remember" 33
A Student's Model: "In the Net," Anthony C. Rodrigues 35

Revising 36
First Reading: *Content and Organization*
Second Reading: *Style*
   Focus on Word Choice: *Exact Verbs*

Publishing 39
Proofreading: Grammar Link—*Capitalizing Proper Nouns*
Test-Taking Mini-Lesson: *Writing Description for Tests* 41
Connections to Literature: *Writing a Narrative Poem* 42

Focus on Speaking and Listening: *Telling a Story* 45

Choices: *Careers • Speech • Drama • Writing • Technology* ... 47

CHAPTER 2

Reporting the News 48

Connecting Reading and Writing 49

Informational Text
Exposition

READING WORKSHOP: *A Newspaper Article* 50
Preparing to Read 50
READING SKILL ■ Main Idea
READING FOCUS ■ Inverted Pyramid Structure

Reading Selection: "Whale Watch: Kids Use Internet to Track Progress of Newly Freed J. J.," Lisa Richardson from the *Los Angeles Times; Orange County Edition* 51
Vocabulary Mini-Lesson: *Multiple-Meaning Words* 56
Test-Taking Mini-Lesson: *Answering Main Idea Questions* 57

WRITING WORKSHOP: *A Newspaper Article* 58
Prewriting 58
Critical-Thinking Mini-Lesson: *Analyzing Cause and Effect*

Writing 66
Framework for a News Article
A Writer's Model: "Principal Approves Longer Passing Period" 67
A Student's Model: "Mr. Sagers Moves to Cyprus High," Natalie Banta and Amy Tidwell 68

Revising 69
First Reading: *Content and Organization*
Second Reading: *Style*
    Focus on Sentences: *Varying Sentences*

Publishing 72
Proofreading: Grammar Link—*Correcting Run-on Sentences*
Connections to Life: *Writing a Newspaper's Advice Column* 74

Focus on Viewing and Representing
Producing a Newspaper 76

Focus on Viewing and Representing
Producing a TV News Segment 79

Choices: *Careers • Crossing the Curriculum: Art, Science, Writing* 83

ix

CHAPTER 3

Informational Text
Exposition

Explaining How 84

Connecting Reading and Writing 85

READING WORKSHOP: *A "How-to" Article* 86
Preparing to Read 86
READING SKILL ■ Making Predictions
READING FOCUS ■ Forming Mental Images

Reading Selection: "Making a Flying Fish," Paula Morrow
from *Faces: Happy Holidays* 89
Vocabulary Mini-Lesson: *Compound Words* 92
Test-Taking Mini-Lesson: *Making Predictions* 93

WRITING WORKSHOP: *A "How-to" Paper* 94
Prewriting 94
Writing Mini-Lesson: *Elaboration—Using Specific Language*

Writing 98
Framework for a "How-to" Paper
A Writer's Model: "A Snowman of Style" 99
A Student's Model: "Make It Grow," Stephanie Thompson 102

Revising 103
First Reading: *Content and Organization*
Second Reading: *Style*
   Focus on Sentences: *Transitional Words*

Publishing 106
Proofreading: *Grammar Link—Using Commas in a Series*
Test-Taking Mini-Lesson: *Writing Instructions* 108
Connections to Literature: *Writing a Descriptive Paragraph* 109

Focus on Viewing and Listening
Viewing and Listening to Learn 112

Choices: *Crossing the Curriculum: Science, Speech • Careers • Writing* 117

Comparing and Contrasting 118

CHAPTER 4

Informational Text

Exposition

Connecting Reading and Writing 119

READING WORKSHOP: *A Comparison-Contrast Essay* 120

Preparing to Read 120
READING SKILL ■ Points of Comparison
READING FOCUS ■ Comparison-Contrast Structure

Reading Selection: "The Nixon-Kennedy Presidential Debates,"
Edward Wakin from *How TV Changed America's Mind* 121
Vocabulary Mini-Lesson: *Prefixes and Suffixes* 126
Test-Taking Mini-Lesson: *Recognizing Supporting Details* 127

WRITING WORKSHOP: *A Comparison-Contrast Essay* 128

Prewriting 128
Critical-Thinking Mini-Lesson: *Evaluating Details*

Writing 136
Framework for a Comparison-Contrast Essay
A Writer's Model: "Puppy Love or Hamster Heaven" 137
A Student's Model: "A Collection Question," Matthew Hester 138

Revising 139
First Reading: *Content and Organization*
Second Reading: *Style*
    Focus on Sentences: *Combining Sentences*

Publishing 142
Proofreading: Grammar Link—*Using Comparatives Correctly*
Test-Taking Mini-Lesson: *Writing a Classification Essay* 145
Connections to Life: *Comparing Documentaries* 146

Focus on Viewing and Representing
Comparing Ideas in Photographs 147

Choices: *Careers • Viewing and Representing •
Creative Writing • Crossing the Curriculum: Music* 151

CHAPTER 5

Informational Text — Exposition

Responding to a Novel 152

Connecting Reading and Writing 153

READING WORKSHOP: *A Book Review* 154

Preparing to Read 154
READING SKILL ■ Point of View
READING FOCUS ■ Elements of a Novel

Reading Selection: Review of *Catherine, Called Birdy*, Kathleen Odean from *Great Books for Girls* 155

Vocabulary Mini-Lesson: *Wordbusting Strategy (CSSD)* 159
Test-Taking Mini-Lesson: *Answering Questions About Unfamiliar Vocabulary* 160

WRITING WORKSHOP: *A Book Review* 161

Prewriting 161
Critical-Thinking Mini-Lesson: *Identifying the Elements of a Plot*

Writing 168
Framework for a Book Review
A Writer's Model: "A Review of Natalie Babbitt's *Tuck Everlasting*" 169
A Student's Model: "A Review of *Out of the Storm* by Patricia Willis," Diana DeGarmo 170

Revising 171
First Reading: *Content and Organization*
Second Reading: *Style*
  Focus on Word Choice: *Clichés*

Publishing 174
Proofreading: Grammar Link—*Using Appositives*
Connections to Literature: *Writing a Short Story* 176
Connections to Literature: *Writing an Essay About a Poem's Sound Effects* 178

Focus on Viewing and Representing
Comparing Media: Film, TV, and Literature 181

Choices: *Viewing and Representing • Writing • Connecting Cultures • Technology • Creative Writing* 185

CHAPTER 6

Sharing Your Research 186

Connecting Reading and Writing 187

READING WORKSHOP: An Informative Article 188
Preparing to Read 188
READING SKILL ■ Making Inferences: Drawing Conclusions
READING FOCUS ■ Author's Purpose

Reading Selection: "The California Gold Rush," Kathy Wilmore
from *Junior Scholastic* 189
Vocabulary Mini-Lesson: *Word Roots* 196
Test-Taking Mini-Lesson: *Answering Questions About Tables* 197

WRITING WORKSHOP: A Research Report 198
Prewriting 198
Critical-Thinking Mini-Lesson: *Searching the World Wide Web for Information*
Writing Mini-Lesson: *Paraphrasing*

Writing 210
Framework for a Research Report
A Writer's Model: "The South American Guanaco" 211
A Student's Model: "Billiards," Genna Offerman 213

Revising 214
First Reading: *Content and Organization*
Second Reading: *Style*
    Focus on Word Choice: *Using Precise Nouns*

Publishing 217
Proofreading: Grammar Link—*Capitalizing and Punctuating Titles*
Test-Taking Mini-Lesson: *Writing an Informative Essay* 219
Connections to Life: *Creating Visuals to Share Information* 220

Focus on Speaking and Listening
Giving and Evaluating a Research Presentation 222

Choices: *Careers • Listening • Crossing the Curriculum: Physical Education • Creative Writing* 225

Informational Text
Exposition

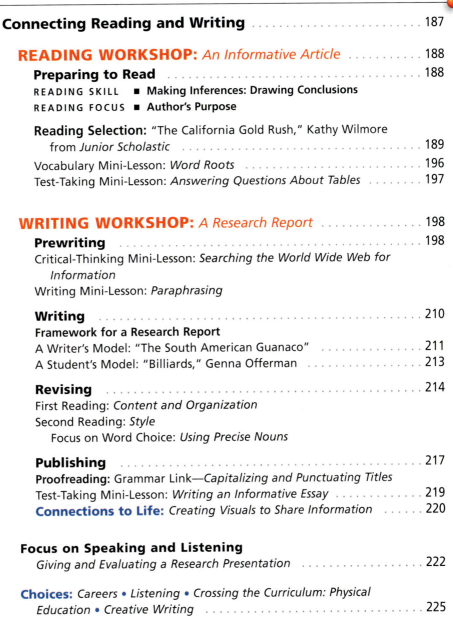

CHAPTER 7

Informational Text

Persuasion

Making a Difference 226

Connecting Reading and Writing 227

READING WORKSHOP: *A Persuasive Essay* 228
Preparing to Read 228
READING SKILL ■ Fact and Opinion
READING FOCUS ■ Reasons and Evidence

Reading Selection: "The U.S. Has a Garbage Crisis," William Dudley from *The Environment: Distinguishing Between Fact and Opinion* .. 229
Vocabulary Mini-Lesson: *Dictionary and Thesaurus* 235
Test-Taking Mini-Lesson: *Answering Questions About Fact and Opinion* 236

WRITING WORKSHOP: *A Persuasive Letter* 237
Prewriting 237
Critical-Thinking Mini-Lesson: *Understanding Your Audience*

Writing 244
Framework for a Persuasive Letter
A Writer's Model: "Dear Mr. Matsuo" 245
A Student's Model: A Letter to the President, Tyler Duckworth 247

Revising 248
First Reading: *Content and Organization*
Second Reading: *Style*
    Focus on Sentences: *Eliminating Stringy Sentences*

Publishing 251
Proofreading: Grammar Link—*Punctuating Possessives Correctly*
Test-Taking Mini-Lesson: *Answering Questions That Ask You to Persuade* 253
Connections to Life: *Writing a Humorous Advertisement* 254

Focus on Listening
Evaluating a Persuasive Speech 256

CHOICES: *Editorial Cartoons • Careers • Crossing the Curriculum: Social Studies • Speaking* 259

PART 2 | Quick Reference Handbook 261

THE DICTIONARY 262
Types and Contents 262

DOCUMENT DESIGN 264
Manuscript Style 264
Desktop Publishing 265
Graphics 269

THE HISTORY OF ENGLISH 272
Origins and Uses 272

THE LIBRARY/MEDIA CENTER 276
Using Print and Electronic Sources 276

READING AND VOCABULARY 286
Reading 286
Vocabulary 295

SPEAKING AND LISTENING 301
Speaking 301
Listening 309

STUDYING AND TEST TAKING 315
Studying 315
Test Taking 319

VIEWING AND REPRESENTING 325
Understanding Media Terms 325

WRITING 337
Skills, Structures, and Techniques 337

Index 350

Acknowledgments 369

Photo and Illustration Credits 370

MODELS

READING SELECTIONS

- William Dudley, **"The U.S. Has a Garbage Crisis,"** from *The Environment: Distinguishing Between Fact and Opinion*
- Paula Morrow, **"Making a Flying Fish,"** from *Faces: Happy Holidays*
- Kathleen Odean, Review of ***Catherine, Called Birdy,*** from *Great Books for Girls*
- Rosa Parks with Jim Haskins, from ***Rosa Parks: My Story***
- Edward Wakin, **"The Nixon-Kennedy Presidential Debates,"** from *How TV Changed America's Mind*
- **"Whale Watch: Kids Use Internet to Track Progress of Newly Freed J. J.,"** from the *Los Angeles Times*; Orange County Edition
- Kathy Wilmore, **"The California Gold Rush,"** from *Junior Scholastic*

WRITING MODELS

- Lewis Carroll, **"How Doth the Little Crocodile"**
- Edwin A. Hoey, **"Foul Shot"**
- Jack Prelutsky, **"Last Night I Dreamed of Chickens"**
- Robert Louis Stevenson, **"Windy Nights"**
- Mary Whitebird, **"Ta-Na-E-Ka"**

STUDENT MODELS

- Natalie Banta and Amy Tidwell, **"Mr. Sagers Moves to Cyprus High"**
- Diana DeGarmo, **"A Review of *Out of the Storm* by Patricia Willis"**
- Tyler Duckworth, **A Letter to the President**
- Matthew Hester, **"A Collection Question"**
- Genna Offerman, **"Billiards"**
- Anthony C. Rodrigues, **"In the Net"**
- Stephanie Thompson, **"Make It Grow"**

STUDENT'S OVERVIEW

The *Elements of Language* **Holt Literacy Handbook** contains two major parts:

PART 1 Communications

This section ties together the essential skills and strategies you use in all types of communication—reading, writing, listening, speaking, viewing, and representing.

Reading Workshops In these workshops, you read an article, a story, an editorial—a real-life example of a type of writing also featured in the Writing Workshop in the same chapter.

Writing Workshops In these workshops, you brainstorm ideas and use the writing process to produce an article, story, editorial, or other piece of your own.

Focus on Speaking and Listening & Focus on Viewing and Representing
These features help you sharpen your skills in presenting your ideas visually and orally. They also show you how to take a more critical view of what you hear and see.

PART 2 Quick Reference Handbook

Use this handy guide anytime you need concise tips to help you communicate more effectively—whether you need to gather information from a variety of media, make sense of what you read, prepare for tests, or present what you know in a document, a speech, or a visual.

Elements of Language on the Internet

Put the communication strategies in *Elements of Language Holt Literacy Handbook* to work by logging on to the Internet. At **go.hrw.com**, you will find online resources to help you enjoy and master reading and writing.

Student's Overview

The Reading and Writing Processes

Do these situations sound familiar? While reading, you suddenly realize you have read the same sentences several times without gaining any meaning from them. While writing, you stare at the single sentence you have written, unable to think of anything else to write. When you find yourself stuck, step back and look at the processes of reading and writing.

Reading

The reading you do in school requires you to think critically about information and ideas. In order to get the most from a text, prepare your mind for the task before you read, use effective strategies while you read, and take time to process the information after you read.

- **Before Reading** Get your mind in gear by considering your purpose for reading a particular piece of writing and by thinking about what you already know about the topic. Preview the text by skimming a bit and considering headings, graphics, and other features. Use this information to predict what the text will discuss and how challenging it will be to read.

- **While Reading** As you read, figure out the writer's main idea about the topic. Notice how the text is organized (by cause and effect or in order of importance, for example) to help you find support for that point. Connect the ideas to your own experiences when you can. If you get confused, slow down, re-read, or jot ideas in a graphic organizer.

- **After Reading** Confirm and extend your understanding of the text. Draw conclusions about the writer's point of view, and evaluate how well the writer communicated the message. Use ideas in the text to create a piece of art, to read more on a related topic, or to solve a problem.

Writing

A perfect text seldom springs fully formed from your mind; instead, you must plan your text before you write and work to improve it after drafting.

TIP Reading and writing are both recursive processes—that is, you can return to earlier steps when needed. For example, you might make new predictions while you are reading a text or you might develop additional support for ideas when you are revising a piece of writing.

xviii Reading and Writing

- **Before Writing** First, choose a topic and a form of writing, such as a poem or an editorial. Decide who your readers will be and what you want the text to accomplish. Develop ideas based on your knowledge and on research. Organize the ideas, and jot down your main point.
- **While Writing** Grab attention and provide background information in an introduction. Elaborate your ideas to support your point, and organize them clearly. Then, wrap things up with a conclusion.
- **After Writing** To improve a draft, evaluate how clearly you expressed your ideas. Ask a peer to suggest areas that need work. Then, revise. Proofread to correct mistakes. Share your finished work with others, and reflect on what you learned.

You may have noticed that the reading and writing processes involve similar strategies. The chart below summarizes these similarities.

The Reading and Writing Processes

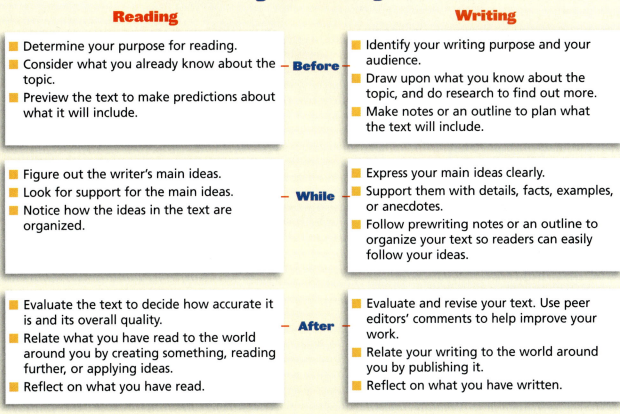

Reading		Writing
■ Determine your purpose for reading. ■ Consider what you already know about the topic. ■ Preview the text to make predictions about what it will include.	Before	■ Identify your writing purpose and your audience. ■ Draw upon what you know about the topic, and do research to find out more. ■ Make notes or an outline to plan what the text will include.
■ Figure out the writer's main ideas. ■ Look for support for the main ideas. ■ Notice how the ideas in the text are organized.	While	■ Express your main ideas clearly. ■ Support them with details, facts, examples, or anecdotes. ■ Follow prewriting notes or an outline to organize your text so readers can easily follow your ideas.
■ Evaluate the text to decide how accurate it is and its overall quality. ■ Relate what you have read to the world around you by creating something, reading further, or applying ideas. ■ Reflect on what you have read.	After	■ Evaluate and revise your text. Use peer editors' comments to help improve your work. ■ Relate your writing to the world around you by publishing it. ■ Reflect on what you have written.

The Reading and Writing Workshops in this book provide valuable practice for strategies that will help you effectively use these related processes.

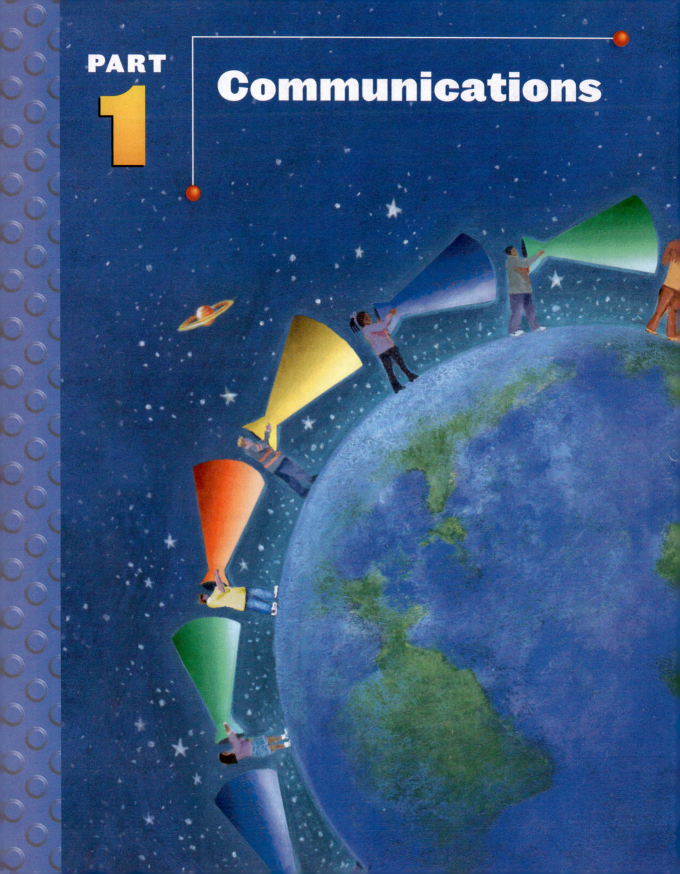

PART 1 Communications

**Taking Tests:
Strategies and Practice** 2

**1 Narration/Description:
Sharing Our Stories** 16

**2 Exposition:
Reporting the News** 48

**3 Exposition:
Explaining How** 84

**4 Exposition:
Comparing and Contrasting** ... 118

**5 Exposition:
Responding to a Novel** 152

**6 Exposition:
Sharing Your Research** 186

**7 Persuasion:
Making a Difference** 226

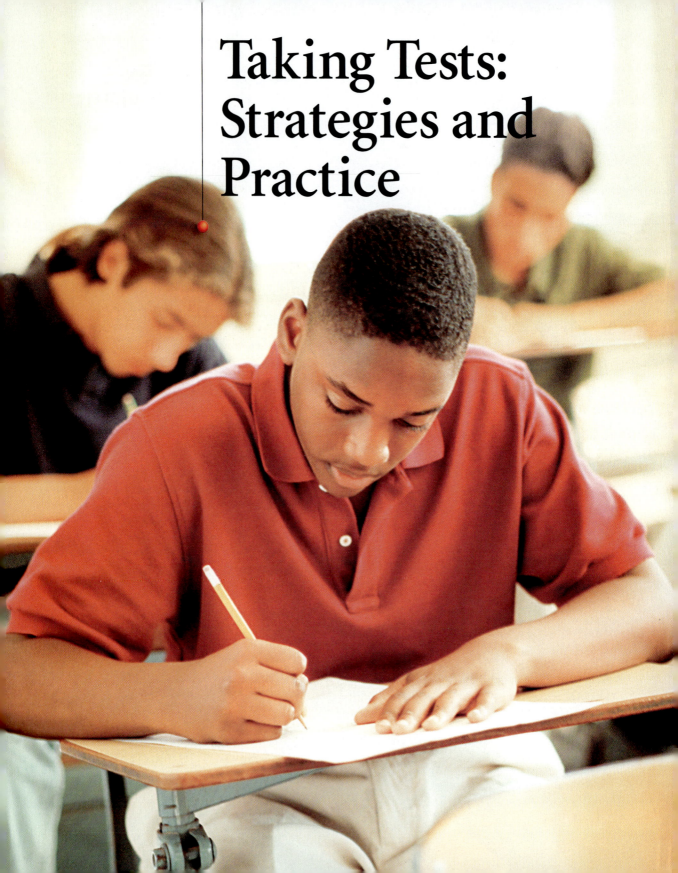

Taking Tests: Strategies and Practice

Taking Reading Tests

In the years ahead, you'll probably take many **standardized tests**. A standardized reading test contains **reading passages** followed by **multiple-choice questions**. Some tests also have an open-ended **essay question**. The following strategies and practice will help you boost your scores on the reading sections of standardized tests.

THINKING IT THROUGH

Reading Test Strategies

▶ **STEP 1** **Watch your time.** Divide the test time by the number of questions to estimate how much time you can spend on each question. Check as you work to see if you need to speed up.

▶ **STEP 2** **Concentrate.** Carefully read the directions and any introduction to the reading passage. As you read the passage, don't let your attention wander. If you're allowed to mark the test booklet, underline or circle key words.

▶ **STEP 3** **Understand the question.** Look for tricky words like *not* and *except;* they require you to choose an answer that is false or opposite in some way. Don't fall for answers that make true statements but don't answer the question that's being asked. Never choose an answer until you've read *all* of the choices.

▶ **STEP 4** **Make educated guesses.** You may recognize the correct answer easily. If not, first get rid of the one or two answers you know are wrong. Then, from the remaining answers, choose the one you think is most likely to be right.

▶ **STEP 5** **Keep going.** Don't get stuck. Skip difficult questions, and go back to them later if you have time at the end.

▶ **STEP 6** **Don't lose your place.** Match each question to the number on the answer sheet. If you skip a question, be sure to skip that number on the answer sheet.

▶ **STEP 7** **Take another look.** Before time runs out, try answering questions you skipped the first time round. Be sure to check your answer sheet carefully, and erase any stray pencil marks.

> **TIP** Before the test, ask about how the test is scored. If no points are taken off for wrong answers, plan to answer every question. If wrong answers count against you, answer questions you know and those you can answer with an educated guess.

Comparing Texts

Read the following passages carefully. Then, choose the **best** answer to each question.

Do Animals Think?

by Ellen Lambeth

This panther looks deep in thought. But don't let that pose fool you. Animals often do things that may make you think they're thinking.

Thinking about thinking is tricky, because thinking isn't something you can see. It goes on inside the brain. We know when we're doing it. But who can tell if an animal is thinking? It's not easy.

For example, check out the animal actions below. Do they show that the animals are thinking—or not thinking? What do you think? (We'll tell you later what scientists think.)

- A bird builds a nest that's just right for its eggs and babies.
- An octopus uses its arms to open a jar with food inside.
- A lion sneaks around behind its prey and then chases it toward another lion that's hiding and waiting.
- A salmon returns from the ocean to the same stream where it hatched.

"Do Animals Think?" by Ellen Lambeth from *Ranger Rick*, vol. 31, issue 3, March 1997. Copyright © 1997 by **National Wildlife Federation**. Reprinted by permission of the publisher.

What Is Thinking?

It may be easier to first explain what thinking isn't. For example, it isn't needed for things animals do automatically—like when a beaver dams a stream with sticks, mud, and grasses.

The beaver is making a pond, but it didn't learn how to do that. It doesn't think about doing it, either. Some animals just do what they do—kind of like robots—and they do it the same way every time. Scientists call this kind of behavior instinct.

But what about when an animal does learn to do something? Is that thinking? For example, you can teach a dog to give you its paw and "shake hands" for a treat. Even a worm can learn to follow a maze! But most scientists don't believe that the worm—or even the dog—is thinking when it learns such tricks.

A sheepdog at work, though, is a different story. One of the dog's jobs is to single out one sheep from a flock. The dog knows how to do that because it was trained.

But say the sheep doesn't want to leave the flock. It moves this way or that, or tries to duck behind another sheep. The dog must figure out a plan and keep changing that plan until it "outsmarts" the sheep, cutting it away from the others. Many people would agree that the sheepdog must be thinking about what it's doing.

Thinking Tests

For a long time, scientists didn't study animal thinking. Most of them didn't believe that animals could think. They thought humans were the only thinking animals.

Now more scientists are studying this subject. But it's very hard to prove things that no one can see or measure. So some scientists decided to take a look at brains.

Is bigger better? No. Cow brains are bigger than dog brains, but that doesn't make cows smarter than dogs. And squirrels have some of the biggest brains of all for their body size. But squirrels aren't even close to being the smartest animals in the world. So the size of a brain may give some clues about brain power, but it doesn't prove anything.

Other scientists study thinking by watching how animals solve problems. They watch animals in the wild. Or they set up thinking tests in a lab.

For example, a scientist might put some food just out of an animal's reach. One kind of animal may grab a stick and use it to slide the food over. Another kind might not be able to figure out a way to get the food. Some scientists think animals that have lots of problems to solve must be smarter than animals with simple lives.

Scientists also study certain kinds of behavior for clues about thinking. They watch for three things: whether animals use tools, how they act with each other, and how they communicate. . . .

So, Think About It

What did you decide about the animals in the beginning of this story? Well, the bird and salmon are using instinct. Their behaviors are amazing, but they stay the same, no matter what. The lion and octopus are most likely thinking. Why? Because each is carrying out some kind of plan to solve a problem. And if things were different, they could change their plans and solve their problems in different ways.

Many people think certain animals—such as whales and dolphins, monkeys and apes, wolves and dogs, crows and jays—are especially smart. But each might be smart at some things and not at others. It all depends on the lives they lead.

More and more scientists are coming up with new ways to study animal brain power. They often disagree. But many are sure that we humans aren't the only thinkers. And that leaves us with plenty to think about!

1. What is the main idea of this passage?
   A. There is evidence that some animals can think.
   B. Smarter animals have bigger brains than less intelligent animals.
   C. Nearly all animals have the ability to solve problems.
   D. Some animals can use man-made tools.

2. Which of the following actions shows that the animal might be thinking?
   F. A bird living in the north migrates to a warm climate in the fall.
   G. A bird speaks in return for a treat from its owner.
   H. A bird soaks dog food in water to soften it.
   J. A baby bird flies for the first time.

3. Which experiment might a scientist use to determine whether an animal is thinking?
   A. putting food for it in a maze
   B. teaching it to perform a trick
   C. setting up a problem and giving it a tool
   D. watching it raise its young in the wild

4. *Instinct* is repeated behavior that
   F. parents must teach their young
   G. requires thinking and problem solving
   H. imitates what everyone else is doing
   J. is not learned and does not change

5. According to the passage, how do the beaver and the sheepdog differ?
   A. Both animals think, but the sheepdog's actions prove it is smarter.
   B. The sheepdog thinks while herding, but the beaver uses instinct to build a dam.
   C. Scientists believe that the sheepdog is working and the beaver is not.
   D. The beaver is less intelligent than the sheepdog because its brain is smaller.

6. What does *cutting* mean in the following sentence?
   > The dog must . . . keep changing that plan until it 'outsmarts' the sheep, cutting it away from the others.
   F. piercing with a sharp object
   G. separating something from a group
   H. pretending not to see someone
   J. shortening or making less

7. Why does the writer include the bulleted (•) items on the first page of the passage?
   A. to prepare readers by making them think about specific animal behaviors
   B. to show readers how the rest of the passage will be organized
   C. to give readers examples of experiments scientists have done
   D. to test whether readers are paying attention to the topic

8. From studying animals' brains, scientists have concluded that
   - F. bigger brains indicate higher intelligence
   - G. smaller brains indicate higher intelligence
   - H. smaller brains indicate less intelligence
   - J. brain size is not directly related to intelligence

Write several paragraphs in response to *one* of the following questions:

9. The passage talks about three kinds of animal behavior: instinct, trained behavior, and thought. Explain the differences among these behaviors, and give an example of each kind.

10. So, what is your answer—*do* animals think? State your opinion and support it with your own observations and with details from the article.

CRITTER CREW

by Anna Mearns

When Hurricane Andrew hit South Florida, it wiped out the homes, food, and water supplies of thousands of people.

That was bad enough. But just imagine what a hurricane can do to the cage of a wild animal. R-i-p! Many cages were torn open by the storm. And out dashed the animals!

"It was like a nightmare," says Todd Hardwick. Todd runs a business in Miami, Florida, called Pesky Critters. He and his

"Critter Crew" by Anna Mearns from *Ranger Rick*, vol. 27, issue 9, September 1993. Copyright © 1993 by **National Wildlife Federation**. Reprinted by permission of the publisher.

helpers recapture escaped animals. They also take away wild animals that have gotten into people's homes.

"In the first few days after the hurricane," Todd says, "we saw thousands of monkeys running loose. One day we saw 400 of them up in the trees! And we saw strange animals that looked like tiny reindeer.

"They were running and jumping over fences in backyards." Todd also found boa constrictors, parrots, lizards—and one very hungry cougar (mountain lion).

Cougar Capture

Just after the hurricane, Todd got a call from a man looking for his lost female cougar. Todd looked for the cougar for almost a month, but couldn't find her.

Finally, Todd explains, he got a call from the mother of a three-year-old girl. The girl had found a huge, wild cat under her house! The frightened mother called Todd for help.

Todd and his assistant, Jill Voight, came right away. Just as they suspected, it was the missing cougar.

The only way to get close to the animal was to crawl under the house. So Todd went in on his hands and knees and shot the cougar with a tranquilizer (TRANK-weh-lie-zer) dart. The dart contained medicine to put her to sleep.

The cougar dashed out as soon as she was shot. Then the medicine started to work. When the cougar became very sleepy, Todd put on special long gloves and caught her.

Finally, with Jill's help, he put her in a cage. When he delivered the cougar to her owner, the man started to cry for joy. He was so happy to see her alive!

Python Under the House

Recapturing escaped cougars is all in a day's work for Todd. He's used to it—there are lots of weird animals where he lives. That's because lots of people bring wild animals into Miami by plane and by boat. And it's easy to keep animals there because the climate is warm year round.

But sometimes the new owners get tired of caring for wild pets and let them go. Todd thinks that's what may have happened to the huge python he found hiding under a house in the suburbs. The snake's owners had let it go in a local state park, where it lived for eight years.

Then one night, a family that lived next to the park heard an animal scream. When they looked out, they saw a huge snake with its mouth around a full-grown raccoon. After it finished eating, the snake went into a burrow it had dug under their house.

Todd and three friends spent two whole days digging out the snake. They widened the snake's burrow, which ran from the front of the house to the back. Then Todd put two friends on one side of the house. He put himself and a friend on the other.

Todd lowered himself toward the snake while his friend hung onto his legs. Todd was carrying a stick with a loop of rope at the end. When the snake started to strike at his face, Todd quickly flipped the rope over its head.

He and his friends then pulled the snake out. It was huge—22 feet (7 m) long and 250 pounds (113 kg). Finally, Todd took the snake home. He kept it there until he found someone who could care for it.

Alligators at Home

The python fit right into Todd's zoo-like home. He has permits to keep many different kinds of animals. He has four monitor lizards there. (He found one of the lizards stuck in a car engine.) He has nine iguana lizards. He has an ostrich-like bird from South America called a rhea (REE-uh)—which he named "Pizza Rhea." Then there are the two alligators, the tortoise, the flamingo, the Asian deer, and the 50 parrots.

Todd likes animals.

When he was 12, Todd found an orphaned mockingbird and helped raise it. That's when he got really interested in animals. "I used to track animals in my area. I'd catch live raccoons and opossums just to look at them," he says. "But I always put them right back in the wild."

People got to know about Todd and his love for wild animals. "They'd call me and say, hey, we have a raccoon in our attic, or a snake in our pool—could you come get it out?" he says.

Todd got very good at live-trapping animals. When he was 18, he became an official "nuisance wildlife trapper." That means the state of Florida gave him a license to start a business helping people get rid of pesky wildlife.

---

11. Which sentence gives the **best** description of Todd Hardwick's job?
   A. He rescues pets separated from their owners during hurricanes.
   B. He uses tranquilizer darts to rescue lost pets.
   C. He finds and rescues escaped pets and wild animals.
   D. He traps wild animals and sells them to zoos.

12. What is the difference between how Todd caught the cougar and the python?
   F. He had to crawl under a house to get the cougar, but the python was in a cage.
   G. He used a steak to tempt the cougar and a raccoon to tempt the python.
   H. He used his assistant to catch the cougar but caught the python himself.
   J. He used a tranquilizer dart for the cougar and a roped stick for the snake.

13. Unlike some pest-control companies, Todd's company, Pesky Critters,
   A. does all of its work after hurricanes
   B. works only with rescuing lost pets
   C. traps wild animals and pets alive
   D. exterminates pests

14. Why did the owner of the cougar cry?
   F. The cougar died during a hurricane.
   G. Todd sold the cougar for a lot of money.
   H. The cougar had been shot and was badly wounded.
   J. Todd rescued the cougar and returned it to its owner.

continued

15. From the types of animals Todd traps in Miami, we can predict that his business would probably be
    A. more successful in a northern city
    B. less successful in a northern city
    C. successful anywhere in the country
    D. more successful in a rural area

16. We can infer that Todd is good at
    F. solving problems
    G. organizing large groups of people
    H. treating sick animals
    J. attracting new customers

17. What conclusion can you make based on this passage?
    A. People should learn how to protect themselves from wild animals.
    B. A person's childhood interest may lead to a career.
    C. No one should have a wild animal as a pet.
    D. A pet that is well cared for will never leave its owner.

Comparing the Passages

18. How are the topics of these two passages similar?
    F. Both discuss the behavior of animals.
    G. Both ask whether animals think.
    H. Both tell about animal rescues.
    J. Both show that animals have feelings.

Write several paragraphs in response to *one* of the following questions:

19. Different types of articles appear in different types of magazines. Explain why the first passage might be published as an article in a science magazine. Then, explain why the second one might be published in a more general magazine. Use details from the passages to explain your ideas.

20. Both the scientists in the first passage and Todd Hardwick in the second passage are interested in animals, but in different ways. Use details and information from the passages to contrast their interests (explain the differences between them).

Taking Writing Tests

Standardized tests measure your writing skills in two ways:

- An **on-demand writing prompt** gives you a situation and asks you to write a coherent, well-developed **essay** in a limited time, perhaps less than an hour. The prompt may ask you to write a narrative, expository, or persuasive essay.
- **Multiple-choice questions** test your knowledge of sentence construction and revision and of paragraph content and organization.

Use the following strategies to write any type of essay. You'll recognize these steps—you know them already as the steps in the writing process.

THINKING IT THROUGH  Writing Test Strategies

▶ **STEP 1 Read the writing prompt carefully.** Underline key verbs (such as *analyze, argue, explain, discuss*) that tell you what to do. (Before the test, review the chart of **key verbs that appear in essay questions,** page 320.) A prompt may ask you to do more than one thing. Cover all parts of the prompt—including addressing the correct audience—or you'll lose points.

▶ **STEP 2 Think before you write.** If you have forty-five minutes to write an essay, take ten minutes or so for prewriting. Use scratch paper to brainstorm ideas, make a cluster diagram or a rough outline, and gather details. Plan how to organize and support ideas.

> **TIP** Don't skip this prewriting step. Using prewriting strategies will result in a stronger, more interesting essay.

▶ **STEP 3 Draft your essay.** Spend about two thirds of your time drafting your essay. Express your ideas as clearly as you can. Write a strong opening paragraph and a definite closing, and add many specific details to support and elaborate your main points.

▶ **STEP 4 Edit and revise as you write.** Leave enough time at the end to re-read your draft and make your ideas easier to follow. To add a word or a sentence, mark a caret (∧) and insert it neatly.

▶ **STEP 5 Proofread your essay.** Find and correct all errors in grammar, punctuation, capitalization, and spelling.

Reference Note

For more on writing an **autobiographical incident,** see pages 27–40.

Narrative Writing

Sample Writing Prompt *Describe an experience you had that changed your perspective—that made you see the world or yourself differently. As you retell your experience, add details that make clear where the story takes place and who the characters are. Be sure to tell how the incident changed you or what you learned.*

A story map like the one below can help you plan to write about an autobiographical incident. Be sure to do what the prompt asks you to do—add details of setting and characters.

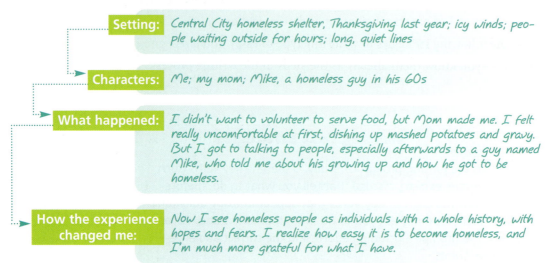

Setting: Central City homeless shelter, Thanksgiving last year; icy winds; people waiting outside for hours; long, quiet lines

Characters: Me; my mom; Mike, a homeless guy in his 60s

What happened: I didn't want to volunteer to serve food, but Mom made me. I felt really uncomfortable at first, dishing up mashed potatoes and gravy. But I got to talking to people, especially afterwards to a guy named Mike, who told me about his growing up and how he got to be homeless.

How the experience changed me: Now I see homeless people as individuals with a whole history, with hopes and fears. I realize how easy it is to become homeless, and I'm much more grateful for what I have.

Expository Writing

Sample Writing Prompt *A time capsule is being buried in the cornerstone of the new city hall, and it won't be opened for one hundred years. Describe three objects you would place in the time capsule that will tell people of the future what life is like where you live at the beginning of the twenty-first century. Tell why you've chosen each object.*

One writer gathered his ideas by using a chart:

Object	Why I Chose It
cell phone	Instant phone contact; can stay in touch with family and friends anywhere you go; some have Internet access

portable CD player and four favorite CDs	Your own personal great music wherever you go. This will give an idea of the many kinds of music we have.
laptop computer	The Internet is the biggest thing of the early 21st century. People use it for fun, for e-mail, and for research.

An expository writing prompt may ask you to explain parts of a topic, as in the example above, or to explain a process, causes and effects, or problems and solutions. To make your ideas clear to readers, always include plenty of facts, examples, and other kinds of details as support.

Persuasive Writing

Sample Writing Prompt   *A neighbor has asked your advice about what kind of pet to adopt. Should she have a cat, a dog, or another kind of pet? State your opinion, and give at least two reasons to support your view.*

You probably already know what kind of pet you'll recommend. (With some issues, you need to carefully consider both sides—the pros and cons—before you decide what you think.) Here's a cluster diagram by a student who thinks her neighbor should adopt a cat and who is trying to think of reasons and evidence to support her opinion.

Reference Note

For more on **persuasive writing,** see pages 237–252.

> **TIP** Review the strategies on page 3, which also apply to multiple-choice writing questions.

Multiple-Choice Writing Questions

Multiple-choice writing questions like the ones below are another way to test your understanding of sentence and paragraph structure and of the conventions of standard English (grammar, usage, punctuation, capitalization, and spelling).

Read the following paragraph. Then, choose the best answer for each question.

(1) For most living things, danger is all around. (2) Often it strikes suddenly when a predator launches a surprise attack. (3) In other cases it develops slowly—the onset of disease or threat of starvation, for example. (4) Living things defend themselves from danger in countless ways. (5) Many animals have sharp senses and take emergency action at the first sign of trouble. (6) Most try to escape, but some have special protection that allows them to withstand an attack. (7) Plants also need defenses, particularly against hungry animals. (8) However, they are rooted to the ground and cannot run away as animals can. (9) Instead, they use spines, thorns, and special chemicals to make themselves unpleasant or dangerous to eat.

From *DK Nature Encyclopedia*. Copyright © 1998 by **Dorling Kindersley Ltd.** Reprinted by permission of the publisher. All rights reserved.

1. The **best** topic sentence for this paragraph is
   A. sentence 2
   B. sentence 3
   C. sentence 4
   D. sentence 9

2. Where is the **best** place to add this sentence?
   > A porcupine, for instance, is covered with sharp spines that discourage predators.

   F. after sentence 4
   G. after sentence 5
   H. after sentence 6
   J. Nowhere; it destroys unity.

3. A *predator* (sentence 2) is
   A. a natural disaster
   B. any plant or animal
   C. a disease or injury to an animal
   D. an animal that kills another animal

4. Sentences 5 and 6 elaborate (by giving examples) the statement made in
   F. sentence 1
   G. sentence 3
   H. sentence 4
   J. sentence 7

5. In sentence 2, the word *Often* is
   A. a noun
   B. a pronoun
   C. an adjective
   D. an adverb

6. What is the direct object in sentence 7?
  F. plants
  G. defenses
  H. against
  J. animals

7. What is the **best** way to combine these two sentences?
> Turtles protect themselves. They withdraw their heads and limbs under a tough shell.

  A. Turtles protect themselves; and they withdraw their heads and limbs under a tough shell.
  B. Turtles protect themselves, they withdraw their heads and limbs under a tough shell.
  C. Turtles protect themselves by withdrawing their heads and limbs under a tough shell.
  D. Turtles protect themselves in order to withdraw their heads and limbs under a tough shell.

8. How should the following sentence be corrected?
> A ladybug uses it's bright colors and pattern to warn predators that it tastes terrible.

  F. Change *it's* to *its*.
  G. Add a comma after *colors*.
  H. Change *it tastes* to *they taste*.
  J. Make no change; the sentence is correct.

9. Which word is misspelled?
> Some <u>butterflies</u> and moths <u>wear</u> colors
>   **A**   **B**
> and patterns that mimic <u>there</u> poisonous,
>   **C**
> bad-tasting relatives. NO ERROR
>   **D**

10. Andre has found a book about insects. Which of the following would **most** quickly show him where the book discusses how insects use camouflage as a defense?
  F. the table of contents
  G. the index
  H. the introduction
  J. the glossary

Reference Note

For more on preparing for reading and writing tests, see the **Test-Taking Mini-Lesson** in each Part 1 chapter and **Studying and Test Taking** on pages 315–324.

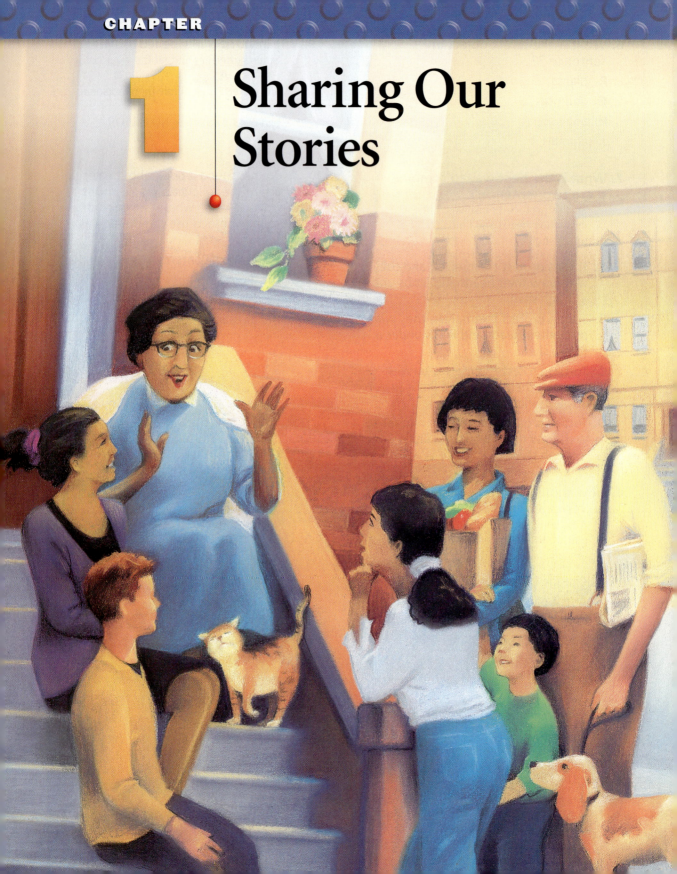

CHAPTER 1

Sharing Our Stories

CONNECTING READING AND WRITING

Reading Workshop

Reading an Autobiographical Incident

Writing Workshop

Writing About a Life Experience

Speaking and Listening

Telling a Story

Do you wonder what it is like to fly over the ocean alone in a small plane? Would you like to know what it is like to live in a different country? You can learn about these experiences by reading *autobiographical incidents.* An **autobiographical incident** is a true story about a specific event in a writer's life. Not only do you learn about the event, but you also learn why the experience is important to the writer. Because writers share, or express, their thoughts and feelings, an autobiographical incident is an example of **expressive writing.**

You also share autobiographical incidents. When you talk with your grandmother about your track meet, for example, you are telling a story about yourself. Writing an autobiographical incident is a great way to express what you think and feel.

> Narration/Description

YOUR TURN 1 — Sharing Experiences

List the topics of three memorable experiences that you would not mind sharing. Then, discuss the following questions with a partner.

- Why are these experiences memorable?
- What did you learn about yourself from these experiences?

internetconnect

GO TO: go.hrw.com
KEYWORD: EOLang 6-1

Reading Workshop

Reading an Autobiographical Incident

WHAT'S AHEAD?

In this section you will read an autobiographical incident. You will also learn how to
- form generalizations
- construct a flowchart to understand chronological order

If you want to bring about a change, you have to take action. Many people throughout the history of the United States have dared to do just that. These people stood up for what they believed, and their actions led to positive changes in U.S. society. Rosa Parks is one of those people. On December 1, 1955, in Montgomery, Alabama, Rosa Parks challenged a law that said African Americans must sit in a separate section from whites on public buses. Read about the incident in the excerpt from her autobiography on the next page.

Preparing to Read

READING SKILL

Making Inferences: Forming Generalizations   A **generalization** is a statement that applies to many individuals or experiences, not just a specific person or experience. As you read the following excerpt, think about what you could say about Rosa Parks's experience that would also be true for others who have experienced discrimination.

READING FOCUS

Chronological Order   Rosa Parks tells her story in **chronological order.** She starts with the first event and ends with the last. As you read, pay attention to the order, or **sequence,** of events. How does chronological order help you understand the story?

18   Chapter 1   Narration/Description: Sharing Our Stories

Jot down answers to the numbered active-reading questions in the shaded boxes. The underlined words will be discussed in the Vocabulary Mini-Lesson on page 25.

from Rosa Parks: My Story

BY ROSA PARKS
with Jim Haskins

When I got off from work that evening of December 1, I went to Court Square as usual to catch the Cleveland Avenue bus home. I didn't look to see who was driving when I got on, and by the time I <u>recognized</u> him, I had already paid my fare. It was the same driver who had put me off the bus back in 1943, twelve years earlier. He was still tall and heavy, with red, rough-looking skin. And he was still mean-looking. I didn't know if he had been on that route before—they switched the drivers around sometimes. I do know that most of the time if I saw him on a bus, I wouldn't get on it.

> **1.** What is the first event in Rosa Parks's story?

I saw a vacant seat in the middle section of the bus and took it. I didn't even question why there was a <u>vacant</u> seat even though there were quite a few people standing in the back. If I had thought about it at all, I would probably have figured maybe someone saw me get on and did not take the seat but left it vacant for me. There was a man sitting next to the window and two women across the aisle.

> **2.** Do you think the order of the first two paragraphs could be switched? Why?

The next stop was the Empire Theater, and some whites got on. They filled up the white seats,[1] and one man was left standing. The driver looked back and noticed the man standing. Then he looked back at us. He said,

---
1. **white seats:** seats on a public bus that only white people could occupy.

"Let me have those front seats," because they were the front seats of the black section.[2] Didn't anybody move. We just sat right where we were, the four of us. Then he spoke a second time: "Y'all better make it light on yourselves and let me have those seats."

> **3.** Why did the bus driver tell the black passengers to give up their seats?

The man in the window seat next to me stood up, and I moved to let him pass by me, and then I looked across the aisle and saw that the two women were also standing. I moved over to the window seat. I could not see how standing up was going to "make it light" for me. The more we gave in and <u>complied</u>, the worse they treated us.

> **4.** How many seats did the bus driver need so all the white passengers could sit down?

I thought back to the time when I used to sit up all night and didn't sleep, and my grandfather would have his gun right by the fireplace, or if he had his one-horse wagon going anywhere, he always had his gun in the back of the wagon. People always say that I didn't give up my seat because I was tired, but that isn't true. I was not tired physically, or no more tired than I usually was at the end of a working day. I was not old, although some people have an image of me as being old then. I was forty-two. No, the only tired I was, was tired of giving in.

The driver of the bus saw me still sitting there, and he asked was I going to stand up. I said, "No." He said, "Well, I'm going to have you arrested." Then I said, "You may do that." These were the only words we said to each other. I didn't even know his name, which was James Blake, until we were in court together. He got out of the bus and stayed outside for a few minutes, waiting for the police.

> **5.** Why do you think the bus driver insisted that Rosa Parks move?

As I sat there, I tried not to think about what might happen. I knew that anything was possible. I could be <u>manhandled</u> or beaten. I could be arrested. People have asked me if it <u>occurred</u> to me then that I could be the test case the NAACP[3] had been looking for. I did not think about that at all. In fact if I had let myself think too deeply about what might happen to me, I might have gotten off the bus. But I chose to remain.

> **6.** Why do you think Rosa Parks decided not to give up her seat?

---

2. black section: the back of a public bus, where African Americans were allowed to sit.
3. NAACP: National Association for the Advancement of Colored People, an organization that fights for the equal treatment of African Americans and other minority groups.

> **First Thoughts on Your Reading**
>
> 1. Based on what you have read, how were Rosa Parks and other African Americans treated during the 1950s?
> 2. How would you tell Rosa Parks's story in your own words?

Making Inferences: Forming Generalizations

 READING SKILL

Read Between the Lines An author will not always give you every detail of a story. Sometimes you will need to make educated guesses about what is happening. Educated guesses are called **inferences**. To make inferences, combine clues that the author provides with what you already know about the subject.

Example: **What you read:** The little boy fell on the floor kicking and screaming while his mother held the football.

+ **What you know:** My mother took my toys away when I was in trouble, and I would get very mad.

Inference: The little boy misbehaved, so his mother took the football away from him.

Reference Note

For more on **inferences**, see page 288 in the Quick Reference Handbook.

One type of inference is a *generalization*. A **generalization** is a statement that applies to many different situations or people even though it is based on specific situations or people.

Example: **What you read:** Emma and Miguel do their math homework. Emma and Miguel make *A's* in math.

+ **What you know:** I do my homework in science, and I make good grades.

Generalization: Doing your homework usually leads to good grades.

TIP Generalizations use words like *many, usually, some, overall, most,* and *generally*. What clue word does the generalization in the example use?

Notice that the generalization above doesn't apply just to Emma and Miguel or to math homework. It is a general statement that is true for many different people and school subjects.

Read the paragraph on the next page. Then, form a generalization by using personal knowledge as well as information in the paragraph. Use the steps that follow the paragraph if you need help.

TIP Be careful not to make *faulty generalizations*. If you can find an exception to your generalization, then it is faulty. Faulty generalizations tend to include words like *all, none, never, always,* and *every*.

Faulty Generalization: Doing your homework *always* leads to good grades.

In 1848, Elizabeth Cady Stanton and Lucretia Mott organized the first women's rights convention. Through their efforts and the persistence of women after them, women eventually gained the right to own property and to vote. In the 1960s, Cesar Chavez helped migrant workers by forming a union, the United Farm Workers. He began strikes and boycotts that won union members better wages and working conditions. Ed Roberts began the movement for the rights of the disabled when he started a program to help disabled students in the 1960s. Other people joined the cause, and eventually Congress passed the Americans with Disabilities Act in 1990. This act made it illegal to discriminate against people with mental or physical disabilities.

Reference Note

For more on **generalizations,** see page 287 in the Quick Reference Handbook.

THINKING IT THROUGH

Forming Generalizations

▶ **STEP 1** Read the entire passage. Look for similarities and connections between the details in the passage.

Stanton and Mott helped women. Chavez helped migrant workers. Roberts helped disabled people. They all made a difference.

▶ **STEP 2** Connect the details in the passage to something you already know.

My parents organized a petition to keep a park from becoming a parking lot. The mayor agreed.

▶ **STEP 3** Form a generalization that combines what you read with what you know.

People can often make a difference when they stand up for what they believe.

▶ **STEP 4** Check your answer. Make sure your generalization
- is not faulty (look for a faulty generalization clue word)
- is reasonable, based on the information in the passage.

I say <u>often</u>, not <u>always</u>. My generalization is reasonable because all the details I read were about people who did something and made a difference.

YOUR TURN 2 Forming Generalizations

Re-read the reading selection on pages 19–20. Using the steps in the Thinking It Through on page 22, form a generalization about what sometimes happens when people take a stand against something they believe is unfair. Be prepared to support your generalization with information from the reading selection and from your own knowledge.

Chronological Order

READING FOCUS

It Goes Like This   Like a fictional story, an autobiographical incident has a beginning, middle, and end. The writer uses **chronological** (or time) **order** to tell which event happened first, second, third, and so on. If the events were not written in chronological order, you might have a hard time picturing the story in your mind. Read the following autobiographical incident. Which event happened first? second? third?

> While visiting our grandmother, my sister and I decided we would have a picnic lunch. We packed a bag and walked to the field behind my grandmother's house.
> We chose a nice, shady spot under a big tree. Tamara had started to spread out the blanket when all of a sudden she began to scream and fling her arms wildly. Before I could ask her what was wrong, I was screaming, too. We both ran to the house.
> My grandmother heard the noise and came out to see what was wrong. She found that Tamara and I had been stung several times. We definitely upset a family of yellow jackets when we laid our blanket on top of their nest.

Flowcharts are graphic organizers that can help you see the events of an autobiographical incident in the order in which they occurred. In the flowchart on the next page, notice that only major events of the incident above are listed. Details are left out.

To tell the difference between a major event and a supporting detail, look for action. For instance, what is more important: that the picnic spot was nice and shady, or that the narrator and her sister screamed and ran to the house? The main event in that paragraph is the action of the narrator and her sister.

YOUR TURN 3 Charting Chronological Order

Copy the following flowchart onto your paper. Then, read the list of events and details taken from *Rosa Parks: My Story* below. Decide which sentences are supporting details and which are major events. Place the major events in the flowchart. When you are done, re-read the reading selection on pages 19–20 to see if you listed the major events in the correct order.

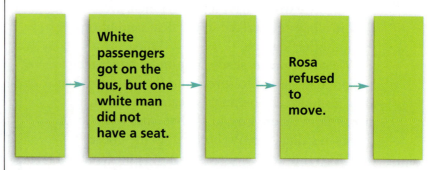

The bus driver told the African American passengers to move.
The bus driver's name was James Blake.
Rosa waited for the police.
Rosa got on the bus after work to go home.
The bus driver was tall, heavy, and had a red face.

MINI-LESSON VOCABULARY

Context Clues

As you read an autobiographical incident, you may discover that the author uses unfamiliar words to tell about his or her experience. One way to determine the meaning of an unfamiliar word is to use *context clues*. A word's **context** is made up of the words and sentences that surround it. Try using context clues to understand the underlined word in this passage taken from Rosa Parks's autobiography.

> I wasn't frightened at the jail. I was more <u>resigned</u> than anything else. I don't recall being real angry, not enough to have an argument. I was just prepared to accept whatever I had to face. I asked again if I could make a telephone call. I was ignored.
>
> Rosa Parks, *Rosa Parks: My Story*

THINKING IT THROUGH — Using Context Clues

▶ **STEP 1** Look at the context of the unfamiliar word. See if the words and sentences around it provide clues to the word's meaning.

The passage says that Rosa was not frightened or angry. It also says she was "prepared to accept" anything.

▶ **STEP 2** Use the context clues to make a guess at the unfamiliar word's meaning.

Since Rosa was not frightened or angry, and she could accept anything, I think resigned means "prepared to accept whatever happens."

▶ **STEP 3** Check your definition by inserting it in the passage in place of the unfamiliar word.

"I wasn't frightened at the jail. I was more <u>prepared to accept whatever happened</u> than anything else." That makes sense.

PRACTICE

Using context clues, figure out the meanings of these words. The words are underlined in *Rosa Parks: My Story*.

1. recognized (page 19)
2. vacant (page 19)
3. complied (page 20)
4. manhandled (page 20)
5. occurred (page 20)

Reading Workshop 25

MINI-LESSON TEST TAKING

Making Inferences

When you take a reading test, you may be asked to make an inference. Read the passage below and the question following it. How would you answer the question?

Citizens in Montgomery organized a bus boycott to protest the arrest of Rosa Parks. Leaflets were distributed encouraging African Americans not to ride the bus. Not using public transportation was very difficult for families without cars, so other means of transportation were made available. Black-owned cab companies helped those without cars by charging cheap fares. In addition, car owners and local churches formed car pools.

You can tell from the passage that during the Montgomery bus boycott

A. most African Americans stayed home
B. all African Americans refused to ride the bus
C. many African Americans supported one another
D. all African Americans used taxis to get around

THINKING IT THROUGH: Making Inferences

▶ **STEP 1** Read the passage and the question to see what it is asking you.

"You can tell" tells me I will make an educated guess, or an inference.

▶ **STEP 2** To identify the best response, look at each of the answer choices and ask yourself these questions:
- Is there information in the passage that supports this answer choice?
- Does this statement cover all the information in the passage?
- Is the answer free of faulty generalization words such as *all, none, never, always, every*?

Answer A—The passage does not mention African Americans staying home.

Answer B—Right away I see a faulty generalization clue word—<u>all</u>. I don't know if all African Americans refused to ride the bus.

Answer C—I can find specific information to support this choice.

Answer D—Yes, they did use taxis, but they also carpooled. D also has a faulty generalization word—<u>all</u>.

▶ **STEP 3** After evaluating each answer choice, choose the best one.

I think answer C is the best answer. I can support it with information from the passage.

Writing Workshop

Writing About a Life Experience

On the first day of school, you are given your first assignment—*Tell the class one thing you did this summer.* "This is easy," you think. "I'll talk about my rafting trip." You begin by telling when and where you went, and who was with you. Then, you describe the trip, particularly the dangerous parts. As you share your experience, your teacher and classmates learn something about you. You discover something about yourself, too. It is obvious that you like rafting, but your story also reveals that you like action.

You can discover more about yourself through **expressive writing.** In this workshop you will have an opportunity to share your thoughts and feelings about a single experience from your life by writing an **autobiographical incident.** You will use details that tell the reader what happened and how you felt about the incident.

WHAT'S AHEAD?

In this workshop you will write an autobiographical incident. You will also learn how to

- include background information
- create a detail chart
- arrange ideas in chronological order
- choose exact verbs
- capitalize proper nouns

Choose an Experience

Who? Me? What is the one subject you know the best? Why, *you* are, of course. You have probably had many experiences that you can write about. The first step in writing an autobiographical

incident is choosing one particular experience. If you need help coming up with one, consider these suggestions.

- Think about an experience that defines an emotion. When were you most happy, scared, surprised, sad, or angry?
- Brainstorm with your friends and family members. Ask them to recall a memorable experience that involves you.
- Look at your journals and at letters or pictures you have saved.
- Draw a road map of your life like the one to the left. Start with your birth and list all the important events that have happened to you up to now, such as your first day of kindergarten, the day your little sister was born, and the time your baseball team won the city championship.

KEY CONCEPT

You Be the Judge Once you have a list of experiences, you want to choose the one that will make the best autobiographical incident to share with an audience. **The best experience is one that is meaningful, or important, to you.** Ask yourself the questions below to decide which experience is most meaningful.

Question	Example
Do I remember the experience well?	If you cannot remember all the details, you will not be able to provide a complete picture of the experience. For instance, family members may have told you about your first step, but do *you* remember all the details?
Why is this experience important?	The reader should know how you felt about this experience or what you learned from it. For example, you might say that forgetting your lines in the school play was your most embarrassing moment.
Am I willing to share this experience?	You should feel comfortable letting other people read about your experience. For example, you might not want to share your first crush with the whole class.

 Choosing an Experience

Make a list of your experiences. Then, choose one experience to share by answering the questions in the chart above.

Think About Purpose and Audience

FYI... You are telling a story to a group of people when someone interrupts to ask, "How old were you?" Before you can speak, your best friend answers, "Third grade, right?" You agree and continue, only to be stopped again with another question. Again, your best friend answers. Why does your best friend understand the story when everyone else does not?

Before you begin writing your autobiographical incident, think about your purpose and audience. **Your purpose is to express your thoughts and feelings by sharing an experience with an audience.** Because you may not know exactly who your audience is, you should write as if your audience knows nothing about you. In order for your audience to understand your incident fully, you will need to provide **background information,** facts that set up the story. The four *W*'s—*What? When? Who? Where?*—will help you think about the information your audience needs.

- **What:** What is the incident? What happened?
- **When:** When did this event happen? How old were you?
- **Who:** Besides you, who was involved?
- **Where:** Where did this event take place? What was this place like?

KEY CONCEPT

> <u>What</u>? slipped during a dance recital
>
> <u>When</u>? an October night when I was seven years old
>
> <u>Who</u>? me, my parents, my dance teacher, my classmates, and their friends and families
>
> <u>Where</u>? on an auditorium stage that had very bright lights

TIP Part of your **style**—how you say things—is your **voice**—the *sound* of your writing. Most good writing sounds like speech. You can develop your voice by choosing words that sound like you yet fit your audience and purpose.

Describe the voice in each sentence below:

1. I was so embarrassed! I wanted to crawl under the stage.
2. I doubt that I had ever been as embarrassed as I was at that moment.

YOUR TURN 5 Thinking About Your Audience

Ask yourself *What? When? Who? Where?* to help you think of background information you should give your audience. Write your answers on a sheet of paper or in a learning log.

Recall Descriptive Details

You Had to Be There   You ask a friend about the movie he saw the other night. "Oh, it was great! First, the bad guy terrorizes the city. In the end, though, the good guy wins." It doesn't sound so great to you. Why not? Your friend left out the details.

KEY CONCEPT

Details will allow your readers to experience an incident just as if they were there. Two types of details that you should include in your essay are *action details* and *sensory details*.

- **Action details** tell what events occurred and what people said.

    > After waiting thirty minutes, I finally made it through the ticket line. I raced to the roller coaster only to find another long line.
    >
    > "Will I ever get to have fun?" I moaned to my friend.

- **Sensory details** describe what you see, hear, taste, feel, and smell.

    > The coaster went click, click, click as it slowly went uphill. Sweat trickled down my neck as we reached the top.

TIP   You can decide if a detail is necessary by asking yourself, "What was most important about my experience?" For instance, if the most important part of your vacation was going whale watching, then your details should be about whales. Leave out the details that do not describe the whales.

To re-create your memory, picture the incident in your mind. In a chart like the one below, record the details that you "see."

Action Details	Sensory Details
Beginning: lined up backstage, then walked onto stage. My dance teacher said, "Break a leg!"	black leotard, sequined belt flowery smell of hair spray announcer's booming voice
Middle: doing a routine with wooden boxes, was supposed to put one foot on the box next to me, missed and slipped—everyone else was on their box except me	heard audience laughing felt hot, face turned red dance teacher had said if we made a mistake to keep smiling
End: curtain dropped, I cried	sobbing, salty tears

YOUR TURN 6   Recalling Details

Create a detail chart like the one above. List action and sensory details from the beginning, middle, and end of your incident.

MINI-LESSON: CRITICAL THINKING

Arranging Ideas

My mom was not happy. Tony and Najla stared at me with open mouths. I hit the ball. It went crashing into the living room window. Tony, Najla, and I were playing baseball in the street. Najla pitched the ball. "I'm in trouble now," I said.

Wait a minute. What just happened? The mother was angry before the ball broke the window? The narrator is in trouble for playing in the street or because the ball crashed into the living room? This story is confusing.

In order to help their readers understand an incident, writers usually tell events in *chronological order*. Using **chronological order** means telling the events of a story in the order that they happened, starting with the first event, going to the second, then the third, and so on. Chronological order helps the reader follow the action of the incident. You can see that a story written chronologically is much easier to understand than one that is not.

Tony, Najla, and I were playing baseball in the street. Najla pitched the ball to me. I hit the ball, and it went crashing into the living room window. Tony and Najla stared at me with open mouths. "I'm in trouble now," I said. My mom was not happy.

PRACTICE

Read the following list of events. Then, rewrite the events in chronological order on your own paper.

look at the clock, it is 6:50 A.M.
get dressed, it is 6:55 A.M.
alarm goes off at 6 A.M.
grab my books, it is 6:59 A.M.
get on the bus at 7 A.M.

take a shower
jump out of bed
hit the snooze button
breathe a sigh of relief, "I barely made it!"

TIP To arrange events in chronological order, you can create a numbered list, draw a **flowchart,** or make a **time line.** Choose one of these methods when you write your answer.

Reference Note
For more on **flowcharts,** see page 23. For more on **time lines,** see page 96.

Autobiographical Incident

Framework | **Directions and Explanations**

Introduction
- Attention-grabbing opening
- Background information

Start your paper with an **interesting opening.** You might ask a question or give a hint about why this incident is important to you. Or, like the writer of the model to the right, you might set the scene. Provide **background information** by telling your reader what the incident is, who was involved, where the incident took place, and when it happened.

Body
- Beginning of incident (action details and sensory details)
- Middle of incident (action details and sensory details)
- End of incident (action details and sensory details)

- Write the events in **chronological order.**
- Write about the beginning of your incident in the first paragraph of the body, the middle of the incident in the second paragraph, and the end of the incident in the third paragraph.
- Describe each part of the incident using **action details** and **sensory details.**

Conclusion
- Reason this incident is important to you

Explain how this incident affected you. **Why is it important? What does it mean to you?** Leave your reader with a complete picture of what occurred and how you felt.

 Drafting Your Autobiographical Incident

Now it is your turn to write an autobiographical incident. As you write, refer to the framework above and the Writer's Model on the next page.

A Writer's Model

The final draft below closely follows the framework for an autobiographical incident on the previous page.

A Night to Remember

    It was a cool October evening. Excitement and family members filled the auditorium. I was only seven years old, but I was the center of attention. Finally, after weeks of preparation, I would show off all my hard work in a dance recital. Everything would be perfect—so I thought.

    I waited backstage all dressed up in my black leotard and tights with a gold sequined belt. My hair was pulled back in a French braid, and a strong flowery smell of hair spray hung around me. In a booming voice, the master of ceremonies announced that my class was next. As I pranced proudly onto the stage and into the hot, bright stage lights, my dance teacher whispered, "Break a leg!"

    My dance class was doing a routine with boxes two feet by two feet, made of wood. During part of the routine, the entire class was standing in a line on top of our boxes facing the audience. All I had to do in the next move was put one foot on the box next to mine and keep my other foot on my box. It really was an easy move. I was concentrating so much on maintaining the huge smile I had plastered on my face and keeping my head up that I did not look where I was going. I missed my partner's box altogether and slipped. There I was standing on the stage floor when my classmates were on top of their boxes. I could hear giggles coming from the audience, and I felt the heat rush to my face. I remembered my dance teacher had told my class during rehearsal, "If you make a mistake, keep smiling so the audience will not notice." I did my best to follow her advice as I continued with the routine.

(continued)

Side annotations:
- Attention-grabbing opening
- Background information
- Beginning of incident
- Sensory details
- Action details
- Middle of incident
- Action details
- Sensory details

(continued)

End of incident Sensory details Action details	When the curtain dropped, so did my hopes for the evening. I sobbed loudly, tasting the salt from the tears that streamed down my face. I ran backstage, but no one could console me. I just wanted to be left alone.
Reason this incident is important	Recently I realized I *had* been a star that night. I was embarrassed, but I fought the urge to run off the stage. Instead, I finished the routine with a smile on my face. Now when friends and family laugh about the time I slipped during a dance recital, I can laugh too.

Designing Your Writing

Illustrating Your Autobiographical Incident   Illustrations, such as drawings or photographs, can enhance your written description and show why an incident is important and meaningful to you. For instance, say you are writing about the time you received your best present—a puppy. You could include a picture of yourself hugging the puppy with a red ribbon around its neck. The picture shows how excited you were when you got your dog. The writer of the Writer's Model included a photo that was taken the exact moment she slipped during the dance recital. The picture definitely illustrates her embarrassment. There are several ways you can include pictures in your paper. You can paste snapshots on a piece of paper, scan pictures on the computer, or even draw your own illustrations.

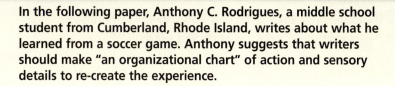

In the following paper, Anthony C. Rodrigues, a middle school student from Cumberland, Rhode Island, writes about what he learned from a soccer game. Anthony suggests that writers should make "an organizational chart" of action and sensory details to re-create the experience.

In the Net

It was two o'clock on a Sunday afternoon, and I was on my way to my championship soccer game. As I rode up to the field and entered the parking lot, I wondered if this game was going to be like the other years when our team made it to the semifinals but then lost in the championship game. I looked at the field and I remembered seeing the pine trees in the background, but it was difficult to concentrate on their beauty because I was so nervous. — **Background information**

One by one the players arrived and the coach told us to begin our warm-up drills and to take shots on our goaltender. I wondered if during the game I was going to shoot as well as I had in warm-ups. — **Beginning of incident**

Finally, it was time. I was in the starting lineup, playing halfback. The whistle blew and the game had officially started. In the first half our team played exceptionally well, but at half time the score was 0–0, and we were all exhausted and cold. In the beginning of the second half we scored a goal. The crowd went up with a roar, and the players were running down the field yelling and screaming. I started to believe that maybe we would win. The second half went on and on. We maintained our 1–0 lead. — **Middle of incident**

We went on to win the game 1–0. I was so excited that I had won my first championship game in all of my six years playing soccer. I learned that anything is possible if I put my mind and soul into it. — **End of incident** / **Reason this incident is important**

Revising

Evaluate and Revise Content, Organization, and Style

Take Two When you are ready to evaluate your essay or a classmate's, you should read the essay twice. In the first reading, look at the essay's content and organization, using the guidelines below. In the second reading, focus on the sentences, using the Focus on Word Choice on page 38. For both readings, be sure to **collaborate** or have a **writing conference** with a classmate to discuss your evaluation.

▶ **First Reading: Content and Organization** Use the chart below to evaluate and revise your autobiographical incident.

Guidelines for Self-Evaluation and Peer Evaluation		
Evaluation Questions	**Tips**	**Revision Techniques**
❶ Does the introduction grab the reader's attention?	**Underline** the question or hint that makes the beginning interesting.	If needed, **add** a question or a hint about the incident's importance.
❷ Does the introduction include enough background information to help the reader understand this incident?	**Circle** information about what the incident is, who was involved, where it took place, and when it happened.	If necessary, **add** sentences that provide background information for the reader.
❸ Are the action details in chronological order?	**Put a number** by each action detail and check that the numbers match the order in which the action happened.	If necessary, **rearrange** action details so that they are in chronological order.
❹ Do sensory details help the reader experience the incident?	Use a colored marker to **highlight** the sensory details.	**Elaborate** on each action detail as needed by adding sensory details that describe what was seen, heard, tasted, felt, or smelled.
❺ Does the conclusion tell why the incident is important to the writer?	**Put a check mark** next to the passage that explains why the event is important.	If needed, **add** thoughts or feelings that will relate the importance of the incident.

36 Chapter 1 **Narration/Description:** Sharing Our Stories

ONE WRITER'S REVISIONS This revision is an early draft of the autobiographical incident on page 33.

> There I was standing on the stage floor when my class-mates were on top of their boxes. I missed my partner's box altogether and slipped. I could hear giggles coming from the audience, *, and I felt the heat rush to my face.* I remembered my dance teacher had told my class during rehearsal, "If you make a mistake, keep smiling so the audience will not notice."

move

elaborate

Responding to the Revision Process

1. Why do you think the writer moved a sentence?
2. Why do you think the writer added information to the paragraph above?

> **PEER REVIEW**
>
> As you look at your peer's autobiographical incident, ask yourself:
>
> - Could the writer add dialogue to elaborate on an event? If so, where?
> - What do I think of the writer's experience? Do I know why it is important to the writer?

▶ **Second Reading: Style** You have revised your essay so that it is well organized and complete. Now, you will check that you have written your autobiographical incident using the best possible sentences. One way to improve your sentences is to use *exact verbs*. **Exact verbs** make your writing better because they accurately express a specific action.

When you evaluate your autobiographical incident for style, ask yourself whether your writing includes verbs that accurately describe certain actions. As you re-read your incident, mark an *X* through ordinary verbs that are not very descriptive. Then, replace the dull verbs with more descriptive ones. The Focus on Word Choice on the next page can help you learn to use exact verbs.

Writing Workshop

Focus on Word Choice

Exact Verbs

One of your purposes when you are writing an autobiographical incident is to help your readers see the action. Exact verbs can help you accomplish your goal. Exact verbs make your writing style more vivid and precise. Look at the following examples. Notice how exact verbs paint a more specific picture of an event in your mind—they make the action come alive.

Dull Verbs
Jesse *ate* his dinner.
Natalie *said*, "I'm leaving!"
Brian *went* to the store.

Exact Verbs
Jesse *gobbled down* his dinner.
Natalie *screamed*, "I'm leaving!"
Brian *raced* to the store.

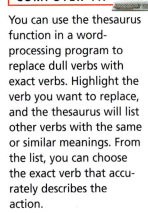

COMPUTER TIP

You can use the thesaurus function in a word-processing program to replace dull verbs with exact verbs. Highlight the verb you want to replace, and the thesaurus will list other verbs with the same or similar meanings. From the list, you can choose the exact verb that accurately describes the action.

ONE WRITER'S REVISIONS

As I ~~walked~~ *pranced* proudly onto the stage and into the hot, bright stage lights, my dance teacher ~~said~~ *whispered*, "Break a leg!"

Responding to the Revision Process

How did replacing dull verbs with exact verbs improve the sentence above?

YOUR TURN 8 — Evaluating and Revising Your Autobiographical Incident

- First, evaluate and revise the content and organization of your paper, using the guidelines on page 36.
- Next, use the Focus on Word Choice above to see if you need to replace dull verbs in your paper with exact verbs.
- If a peer evaluated your paper, think carefully about your peer's comments as you revise.

Proofread Your Narrative

Correctness Counts Errors in your final draft will be distracting to your readers. If you have another person proofread your narrative, you will be less likely to overlook mistakes.

Grammar Link

Capitalizing Proper Nouns

As you write your autobiographical incident, you will use **nouns,** words that name people, places, things, and ideas. There are two kinds of nouns: *common* and *proper*. A **common noun** names any one of a group of persons, places, things, or ideas. A **proper noun** names a particular person, place, thing, or idea, and begins with a capital letter. Here are some examples of common and proper nouns.

Common Nouns	Proper Nouns
city	Boston
religion	Judaism
basketball player	Michael Jordan
teacher	Mr. Williams

Notice that the title *Mr.* is capitalized in the example above. Capitalize a title that comes *immediately* before the person's name.

Example:
Washington, D.C., was named after President George Washington.

Most titles are not capitalized when they are not immediately followed by a name.

Example:
The first president was George Washington.

PRACTICE

Capitalize the proper nouns in the following sentences.

Example:
1. My vacation to visit aunt sue in england was the best.

1. aunt sue ➤ Aunt Sue
   england ➤ England

1. I spent the entire month of july living in london.
2. In one day, we visited the tower of london and buckingham palace.
3. Riding on a boat down the thames river was exciting for my aunt and me.
4. I was hoping to see prince william, but he was in scotland with his father.
5. It took over ten hours for me to travel from london's gatwick airport to george bush intercontinental airport.

Publish Your Essay

Extra, Extra Read All About It   You are finally ready to share your experience with others. After all, that is the purpose of writing an autobiographical incident. How do you go about getting an audience to read your essay?

- One audience could be an older you. Create a scrapbook of your life with the first entry being your autobiographical incident. It will be fun to look back on these memories later in life.
- Make an illustrated book of all the autobiographical incidents from your class. Place the book in your school library for other students to read.
- Create a "Me" poster you could share with your class. Include your autobiographical incident along with pictures and mementos that tell your hobbies, likes and dislikes, and plans for the future.

Reflect on Your Essay

Building Your Portfolio   Your essay is finally written and published. Now, take the time to think about *what* you wrote and *how* you wrote. Reflecting on work that you have completed will make you a better writer in the future.

- What did you find difficult when writing about yourself? What did you find easy?
- Think back on all the steps you took before you actually began writing your autobiographical incident. Which of these steps would you use again when writing another paper?

TIP   As you proofread your essay, use a dictionary to make sure you have spelled words correctly. Don't guess about the correct spelling.

YOUR TURN 9 Proofreading, Publishing, and Reflecting on Your Essay

- Correct grammar, usage, and mechanics errors. Pay particular attention to the capitalization of proper nouns.
- Publish your essay using one of the suggestions above.
- Answer the Reflect on Your Essay questions above. Write your responses in a learning log, or include them in your portfolio.

MINI-LESSON: TEST TAKING

Writing Description for Tests

In an essay test, you may be given a question that asks you to describe a person, place, or thing. Your description should include action details and sensory details. Read the following descriptive writing prompt. How would you answer this type of essay question?

> Think about your friends. Choose one and write a letter to your teacher in which you describe your friend. In your letter, describe in detail what your friend looks like and how your friend acts.

TIP Handwriting is important when answering an essay question. Your teacher or another test grader will not be able to read your answer if your handwriting is not **legible,** or easy to read. To make sure your answer is legible, use your best handwriting. You can print or write in cursive. Choose the style that will be easier for others to read.

THINKING IT THROUGH — Writing a Description

▶ **STEP 1** Read the prompt to see what it is asking you to do. What is your topic? Who is your audience?

The prompt is asking me to write a letter describing a friend. I will describe how my friend Reggie looks and acts. The audience is my teacher.

▶ **STEP 2** List action and sensory details that describe your subject. To picture the details, close your eyes and imagine the subject right in front of you.

<u>Action details</u>: makes good grades, does nice things (shared his sandwich), plays baseball

<u>Sensory details</u>: has curly, short, black hair and brown eyes, is tall (5 feet 3 inches) and thin (about 95 pounds), has a squeaky voice, smells like apples because he always uses apple shampoo

▶ **STEP 3** Decide how you will organize your details. Then, write your description.

First paragraph: I will tell what Reggie looks like.
Second paragraph: I will tell how he acts.

▶ **STEP 4** Read your description, checking for details that allow your reader to see your subject clearly.

I will check to see that I have a really good description of what Reggie looks like and how he acts.

Connections to Literature

Writing a Narrative Poem

Just as there are different types of stories—funny, sad, scary—there are different ways to present them to an audience. One way to present a story is by writing a narrative poem. A **narrative poem** has characters and a beginning, middle, and end. When you wrote your autobiographical incident, you wrote a *prose* narrative. Now you have a chance to be a poet by writing a narrative *poem*.

Start with the Basics It is not difficult to create a poem once you understand how poems are written. Poets say things in unusual ways. They often use very few words, so they have to select their words very carefully. Poets use sounds and figurative language to express their thoughts and feelings and to paint a picture of people, places, things, and actions.

The following list will provide you with the definitions and examples of the most common poetic elements.

Alliteration is the repetition of consonant sounds, especially sounds at the beginning of words.

S̲ara c̲ertainly s̲aw S̲am s̲ail to S̲ardinia.

B̲obby b̲uilt r̲ubber b̲aby b̲uggy b̲umpers.

Figurative Language is descriptive language that is not meant to be taken literally. Figurative language is used to express an idea by making a comparison that will give readers a clearer picture of the idea. For example, saying a noise is loud is not as clear as comparing the noise to eighty bowlers all making strikes at the same time. Three types of figurative language are *personification*, *simile*, and *metaphor*.

- **Personification** is describing something that is not human, such as an animal or object, as if it were human by giving it human qualities.

  The *joyful* sparrow chirped *hello*.

  Each morning the alarm clock *screams* at me to get out of bed.

- **Simile** compares two different things using the word *like* or *as*.

  Like a statue, I sat motionless.

  The leaves fell as quietly *as* a whisper.

- **Metaphor** compares two different things by saying one is the other.

  He *is* a bottomless pit, eating everything in sight.

  When she first wakes up in the morning, her hair *is* a tangled bird's nest.

Seeing Is Believing Read the narrative poem on the next page. What event is the poet relating? What are his thoughts and feelings? What other examples of alliteration or figurative language can you find?

Foul Shot
by Edwin A. Hoey

With two 60's stuck on the scoreboard
And two seconds hanging on the clock,
The solemn boy in the center of eyes,
Squeezed by silence,
Seeks out the line with his feet,
Soothes his hands along his uniform,
Gently drums the ball against the floor,
Then measures the waiting net,
Raises the ball on his right hand,
Balances it with his left,
Calms it with fingertips,
Breathes,
Crouches,
Waits,
And then through a stretching of stillness,
Nudges it upward.
The ball
Slides up and out,
Lands,
Leans,
Wobbles,
Wavers,
Hesitates,
Exasperates,
Plays it coy
Until every face begs with unsounding screams—
And then
        And then
                And then,
Right before ROAR-UP,
Dives down and through.

Figurative language: personification—silence is squeezing the boy

Alliteration—lands and leans

Alliteration—wobbles and wavers

Figurative language: personification—the ball is playing it coy

---

TIP As you read the narrative poem, notice that
- the incident can be the title of the poem
- a narrative poem does not have to be auto-biographical
- events are written in chronological order so the reader can understand the incident
- placing one word on a line can emphasize that word or thought
- exact verbs provide an accurate description of the action

Got the Idea? How did the author of "Foul Shot" fit a story into a poem? As you can see, the author based his poem on a specific incident. The poem describes, in order, the events that happened during a free-throw shot. The poet did not take five pages to describe the incident, nor did he just list the events by saying, "The boy bounced the ball a few times, threw it, and it went into the basket." Instead, he selected his words carefully and used alliteration and figurative language. The poet's words put you there in the gym. You can see the action clearly and feel the crowd's hopes and the boy's nervousness.

The Ball Is in Your Court Now that you have read an example, try writing your own narrative poem by following the steps below.

1. Brainstorm an incident to write about that you don't mind sharing with others. The incident could be the title of your poem.
2. In the first stanza (group of lines), describe where the character is and how he or she feels. You can write about yourself or a **fictional,** or made-up, character.
3. In the second stanza, describe what the character is doing and what he or she is thinking. Remember, each line does not have to be a complete sentence. You can write a phrase or one word on a line.
4. In the last stanza of your poem, tell how the incident ends.

Making It Better Once you have written the basic events that make up your narrative poem, you can revise your poem. You want to make sure you have used the best words to relate your ideas and feelings. Use the following suggestions to add poetic sounds and descriptions to your poem. Remember, a poem does not have to rhyme unless you want it to. There are other poetic elements you can use. Look for places where you can

- make several words that are near each other all begin with the same sound
- give human qualities to a feeling, animal, or object
- compare two unlike things using *like* or *as*
- compare two unlike things by saying one *is* the other

YOUR TURN 10 **Writing and Revising a Narrative Poem**

Write a narrative poem using the steps above. Then, revise your poem by adding as many of the poetic elements on page 42 as you can. Make a clean copy of your narrative poem and share it with a friend or give a **dramatic presentation** of your poem to your class.

Focus on Speaking and Listening

Telling a Story

The art of storytelling has been around for a very long time. Before people could write, they told stories. Early storytellers would explain things in nature, teach lessons, and retell historical events. The **oral tradition** continued as these stories were passed from one generation to the next.

People still enjoy listening to a good story. In order to make a story entertaining, storytellers plan and practice before sharing a story with an audience. You can use the following guidelines as you prepare to tell a story.

WHAT'S AHEAD?

In this section you will tell a story. You will also learn how to
- keep your audience's attention
- make your story entertaining
- understand your audience's needs

Plan Your Story

To keep your audience's attention, plan to give them what they want—action. Choose an incident that has more "doing" than "describing." Your story will be more interesting if it keeps moving with action details.

You should also plan to tell your story in **chronological order**. You want your audience to be eager to find out what will happen next. Build **suspense** by saving the outcome until the very last moment. Jotting down the events on note cards will help you. Use three note cards, one each for the beginning, middle, and end of your story.

Your audience will also want **background information**. What will the audience need to know to understand your story? Answer this question before you begin practicing.

TIP Use formal language when telling your story. Use informal language, such as slang, only when a character is speaking and you are sure your audience will understand it.

Practice Your Story

Before you tell your story in front of an audience, you will need to practice what you have planned. You will also need to practice making your story entertaining. How do you do that? It's simple.

TIP Language, especially sayings or names for things, reflects different regions and cultures. For example, do you say *you*, *y'all*, or *you guys* when talking to a group? If possible, include in your story the specific words and phrases that a character from a different culture or part of the country might say.

Speak Out Your voice is the most important tool when telling a story, so use it. Practice speaking loudly enough for the people in the back row to hear; talk slowly and clearly enough for your audience to understand you. Also, practice changing the levels of your voice to change the mood. For instance, whispering adds suspense, and yelling suddenly can show surprise. You can even change your voice entirely. Try using different voices so the audience will know when different characters are speaking.

Show and Tell Words alone cannot express a story fully. Facial expressions and gestures are important as well. Don't tell everything; practice showing your actions. If you were telling a story about falling off your mountain bike, you might fall to the floor, grab your knee, and grimace as if in pain. You can include **sensory details** in your story by using gestures, too. For example, covering your ears shows that you heard a loud noise.

Practice Makes Perfect Practice telling your story in front of a friend and let your friend make suggestions on how you can improve your presentation. Make sure that you tell your story to your friend the same way you would tell it to a real audience. Keep the events in order, include background information, and use your voice and gestures.

Share Your Story

As you share your story, maintain eye contact with your audience. By looking at your audience, you can tell what they need. If the faces in your audience look puzzled, give background information or a more detailed explanation. If your audience is distracted or, worse, falling asleep, wake them up by performing an action or speaking in a different voice. The more lively you are, the more your audience will enjoy your story. Have fun. Telling a story should be an enjoyable experience for the audience and for you.

Reference Note
For more on adjusting **volume, rate, pitch** (your voice's highs and lows), and **tone** (or mood), see page 304. For more on **oral interpretation**, see page 307.

YOUR TURN 11 **Telling a Story**

Follow the guidelines above to share a story and make connections with your classmates. As you tell your story and listen to your classmates' stories, do you notice similar experiences?

CHAPTER 1 Choices

Choose one of the following activities to complete.

▶ CAREERS
1. When I Grow Up Read an autobiography or biography about a person who has a career that interests you. When you are finished, write a **journal entry** telling one thing that surprised you about the person and the career.

▶ SPEECH
2. Telling Tales All cultures have stories that are passed on from one generation to the next. These stories, called folk tales, come from the **oral tradition.** Even though folk tales reflect the particular culture that created them, tales from different cultures have common features, such as talking animals. Compare two folk tales from different cultures, and present your findings to your class in an **oral report.**

▶ DRAMA
3. Another Life With a few other classmates, present a **dramatic interpretation** of a play based on the life of a real person. For example, *The Miracle Worker* is about Helen Keller. You can find plays in the drama section of your school or local library.

▶ WRITING
4. Larger Than Life Write a **tall tale,** a story full of exaggerations, by taking a real incident and describing it with larger-than-life details. For instance, say you went fishing and caught a two-pounder that did not put up much of a fight. In your tall tale, however, the fish weighed twenty pounds, and it took you *and* a friend to drag it into the boat! If you wish, produce your tale as a **puppet show** or **skit.**

▶ TECHNOLOGY
5. You've Got Mail If you have access to e-mail, send an **e-mail message** to a friend describing an event that has just occurred in your life. Give background information so your friend will understand what happened.

PORTFOLIO

Choices 47

CHAPTER 2

Reporting the News

CONNECTING READING AND WRITING

Reading Workshop

Reading a Newspaper Article

Writing Workshop

Writing a Newspaper Article

Viewing and Representing

Producing a Newspaper

Viewing and Representing

Producing a TV News Segment

Informational Text

Exposition

You and your classmates are riding the bus to school when suddenly the bus stalls. The bus driver tries to start the bus, but is unsuccessful. A trip that normally takes thirty minutes has turned into a two-hour ordeal. This event has made a big impression on you, but you probably will not see it reported on tonight's newscast or in tomorrow's newspaper. What makes some events worth reporting in the news and others not? Newsworthy events are not just recent events. They must also affect many people or simply grab people's attention.

YOUR TURN 1 Looking at the News

Find an example of a news story. You can watch the news on television, listen to the news on the radio, or find a news article in a newspaper or magazine. Then, answer the following questions about the story you found.

- What event is the news story about?
- Who would want to know about this event?
- Why do you think this event made the news?

GO TO: go.hrw.com
KEYWORD: EOLang 6-2

Reading Workshop

Reading a Newspaper Article

WHAT'S AHEAD?

In this section you will read a news article. You will also learn how to

- identify the main idea of a news article
- recognize the pattern of a news article called inverted pyramid structure

Can an orphaned baby whale survive without its parents? Students in California are asking the same question. They have been logging onto the Internet to check the status of the baby whale ever since she was returned to the ocean. What started as a history project focusing on current events has turned into something more. Find out what students have learned from this project by reading the news article on the next page.

Preparing to Read

READING SKILL

Main Idea   The **main idea** is the most important point a writer wants to make. Sometimes the main idea is *stated*. This means it will be written in a sentence or two. Other times the main idea is *implied*, or suggested. In that case, you will have to look for clues to figure out the writer's most important point. As you read the following article, see if you can figure out the main idea.

READING FOCUS

Inverted Pyramid Structure   A news event is made up of many details that answer the *5W-How?* questions.

- *Who* was involved?
- *What* happened?
- *When* did the event take place?
- *Where* did the event occur?
- *Why* did the event happen?
- *How* did the event happen?

News writers organize these details in an **inverted pyramid** (upside-down triangle) **structure** that begins with the most important details and ends with the least important details. Why do you think news articles are organized this way?

Chapter 2   **Exposition:** Reporting the News

Reading Selection

Read the following news article. In a notebook, write the answers to the numbered active-reading questions in the shaded boxes. The underlined words will be discussed in the Vocabulary Mini-Lesson on page 56.

FROM LOS ANGELES TIMES; ORANGE COUNTY EDITION

Whale Watch: Kids Use Internet to Track Progress of Newly Freed J. J.

BY LISA RICHARDSON

MISSION VIEJO—Marine experts from Sea World are using the latest radio transmission technology to monitor J. J., the newly freed gray whale.

Ten sixth-graders at Barcelona Hills Elementary School in Mission Viejo are doing the same thing, using the Internet.

Since the fifteen-month-old whale was orphaned last year, the group has followed her arrival at Sea World, how she has adapted to her handlers and, most recently, her return to the ocean and ride to freedom Tuesday.

The group has amassed an encyclopedic amount of whale knowledge over the months, and students can spout whale family classifications, whale dietary habits, and whale growth patterns with ease.

The group, students of history teacher Kaye Denison, spent most of Thursday morning on the Internet, checking reports on the whale's progress.

Having followed J. J. for so long, the eleven- and twelve-year-olds have put some thought into why—beyond scientific reasons—saving her life and studying her is important.

They have concluded that even if animals and mammals don't love human beings, it's natural for humans to love them.

At their school, the kids care for frogs, snakes, a chameleon, a skunk, an iguana, fish, and water turtles. They are sure the animals are indifferent toward them, but it doesn't stop them from liking the creatures.

"I heard on the news that you're not lonely and your life is not so stressful with animals in it, and I think it's true," said Sean Kingsmill, twelve.

"I mean, people are lonely," A. J. Young said.

1. What have the sixth-graders been doing for several months?

2. How are the students keeping track of J. J.'s progress?

"For example, wouldn't you be lonely if you didn't live at all with anybody, and wouldn't you want a dog or something?"

Learning about the whale has been fun. They know that J. J. weighs more than 17,000 pounds, is 29 feet long, and gains 2 pounds every hour. Killer whales are natural enemies of gray whales, and while adults eat plankton,[1] J. J. existed mostly on a mixture of milk, powdered fish, and warm cream passed through a tube into her stomach.

"It's important to save her because they come from an extinct [endangered] species, and it's good since they're coming back up," said Danielle Howannesian, eleven. "Besides, babies are always cute."

---

1. **plankton:** microscopic animals and plants.

It is largely affection for the baby whale that keeps them interested in her plight.

They sympathized with J. J.'s orphanhood and her efforts to learn survival skills. When she was released, the group felt bad for the whale's disappointed handlers, who said J. J. did not make her typical sound of gratitude before swimming away. But they believe J. J. will miss her handlers after awhile. . . .

For now the group relies on updates posted to the Sea World Web site . . . , but by next Friday, the satellite tracking system should begin receiving transmissions directly from J. J., and the students will have access to more current information.

But the class doesn't spend all its time on J. J. For another project in Denison's class, the children had to pretend they were Hollywood location <u>scouts</u> and, using computers, map important sites in ancient Egypt. The project was coupled with lessons on chemical warfare in neighboring Iraq and political tension in the region.

"My class is actually an ancient history class, but because we're really involved in current events, we tie in whatever is happening in the world," Denison said.

Members of the "Barcelona Hills J. J. Fan Club"—what one student <u>dubbed</u> the group—say they will follow the whale's progress until they are sure she is safe or has joined a <u>pod</u> of whales.

"We've been with it this long," said Lindsay Murray, twelve. "We have to make sure that she's going to be OK."

---

3. Do you think the information in the second paragraph above should appear earlier in the article? Why or why not?

4. According to the first paragraph above, why does this project interest students?

5. Is the information in the two paragraphs at the top of this column necessary to understand the class's "J. J." project? Why or why not?

> **First Thoughts on Your Reading**
> 1. What is this article about?
> 2. Where are the most important details in the article located?

Main Idea

Behind the Wheel   What do a bicycle wheel and a news article have in common? You may have noticed that the spokes on a bicycle wheel lead directly to the hub, which is the central point of the wheel. News articles also have a central point, or **main idea**. All the details lead the reader to the main idea, which can be stated or implied. A **stated main idea** is one that is written out in a sentence or two.

Example:
Brian Caspar's quick thinking saved his friend's life.

An **implied main idea,** or suggested main idea, is not found in a specific sentence. The reader must look at how the supporting details are related to figure out the implied main idea.

Example:
Brian Caspar found his friend lying unconscious on the floor. After calling 911, Brian began CPR before paramedics arrived. His friend is now in stable condition.

All the details in the example above support the main idea: Brian thought quickly and saved his friend's life.

Read the news article below. Can you identify the main idea? Use the Thinking It Through steps on the next page if you need help.

> To make room for a new playground, Urban Demolition, Inc., used dynamite to demolish the old Paramount Theater on Elm Avenue last Wednesday.
> The demolition took approximately nine seconds from start to finish. Dust hovered over Elm Avenue and the surrounding areas for several hours.
> Urban Demolition crews estimate that it will take a week for them to clear the rubble.

TIP   Whether you are reading a newspaper article, a short story, or a research report, you should look for a main idea. Finding the main idea will help you understand the supporting details.

THINKING IT THROUGH

Identifying the Main Idea in a News Article

▶ **STEP 1** Identify the main idea by asking, "*Who* (or *what*) did *what* and *why?*"

Urban Demolition, Inc., demolished the Paramount Theater to make room for a playground.

▶ **STEP 2** Check to see that you identified the main idea by asking, "Do all the details support my answer?"

The details tell me how long it took, what happened afterward, and what will happen in the future. They all relate to the demolition.

YOUR TURN 2 Identifying the Main Idea

Re-read the news article on pages 51–52. Then, use the Thinking It Through steps above to identify the article's main idea.

| READING FOCUS |

Inverted Pyramid Structure

Why Save the Best for Last?   After dinner, you can have dessert. After you clean your room, you can see your friends. Have you ever asked yourself, "Why do I have to *wait* for all the good stuff?" You don't have to wait when you read a news article.

News articles are arranged in an **inverted pyramid structure.** An inverted pyramid is an upside-down triangle. The wide part of the triangle holds the *lead.* The **lead,** which can be more than one paragraph long, is the beginning of a news article. It summarizes the most important information about an event by answering the *5W-How?* questions: *Who? What? When? Where? Why?* and *How?* Readers who are in a hurry can understand the event by reading just the lead.

The rest of the news article provides readers with more information about the event. The details are presented in order from most important to least important. Why? If an article is longer than the amount of space the news editor has set aside for it, some of the information will need to be cut. Cutting is easy when the least important details are at the end of the article. The news

Lead
(5W-How?
questions)
Details
Details
Details

editor can start at the end and cut details until the article fits its assigned space. An inverted pyramid structure saves time for both the reader and the news editor.

Cut to Fit   Edie, a newspaper editor, has room for a four-paragraph article, but the following article has five paragraphs. Notice how Edie rearranged the details so that the important ones are at the beginning, then cut the unimportant details so the article now has only four paragraphs.

> Malcolm Scott, CEO of Happy Faces Corporation, announced plans today to build a new amusement park west of downtown.
>
> ~~"I can't wait for the park to open," said eleven year old Hector Garza. "I will be the first one in line."~~
>
> "We want to give people, especially kids, a fun and exciting place to visit," said Scott.
>
> The park will be a good source of entertainment, say city officials. It will also create jobs and bring additional money to the community from tourists.
>
> Construction for the new amusement park will begin in September and should be completed by the end of April. The grand opening is scheduled for the beginning of May.

Answers to *who, what,* and *where*

Answers to *why*

Answers to *how* and *when*

TIP   The paragraphs in a newspaper article are usually very short, sometimes only one or two sentences. Shorter paragraphs with fewer details make reading a news article easier and more efficient.

TIP   How does an editor decide which details are less important than others? You already know that the *most* important details answer the *5W-How?* questions about the topic. Among the details that follow the lead, those judged more important than others might be ones that

- are more recent
- concern more readers
- are more attention-grabbing

YOUR TURN 3   Editing a News Article

Make a copy of the news article on pages 51–52. In a group, re-read it with news editors' eyes.

- After reading, discuss whether the answers to the *5W-How?* questions are in the lead. If they are not, rearrange the paragraphs so that the answers are at the beginning.
- Then, cut the least important details in the article so it will fit in a space for a fifteen-paragraph article. You will need to cut four paragraphs. Use the second Tip in the margin above to decide which details are less important.

Reading Workshop

MINI-LESSON VOCABULARY

Multiple-Meaning Words

When you read the newspaper, do you ever get confused by a word you have known for years? When that happens, you have probably stumbled upon a **multiple-meaning word,** a word with more than one meaning.

- A multiple-meaning word can have two or more very different definitions.

  Examples:
  Marcus *filed* the papers. (to put in place)

  The band members *filed* onto the field. (to move in a line)

- A multiple-meaning word can be used as more than one part of speech.

  Examples:
  If you know the answer, raise your *hand*. (part of the body—noun)

  Can you *hand* me the hammer, please? (to give by hand—verb)

THINKING IT THROUGH — Understanding Multiple-Meaning Words

The following steps can help you find the correct meaning of a multiple-meaning word. The example below is from the reading selection.

Example:
"Members of the 'Barcelona Hills J. J. Fan Club'—what one student <u>dubbed</u> the group . . ."

I think <u>dubbed</u> means "you record over the original," but that definition doesn't make sense here.

▸ **STEP 1** Look at how the word is used in the passage. What do the words and sentences around it tell you?

The sentence says that one student <u>dubbed</u> the class the "Barcelona Hills J. J. Fan Club." It sounds like <u>dubbed</u> means "to name."

▸ **STEP 2** Check your definition in the original sentence. Ask yourself, "Does this definition make sense?"

"Members of the Barcelona Hills J. J. Fan Club—what one student <u>named</u> the group . . ." That makes sense to me.

PRACTICE

Use the steps above to define the following multiple-meaning words. The words are underlined for you in the reading selection.

1. marine (page 51)
2. spout (page 51)
3. concluded (page 51)
4. scouts (page 52)
5. pod (page 52)

MINI-LESSON TEST TAKING

Answering Main Idea Questions

Just as a lead will tell you the most important points of a news article, a main idea will tell you the central point of a reading passage. When you take a reading test, you may be asked to identify the main idea of a reading selection. Read the following passage and question. How would you answer the question?

> Gray whales exhibit a number of interesting behaviors. They often show their flukes, or tails, when they dive. A diving whale is said to be *sounding*. Gray whales can also leap out of the water and fall back, creating a big splash. This type of behavior is called *breaching*. *Spyhopping* occurs when a whale peeks its head vertically out of the water, possibly to see above the surface. You can see the behaviors of gray whales off the west coast of the United States from late fall until early spring.

What is the main idea of this passage?

A. Whale watching is a fun activity.
B. Whales can leap out of the water.
C. Spyhopping allows whales to see above the surface.
D. Gray whales display many interesting behaviors.

THINKING IT THROUGH | Identifying the Main Idea

▶ **STEP 1** Decide what the question asks.

I need to find the main idea.

▶ **STEP 2** Look at what all the details have in common. The details should point to the main idea. **Hint:** Pay attention to the first and last sentences. Sometimes you may find a sentence that states the main idea.

All of the details describe the behaviors of gray whales. The first sentence tells me that gray whales have different behaviors, and the last sentence tells me where and when I can see them.

▶ **STEP 3** State the main idea in your own words. Then, look for an answer that closely matches your own. Rule out answers that are obviously wrong.

Gray whales exhibit three different behaviors. Answer choice D says something like that.

▶ **STEP 4** Check to make sure that the details in the paragraph or passage support your answer.

The different behaviors of gray whales are sounding, breaching, and spyhopping. Those details support my answer.

Writing Workshop

Writing a Newspaper Article

WHAT'S AHEAD?

In this workshop you will write a newspaper article. You will also learn how to

- choose a news-worthy event
- organize and evaluate details
- analyze cause and effect
- vary sentence structure
- correct run-on sentences

The headlines read "Mayor Honors Sixth-Grade Student," "Wind Rips Roof off Middle School," and "Girl Saves Brother from Shark Attack." Interesting events occur every day everywhere—even where you live. Would you like to be the one to tell the story? You can, by writing a news article.

News articles are a form of **expository,** or **informative,** writing. They provide readers with information about events that have happened recently. In this Writing Workshop you will write a newspaper article. Your article will explain an interesting event of your choice.

Prewriting

Choose and Evaluate an Event

Look and Listen Interesting events will not just fall into your lap. To find one, you may need to do a little digging. You won't be digging with a shovel, though. Instead, you will use your eyes and ears. Here are some suggestions you can use to find an event that has already happened.

- Talk to presidents and sponsors of clubs at your school about events that have happened recently.
- Ask members of local organizations, such as the PTA or city council, about recent decisions they have made.
- Make a list of recent events you have observed firsthand.

Is It Worth It? Would you spend all your time gathering, organizing, writing, revising, and publishing information about an event if no one is going to find your article interesting? Of course not. **Make your time and the readers' time worthwhile by writing about an event that is newsworthy.** An event is newsworthy if it has at least one of the following characteristics.

KEY CONCEPT

Newsworthy Characteristic	Example
The event . . .	
makes a difference in people's lives	World leaders announce plans to help nations' starving people.
is current	A hurricane slams into the East Coast.
involves people who are famous or in power	A famous singer gives a free concert.
touches people's emotions	Students organize a fund-raiser to help an animal shelter buy supplies.

TIP Events can have more than one newsworthy characteristic. For instance, a school newspaper's story about the volleyball team's win in the state tournament is current *and* touches people's emotions. Reporters look for events with more than one newsworthy characteristic so more people will read their articles.

An article's newsworthiness also depends on the purpose of the newspaper. For example, school or community newspapers generally focus on local events. However, city and national newspapers focus on a range of events, from local to worldwide.

YOUR TURN 4 Choosing and Evaluating an Event

- Make a list of events that have happened recently in your school or community.
- Then, evaluate each event on your list by looking for newsworthy characteristics. (Assume you are writing for a community or school newspaper.)
- Choose the event with the greatest number of newsworthy characteristics as the subject of your news article.

Writing Workshop   59

Identify Your Audience

Who Wants to Know?   The school board meeting is over. Your teacher wants to know if the school board approved a pay raise for teachers, but you want to know what the board decided about school uniforms.

Different events interest different people. The people who will be interested in the event you have chosen are your **audience**. To figure out the audience for your news article, ask yourself, "Who will be interested in this event, and why?"

Here is how a student identified his news article's audience.

> Event: I am writing about the principal approving a longer passing period between classes at my school.
>
> Audience: I think teachers and students will be interested because this event happened at school, and the longer passing period will affect them.

YOUR TURN 5 Identifying Your Audience

In your notebook, complete the sentences below to identify the audience for your news article.

Event: I am writing about _____.

Audience: I think _____ will be interested because _____.

Gather Details

Just the Facts   Your friend tells you he saw a famous sports star. You want to know all about it. "Who? When? Where? Tell me!" you beg.

KEY CONCEPT

Just as you want all the facts of your friend's encounter with a sports star, **your audience will want all the facts of the newsworthy event.** Answers to the *5W-How?* questions will provide your readers with the facts, or details, of the event. The following chart shows specific questions you should try to answer as you gather the details for your news article.

Who?	Who was involved in the event? (Names are important, but also try to get other details about the people involved, such as titles, ages, or professions.)
What?	What was the event?
When?	When did the event occur? (Get the time and date of the event.)
Where?	Where did the event take place? (Find out the address or location.)
Why?	Why did the event happen?
How?	How did the event happen? (List the smaller events that made up the event.)

The *5W-How?* questions will give your audience the basic information about the event, but some readers will want to know even more. To help your audience fully understand the event, find the answers to these questions as well.

- What are the effects of the event?
- How do people feel about the event?

> **TIP** A news article's **voice** is *objective*, or factual. When you write a news article, use words that simply state the facts. For instance, instead of writing about a "cute cocker spaniel," stick to the facts and write about a "one-year-old cocker spaniel." The dog's age is a fact because it can be proven. "Cute," on the other hand, is a matter of opinion.

Get to the Source You know what information you need, but how do you go about getting the answers to your questions? **Gather details for your news article by interviewing people who witnessed the event or played a part in it.** Even if *you* observed the event firsthand, you should still talk to other people.

As you interview, take notes about what people say, but also record a few direct quotations. In other words, write down what people say word-for-word instead of summarizing. Readers find direct quotations interesting because they have more force than a summary. You can see the power of a direct quotation in the example on the next page.

KEY CONCEPT

> **TIP** In an interview, avoid asking questions with *yes* or *no* answers. Instead, ask questions that will give you more information, such as, "What do you think about the longer passing period?"

Summary: Neil Armstrong was the first man to walk on the moon. Armstrong felt his first step was an exciting moment not only for him but for the rest of the world as well.

Direct Quotation: Neil Armstrong was the first man to walk on the moon. As he made his first step he said, "That's one small step for [a] man, one giant leap for mankind."

The following example shows the notes one student took as he interviewed people. Notice that he includes details that answer the *5W-How?* questions, information about the effects of the event, and people's reactions to it. The student also recorded direct quotations that support some of the details.

TIP Your job as a reporter is to present a balanced picture of news events. That means you should present a range of different opinions. You will not include your *own* opinions about the event. To give his audience a balanced picture of the event, the student reporting on the extended passing period got direct quotations from people on both sides of the issue.

Who? Principal Reyes

What? He approved a longer passing period between classes.

When? He announced it at today's pep rally.

Where? Main Street Middle School

Why? Principal Reyes agreed that students needed more time to go to their lockers and the restroom between classes.

How? Morgan Sykes passed a petition around last Wed. and Thurs. It was given to Principal Reyes on Fri.—134 people signed it.

What are the effects of the event? Starts Oct. 7. Classes—5 minutes shorter except 7th period. Passing period—5 minutes longer. School is still over at 3:00 P.M.

How do people feel about the event?
Negative reaction: Toby Washington, 7th grade: "I like my classes. I don't want them to be five minutes shorter. Those five minutes give me a chance to start my homework."

Positive reaction: Paul Brook, 6th-grade history teacher: "I'm so happy that instruction will not be interrupted by students leaving class to go to the restroom or their lockers."

Positive reaction: Joanna Tran, 6th grade: "The extra time will help me clear my head after one class and gear up for the next."

YOUR TURN 6 — Gathering Details

Gather details and direct quotations for your news article by interviewing people involved in and affected by the event. Remember that you are looking for answers to the *5W-How?* questions, information about the effects of the event, and people's reactions to the event.

Organize and Evaluate Details

Go Ahead, Spoil Them!   Your readers not only want information about an event, they want to read the most important information first. Give your readers what they want by organizing the details you have gathered in a logical progression—an inverted pyramid structure. **In an inverted pyramid structure, the most important details appear at the beginning of a news article, and the least important details appear at the end.** The inverted pyramid structure of a news article looks like this:

Reference Note

For more on **inverted pyramid structure,** see page 54.

KEY CONCEPT

> Lead (answers the *5W-How?* questions)
> Most important details
> Less important details
> Least important details

To arrange your details in an inverted pyramid structure, start by identifying the details that will go in the *lead*. The **lead** is the beginning of an article, and it provides the answers to the *5W-How?* questions. If your audience reads only the lead, they will still have an idea of what happened.

Once you know which details go in the lead, evaluate the remaining details, and arrange them in descending, or decreasing, order of importance. How do you organize details from most important to least important? Look at your details about the effects of the event and people's reactions to it. Think about your audience and ask yourself the questions on the following page.

- **Which details would give my audience a better understanding of the event?** The answer to this question will point to the most important details, the ones that will follow the lead.
- **What additional information is likely to interest my *whole* audience?** You have identified information for the lead and other important details of the event. Look over your remaining notes. What *other* information is likely to interest *all* your readers? This information, though less important than the lead, is important enough for the middle of the article.
- **What information might interest *just a few members* of my audience?** Your audience may contain a group with a special interest in certain details. The "least important" details may still be of interest to this group. These types of details go at the end of the article.

Reference Note
For more on **evaluating details,** see the second Tip on page 55.

This is how the student writing about the passing period change arranged the details for his news article.

Lead: answers to the 5W-How? questions

Most important details:
—information about when the passing period starts and the effect on class time, passing period time, and school hours

Less important details:
—information about how students feel about the longer passing period
—positive quotation from Joanna Tran and negative quotation from Toby Washington

Least important details:
—information about teachers appreciating the extra time as much as the students do and positive quotation from Paul Brook

---

YOUR TURN 7 Organizing and Evaluating Details

Organize your details in an inverted pyramid structure. First, place the answers to the *5W-How?* questions in the lead. Then, arrange the remaining details from most important to least important by asking yourself the questions that appear at the top of this page.

MINI-LESSON: CRITICAL THINKING

Analyzing Cause and Effect

Have you ever set a series of dominoes upright in a row? When the first domino in line tips over, it causes the next one to fall, which causes the next one to fall, and so on. Analyzing a cause-and-effect chain is like watching a chain of dominoes, because it involves looking at how one thing leads to another.

Below is an example of a cause-and-effect chain. Can you see how each cause leads to an effect, which then causes another effect, and so on?

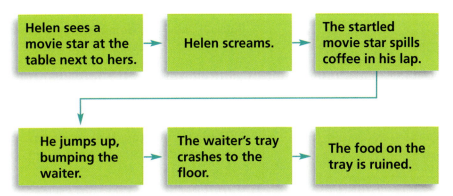

Your news article will explain the causes and the effects of an event. As you write, make sure that the relationships between the causes and effects are clear. If you leave out a portion of the cause-and-effect chain, your audience may not fully understand the event. For example, suppose your little brothers are happily playing together in the living room. You leave to get a snack. When you come back, one brother is crying, and the other brother is yelling. What happened? You missed what caused your brothers to fight. Causes and effects need to be connected clearly in order for them to make sense.

PRACTICE

Create five cause-and-effect chains. The following causes will be the first step in each chain. Use your imagination and experience to complete the chains. Each chain should have at least three steps.

1. A river overflows due to heavy rain.
2. A tornado is seen near town.
3. Sixth-grade students take snacks to a local nursing home.
4. Ms. Martinez, a science teacher, wins the Teacher of the Year award.
5. Greg Goldstein sings off-key during the choir's concert.

Writing Workshop

News Article

Framework | **Directions and Explanations**

Lead
- Attention-grabbing opening
- Answers to the *5W-How?* questions

Capture your audience's attention by beginning your article with an unusual or interesting detail.

Detail	Several animals escaped from Pete's Pets on Friday.
Unusual Detail	Charlie the chimpanzee led several of his animal friends on a daring escape from Pete's Pets on Friday.

Then, write a sentence that answers, at least, "*Who did what?*" Finally, give the remaining answers to the *5W-How?* questions.

Keep in mind your lead may be one to three short paragraphs, depending on the amount of information you gathered.

Body
- Most important details
- Less important details
- Least important details

- Organize the remaining **details** in an inverted pyramid structure. Refer to your responses to Your Turn 7 for the order of these details. Be sure the remaining details include information about the effects of the event and people's reactions to it.
- Group the details in short paragraphs.
- Place **direct quotations** after the details they support.

YOUR TURN 8 Writing Your News Article

Now it is your turn to write a news article. As you write,
- keep your audience in mind
- order your details so that the most important ones come first and the least important ones come last
- refer to the framework above and to the Writer's Model on the next page

66   Chapter 2   **Exposition:** Reporting the News

A Writer's Model

The final draft below closely follows the framework for a news article on the previous page.

Principal Approves Longer Passing Period

A major change has taken place at Main Street Middle School: The period between each class is now five minutes longer. Principal Alan Reyes approved the longer passing period. His decision was announced at today's pep rally in Loftus Gymnasium. *[Attention-grabbing opening / Answer to where / Answers to what and who / Answer to when]*

Eighth-grader Morgan Sykes started the petition that led to the longer passing period. She passed the petition to other students last Wednesday and Thursday. When Principal Reyes received it last Friday, 134 students had signed it. *[Answer to how]*

Principal Reyes agreed that students need extra time between classes. With a longer passing period, students will not have to leave class to go to their lockers or the restroom. *[Answer to why]*

The longer passing period will go into effect on Monday, October 7. From now on, each class except seventh period will be five minutes shorter, and the passing periods will be five minutes longer. School will still be over at 3:00 P.M. *[Most important details]*

Most students are happy about the change, and they are already making plans for the extended passing time. Sixth-grader Joanna Tran said, "The extra time will help me clear my head after one class and gear up for the next." *[Less important details / Quotation]*

At least one student disapproved of the new passing period. "I like my classes. I don't want them to be five minutes shorter," said seventh-grader Toby Washington. "Those five minutes give me a chance to start my homework." *[Quotation]*

Most teachers will enjoy the extra time as much as the students will. "I'm so happy that instruction will not be interrupted by students leaving class to go to the restroom or their lockers," said sixth-grade history teacher Paul Brook. *[Least important details / Quotation]*

A Student's Model

When you write a news article, you want to choose a newsworthy topic. Natalie Banta and Amy Tidwell, reporters for Olympus Junior High's online newspaper the *Olympian,* write about an important school event—the principal leaving.

Mr. Sagers Moves to Cyprus High

Attention-grabbing opening

Maybe you have heard the rumor about Principal Sagers leaving Olympus Junior High School. Well, it is true. Mr. Sagers was promoted to be the principal of Cyprus High.

Answers to *who,* *what, why,* and *how*

The new principal of Olympus Junior High (OJH) will be Linda Mariotti. She has been the assistant principal at Bonneville and at Granite High, a coordinator at the Jones Center, and a language specialist. We will meet her next September.

Answer to *when*
Most important details

When we asked Principal Sagers what he would miss the most about OJH, he answered that he would miss the attitude of the community. "Everyone seems to have high expectations of learning," he said.

Less important details

Some of Principal Sagers's greatest accomplishments have been in the area of technology. He said, "We've achieved a lot [in the area of technology] in the last two years. We've also tried to create a positive climate and beautify the school." If Principal Sagers were not leaving, he would continue increasing literacy. "The goal was to identify all students not reading on their grade level. We're using technology as a vehicle to enhance instruction," he said.

Least important details

It is hard to go to a new school for everyone, but Principal Sagers said, "The first year at a new high school [for a principal] is extremely difficult. It's always hard to start over as a new leader."

Revising

Evaluate and Revise Content, Organization, and Style

Check and Check Again As you look over a peer's article or your own, you should do at least two readings. First, focus on the article's content and organization. The guidelines below will help you edit your article. Then, in your second reading, go back and look for ways to make sentences stronger by using the Focus on Sentences on page 71.

▷ **First Reading: Content and Organization** Use the chart below to look for ways to improve the content and organization of your news article. Respond to questions in the left-hand column. If you need help answering the questions, use the tips in the middle column. If necessary, make the changes suggested in the right-hand column.

TIP Try using a **reference source** when you revise the content and organization of your article and edit it for style. Reference sources such as the dictionary, a thesaurus, and Part 2 of this book can help you improve your article.

Guidelines for Self-Evaluation and Peer Evaluation

Evaluation Questions	Tips	Revision Techniques
❶ Does the lead answer the 5W-How? questions?	**Circle** the answers to the questions *who, what, when, where, why,* and *how.*	If needed, **add** answers to the 5W-How? questions at the beginning of the news article.
❷ Are details in the body given in order from most important to least important?	**Put a star** next to the details that help the reader better understand the event. **Put a check** next to the details that are not as important and could be cut.	If necessary, **rearrange** the details so those with a star next to them directly follow the lead and those with a check are at the end of the article.
❸ Does the body include details that explain the effects of the event and people's reactions to it?	**Underline** the details that explain the effects. **Put a box** around the details that show people's reactions.	**Add** details that explain the effects and people's reactions if these details are missing.
❹ Does the article include quotations that support the details of the article?	**Highlight** each quotation. **Draw an arrow** to the detail each quotation supports.	If needed, **elaborate** the details by adding quotations.

Writing Workshop   69

ONE WRITER'S REVISIONS This revision is an early draft of the news article on page 67.

> The longer passing period will go into effect on Monday, October 7. From now on, each class except seventh period will be five minutes shorter, and the passing periods will be five minutes longer. School will still be over at 3:00 P.M.
>
> Principal Reyes agreed that students need extra time between classes. *With a longer passing period, students will not have to leave class to go to their lockers or the restroom.*

rearrange (first paragraph moved)

add (sentence added)

Responding to the Revision Process

1. Why do you think the writer changed the order of the two paragraphs?
2. How did adding a sentence improve the writing?

PEER REVIEW

As you look at a peer's news article, ask yourself these questions:

- What makes this article newsworthy?
- How do people feel about this event? Is more than one viewpoint presented?

▶ **Second Reading: Style** Now that you have revised the content and organization of your news article, you can **edit** the individual sentences. You can improve your sentence style by using a variety of sentences—short sentences and long sentences. An article with too many short, choppy sentences or too many long, complex sentences will be difficult to read.

When you evaluate your news article for style, ask yourself whether your writing has a variety of sentences—both short and long. As you re-read your article, draw a wavy line under short sentences, especially ones that contain eight words or fewer. Look over your work. Does your news article seem to have mainly short sentences? If so, combine some of the short sentences by using *and,* *but,* or *or.* (Keep some short, effective sentences for variety, though.)

Varying Sentences

A news article presents the facts simply and quickly. That does not mean, however, that all its sentences will be short. A series of short sentences can bore the audience. To vary your sentences, use *and*, *but*, or *or* to combine two short sentences.

Focus on Sentences

All Short Sentences: An ice storm surprised downtown workers last night. Road crews responded. They were not prepared for the severity of the storm. The storm continued until 10:00 P.M. Roads remained icy. Workers found they had two options. They could risk driving. They could stay in their offices.

A Variety of Sentences: An ice storm surprised downtown workers last night. Road crews responded**,** **but** they were not prepared for the severity of the storm. The storm continued until 10:00 P.M.**,** **and** roads remained icy. Workers found they had two options. They could risk driving**,** **or** they could stay in their offices.

TIP A comma generally comes before the *and, but,* or *or* that connects two short sentences.

ONE WRITER'S REVISIONS

School will still be over at 3:00 P.M.

Most students are happy about the change. They are ^(, and)

already making plans for the extended passing time.

Responding to the Revision Process
How did combining the sentences improve the writing?

Evaluating and Revising Your News Article

Evaluate and revise the content and organization of your news article, using the guidelines on page 69. Then, use the Focus on Sentences above. If your class did peer evaluations, consider your peer's comments as you revise.

Writing Workshop 71

Publishing

Proofread Your News Article

Upon Close Inspection . . . Mistakes in a news article will distract readers from the facts. Have another person proofread your article to find mistakes you might have missed.

Grammar Link

Correcting Run-on Sentences

Sometimes when you write, your pencil cannot keep up with your thoughts. When this happens, you may write *run-on sentences*. A **run-on sentence** is really two or more sentences that are written as one.

Mick loves old movies he also loves to read.

One way to correct a run-on sentence is to divide the sentence into separate sentences.

Mick loves old movies. He also loves to read.

You can also turn a run-on sentence into a compound sentence by adding a comma and *and*, *but*, or *or*.

Mick loves old movies**,** **but** he also loves to read.

PRACTICE

Correct the run-on sentences to the right. First, divide the run-on sentence into separate sentences. Then, rewrite the run-on sentence as a compound sentence by adding a comma and *and, but,* or *or.* If a sentence is correctly punctuated and is not a run-on, write *C* on your paper.

Example:
1. I like the longer passing period my friend does not.

1. *I like the longer passing period. My friend does not.*

   I like the longer passing period, but my friend does not.

1. The passing period will be five minutes longer school will still be over at 3:00.
2. Morgan Sykes talked at the pep rally she received a standing ovation.
3. The students signed the petition asking for a longer passing period the principal agreed with them.
4. Students can use the extra time to go to their lockers they might use the time to go to the restroom.
5. Students will not miss important information by leaving class to go to their lockers or the restroom.

Publish Your News Article

Spread the News   Before you publish your article, you will need to write a *headline*. A **headline** is an attention-grabbing title for a news article. A good headline will summarize the event in a short sentence that contains an action verb. Action verbs are important because they tell the reader specifically what happened. Look at the examples below.

Examples:
Sixth-Graders **Adopt** Terence the Tarantula
Teachers **Ban** Homework Next Week

After writing a headline for your article, publish it using one of the following ideas.

- With your classmates, publish your articles together in a newspaper and distribute it to your class.
- Record your article on videotape and show it to your class as part of a news segment. See pages 79–82 for more information.
- Submit your article to your school or community newspaper.

Reflect on Your News Article

Building Your Portfolio   Now, take time to reflect on what you have done. Answer these questions.

- How is a lead for a news article like other introductions for other types of writing? How is it different?
- Would you use interviewing to gather information for other types of writing? Why or why not?

COMPUTER TIP
Make your news article look like a real one by typing it in **columns,** or vertical rows. Measure the width of a real newspaper column and set the margins of your document to the same width. Then, select the justify option to make straight edges at both the left and right margins.

Before you print your article, use the print preview feature to see what it will look like. You can usually find the print preview feature in the toolbar.

PORTFOLIO

YOUR TURN 10 **Proofreading, Publishing, and Reflecting on Your News Article**

- Correct spelling and punctuation mistakes. Make sure your article does not contain run-on sentences.
- Write a headline for your article and publish your article using one of the suggestions above.
- Answer the questions from Reflect on Your News Article above. Record your responses in a learning log, or include them in your portfolio.

Writing Workshop

Connections to Life

Writing a Newspaper's Advice Column

You have a problem, and you are unsure how to solve it. Of course, you could turn to a friend or relative for help. Would you consider writing to the newspaper? Newspapers feature a special kind of **problem-solution writing** called an advice column. Newspaper advice columns provide information on how to solve all sorts of problems, from personal and financial to car and home repair. They are designed to be entertaining as well as informative.

What Is Your Problem?

Advice columns consist of two parts—the readers' problems and the columnist's answers. Newspapers publish these letters and responses to offer help not only to the person writing the letter but also to other readers who may have a similar problem. Maybe you can identify with this reader's problem below:

> Dear Pat the Problem Solver,
>
> My little brother always gets me in trouble by starting arguments. Then, when my mom comes to see what we are arguing about, he blames me for starting it. I try to explain my side of the story, but it's my word against his. What can I do to keep from being accused of a crime I have not committed?
>
> *Falsely Accused*

Help Is on the Way

What is the solution? An advice columnist does more than just provide the reader with an answer. In a response, you can usually find these items.

- **a restatement of the problem** The first thing an advice columnist does is restate the reader's problem. By restating the problem, the columnist lets the reader know that he or she understands what is wrong.

- **a solution** The next part of the response is the advice. Columnists give readers advice that they can actually use. The advice columnist will offer a solution that the reader can carry out to make the situation better.

- **an example** The final part of the response is an example that shows that the recommended solution really works. The advice columnist may give a personal example or one from someone else who tried the same solution. Readers are more likely to try the advice if they read that the solution has already worked in another situation.

Read the response Pat the Problem Solver wrote to Falsely Accused on the next page. The elements listed above are labeled for you.

Dear Falsely Accused,

    Brothers and sisters often start arguments and then try to pass the blame to someone else. There are two ways you can handle this type of situation. One way is to avoid arguing. When your brother wants to start a fight, walk away and ignore him. However, if you simply cannot hold your tongue, the second way is to discuss (not argue about) the issue in front of your parents. This will keep your little brother (and you) in line. When my little sister wanted to argue, I would ignore her or tell her we should ask our parents what they thought. Suddenly, she would drop the issue. My sister no longer had the fun of seeing me mad or in trouble. Good luck!

Pat

Restatement of the problem

Solution

Example

YOUR TURN 11 — Writing a Newspaper's Advice Column

Pretend you are an advice columnist. Choose one of the following letters. Then, use the guidelines on page 74 to write a response. To publish your response, consider producing a newspaper in which you include an advice column or presenting your response in an oral presentation.

    My father is coach of the soccer team. He made someone else goalie even though he knew that I wanted the position and that I am a good goalie. He said he didn't choose me because he didn't want to show favoritism. Can you help?

A Fan of Fairness

    I just moved to a small school where everyone else has known each other since kindergarten. It has been really hard to make friends, and my shyness doesn't help. Do you have any suggestions?

New Kid in Town

Focus on Viewing and Representing

Producing a Newspaper

WHAT'S AHEAD?

In this section you will produce a newspaper. You will also learn how to

- organize news articles into sections
- write editorials
- design the layout of a newspaper

TIP The outline of an editorial looks like this:

Opinion statement
   First reason
      Fact or example
   Second reason
      Fact or example
   Third reason
      Fact or example
Call to action

Reference Note

For more on **persuasive writing,** see page 237. For more on **editorial cartoons,** see page 334 in the Quick Reference Handbook.

You and your classmates have written a variety of news articles that would interest others, so why not publish them in your own newspaper? Working with a small group, you can follow the guidelines below to produce a newspaper.

Make a Plan

Use What You Have To fill the pages of your newspaper, you can use the articles you and your group members wrote in the Writing Workshop. First, gather the articles together. Then, put the ones about school events in one stack and ones about community events in another stack.

Hand Out Assignments Your newspaper should include school articles and community articles. If you need more of one type of article, brainstorm a list of story ideas and choose a "reporter" to investigate and write an article.

In addition to school and community news, you will also need two *editorials* and an *editorial cartoon.* **Editorials** are articles that try to persuade readers to think or act a certain way. For instance, you may want to persuade others that your community needs to create bike lanes on busy streets. In the editorial, you would clearly state your opinion and support it with evidence—facts and examples. At the end of the editorial, you would ask your readers to take some action, such as signing a petition or changing a habit. You can also express your opinion in an **editorial cartoon.** Drawing a cyclist riding on top of cars because no room is available on the street would show that bike lanes are needed.

The Name Game Before you put your paper together, you should decide on an original name for your newspaper. The name should be related to your school or community and appeal to readers. For example, if your school's mascot is an alligator, you could call your newspaper the *Gator Gazette*.

Put It Together

To put your newspaper together, use the instructions in Designing Your Writing below.

Designing Your Writing

Newspaper Layout If your newspaper is clearly organized and appeals to the eye, people will be eager to read it. Your newspaper will consist of four pages. Each page will represent a section.

Page 1—The front page will have a **flag,** the title of the newspaper and the date of publication, across the top. It will also include the most newsworthy school article and the most newsworthy community article.

Page 2—School news section

Page 3—Community news section

Page 4—Editorial section

Follow these steps to design the layout of your newspaper.

- First, draw what each newspaper page will look like on an $8\frac{1}{2}'' \times 11''$ piece of paper. Use ××× to represent headlines, ≡ to indicate articles written in columns, and ⊠ to stand for pictures or graphics. As you design the layout, keep in mind the following guidelines.

  1. Articles in a newspaper should fill a square or rectangular block. Blocks help readers know where an article begins and ends. Look at the examples to the right.
  2. Generally, headlines should not be placed side by side. Headlines attract readers to the article because they are written or typed in a larger size than the articles. If two headlines are next to one another, readers will have difficulty separating them. Look at the difference in the examples to the right.
  3. Each page should have one image. Your group can paste or scan actual photographs onto the pages. If you do not have photographs, you can draw pictures. Make sure that the picture or photograph is related to the topic of the article.

TIP You can add more pages to your newspaper by including other sections, such as sports, movie reviews, and classified ads.

Poorly Designed

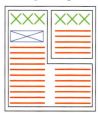

Well Designed

Here is an example of one group's drawing of their newspaper's layout.

Front page   **School news**   **Community news**   **Editorials**

 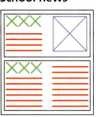 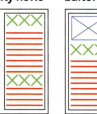 

- After you have decided on the placement of the articles, you can begin to make the pages of the newspaper. Tape two $8\frac{1}{2}'' \times 11''$ pieces of paper together like a book. Fold the taped paper in half to make four pages. Set your newspaper pages aside.
- On separate pieces of paper, write or type the articles in columns that are two or three inches wide. On an $8\frac{1}{2}'' \times 11''$ piece of paper, you can fit three 2-inch columns or two 3-inch columns. You also need to write or type the flag and headlines, and draw or print the images.
- Finally, glue the flag, the articles, the headlines, and the pictures onto the pages of the newspaper.

Reference Note
For more on laying out articles in **columns,** see the Computer Tip on page 73.

TIP If a news article is too long to fit within the block you have assigned to it, you can cut the article from the bottom. The least important details are at the end because you arranged them in an inverted pyramid structure.

YOUR TURN 12   Producing a Newspaper

In a group, use the following steps to produce a newspaper.
- First, decide whether the articles you wrote in the Writing Workshop are school news or community news.
- Next, assign some reporters to write editorials and others to draw editorial cartoons. If you need more school or community articles, assign reporters to write them, too.
- Then, use the guidelines in Designing Your Writing on pages 77–78 to design the layout of your newspaper.
- Finally, when your newspaper is complete, place it in your school's library so other students can read it.

Focus on Viewing and Representing

Producing a TV News Segment

Watching a news segment on TV can affect you differently than simply reading a newspaper article or listening to a news story on the radio. The visual images that you see on TV can make you feel as if you are witnessing an event firsthand. In this section you and a few classmates will work together to produce a short news segment (around three minutes) that will help others experience the excitement of a news event.

WHAT'S AHEAD?

In this section you will produce a television news segment. You will also learn how to

- recognize the different roles of a television production team
- convert a news article into a script
- perform, record, and evaluate your news segment

Reference Note

For more on **newsworthy characteristics,** see page 59.

Select Your Story

Look over the articles you and your group members wrote for the Writing Workshop. Which one is most newsworthy? Which news article has the greatest potential for interesting visuals? Identify the news article that is both newsworthy and has visual interest, and use it as the story for your news segment.

Choose Your Part

In your group, decide who will play each of the following roles.
- **Producer** The producer coordinates the production and is a link between the camera person and the anchor and reporter. The producer signals the camera person to start and stop taping and points to the anchor or reporter to begin talking. He or she also keeps the cue cards ready for the anchor and reporter to use if they need help with their lines.
- **Camera Person** The camera person is responsible for operating the video camera and taping the news segment.

- **Anchor** The anchor introduces the news story and the reporter. The anchor almost always sits behind a desk in the studio. Your group can create a studio by setting up a table or desk and chair in front of a solid-color background.
- **Reporter** The reporter presents the details of the event, usually from the scene where the event occurred. If your group cannot get to the scene, the reporter can sit in the studio. Sometimes the reporter sits beside the anchor. Other times the reporter is located in a different part of the studio. The reporter may also interview people who witnessed or were involved in the event.

Prepare the Script

A script tells what will be *said* and *shown* in the news segment. It consists of two parts, audio and video. The audio part includes the music and words that people will hear in your news segment. The video part shows what people will see as they watch your news segment. Look at the example below.

Video: What Is Seen	Audio: What Is Heard
Shot of the studio with anchor behind desk (Begin taping when music starts.)	Begin music
Move in to a close-up shot of anchor	Fade music
Close-up shot of anchor (Put camera on pause.)	Anchor: Good evening. I'm Fatima Rahman. Tonight we bring you a story about the decision of Main Street Middle School's Principal Reyes to extend the passing period. We go now to our reporter on the scene, Kyle Lucas. Kyle . . .
Close-up shot of reporter outside principal's office (Begin taping when reporter speaks.)	Reporter: Thank you, Fatima. I'm here at Main Street Middle School where today Principal Reyes announced . . .

Chapter 2 **Exposition:** Reporting the News

Your group is now ready to write its own script. To turn the news article you have chosen into a script for the news segment, fold a piece of paper in half to create two columns. Label one column *Video* and the other *Audio*. Then, follow the steps below.

Writing a Script

Step 1	**Write the anchor's dialogue.** In your article's lead, find the answer to the question "Who did what?" The answer will be what the anchor says to introduce the news story. The anchor will also introduce the reporter.
Step 2	**Write the reporter's dialogue.** The reporter will tell the remaining information in the lead and the body of the news article. The reporter will also interview the real people involved in the event or classmates playing the parts. This way, the quotes that are in the article will also be in the news segment.
Step 3	**Write the camera shots.** Next to the dialogue, write the directions for the camera person. The camera person will need to know what images to shoot and when to start and stop taping.
Step 4	**Make cue cards.** Transfer the dialogue to large pieces of poster board. Write in big letters so the anchor and reporter can use the cards for reference.
Step 5	**Decide on hand signals.** The producer will give hand signals to tell the rest of the group when to start and stop. That way, the producer's voice will not be heard on the videotape.

TIP Your group may choose to complete the steps in this chart together, or you may assign specific tasks to different group members.

Practice Your Performance

Practice does make perfect, so you should have several practice sessions before filming your news segment. Time your practices so your group can be sure the segment will not run more than the time your teacher allows.

TIP Check with your teacher to see if your school has video equipment. If not, you can perform your news segment live.

All for One and One for All Each group member should practice his or her role.

- The **producer** should be familiar with the script so that he or she knows when to use hand signals. He or she should also keep the cue cards ready and in order during taping so the anchor and reporter can use them.

Focus on Viewing and Representing

- The **camera person** should practice using the video recorder. He or she should know how to start, stop, pause, and focus the camera. The camera person should also practice moving in for close-ups and pulling back for long shots.
- The **anchor** and **reporter** should be familiar with their lines so that they depend on cue cards as little as possible. Unless they are interviewing someone, they should practice looking directly into the camera when speaking. The anchor and reporter should speak slowly, clearly, and loudly enough for the microphone to pick up their voices.

All Together, Now Once your group has practiced a few times and feels confident, do one practice run with the camera. As you watch the video, look for errors your group can avoid the next time you tape. For instance, if the camera person notes problems with shaking or blurring, he or she can try to avoid those same mistakes by holding the camera more steady and focusing more carefully. The anchor and reporter can listen for misreadings or quiet voices. The producer can make sure the transitions between shots are smooth.

Record and Evaluate Your News Segment

Now that you have practiced, make a final tape. Follow the instructions in your script to create your news segment.

When taping is complete, evaluate your news segment. How does it look? With your group, watch the video and ask yourselves the following questions about language, medium, and presentation.

- **Language:** Are the details of the event told clearly and completely?
- **Medium:** Do the sounds and images used enhance the written story?
- **Presentation:** Do the anchor and reporter speak clearly and look directly into the camera? Are camera shots steady and focused?

TIP Anchors and reporters should dress appropriately. Anchors usually dress professionally, and reporters dress for the scene. For instance, a reporter on location at city hall may wear a suit, but a reporter at a football game may wear jeans.

TIP Good news segments flow smoothly from beginning to end. If you notice long shots of the anchor or reporter without audio, you should retape those parts to improve the flow of your segment.

YOUR TURN 13 Producing a TV News Segment

Follow the guidelines beginning on page 79 to produce a TV news segment. When you finish, share it with your classmates.

CHAPTER 2 Choices

Choose one of the following activities to complete.

▶ CAREERS

1. Behind the News There are many careers in the field of journalism, such as newspaper reporter, TV reporter, newspaper editor, TV anchor, and TV producer. Research one of these careers to find out the education and training required and the average salary a person in that position would make. You may call your local TV station or newspaper, contact a university, or use the Internet to find information. Use what you learn to write a **report**.

▶ CROSSING THE CURRICULUM: ART

2. Express Yourself Editorial cartoons use pictures and symbols to express opinions about different events. You can create an **editorial cartoon** about a current situation in your school or community. The cartoon should show the event and your opinion about it. Limit the words in your cartoon to the title and, if necessary, brief dialogue between characters.

▶ WRITING

3. What's the Story? Turn your newspaper article into a **short story**. Your story should include everything that your article does—the details of the newsworthy event and the people involved. However, your purpose will be to entertain rather than to inform. Use plenty of descriptive language and action verbs to make the reader feel as if he or she actually witnessed the event.

▶ CROSSING THE CURRICULUM: SCIENCE

4. Tell Me Why Write a brief **article** that answers a frequently asked *why* question about science. Begin the article with a question, such as "Why do people get the hiccups?" or "Why do leaves change colors and fall in autumn?" Then, do enough research to answer the question. Ask your science teacher to help you find the most up-to-date material. Submit your article to a class or school newspaper.

PORTFOLIO

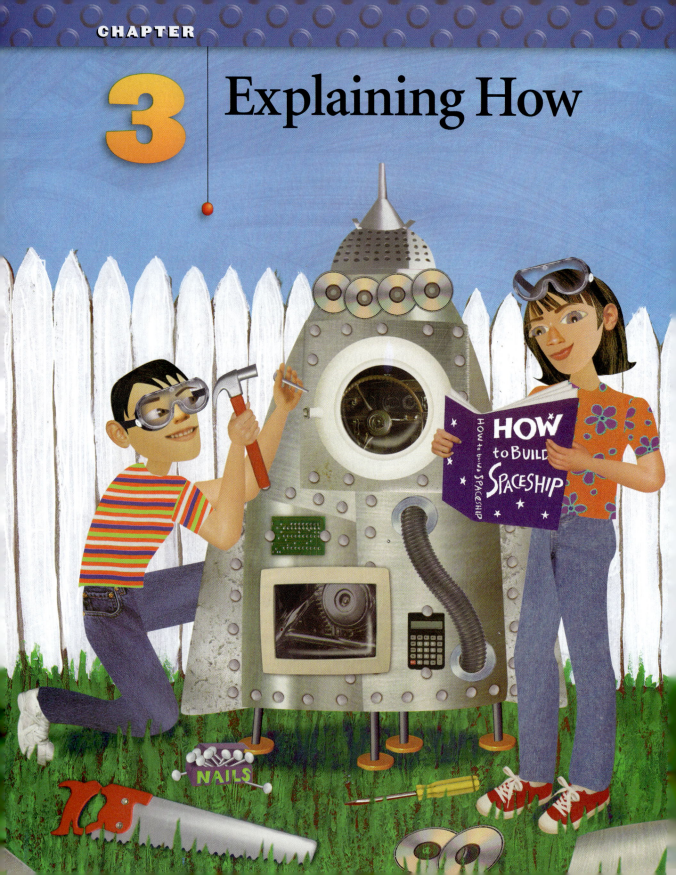

CHAPTER 3

Explaining How

CONNECTING READING AND WRITING

Reading Workshop

Reading a "How-to" Article

Writing Workshop

Writing a "How-to" Paper

Viewing and Listening

Viewing and Listening to Learn

Informational Text

Exposition

Here is a riddle for you: How are you and a computer alike? Computers follow a set of instructions to perform a function, and so do you. Think about it. In math class, for instance, your teacher tells you how to turn an improper fraction into a mixed number. This evening, you may heat up a frozen dinner by following the instructions on the box. The instructions you listen to, view, and read are all designed to teach you to complete a process.

Once you know how a process is done, you can share that information by giving instructions. Whether you share instructions orally, in writing, or through a demonstration, your goal is still the same: to teach others what you know.

YOUR TURN 1 — Examining a Process

Find an example of instructions for how to do or how to make something. Share your example with a partner and discuss the following questions.

- Do the instructions tell you how to do something or how to make something? What process do they explain?
- Do you think you could follow the instructions? Why or why not?

internet connect

GO TO: go.hrw.com
KEYWORD: EOLang 6-3

Connecting Reading and Writing   85

Reading Workshop

Reading a "How-to" Article

WHAT'S AHEAD?

In this section, you will read a "how-to" article. You will also learn how to

- make predictions
- form mental images from specific language

Holidays are a special time for families and friends to gather together and celebrate. Holidays are also a great time to do fun activities. Maybe you have made a card for Valentine's Day, planned a picnic for the Fourth of July, or planted a tree for Earth Day. You will read about one of these activities on the following pages. You will also read about a holiday activity that children take part in halfway around the world. Every May fifth, Japanese children make windsocks called *koinobori* (koi•nō´bô•ri) to hang outside their homes to celebrate Children's Day. The instructions for making *koinobori* appear in "Making a Flying Fish" on page 89.

Preparing to Read

READING SKILL

Making Predictions   A **prediction** is a guess you make about what will happen next. As you read instructions, you may predict what you will do with the supplies that are listed, what the outcome of a step will be, or what the final product will look like. Predictions give you a purpose for reading. You can find out whether your prediction is right by reading further and finding out what happens.

READING FOCUS

Forming Mental Images   Writers of "how-to" articles use **specific language** to name and describe the parts and the activities involved in a process. As you read the "how-to" article on page 89, look for words and phrases that create a picture in your mind of the steps for making a windsock.

86   Chapter 3   **Exposition:** Explaining How

Making Predictions

READING SKILL

I Wonder What Will Happen As you enter your math class, you see that you have a substitute teacher. You go to your seat, get out your review, and begin studying for the test you are about to take. After the bell rings, the substitute announces that the test has been canceled for today. Your friend will have the same substitute teacher later that day, so you go to tell her that her test will be canceled, too. How do you think she will react to the news that the test has been canceled? What if you find out your friend spent four hours studying last night? Now, what do you think her reaction will be? Has your prediction changed?

In life, you are constantly making predictions and adjusting them. For instance, your mind may follow this pattern:

1. what you know	There is no math test today.
2. your prediction	My friend will be happy.
3. new information	My friend studied for four hours.
4. adjusted prediction	My friend will not be happy.

Your mind also makes predictions when you read. The flowchart below shows what your mind is doing as you make a prediction.

Your mind . . .

takes what you already know about the subject → adds information from your reading → forms a prediction that makes sense

As you read on, your mind . . .

checks to see that your prediction is right   **or**   corrects your prediction using new information

Reading Workshop **87**

Try making a prediction now. The following paragraph is from a set of "how-to" instructions for an Earth Day activity. Read the list of materials and steps. Think about what you already know about the subject. Then, make a prediction about what you think the next step will be. If you need help, use the steps in the Thinking It Through below the instructions.

> To plant a tree, you should gather the following materials: tree, shovel, mulch, and a watering can. First, dig a hole twice as deep as the tree's container. The hole should also be twice as wide as the container. Second, remove the container and place the tree in the hole. Then, using the same soil you removed, fill the hole. When the hole is completely filled, apply a two-inch layer of mulch around the base of the tree.

THINKING IT THROUGH — Making Predictions

▸ **STEP 1** Read a part of the passage. Ask yourself, "What is the passage explaining or telling?"

The passage is telling me how to plant a tree.

▸ **STEP 2** Consider the information you have just read. Ask yourself these questions:
- "Does the information remind me of anything?"
- "What do I already know about this information?"

The information reminds me of the time when I helped my mom plant a tree in our backyard. I already know about the materials because we used the same materials.

▸ **STEP 3** Use what you already know, plus clues from the passage, to make a guess about what will happen next.

I have already been told to plant the tree, but I haven't been told to use the watering can yet. I think the next step will tell me to water the tree.

Read the following article. In a notebook, write down the answers to the numbered active-reading questions in the shaded boxes. If necessary, use the Thinking It Through steps on page 88 for the questions that ask you to make a prediction. The underlined words will be used in the Vocabulary Mini-Lesson on page 92.

Making a Flying Fish

by Paula Morrow
from FACES

Japanese boys and girls have their own special day each year on May 5. It is called Children's Day and is a national holiday. This is a time for families to celebrate having children by telling stories, feasting, going on picnics, or visiting grandparents. . . .

A special feature of Children's Day is the *koinobori* (koi•nō´bô•ri) that families display in their yards—one for each child in the family. A tall pole is placed in the garden. . . . Fish made of cloth or strong paper are attached to the pole. Each fish has a hoop in its mouth to catch the wind. The largest fish is for the oldest child, and the smallest is for the youngest.

These fish represent a kind of carp known as a strong fighter. These carp battle their way upstream against strong currents. When the *koinobori* dance in the wind, they remind the children of carp leaping up a waterfall. This is

> **1.** Based on this paragraph, predict what materials might be discussed later in the selection.

Reading Workshop 89

supposed to inspire children to be equally brave and strong.

You can make your own *koinobori* and fly it from a pole or hang it from your window on May 5. In that way, you can share Children's Day with the boys and girls of Japan.

You need an 18- by 30-inch piece of lightweight cloth (cotton, rayon, or nylon), felt-tip markers, a needle and thread, scissors, a narrow plastic headband, and string.

First, choose a piece of cloth with a bright, colorful pattern or decorate it yourself with felt-tip markers. Fold the fabric in half lengthwise, with the bright side on the inside. Sew a seam ½ inch from the long (30-inch) edge, making a sleeve.

On one end of the sleeve, make a 1-inch-wide hem by turning the right side of the fabric over the wrong side. Then, sew the hem, leaving three 1-inch-wide openings about 5 inches apart.

Make cuts 5 inches deep and 1 inch apart all around the unhemmed end of the sleeve to form a fringe. This is the fish's tail.

Next, turn the sleeve right side out. With . . . a felt-tip marker, add eyes near the hemmed (head) end (away from the fringed tail).

Thread the narrow plastic headband into the hem through one of the openings. Continue threading it until the open part of the headband is hidden.

Then, tie a 12-inch-long piece of string to the headband at each of the three openings. Tie the loose ends of the strings together.

Finally, hang your windsock from the strings on a tree limb, a clothes pole, or the eaves of your house. On windy days, it will dance like a carp swimming upstream against a waterfall!

2. Make a prediction about what you might do with the needle and thread based on this paragraph.

3. What do you predict the "sleeve" will be used for?

4. How do you know how long the fringe will be?

5. What word lets you know this is the last step?

one-inch opening

one-inch hem

Sleeve

 right side of fabric

 wrong side of fabric

First Thoughts on Your Reading

1. Could you picture the steps for making a *koinobori*? Why or why not?
2. Were your predictions about the materials, the needle and thread, and the "sleeve" correct? If not, identify the information in the selection that helped you adjust your predictions.

Forming Mental Images

It's All in Your Head   Pictures in your first books probably helped you understand the words. Even though the books you read today may lack pictures, you can create your own **mental images**—pictures in your mind—using the words on a page.

Most writers of "how-to" instructions know that they should use specific language to describe a process. As a reader, you can use these specific words and phrases to come up with a mental image.

The chart below gives examples of different kinds of specific language. As you read, think about how these examples help a reader *visualize*, or create a mental picture of, a process.

READING FOCUS

TIP   Drawing the instructions you read will help you understand a process better. Drawing can make it easier to picture a process. What do you picture when you read, "Turn the poster over and shake gently to remove any excess glitter"? Is it something like this?

Specific Language	Examples
Numbers	12 x 15 inches, 3 pieces, 450 degrees
Descriptive Words	small circle, large piece of fabric, hollow pipe
Exact Verbs	fold, turn, hang, sprinkle, twist
Comparisons	sew cloth like a sleeve, fold like a hot dog bun
Transitions	after, first, next, finally; above, below, behind, into

YOUR TURN 2   Forming a Mental Image

Find examples of specific language in the selection on pages 89–90. Choose one example and draw a picture of what you see in your mind. Share your drawing with a classmate who drew the same example and discuss the similarities and differences.

MINI-LESSON VOCABULARY

Compound Words

As you read a "how-to" article, you may find words that are unfamiliar to you. Some of these unfamiliar words may be *compound words*. **Compound words** are formed by putting together two or more words to make a new word. A compound word might be written as one word, as separate words, or as a hyphenated word.

Examples: roadrunner
free fall
ice-skating
hand-me-down

THINKING IT THROUGH

Discovering the Meanings of Compound Words

Here is one example of a compound word from "Making a Flying Fish":

You need an 18- by 30-inch piece of lightweight cloth.

▶ **STEP 1** Break the compound word down into its parts.

<u>Lightweight</u> breaks down to <u>light</u> and <u>weight</u>.

▶ **STEP 2** Define each of the parts.

The word <u>light</u> means "not very heavy." <u>Weight</u> means "how much something weighs."

▶ **STEP 3** Use the definitions of the parts to come up with a full definition.

Lightweight must mean "not weighing very much."

▶ **STEP 4** Check that your definition makes sense by inserting the definition for the compound word into the sentence.

"You need an 18- by 30-inch piece of <u>not weighing very much</u> cloth." The definition makes sense to me.

PRACTICE

Define the meanings of the following compound words by using the steps in the Thinking It Through above. The words are underlined in "Making a Flying Fish."

1. felt-tip (page 90)
2. headband (page 90)
3. windsock (page 90)
4. upstream (page 90)
5. waterfall (page 90)

MINI-LESSON TEST TAKING

Making Predictions

Some reading tests may ask you to make predictions. Read the following passage and question. How would you answer the question?

> Several Mexican holidays are celebrated in the United States. One is Cinco de Mayo. Cinco de Mayo is a national holiday in Mexico. On May 5, 1862, a small group of Mexican patriots defeated an invasion by the French army in Puebla, Mexico. Today, Cinco de Mayo is recognized as a celebration of not only that victory but also of Mexican culture.

Based on the information in this paragraph, what might the next paragraph be about?

A. how the French invaded Mexico
B. other Mexican victories
C. how Cinco de Mayo is celebrated
D. French holidays

THINKING IT THROUGH — Making Predictions

▶ **STEP 1** Read the passage and the question. Try to answer the question in your own words.

I think the next paragraph will talk more about other Mexican holidays.

▶ **STEP 2** Look for an answer choice that closely matches your own.

The answer choices don't really say the same thing as my prediction, so I will go to the next step.

▶ **STEP 3** If no answer choice matches your prediction exactly, look at each answer choice and ask,

- "Does the choice make sense?"
- "Is this choice supported by information in the passage?" If you cannot support the choice, then it is not the correct one.

If you answer "yes" to both questions, you may have found the right answer.

A—The author has already told me how the French invaded Mexico.

B—The author does not mention other Mexican victories.

C—The passage says that Cinco de Mayo is celebrated to honor Mexican culture. The author could discuss how it is celebrated.

D—The passage is talking about a Mexican holiday, not French holidays.

I think the correct answer is C.

Reading Workshop 93

Writing Workshop

Writing a "How-to" Paper

WHAT'S AHEAD?

In this workshop you will write a "how-to" paper. You will also learn how to

- create a time line
- elaborate ideas with specific language
- use transitional words
- use commas in a series

"Mmm, mmm. No one makes a smoothie as well as you do!" Everyone knows how to make something, whether it is a simple product such as a delicious fruit smoothie or a more complicated one such as a two-level treehouse. Whether the process is easy or difficult, making things takes knowledge and talent. What special skills do you have?

In this workshop you will have an opportunity to share your knowledge with others by writing a "how-to" paper. You will use specific details and **transitional words,** words that connect one idea to another, to give exact instructions for making a product.

Prewriting

Choose a Topic

I Know, I Know Follow the rule successful writers live by: *Write about what you know.* Brainstorm a list of products that you have successfully made before. Consider the following questions.

- Look around your house. What have you built or made?
- What school projects have you made in the past?
- What is your favorite recipe to make?

How Do I Decide? Once you have listed several products, you will need to evaluate them to choose the best one to write about. The chart on the next page shows how one student decided on one of three topics by asking questions about each topic.

Chapter 3 **Exposition:** Explaining How

Topic	Have I made this product before, and do I know the process well?	Does this process have a manageable number of steps (between three and five)?
Paper swan	yes	no—it has over five steps
Snowman decoration ✓	yes	yes—it has about five steps
Soapbox car	not really—I helped my big brother make it	no—this probably takes more than five steps

After evaluating each of his topics, the student whose chart appears above chose the topic that had the most *yes* answers. His "how-to" paper will tell others how to make a snowman decoration.

Think About Purpose and Audience

Show Some Consideration Your friend teaches you a great magic trick. You amaze your little brother with the trick, and he begs you to teach it to him. After you explain it twice, your brother is still confused. Obviously, you need to explain the trick to him in a different way.

Your purpose for writing instructions is to teach someone how to make something. That person could be a teacher, a friend, or even a young child. Before you begin to write, you should consider what information your audience will need. To do that, use the steps in the Thinking It Through below.

KEY CONCEPT

THINKING IT THROUGH
Considering Your Audience

▶ **STEP 1** Identify your audience.

My audience will be fourth-graders.

▶ **STEP 2** What words should you define so your audience can understand the process?

The snowman decoration has a muffler. Fourth-graders may not know that a muffler is a scarf.

▶ **STEP 3** Ask yourself, "What steps caused me trouble?" How can you make those steps clearer?

I had a problem keeping the sequin eyes in place. I used straight pins to hold them until the glue dried.

YOUR TURN 3 — Choosing a Topic and Thinking About Your Audience

Brainstorm a list of products that you have made. Then, make a chart like the one on page 95 and evaluate each product as a possible topic for your "how-to" paper. Choose the product that has the most "yes" answers in the chart.

Once you have a topic, choose an audience. Then, think about the information your audience will need by completing the steps in the Thinking It Through on page 95.

Plan Your Instructions

As Easy as 1, 2, 3 Imagine the frustration of trying to build a model car if the instructions described painting the model before the car was even put together. **Putting steps in the correct order makes the process easier to understand.** Most "how-to" papers are written in **chronological order,** or time order.

One way to think of the steps in chronological order is to imagine yourself making the product. As you perform each step, write it on a time line, recording the **progression,** or order, of the process. Then, look over your steps and add anything you left out.

| KEY CONCEPT |

TIP Look over your time line for steps that may distract the reader. Ask yourself, "Does my audience already know how to do this step?" If the answer is "yes," then you do not need that step.

For example, if you were writing instructions for making a peanut-butter-and-jelly sandwich, it would not be necessary to tell readers to open the jar of jelly. They would already know to do that.

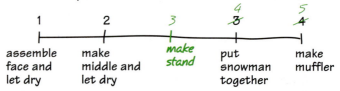

Steps to make a snowman decoration:

1 — assemble face and let dry
2 — make middle and let dry
3 — make stand
4 (3) — put snowman together
5 (4) — make muffler

Next, brainstorm the materials you need to make the product. Think carefully about everything you need. If you forget to list a material, your reader will not be able to make the product.

YOUR TURN 4 — Planning Your Instructions

Write the steps for making your product in chronological order on a time line. Then, list the needed materials.

96 Chapter 3 Exposition: Explaining How

MINI-LESSON WRITING

Elaboration: Using Specific Language

Suppose a friend gave you the following recipe for making Zesty Bagels. Could you follow the directions?

Zesty Bagels

Step 1: Gather materials—pan, bagels, sauce, olives, mushrooms, cheese.

Step 2: Place bagels on pan and pour sauce.

Step 3: Put on toppings.

Step 4: Bake.

As you read the steps, you probably asked yourself many questions. *How many bagels do I need? What are the measurements for the toppings? How long do I bake the bagels and at what temperature?* The recipe leaves you guessing because your friend's directions are not specific.

To help a reader understand a process, you should write your instructions using **specific language.** For example you can give *numbers* to tell how much or how many, such as "six plain bagels." You can also describe supplies using *descriptive words*, such as "finely chopped mushrooms." *Exact verbs* (V) and *transitions* (T) will help tell a reader exactly what to do and where to put supplies.

      V
Sprinkle black olives, mushrooms, and
                  T
cheese evenly **over** the sauce.

Notice how specific language eliminates all guesswork in the recipe below.

Zesty Bagels

Step 1: Gather these materials: a cookie sheet, 6 plain bagels cut in half, 18-ounce jar of spaghetti sauce, ¼ cup chopped black olives, 6 finely chopped mushrooms, and 1 cup grated Parmesan cheese.

Step 2: Place bagel halves on cookie sheet. Evenly spread 1 tablespoon of spaghetti sauce over the face of each bagel.

Step 3: Sprinkle black olives, mushrooms, and cheese evenly over the sauce.

Step 4: Bake in oven at 350 degrees for 15–20 minutes. When done, remove from oven and cool.

PRACTICE

Read the following steps. Then, rewrite the instructions, adding specific language. For more information on specific language, see the chart on page 91.

Directions for Preparing a Can of Soup

Step 1: Gather supplies.

Step 2: Heat soup.

Step 3: Serve.

Writing

"How-to" Paper

Framework	Directions and Explanations
Introduction ■ Attention-grabbing opening ■ Identification of product ■ Reason(s) for making the product	Grab your reader's attention quickly with an interesting introduction. For example, you could **ask questions** to get your reader involved in your paper. Also, **clearly state reasons** why your reader will want to learn to make the product you will explain.
Body ■ List of materials ■ Step 1 (with specific language) ■ Step 2 (with specific language) ■ Step 3 (with specific language) and so on	In the first body paragraph, **list the materials your reader needs** to make the product. One way to list the materials is to put them in the order in which your readers will use them. Another way is to group similar types of materials together. Then, write the steps in the correct **chronological order.** As you write, you should ■ place each step in a **separate paragraph** ■ elaborate on each step with **specific language.** Specific language includes numbers, exact verbs, comparisons, transitions, and descriptive words. (See mini-lesson on page 97.) Transitions are especially useful because they create **coherence.** That is, they show how all the ideas connect.
Conclusion ■ Restatement of reason(s) and/or ■ Suggestions for using or displaying the product	**Restate the reasons** for making the product. You can also suggest **ways to use or display** the product.

YOUR TURN 5 — Drafting Your "How-to" Paper

Now it is your turn to draft a "how-to" paper. As you write, refer to the framework above and the Writer's Model on the next page.

Chapter 3   **Exposition:** Explaining How

A Writer's Model

The final draft below closely follows the framework for a "how-to" paper on the previous page.

A Snowman of Style

Are you at home with nothing to do? Are you eager to do something fun? If so, you can make a snowman. It is easy and fun, and you can make one without snow.

Picture a plump snowman with bright shiny eyes, a muffler, and a black hat. You can make the same winter wonder with these materials, which you can find at many hobby and craft stores:

- a 5-inch, a 4-inch, and a 3-inch foam ball
- two 12-inch black pipe cleaners
- one 1-inch orange pipe cleaner
- a 2-inch piece of black yarn
- three medium-size buttons
- two medium-size sequins
- a 1- × 15-inch piece of bright cloth
- an 8½- × 11-inch piece of black paper
- a 2-inch black pompom
- two straight pins
- scissors
- white glue

The first step is making the snowman's face and hat. The orange pipe cleaner will be the nose. Push the pipe cleaner into the center of the smallest foam ball until it sticks out about ½ inch. Next, make the mouth using the black yarn. Happy snowmen wear smiles. Confused snowmen have mouths like a series of mountain peaks. Choose an emotion for your snowman, and glue the black yarn down to match the feeling you are trying to create. To make the eyes, glue down the two sequins. Use the straight pins to pin the eyes in place while they dry.

(continued)

Annotations:
- Attention-grabber
- Identification of product
- Reasons for making the product
- List of materials
- Step one

(continued)

  Snowmen often wear hats. You can make one by cutting a 3-inch circle of black paper. Pin the circle to the top of the snowman's head. Glue the black pompom to the center of the paper, and set the head aside to dry.

Step two   Next, you will make the snowman's middle using the 4-inch foam ball. Cut one of the black pipe cleaners in half to make the arms. Shape each pipe cleaner like a tree branch or jagged line. Then, push each arm in place on the sides of the ball. The three black buttons will make the snowman's shirt. Glue them down the front of the ball. Set the middle aside to dry.

Step three   While you are waiting for the face and middle to dry, you can make a stand to keep your snowman from falling over. Cut a 1- × 5-inch piece of black paper. Form it into a ring by gluing the ends together.

Step four   When everything is dry, you are ready to put the snowman's body together. Take your last black pipe cleaner and cut four 2-inch pieces. Push two of the pipe cleaners in the top of the 4-inch foam ball 1 inch apart. Push the other two pipe cleaners in the bottom of the 4-inch ball 1 inch apart. Make sure you use two pipe cleaners because they will keep the snowman from wobbling. Then, push the snowman's head on top of the pipe cleaners to attach it to the 4-inch ball. Push the 5-inch ball on the bottom pipe cleaners to finish making the snowman's body.

Step five   The final step is making a muffler for your snowman. A muffler is a long fringed scarf that wraps around the neck. The strip of cloth will make the muffler. Create fringe by making cuts into each end of the fabric. Once that is done, tie the muffler around the snowman's neck.

Suggestions   You can make a variety of snow people by changing the style of the hat and clothing. Make a snow woman or snow child. Give your snow person a job. Doctors wear stethoscopes around their necks, and movie stars wear sunglasses. No matter what type of snowman you choose to create, making one is easy and fun.

Restatement of reasons

Designing Your Writing

Illustrating Steps in a Process When you are writing a "how-to" paper, consider using pictures to help readers understand what you are writing about. You can show readers how to complete individual steps by drawing pictures of the materials and using arrows or lines to show the action that will take place. You can also provide an illustration of the final product so that readers will know what their product should look like. To illustrate your "how-to" paper, you can print or scan images using a computer, cut out pictures from magazines, or even draw graphics by hand. Below is an illustration drawn by the writer of the Writer's Model to help readers understand one step in his "how-to" paper.

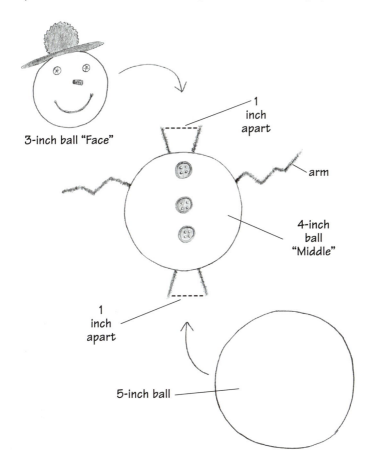

A Student's Model

It is important to have detailed knowledge and enthusiasm about the product you are explaining in your "how-to" paper. Stephanie Thompson wrote the following paper as a middle school student in St. Peters, Missouri. In it, she shares her knowledge and enthusiasm as she provides the instructions for growing ivy.

Make It Grow

Attention-grabbing opener

Have you ever tried growing ivy from a clipping? It is not as hard to do as it might seem. To get started, the following supplies are needed: an existing ivy plant, a fence or trellis for the ivy to climb, a pan about two inches deep, water, and sunlight.

List of supplies

Step one

First, cut about seven or eight leaves from the ivy plant. Make sure that you cut above where the leaf joins the stem, and cut at the same angle as the leaf grows. Then, fill the pan with water and place each leaf in the water. Let the leaves soak until they form roots that are about three to four inches long.

Step two

Step three

When the roots reach the desired length, it is time to find the best location for the ivy to grow. Although ivy is a hardy plant, it does need some care when it is grown from a clipping. Look for a place where there is plenty of sunlight, good drainage, and where no animals can damage it. Make sure that there is a fence or trellis in the location for the ivy to climb.

Step four

Next, hook the ivy leaves on to the fence or trellis so that the roots are almost touching the ground. As they receive sunlight and moisture from the dew, the roots will grow into the ground and the leaves will continue to sprout upward. In no time the ivy will be covering the fence or trellis, and you can start all over again!

Revising

Evaluate and Revise Content, Organization, and Style

Two Is Better Than One When revising your paper or a peer's, you should read the rough draft twice. First, look at the content and organization, using the guidelines below. The second time you read, concentrate on the sentences, using the Focus on Sentences on page 105.

▶ **First Reading: Content and Organization** Use the chart below on your first reading. It will help you evaluate a "how-to" paper and revise its content and organization.

Guidelines for Self-Evaluation and Peer Evaluation

Evaluation Questions	Tips	Revision Techniques
❶ Does the introduction give a reason for making the product?	**Put brackets** around the reason.	If needed, **add** a reason for making the product.
❷ Does the body list all the materials needed to make the product?	**Circle** all the supplies needed to make the product.	**Add** any supplies that have been left out.
❸ Are the steps of the process in the correct chronological order? Is each step in a separate paragraph?	**Write a number** next to each step in the margin of the paper.	If needed, **rearrange** the steps so they are in the correct order and so that each step is in its own paragraph, as needed.
❹ Is each step described with specific language?	**Underline** numbers, descriptions, comparisons, verbs, and transitions.	If necessary, **elaborate** on the steps by adding specific details.
❺ Does the conclusion restate the reason for making the product and/or give suggestions on how to use the product?	**Put a star** beside the sentence that restates the reason. **Draw a wavy line** under the suggestions for using the product.	If needed, **add** a restatement of the reason for making the product. **Add** some suggestions for how to use the product.

Writing Workshop   103

ONE WRITER'S REVISIONS Here is an early draft of the "how-to" paper on pages 99–100.

> Next, you will make the snowman's middle using the 4-inch foam ball. Cut one of the black pipe cleaners in half to make the arms. *Shape each pipe cleaner like a tree branch or jagged line.* Then, push each arm in place on the sides of the ball. The three black buttons will make the snowman's shirt. Glue them down the front of the ball. Set the middle aside to dry. ¶ While you are waiting for the face and middle to dry, you can make a stand to keep your snowman from falling over. Cut a 1- × 5-inch piece of black paper. Form it into a ring by gluing the ends together.

elaborate — (insert of shaped pipe cleaner sentence)
rearrange — (new paragraph break)

Responding to the Revision Process

1. How does adding a sentence improve this part of the instructions?
2. How does breaking the one paragraph into two paragraphs make the instructions clearer?

PEER REVIEW

When looking over a peer's paper, ask yourself these questions:

- Would I be able to make this product? Why or why not?

▶ **Second Reading: Style** You have improved the content and organization of your paper. Now you will concentrate on the style of your sentences. One way to improve your style is to use transitional words, such as *first, next,* and *finally.* Transitional words connect one idea to another.

When you evaluate your "how-to" paper for style, ask yourself whether your writing has transitional words connecting one step to another, creating coherence. As you re-read your paper, highlight each transitional word. Are there any paragraphs with few or no transitional words? If so, add transitional words to paragraphs that need them.

Transitional Words

A reader should be able to follow your ideas as easily as a driver follows road signs. Adding **transitional words** between your thoughts will steer the reader in the right direction. Notice how the underlined transitional words make this paragraph easy to read and understand.

Focus on Sentences

> To make a tie-dyed shirt, <u>first</u> you will need to wrap rubber bands around several parts of a T-shirt. <u>Next</u>, fill a tub or sink with dye. <u>Then</u>, dunk the shirt into the dye. Rinse the shirt with water and hang to dry. <u>Finally</u>, take off the rubber bands when the shirt is completely dry.

TIP Listed below are common transitional words for chronological order, the order used to explain a process.

after	next
before	often
finally	then
first	when

ONE WRITER'S REVISIONS

The orange pipe cleaner will be the nose. Push the pipe cleaner into the center of the smallest foam ball until it sticks out about ½ inch. <s>You will</s> ^Next,^ make the mouth using the black yarn.

Responding to the Revision Process

How did adding a transitional word make this part of the instructions clearer?

YOUR TURN 6 — Evaluating and Revising Your "How-to" Paper

First, improve content and organization using the guidelines on page 103. Then, use the Focus on Sentences above to add transitional words to your paper. If a peer evaluated your paper, consider his or her suggestions as you revise.

Publishing

Proofread Your Paper

Clear the Path Reading a paper full of errors is like running an obstacle course: Progress is often slow. If you *and* a peer proofread your paper, you are more likely to catch distracting mistakes.

Grammar Link

Using Commas in a Series

When you write a "how-to" paper, you may list materials or give directions in a series. A series consists of three or more items written one after the other.

Use commas to separate three or more items in a series.

Incorrect Get out a pen, and paper.

Correct Get out a pen**,** a ruler**,** and paper.

To make the meaning of a sentence clear, use a comma before the *and* or *or* in a series.

Unclear Lori's favorite sandwiches are turkey, ham and cheese. [Does Lori have two or three favorite sandwiches?]

Clear Lori's favorite sandwiches are turkey**,** ham**,** and cheese.

Do not use commas if *all* of the items are joined by *and* or *or*.

Incorrect You can throw, or roll, or bounce the ball.

Correct You can throw or roll or bounce the ball.

PRACTICE

Some of the sentences below need commas. Refer to the rules to the left to decide when to use commas. If a sentence needs commas, rewrite the sentence, adding commas where they are needed. If a sentence is correct, write *C*.

Example:
1. Your snow woman could have long hair a lace collar and earrings.
1. *Your snow woman could have long hair, a lace collar, and earrings.*

1. Glue the eyes hold them with a pin and allow them to dry.
2. My snowman has green eyes a red scarf and blue buttons.
3. Miguel gave his snow teen a headset a T-shirt and a book bag.
4. A snow baby has a bib cap or bow.
5. You can place your snowman on a shelf or a table or a countertop.

Chapter 3 **Exposition:** Explaining How

Publish Your Paper

Tell Them How It Is Done   Since you are the expert, you can share your instructions with others. How do you get your paper to your audience? Use the following suggestions to get people to read your "how-to" paper.

- If you wrote your "how-to" paper for a younger audience, make copies of your instructions and give them to an elementary teacher. If your audience is your classmates, ask your teacher if you can demonstrate how to make your product in class.
- Gather all the "how-to" papers in your class and organize them into categories such as recipes, crafts, and decorations. Compile a "how-to" book and place it in your school's library.

Reflect on Your Paper

PORTFOLIO

Building Your Portfolio   Now that you are finished writing and publishing, take a moment and reflect on your "how-to" paper. Remember your purpose for writing, and think about how your paper will achieve that purpose. Reflecting on a paper you have already completed will help make your next one better.

- Which step in your paper is the easiest to follow? What makes this step clear and easy to understand?
- You created a time line to list your steps in order. In what other types of writing would a time line be useful?
- Take time to examine all the papers in your portfolio. What is one goal you would like to work toward to improve your writing?

> **YOUR TURN 7**
>
> ### Proofreading, Publishing, and Reflecting on Your Paper
>
> - Correct any grammar, usage, and mechanics errors. Pay attention to spelling and punctuation, particularly the use of commas in a series.
> - Publish your paper so others can use your instructions.
> - Answer the questions from Reflect on Your Paper above. Record your responses in a learning log, or include them in your portfolio.

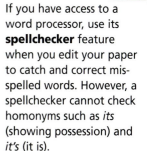

COMPUTER TIP

If you have access to a word processor, use its **spellchecker** feature when you edit your paper to catch and correct misspelled words. However, a spellchecker cannot check homonyms such as *its* (showing possession) and *it's* (it is).

Writing Workshop

MINI-LESSON: TEST TAKING

Writing Instructions

Sometimes an essay test may ask you to write instructions, such as how to do or how to make something. Read the prompt to the right. How would you respond to this prompt on a test?

A new student in your school needs to find the cafeteria. Write the directions for walking from your classroom to the cafeteria.

THINKING IT THROUGH

Writing Instructions for Tests

▶ **STEP 1** Read the prompt. Find out
- what it is asking you to explain
- who your audience is

The prompt is asking me to explain how to get from my classroom to the cafeteria. A new student will be reading my instructions.

▶ **STEP 2** List the materials, if any, you would need to complete the process. Provide definitions of key terms, if necessary.

The new student will not need any materials to learn the way to the cafeteria. There are no terms to define.

▶ **STEP 3** Create a time line to list the steps of the process in order.

Step 1	Step 2	Step 3	Step 4
Turn right out of the classroom door.	Go to the end of the hall and turn right again.	Take the first left.	Go through the double doors, and the cafeteria will be on your left.

▶ **STEP 4** Write your instructions in paragraphs. Remember to use specific language.

I will give specific locations and use directions, such as right and left.

▶ **STEP 5** Review your instructions, checking to make sure that
- you listed any materials needed
- your steps are in order
- you have not left out any steps
- you have included specific language

I don't need materials, and my steps are in order. I can add a specific detail to step 3, though. The first left will come after a water fountain. I also need to explain where the student will find the double doors in Step 4.

108 Chapter 3 **Exposition:** Explaining How

Connections to Life

Writing a Descriptive Paragraph

You are reading instructions for building a basketball backboard. Does having a picture of the backboard in your mind make understanding the instructions easier? It certainly does. You know what the final product looks like, so you already have an idea of what you need to do to make it.

Here's an opportunity for you to help the readers of your "how-to" paper. You will write a **descriptive paragraph** about the product they will make. The written description will help your audience create a mental picture, making the instructions easier to follow.

Do You See What I See? To describe something another person has not seen, you can use descriptive words and phrases to paint a picture in that person's mind. What kinds of descriptive words and phrases help someone picture an object? The following chart provides some examples for you.

Descriptive Words and Phrases	Definitions	Examples
Sensory Details	Details that express what you experience through your five senses—What you hear, see, taste, touch, and smell	sight—blue, tall, leaning hearing—pops, hisses, whispers taste—sweet, salty, sour touch—hot, soft, rough smell—smoky, fresh, spicy
Location Words	Words that describe where something is located	across from next to on the top to the right near to the left
Figurative Language	**Simile**—Language that compares two unlike things using *like* or *as*	The wire is rigid and curled *like* corkscrew pasta. The eyes are *as* shiny *as* emeralds.
	Metaphor—Language that compares two unlike things saying one *is* the other	The string *is* a lifeline keeping the two parts together.

Writing Workshop

First Things First To write a descriptive paragraph, you first need to decide what *spatial order* you are going to use to organize your description. **Spatial order** organizes the details according to their location. You might describe a product from right to left, from top to bottom, or from far away to close up. Choosing an order first will help you be organized as you observe and list all the important details about your product.

For instance, if you choose to describe your product from the left to the right, you will look at the left side of the product and list the details. Then, you will observe the middle of the product, and then the right side, writing down details as you go. You should describe what the product looks like, but you should also consider other sensory details. Does your product make a sound? How does it taste or smell? What does it feel like? Make sure you use location words to tell where the sensory details are located.

To help organize your details in the spatial order that you chose, list them in a chart as you observe your product. The chart below shows a top-to-bottom order for describing a foam snowman.

Spatial Order	Sensory Details and Location Words
Top	small foam ball, black hat on top, fluffy pompom in the center, green sequin eyes, orange nose, black yarn mouth that smiles
Middle	medium foam ball; soft, blue muffler around his neck; three black buttons down the front; black arms stick out
Bottom	large foam ball, black stand made out of paper

Ready, Set, Write Once you have your information in a chart, you are ready to write a descriptive paragraph. All you have to do is follow the order that you chose and write complete sentences using the details that you listed.

When you are finished with your first draft, **elaborate** on your description by adding figurative language. To add figurative language, look at the details to see what comparisons you can make. In the chart above, for instance, the snowman has a mouth that smiles. To whom can a smiling snowman be compared? The snowman smiles like a child with a new toy. The snowman also has green eyes made of sequins. Can you compare his eyes to anything?

Now Picture This The following is an example of a descriptive paragraph that could be included with the Writer's Model on pages 99–100. You can see how the writer uses sensory details, figurative language, location words, and spatial order to describe the snowman decoration. Do you see how adding description will help readers make the snowman?

> My snowman is not a typical snowman made of snow. He does not have to be kept outdoors, and he will not melt. Instead, my snowman is a decoration made of three foam balls, 3 inches, 4 inches, and 5 inches in diameter. He can be placed anywhere and enjoyed anytime. The smallest foam ball is my snowman's head. On top of the head sits a black hat with a fluffy, black pompom in the center. The snowman's eyes are green, sparkling sequins, and his nose is bright orange. The black yarn of his mouth is made to smile like a child with a new toy. The middle foam ball makes his body. He is dressed with a soft, blue muffler around his neck and three shiny black buttons down his front. His arms are also black, and they stick out from his body like branches of a tree. The largest foam ball is on the bottom, and it sits in a circular stand made of black paper. The stand is an anchor keeping the snowman in place.

- description begins at the top
- sensory details and figurative language
- description moves to the middle
- sensory details and figurative language
- description ends at the bottom
- figurative language

Writing and Revising a Descriptive Paragraph

Write a descriptive paragraph using the suggestions above. Remember to

- use spatial order to organize your paragraph
- describe the product with sensory details and location words
- revise your paragraph by adding figurative language

When you have finished writing and revising, make a final draft and include it with your "how-to" instructions.

Focus on Viewing and Listening

Viewing and Listening to Learn

WHAT'S AHEAD?

In this section you will learn how to listen to and watch instructions in different forms. You will also learn how to

- understand instructional charts and graphics
- summarize "how-to" instruction in computer software
- take notes while watching directions on TV or video

You and your friend are neck and neck as you swim to the side of the pool. You both turn at the same time, but you come out ahead. Why? You know how to do a flip turn. You hold on to the lead and declare a victory as you touch the other side.

"Where did you learn to do that?" your friend asks.

You confess, "I learned how from TV."

Instructions come in many forms. Not only can you read a how-to paper, you can also learn how to do or make something from **charts and graphics, computer software,** and **"how-to" videos** or **TV shows.** To follow instructions in these forms, you will need to work on your viewing and listening skills.

Charts and Graphics

Charts and graphics provide you with the same information as a "how-to" paper. Both tell the materials, the instructions, and the order in which you should do the instructions. However, charts and graphics do not rely only on words. They *show* the steps in a process by using pictures, symbols, and labels.

One type of chart is a flowchart. Look at the flowchart on the next page. The steps are easy to follow because arrows direct you from one step to another. Labels, such as Step 1, Step 2, and Step 3,

Chapter 3   **Exposition:** Explaining How

also help you see the order of the steps, and the instructions are brief and to the point.

How to Make a Friend

| Step 1: Introduce yourself to someone new by smiling, giving your name, and asking the new person his or her name. | → | Step 2: Begin a conversation. You might offer help or make a friendly joke. | → | Step 3: Plan to talk or meet again. You could ask for the new person's phone number or an e-mail address, or name a date and time for your next meeting. |

Now, look at the graphic below. This type of graphic is called a diagram. The diagram shows how to fold a blanket like a sleeping bag. As on the flowchart, the steps are labeled, but pictures and symbols give the instructions. These features make it easy to understand what the diagram is demonstrating.

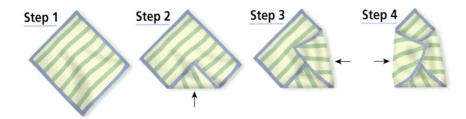

YOUR TURN 9 Understanding Charts and Graphics

Answer the following questions about the flowchart and diagram above.

- What material do you need to make the sleeping bag? How is the material presented?
- How are the instructions presented in the flowchart and the graphic? Do words, pictures, or symbols tell you what to do?
- What order is used in the flowchart and the graph (chronological? spatial?)? How is that order shown in each?

Focus on Viewing and Listening

Computer Software

Most software, including word-processing programs, computer games, and encyclopedias, comes with built-in "how-to" instructions, usually called a help menu. Help menus are set up differently from one program to another, but you can usually get to one by using the help button in the toolbar or on the keyboard. The help menu will list the features of the program. Click on the feature you are interested in, and a help box will appear, giving you specific directions. Here is an example of a help box.

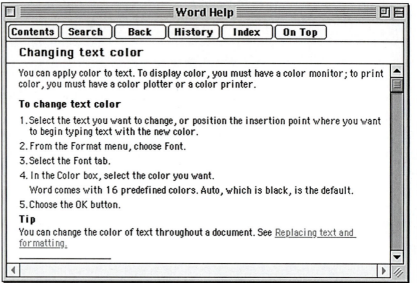

You may find that you go to the same item in a help menu again and again. How can you remember the steps in a process so that you don't have to keep returning to the menu? Summarizing the instructions in a flowchart can help you remember them. To do that, read each step and write down only the important words and details. Use arrows to show the sequence of steps. A flowchart for the instructions in the help box above might look like this:

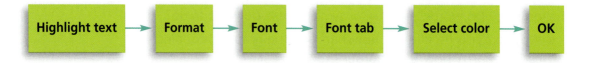

 **Summarizing Instruction**

Create a flowchart that summarizes the steps in the following help box.

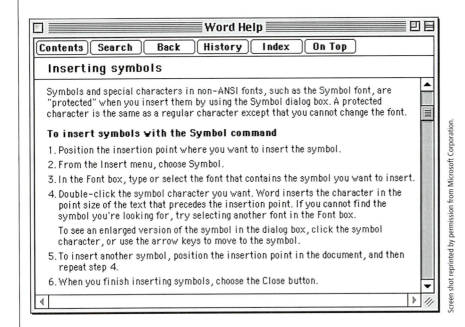

TV and Video

There are "how-to" programs and videos about a variety of topics, but popular ones include cooking, exercise, and home repair. "How-to" programs and videos are very helpful—not only do you *hear* the directions, you also *see* the steps.

When you watch "how-to" instructions on TV or on video, you are doing two things at once. First, you are *listening to* and *viewing* the information. At the same time, you are *trying to understand* how to do the steps in the process. If you are watching a TV program, you cannot ask questions. If you are watching a video, you might hit "pause" or "rewind," but having control over the VCR is not always possible. However, you can get a better understanding of the steps of a process if you take notes. The

Focus on Viewing and Listening 115

following chart gives useful suggestions for taking quick and complete notes while viewing "how-to" instructions.

> **TIP** The guidelines below can apply to viewing *any* informative video. Always watch for important facts, on-screen graphics, and ideas emphasized through repetition or dramatic phrasing. In addition, always take a minute after viewing to record important points and to think about the video producer's purpose.

Note-Taking Guidelines

Guidelines	Tip
Prepare to listen.	Think about your purpose for listening, and prepare to focus on the message by eliminating distractions.
Listen to each step.	Clue words such as the transitions *first, second, then,* and *finally* will let you know when a step begins and ends.
Create an outline of the steps.	Organize your notes by numbering steps as they are presented.
Take notes on each step.	Do not try to write every word. Instead, make a note of each major idea and its support. Listen for words and phrases that are repeated. Watch for on-screen graphics.
Listen for a conclusion.	Major points may be repeated.
Check your notes.	Make any necessary additions or corrections. Summarize the information while it is still fresh in your mind. If possible, discuss the message with others who viewed it. Compare your different perceptions of the message, and add to your notes any points you may have missed.

YOUR TURN 11 Taking Notes to Learn

- Watch a "how-to" program on TV or find a "how-to" video at a video rental store or at your local library.
- Use the note-taking guidelines above to take notes.
- After viewing the video, take five minutes to complete the following sentence starters:

  The producers created this video to ____.

  The most important facts or ideas were ____.

CHAPTER Choices

Select one of the following activities to complete.

▶ CROSSING THE CURRICULUM: SCIENCE

1. How Did That Happen? Use your science book to find information on how something occurs, such as how fish breathe underwater or how taste buds work. Create a **flowchart** or **graphic** that shows the steps of the process. You can use drawings, magazine cutouts, or computer art to illustrate the steps.

▶ CROSSING THE CURRICULUM: SPEECH

2. You Be the Teacher Choose a product and learn how to make it by listening to someone or by watching a "how-to" program. Then, demonstrate how to make it for your class. Select something entertaining, unique, or appealing to others your age.

Give clear, precise **directions** as you show classmates how to make the product. Use visuals to help your audience understand the process.

▶ CAREERS

3. Do You Have What It Takes? Choose a career that interests you. Find out what sort of training, education, and skills you would need to pursue that career by looking in books in the library, using informational Web sites, or interviewing people who are in that career field. Write a **letter** to a friend explaining how to enter the profession you choose.

▶ WRITING

4. Games People Play Invent a game. Your game could be a board game, an athletic game, a card game, or any other type of game. Write the **instructions** for playing your game. First, state the goal of the game. Is the goal to advance to the center of the board, put a ball through a basket, or get rid of all of your cards? Next, write all the steps required for playing the game. Finally, provide the instructions and materials needed to play the game for a group of your classmates.

 PORTFOLIO

CHAPTER 4
Comparing and Contrasting

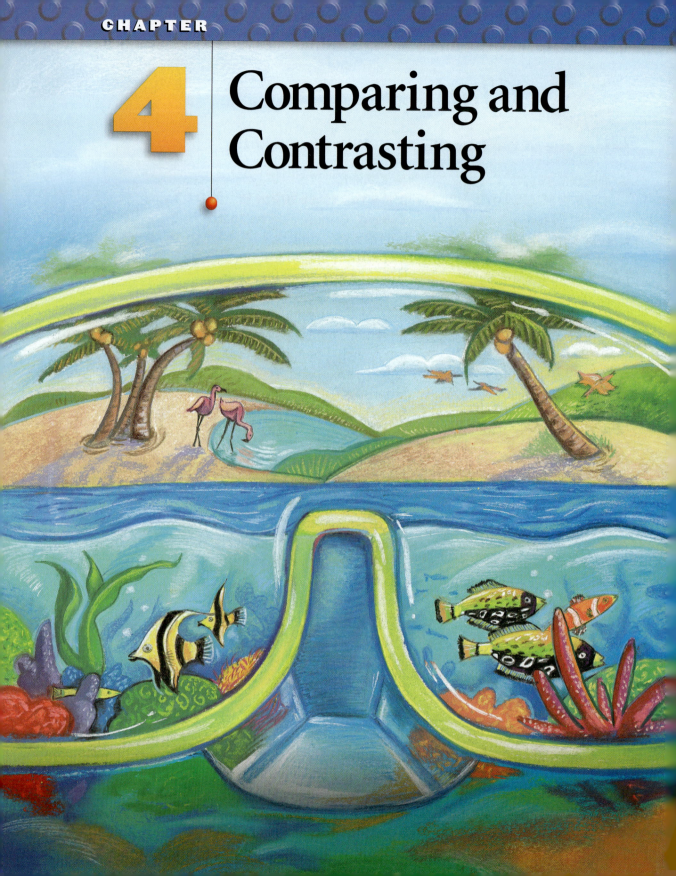

CONNECTING READING AND WRITING

Reading Workshop

Reading a Comparison-Contrast Essay

Writing Workshop

Writing a Comparison-Contrast Essay

Viewing and Representing

Comparing Ideas in Photographs

> **Informational Text**
>
> Exposition

Baked potato or salad? Art or band? You make choices every day. Sometimes those choices are easy, such as deciding on a baked potato for lunch. Other choices require more thought, such as choosing an elective in school. How do you make these important decisions? One way is to **compare** and **contrast** the two choices: You can look at how the two things are alike and how they are different. Once you understand the similarities and differences, you are ready to make a decision.

Comparing and contrasting is useful in other ways, too. Comparison-and-contrast structure may be used to define something unfamiliar by comparing it to something well known. For instance, did you know that the English sport rugby is like American football? Comparing and contrasting two subjects is a great way to share useful or interesting information with others.

YOUR TURN 1 Practicing Comparing and Contrasting

Answer the following questions, and then discuss them with a few classmates. Share your group's findings with the class.

- How are fifth grade and sixth grade different?
- How are fifth grade and sixth grade alike?

Reading Workshop

Reading a Comparison-Contrast Essay

WHAT'S AHEAD?

In this section you will read a comparison-contrast essay. You will also learn how to

- identify points of comparison
- examine two comparison-contrast structures

The two men faced each other down, ready for the big fight. One was the clear favorite; the other was a rookie. Who would win? The event had all the drama of a boxing match, but this was a debate. The following comparison-contrast essay shows how television made the presidential debate between John F. Kennedy and Richard M. Nixon different from previous ones. The debate was not just a war of words. Other elements made one candidate more successful than the other. Read on to see if you can identify those winning elements.

Preparing to Read

READING SKILL

Points of Comparison   Not every similarity and difference between two subjects is important, so an author must choose the most important areas to compare and contrast. These areas are called the author's **points of comparison.**

READING FOCUS

Comparison-Contrast Structure   The **structure,** or organization, of a comparison-contrast essay can help a reader see the similarities and differences more clearly. A writer may give all the information about one subject and then all the information about the other subject, or the writer may shift back and forth between the subjects. As you read Edward Wakin's essay on the next page, try to follow the organization he uses.

120   Chapter 4   **Exposition:** Comparing and Contrasting

Read the following essay. In a notebook, jot down answers to the numbered active-reading questions in the shaded boxes. The underlined words will be discussed in the Vocabulary Mini-Lesson on page 126.

from HOW TV CHANGED AMERICA'S MIND

THE  PRESIDENTIAL DEBATES

BY EDWARD WAKIN

A trim, tanned presidential candidate dressed smartly in dark suit, dark tie, and blue shirt stood at the podium on the left in the Chicago studio of WBBM–TV. He looked <u>vigorous</u>, confident, and businesslike.

His opponent at the other podium wore a light suit, pale tie, and a shirt with a collar that was too big for him. He looked tired, nervous, and in need of a shave.

> **1.** In the first two paragraphs, are the two candidates shown as being similar or different? How?

Both faced the <u>pitiless</u> eye of TV cameras carrying the first televised presidential debate. For one hour of prime time on all three networks, 75 million Americans watched on the evening of September 26, 1960.

The candidate on the left side, Democrat John F. Kennedy, looked nothing like the underdog he was supposed to be. An <u>unproved</u> junior senator from Massachusetts, he faced the highly experienced Republican candidate, Richard M. Nixon.

> **2.** Whose appearance does the writer describe first, Nixon's or Kennedy's? Whose experience does he describe first?

Kennedy needed national exposure. Nixon was seasoned and already nationally known. Twice elected vice president, Nixon had prepared himself for eight years to take over from President Dwight D. Eisenhower.

TV critic Robert Lewis Shayon described the televised debate as if it were a boxing match: "The atmosphere was clearly that of a prizefight: the referee (producer) instructing the champ and the challenger (the candidates), the seconds (advisors) milling around, and the 'come out fighting' handshake."

The rules of the match called for an eight-minute opening statement by Kennedy followed by eight minutes from Nixon. Then a panel of four reporters would ask questions.

Kennedy won.

He won on style and image—two key ingredients for success on TV. Nixon challenged and rebutted[1] what Kennedy said as if he were out to win debating points. He addressed Kennedy rather than the TV viewers.

3. Whom does each of the candidates address during the debate?

On the other hand, as the celebrated chronicler[2] of presidential campaigns Theodore H. White noted, Kennedy "was addressing himself to the audience that was the nation."

Kennedy came across as assured, energetic, <u>dynamic</u>. The camera was his friend.

4. Are Kennedy and Nixon alike or different in the way they come across to the audience?

Nixon came across as <u>uncomfortable</u> and ill at ease.

Nixon lost not on what he said, but on how he appeared. TV viewers saw Nixon as a gray man against the studio's gray backdrop. They saw Nixon forcing nervous smiles and perspiring under the studio lights. He "looked terrible," historian David Culbert stated.

At one point, the camera showed Nixon wiping perspiration from his brow and upper lip as he listened to Kennedy. When the camera was on Kennedy listening, he looked attentive, alert, and self-assured.

5. When listening, what does each candidate do?

Neither candidate said anything that was memorable or headline making. The importance of style and image became obvious when audience <u>reactions</u> to the televised and radio versions were compared. Those who heard the debate on radio thought Nixon had won!

6. What similarity do Kennedy and Nixon share?

But what counted was the televised debate. Half the country had watched it. White had a clear verdict: "In 1960 television had won the nation away from sound to images, and that was that."

---

1. **rebutted:** provided opposing arguments in a debate.
2. **chronicler:** person who records historical events.

First Thoughts on Your Reading

1. Name one thing about Kennedy and Nixon that the author compares.
2. Was the article's organization easy to follow? Why or why not?

Points of Comparison

READING SKILL

The Same, Only Different? Your two closest friends are probably both alike and different. To help someone understand these two friends, however, you wouldn't discuss every similarity and difference. Is it really important to know that one friend has a blue bike helmet while the other has a white bike helmet? You would focus on more important areas, such as personality and hobbies. These main areas would be your **points of comparison.**

A writer does not always announce points of comparison directly. A reader can usually figure out what they are, though, by looking at the details the writer provides.

Look back at the first two paragraphs of "The Nixon-Kennedy Presidential Debates" on page 121. Can you identify the first point of comparison? If you have trouble, look at the chart below.

THINKING IT THROUGH

Identifying Points of Comparison

▶ **STEP 1** Does the first paragraph talk about one subject or both? Write down the topic of the paragraph.

The first paragraph is about what Kennedy wore and how he looked confident.

▶ **STEP 2** Read the next paragraph and write down what it is about.

This paragraph is about what Nixon wore and how he looked tired and nervous.

▶ **STEP 3** Identify the author's first point of comparison. Repeat the process until you have identified all points of comparison.

The author talks about the candidates' overall appearance. This is the first point of comparison.

TIP Sometimes you can identify the point of comparison by reading one paragraph. If an author provides information about both subjects in one paragraph, you can skip Step 2.

Reading Workshop **123**

TIP Paragraphs providing background information may interrupt the author's points of comparison. You should keep reading to find details that describe one subject or both.

 Identifying Points of Comparison

Use the steps in the Thinking It Through on page 123 to identify and list the points of comparison in the reading selection that begins on page 121. You will use your list of points of comparison in the Your Turn on the next page. **Hint:** You should find at least four points of comparison.

READING FOCUS

Comparison-Contrast Structure

A Question of Style Everything has a style. Sports cars have a specific look. You dress in a certain way. Even a comparison-contrast piece has a particular appearance. Not all comparison-contrast writings look just alike, though, because they can be organized in different ways. Two common patterns of organization for comparison-contrast writing are the *block style* and the *point-by-point style*. You can identify the structure of a comparison-contrast piece by looking at the points of comparison.

Block Style A comparison-contrast piece organized in the **block style** discusses all the points of comparison for the first subject and then all the points of comparison for the second subject. Suppose you are reading a comparison-contrast article about going to the movies versus renting a video. The points of comparison are *cost* and *choice of movies*. Here is how a writer using the block style would organize the article.

Subject 1: going to the movies	cost
	choice of movies
Subject 2: renting a video	cost
	choice of movies

In block style, the writer would first discuss going to the movies. The writer would tell about the ticket prices and the choices of movies available. Then, the writer would discuss renting a video. You would read about how much a video costs and what choices you have when renting a video.

124 Chapter 4 **Exposition:** Comparing and Contrasting

Point-by-Point Style   A comparison-contrast piece organized in the **point-by-point style** goes back and forth between two subjects. It explains how the two subjects are alike and different for *one* point of comparison. Then, it explains how they are alike and different for the *next* point of comparison, and so on. The example below shows how the movies-versus-video comparison would be organized in point-by-point style.

Point of Comparison 1: cost	going to the movies
	renting a video
Point of Comparison 2: choice of movies	going to the movies
	renting a video

In point-by-point style, the writer would discuss cost first. You would read about how much going to the movies costs in comparison to renting a video. Then, you would read about the choice of movies you have when you go to the movies, followed by a discussion of the choice of movies available at a video store.

TIP   Did you notice how the point-by-point style always discussed movies first and videos second? This **predictable order** makes it easy for a reader to understand and follow the points of comparison.

? Look back at the block style organization on the previous page. What is predictable about the order in the block style?

YOUR TURN 3   Identifying Comparison-Contrast Structure

Use your list of points of comparison from Your Turn 2 to identify the organization of the reading selection. Overall, does the article tend to use the block style or the point-by-point style? Support your answer with examples from the essay. **Hint:** Do all the details about Kennedy come before the details about Nixon (block style), or do the details switch back and forth between Kennedy and Nixon (point-by-point style)?

Reading Workshop   **125**

MINI-LESSON VOCABULARY

Prefixes and Suffixes

A comparison-contrast piece may contain unfamiliar words. Knowing the meanings of common *prefixes* and *suffixes* may help you figure out these words' meanings. A **prefix** is a word part added *before* the root. A **suffix** is a word part added *after* a root. The **root** is the main part of the word. The charts below provide you with the definitions of common prefixes and suffixes.

Prefix	Definition	Example
un–	not	uneven
re–	again	rerun
pre–	before	preview
semi–	half	semifinals

Suffix	Definition	Example
–ous	characterized by	victorious
–ion	act or condition of	inspection
–ic	nature of	angelic
–less	without	careless

THINKING IT THROUGH Using Prefixes and Suffixes

Here is an example based on the word *uncomfortable* from page 122.

▶ **STEP 1** Separate any prefixes or suffixes from the word's root. Define the root.

Un– is a prefix and –able is a suffix. Comfort is the root. It means "free from worry."

▶ **STEP 2** Add the prefix or suffix to the root, and define the word. If you have another prefix or suffix, add it and define the word.

I'll add –able. Comfortable means "able to be free from worry." I'll add un–. Uncomfortable means "not able to be free from worry."

▶ **STEP 3** Check your definition by placing it in the original sentence.

"Nixon came across as not able to be free from worry and ill at ease." That works.

PRACTICE

Using the steps above, figure out the meanings for the following words underlined in "The Nixon-Kennedy Presidential Debates."

1. vigorous (page 121)
2. pitiless (page 121)
3. unproved (page 121)
4. dynamic (page 122)
5. reactions (page 122)

MINI-LESSON: TEST TAKING

Recognizing Supporting Details

Maybe you have had this experience: Your friend tells you, "I met this person the other day who reminds me so much of you." Your first question would probably be "How are we alike?" You want **supporting details** that show how this other person is like you. A reading test may ask you to identify supporting details that show how two subjects are alike or different. Suppose the following passage and the question below it were in a reading test. How would you answer the question?

> Sonja and Maria sometimes seem like the same person. First, they look alike, since each has shiny black hair and big brown eyes. They also have the same interest in collecting stamps from all over the world. They have similar families, too. Sonja has four brothers and Maria has three brothers. Although they complain about their brothers sometimes, each is proud to be the only sister.

What is similar about Sonja and Maria's appearance?

A. They like to wear the same clothes.

B. They both have dark hair and brown eyes.

C. They both have beautiful curly hair.

D. They both are the only sister.

THINKING IT THROUGH

Recognizing Supporting Details

STEP 1 Identify what detail the question is asking about.

This question asks about the girls' appearance.

STEP 2 Scan the passage to find the section where this detail is discussed.

The passage doesn't use the word "appearance," but it talks about what the girls look like.

STEP 3 Find the place in the passage that gives you the answer.

The sentence about their "shiny black hair and big brown eyes" holds the answer.

STEP 4 Look for the choice that best matches your answer. It may not be stated in the same words, but it should mean the same thing.

Choice D talks about their families. That leaves choices A, B, and C. Clothes are not mentioned, so choice A is not right, and choice C does not match the information in the passage. Choice B is the correct answer.

Writing Workshop

Writing a Comparison-Contrast Essay

WHAT'S AHEAD?

In this workshop you will write a comparison-contrast essay. You will also learn how to

- choose and narrow two subjects
- find points of comparison
- evaluate supporting details
- improve choppy sentences
- use comparatives correctly

You and your best friend wear the same brand of tennis shoes, save your allowances, and spend too much time on the phone. You seem exactly alike, but are you really? You keep your room neat and organized, while your friend's room is always messy. You love Mexican food, but your friend prefers Thai food. You and your friend share many similarities, but you also have differences. Whenever you recognize that two things are both alike and different, you are comparing and contrasting.

You can understand many things by comparing and contrasting two subjects. In letters, reports, journal entries, and tests, you will find many occasions to write about how two subjects are alike and different. This workshop will prepare you.

Prewriting

Choose and Narrow Two Subjects

Apples and Oranges? Maybe you have heard this statement: "That's like comparing apples and oranges!" This expression means that you should only compare things that are alike, such as a red apple with a green one. If you think about it, though, comparing apples and oranges makes sense. They are similar enough to be compared, yet different enough to contrast with each other. **When you choose two subjects for your comparison-contrast essay, make sure they have basic similarities as well as differences.**

You should also choose two subjects you know well. For example, you probably know apples and oranges well enough to give specific details about their similarities and differences. What other subjects do you know well? **Brainstorm** about these categories:

- two TV shows
- two people, such as relatives, friends, or movie or sport stars
- two holidays
- two sports
- two musical groups

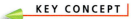
KEY CONCEPT

TIP One way to choose two subjects for a comparison-contrast essay is to pick a category first. Then, select two subjects within that category. For example, apples and oranges are part of the same category—fruit. Apples and motorcycles are from two different categories—food and transportation—so comparing them would be difficult.

Set Your Limits The two subjects you choose should be narrow enough for you to write about in an essay. For instance, you could compare apples and oranges in a short essay, but to compare fruits and vegetables, you would need to write a book. Use the steps in the following Thinking It Through to figure out if you need to narrow your subjects.

THINKING IT THROUGH Narrowing Your Subjects

▶ **STEP 1** Write down a possible subject you know well.

big pets and small pets

▶ **STEP 2** Ask yourself, "Can I break down my subjects into smaller or more specific groups?"

These subjects seem too big. Maybe I should focus on pets I have actually had, like dogs, cats, fish, hamsters, and hermit crabs.

▶ **STEP 3** Choose two specific groups that could be discussed in an essay. These are your narrowed subjects.

Since I have a dog and a hamster as pets, I can talk about those in a short essay. They will be my two subjects.

Choosing and Narrowing Subjects

Make a list of possible subjects to compare and contrast. Consider the following questions to help you choose two subjects you can write about in your essay.

- Are the subjects alike enough to make a comparison?
- Do I know enough about the subjects to provide details?
- Are the subjects narrow enough to discuss in an essay? (Use the Thinking It Through steps on page 129.)

Consider Purpose and Audience

A Reason for Everything   Comparing apples and oranges might make sense, except for just one thing: Who cares about them? Most people already know how apples and oranges are alike and different. In other words, there is no strong **purpose** or **audience** for the essay. To determine a specific purpose and audience, first ask yourself the reason for comparing and contrasting the two subjects. Then, ask yourself who would be able to use the information.

Subjects: dogs and hamsters

Purpose: What is the reason for comparing and contrasting dogs and hamsters?	✓ to help people choose a family pet to help students from other countries understand two American pets
Audience: Who would be able to use this information?	✓ students and families who want a pet students from other countries who do not have dogs or hamsters as pets

The student whose chart is shown above chose to help other students and families decide on a family pet. Because her essay will help readers choose a pet, the student will need to provide more information about caring for these pets. Once you have identified your purpose and audience, you can decide what background information or definitions to include in your essay.

YOUR TURN 5 — Considering Purpose and Audience

Determine your specific purpose and audience for the subjects you have chosen. Create a chart like the one on page 130. Then, think about the background information and definitions your audience will need. Use the following questions to guide you.

- What is the reason for comparing and contrasting the two subjects you have chosen?
- Who would be able to use this information?
- What background information will I need to provide?
- What words will I need to define?

> **TIP** The **voice** of your essay should match your purpose. For example, with a serious purpose such as helping families choose a dog, you would choose words that give specific, direct information: You might refer to a "Lab-Poodle mix" instead of "a mutt." If you want to show the humor in caring for dogs, you might use words that express a lighter tone, such as *pooch, pup,* or *canine comrade.*

Think of Points of Comparison

Generally Speaking How are your two subjects alike? How are they different? As you answer these questions, **begin to notice the larger areas in which you find both similarities and differences.** These areas will be the points of comparison that will help you organize your essay.

THINKING IT THROUGH — Choosing Points of Comparison

Here is how to choose the points of comparison for your comparison-contrast essay.

▶ **STEP 1** Think about the subjects of your comparison-contrast essay. What points do they share?

When I think of dogs and hamsters, I think about how they look and act, what they need to survive, how they relate to people, and how long they live.

▶ **STEP 2** Choose two or three of these points of comparison for your essay. Select the ones that you know well so you can provide specific details.

Because I take care of both pets, I can give lots of details about what they need. I also know how they relate to people.

Writing Workshop 131

> **YOUR TURN 6** **Choosing Your Points of Comparison**
>
> Decide on the points of comparison you will use by following the steps in the Thinking It Through on page 131.

Gather Support and Organize Information

A Leg to Stand On Strong bones support your body just as details support a good essay. How do you get details that will provide the support your ideas need? Start by listing as many details as possible for each point of comparison. Just be sure each detail relates directly to your point of comparison. If it does not, it will weaken, not support, your point.

Getting Organized A Venn diagram can help you organize your details. To make a Venn diagram, draw two overlapping circles like the ones in the student's example below. In the example, the points of comparison are listed to the left of the circles. Each circle represents one of the subjects. The overlapping section includes the details that the subjects have in common. The sections that do not overlap include the details that make each subject different.

TIP Since you are writing to inform, you want to be sure your details are accurate. If you are unsure about a detail, use **reference materials** and other **resources**. Look up and verify your information in books, in magazines, or on the Internet. You can also verify information by asking teachers or friends who are experts on the subjects you have chosen.

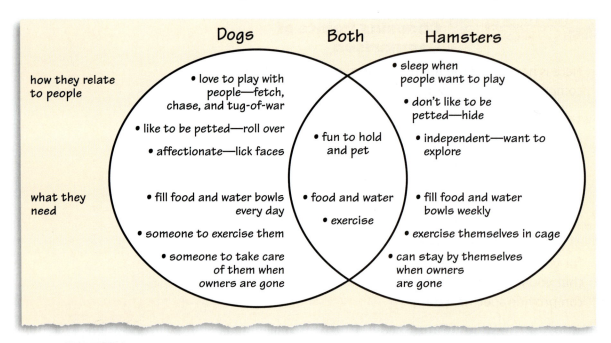

132   Chapter 4   **Exposition:** Comparing and Contrasting

Gathering and Organizing Support

Reference Note

For more on **evaluating details,** see page 135.

Brainstorm a list of details for your two points of comparison. Organize your details in a graphic organizer like the Venn diagram on page 132.

Develop a Main Idea Statement

My Point Is . . .   Have you ever had a conversation with someone who gives you an endless list of details? The entire time that person is talking, you are thinking, "What is the point of all this?" In an essay, you can get to the point by writing a **main idea statement,** or **thesis.** This statement is similar to a topic sentence for a paragraph except that it summarizes the main idea of the entire essay. The main idea statement for your comparison-contrast essay will tell readers the subjects you are comparing and contrasting, the purpose of your essay, and your points of comparison. You can write a main idea statement in one or two sentences. See how one student wrote a main idea statement in the example below.

> **Subjects:** dogs and hamsters
>
> **Purpose:** helping students and families decide on a family pet
>
> **Points of comparison:** how dogs and hamsters relate to people and what dogs and hamsters need
>
> **Main idea statement:** Dogs and hamsters both make good family pets, but they are different in the way they relate to people and in their needs.

 Writing a Main Idea Statement

Think about the subjects, purpose, and points of comparison for your comparison-contrast essay. Then, write a main idea statement to communicate these ideas.

Arranging Details

What Goes Where? You will organize your essay using the block style, which presents all the information about one subject and then all the information about the other subject. Here is how the student using the block style would arrange the points of comparison for dogs and hamsters.

> Subject 1: Dogs
> > how they relate to people
> >
> > what they need
>
> Subject 2: Hamsters
> > how they relate to people
> >
> > what they need

As you can see, the block style presents the points of comparison in the same order for both subjects. For each subject, how the pet relates to people is discussed first, and what the pet needs is discussed second. Follow the same structure in your essay.

TIP For short comparison-contrast essays, the block style is a good way to group similar ideas together. The arrangement of ideas based on similarities is called **logical order**. However, there are other ways to achieve logical order. The chart on page 125 shows the point-by-point style. Still another type of structure is the **modified block style**. In this style, all the *similarities* for the points of comparison are discussed. Then all the *differences* for the points of comparison are discussed. The modified block style looks like this:

Similarities of rugby and football:	rules
	equipment
Differences between rugby and football:	rules
	equipment

 **Arranging Details**

Arrange the points of comparison for your comparison-contrast essay as in the student example above. Check to see that the points of comparison are in the same order for each subject.

Chapter 4 Exposition: Comparing and Contrasting

MINI-LESSON CRITICAL THINKING

Evaluating Details

When you write a comparison-contrast essay, it is important that your details provide **logical support** for the points of comparison. A feature of logical support is *relevance*. **Relevant details** are related to the point they support. Examine the Venn diagram to the right. Can you identify any details that do not support the point of comparison "appearance"? The details that do not support the point of comparison "appearance" would be either listed with a different point of comparison or removed from the essay.

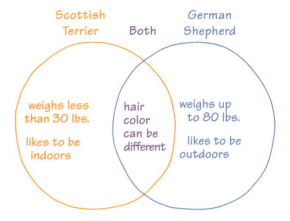

PRACTICE

Look at the example below and evaluate the details for each point of comparison. Decide whether any detail does not belong with the point of comparison where it is listed.

Comparison-Contrast Essay

Framework	**Directions and Explanations**

Introduction
- Attention-grabbing opener
- Main idea statement

Pull your reader in right away with an **interesting beginning.** You could begin with a mysterious statement which you go on to explain, as the writer of the model to the right did. You could also begin with a funny story or a question. Then, include your **main idea statement** so that the reader understands exactly what you are comparing and contrasting.

Body
- Subject #1
  Point of comparison #1
  (with logical support)
  Point of comparison #2
  (with logical support)
- Subject #2
  Point of comparison #1
  (with logical support)
  Point of comparison #2
  (with logical support)

Here you will point out how the two subjects are alike and different for at least two points of comparison.
- Present your first subject by discussing both **points of comparison** in the first body paragraph.
- When you present your second subject in the next paragraph, discuss the **points of comparison** in the same order.

To help you discuss the similarities and differences, use **transitional words.** Transitional words that show similarities are *also, like, in addition,* and *another.* Transitional words that point out the differences are *on the other hand, but, however,* and *unlike.*

Conclusion
- Summary of body paragraphs

Briefly **sum up** the result of the comparison. **Relate** your summary to the main idea you included in the first paragraph.

YOUR TURN 10 Drafting Your Essay

Write a comparison-contrast essay. As you write, refer to the framework above and the Writer's Model on the next page.

A Writer's Model

The final draft below closely follows the framework for a comparison-contrast essay on the previous page.

Puppy Love or Hamster Heaven?

Your friends have one, maybe even two or three. The neighbors have one. Does it seem that everyone has one but you? No, it is not the latest video game, but something much more fun—a family pet. Dogs and hamsters both make good family pets, but they are different in the way they relate to people and in their needs.

Dogs and hamsters are both fun to hold and pet, but they relate to people in different ways. For instance, dogs enjoy human contact. They love to play fetch, chase, and tug-of-war with their owners. Dogs like to be petted, and most dogs will roll over to have their bellies rubbed. Dogs are also affectionate and love licking their owners' faces. However, dogs need lots of care, too. They need fresh food and water every day, and they need regular exercise. They also need someone to take care of them when their owners go out of town.

Hamsters are very different from dogs. Having contact with people is not important to them. They like to sleep when people want to play. Unlike dogs, hamsters do not like being petted. Many will hide when their owners want to pick them up. Hamsters are also very independent. They like to spend their time exploring. Hamsters may be low on affection, but they need less daily care than dogs do. They need food and water just as dogs do, but an owner usually fills up the food and water dishes only once a week. Hamsters need exercise too, but they get their exercise by running on wheels in their cages. If their owners go out of town, hamsters can be left alone.

Dogs and hamsters both make good pets. Dogs provide plenty of affection, but they are also high maintenance. Hamsters are definitely low maintenance, but they are also less cuddly. The choice is yours.

Attention-grabbing opener

Main idea statement

Subject 1: First point of comparison

Supporting details

Second point of comparison

Supporting details

Subject 2: First point of comparison

Supporting details

Second point of comparison

Supporting details

Summary of body paragraphs

Writing Workshop

A Student's Model

When you write a comparison-contrast essay, make sure you have a purpose for writing. Matthew Hester, a middle school student from Laurel Hill, Florida, wants to help his audience make a decision. He compares two types of collections that may interest beginner collectors.

A Collection Question

Attention-grabbing opener

Collecting is very popular today. Collectors have their own magazines, television shows, and Internet sites. If you are thinking about starting a collection, I suggest considering trading cards or airplane models.

Main idea statement

They are both good investments and fun, but they differ in storage and use.

Subject 1: First point of comparison

Collecting trading cards is an enjoyable hobby. They are easy to store and transport in bags, boxes, or notebooks.

Second point of comparison

Trading cards with friends is a super way to spend an afternoon. Cards also provide adventure and challenge as you seek that one card essential to completing your set.

Subject 2: First point of comparison

Model collecting differs from card collecting in several ways. Model airplanes require more storage space than cards do and are more difficult to transport due to their larger size.

Second point of comparison

However, models do allow for more realistic play. The zooming and swooshing of miniature airplanes give the feeling of being in the center of the action.

Summary of body paragraphs

Trading cards and model airplanes both make good collections due to their current and possible future value. This makes them a wise investment for your allowance dollars. Trading cards are excellent choices if you have limited storage space and enjoy a challenge. Model airplanes are better if your storage space is unlimited and you enjoy live-action play. If you have trouble deciding, join me in collecting both. Either way, start your collection today!

Revising

Evaluate and Revise Content, Organization, and Style

Double Vision   Look twice when you evaluate a peer's paper or your own. On the first reading, concentrate on content and organization, using the guidelines below. The second time you read the essay, pay attention to the sentences, using the Focus on Sentences on page 141.

▶ **First Reading: Content and Organization**   Use this chart to evaluate and revise your essay so the ideas are clear.

Guidelines for Self-Evaluation and Peer Evaluation		
Evaluation Questions	**Tips**	**Revision Techniques**
❶ Does the introduction state the main idea?	**Underline** the main idea statement.	**Add** a main idea statement if one is missing.
❷ Does the first body paragraph discuss the first subject with at least two points of comparison?	**Put a star** next to each point of comparison.	If there is no clear point of comparison, **add** one or **revise** an existing one.
❸ Does the second body paragraph discuss the second subject using the same points of comparison in the same order?	**Draw a wavy line** under each point of comparison.	If the same points of comparison are not used, **add** one or **revise** an existing one. **Rearrange** the points of comparison if they are not in the same order.
❹ Do relevant details logically support each point of comparison for both subjects?	**Put a check mark** next to the supporting details for each point of comparison. **Underline** any details that do not support the point of comparison.	If needed, **elaborate** on a point of comparison by adding details. **Delete** details that do not directly support the point of comparison.
❺ Does the conclusion summarize the body paragraphs and refer to the main idea?	With a colored marker, **highlight** the summary.	If needed, **add** a brief summary that is related to the main idea.

ONE WRITER'S REVISIONS This revision is an early draft of the essay on page 137.

> Hamsters are very different from dogs. Having contact with people is not important to them. They like to sleep when people want to play. ~~I have to go to bed by 10:30.~~ Unlike dogs, hamsters do not like being petted. *Many will hide when their owners want to pick them up.* Hamsters are also very independent. They like to spend their time exploring.

delete (annotation for the struck-through sentence)
elaborate (annotation for the inserted sentence)

PEER REVIEW

As you evaluate a peer's paper, ask yourself the following questions:

- What points of comparison does the writer discuss?
- Who will be able to use this information?

Responding to the Revision Process

1. Why do you think the writer deleted a sentence in the paragraph above?
2. Why do you think the writer added a sentence to the paragraph?

▶ **Second Reading: Style** During your first reading, you looked at what you said in your essay and how you organized your ideas. Now, focus on how your essay *sounds*. Good writing has an easy rhythm that is not choppy. To achieve an easy rhythm, writers use a variety of sentences in their essays. They avoid long series of short sentences by combining two short sentences into one sentence.

When you evaluate the rhythm of your comparison-contrast essay, ask yourself whether you have combined sentences so that they are not choppy. As you re-read your essay, underline any short sentence that repeats several words or a phrase from the sentence before or after it. Then, combine sentences by cutting repeated words and inserting necessary words or phrases.

Combining Sentences

Focus on Sentences

Good writers use some short sentences. Too many short sentences are a problem. Many short sentences in a row bore readers. The ideas in the previous three sentences are important for writers to know, but you might have found it difficult to pay attention to them. Their choppy sound and their repeated words and phrases probably bothered you. Combining short, choppy sentences can be as easy as moving a word or phrase from one sentence to another.

Choppy Sentences	~~The car was~~ black. The car was hot. [move a word]
Combined Sentence	The black car was hot.
Choppy Sentences	Jamal played disc golf. ~~He played~~ in the afternoon. [move a phrase]
Combined Sentence	Jamal played disc golf in the afternoon.

ONE WRITER'S REVISIONS

They love to play fetch and tug-of-war with their owners. ~~Dogs also like to play~~ chase.

Responding to the Revision Process
How does combining the two sentences improve the writing?

COMPUTER TIP
If you have access to a computer, speed up the revision process by using the cut-and-paste feature. You can rearrange the details in your comparison-contrast essay by cutting words and sentences and then pasting them in a new location. Cutting and pasting saves you the trouble of typing the information twice.

YOUR TURN 11 — Evaluating and Revising Your Comparison-Contrast Essay

First, evaluate and revise the content and organization of your essay, using the guidelines on page 139. Then, use the Focus on Sentences above to see if you need to combine any choppy sentences. Finally, if a peer evaluated your paper, think carefully about his or her comments as you revise.

Publishing

Proofread Your Essay

Reference Note
For more on **proofreading**, see page 13.

Look Out Two sets of eyes are better than one when trying to find mistakes. After you proofread your essay, see if you can catch more mistakes by enlisting the help of another proofreader.

Grammar Link

Using Comparatives Correctly

In a comparison-contrast essay, you have to make comparisons. When you make comparisons between two subjects, you use the **comparative** form of adjectives and adverbs. To write comparatives correctly, follow the guidelines.

The comparative form of one-syllable modifiers is usually made by adding –*er*.

Modifier	Comparative Form
fast	faster

Some two-syllable modifiers form the comparative by using *more*.

Modifier	Comparative Form
nervous	more nervous

Modifiers with three or more syllables use *more* to form the comparative.

Modifier	Comparative Form
successful	more successful

Be sure not to use –*er* together with *more*. That combination is never correct.

Incorrect Mandy always arrives more earlier than Liza.

Correct Mandy always arrives *earlier* than Liza.

PRACTICE

Complete each of the following sentences with the correct form of the given modifier.

Example:
1. quickly   Sam finished his test ____ than Liam.
1. *more quickly*

1. lovable   I think dogs are ____ than hamsters are.
2. small   Hamsters are ____ than dogs.
3. playful   Hamsters are ____ at night than during the day.
4. frequently   Dogs have to be fed ____ than hamsters.
5. easy   Do you think hamsters are ____ to take care of than dogs?

142   Chapter 4   **Exposition:** Comparing and Contrasting

Publish Your Essay

Experience to the Rescue   Your experience with the two subjects you wrote about in your comparison-contrast essay can provide information that people need and want. What is the best way to reach the audience who will benefit from your experience?

- Does the topic of your comparison-contrast essay relate to a school subject? Did you compare two sports? two artists? two countries? Make copies of your essay and share them with teachers. They might use your essay in their classes.

- Display your essays and those of your classmates on a wall in your school. Invite teachers, parents, and other students to view the "Authors' Wall."

TIP   Grab potential readers by giving your essay an attention-getting title that creatively reflects your topic.

Designing Your Writing

Creating a Bar Graph   A quick and visual way to show your readers the similarities and differences between two subjects is to provide a bar graph. Each point of comparison can be a separate graph. Some word-processing programs allow you to create graphs, or you can draw one by hand. Either way, make sure you use colors and provide a **legend,** or explanation of what each color represents. Colors will help your reader identify each subject in your graph. Below, see how the writer of the Writer's Model used a bar graph that includes a legend to compare the needs of hamsters and dogs.

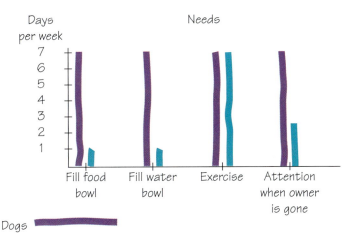

TIP   By looking at the bar graph to the left, readers can tell which pet needs more daily care.
Do you know which pet has more needs?

Writing Workshop

Reflect on Your Essay

Building Your Portfolio   Take time to reflect both on the process of comparing and contrasting two subjects and on the process of writing your essay. Thinking about how you wrote this assignment will help you when you write your next paper.

- Do you think the two subjects you wrote about are more similar or more different? Why?
- Before you wrote your essay, you arranged your ideas in a certain order. Did you find that helpful? Why or why not?
- Think about the reason why you compared the two subjects you chose. How does your essay achieve that purpose?

YOUR TURN 12   Proofreading, Publishing, and Reflecting on Your Essay

- Correct grammar, usage, and mechanics errors.
- Publish your essay by following one of the suggestions on the previous page.
- Answer the questions from Reflect on Your Essay above. Record your responses in a learning log, or include them in your portfolio.

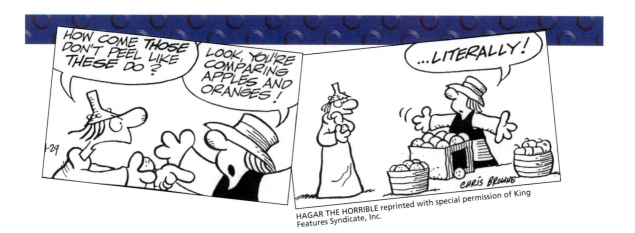

HAGAR THE HORRIBLE reprinted with special permission of King Features Syndicate, Inc.

MINI-LESSON TEST TAKING

Writing a Classification Essay

A common question on essay tests is one that asks you to classify the similarities and differences between two subjects or the good and bad points about one subject. You must quickly determine how to generate ideas. A T-chart can help. Suppose the prompt to the right appeared on a writing test. How would you approach it?

Think about your language arts class and your science class. They are alike in some ways and different in other ways. Write a composition in which you explain how your language arts and science classes are alike and how they are different.

THINKING IT THROUGH — Writing a Classification Essay

▶ **STEP 1** Identify what the prompt is asking you to do.

It asks me to explain how my language arts and science classes are alike and different.

▶ **STEP 2** Think of at least two points of comparison. Then, create a T-chart and fill it in with supporting details.

	Similarities	Differences
What I learn	information about people and events	L. A. — grammar, writing Sci. — plants, animals
What I do	homework write papers read	L. A. — act out plays, write essays Sci. — labs, draw diagrams

▶ **STEP 3** Plan how you will develop your essay.

I'll use block style. I'll talk all about language arts in the first body paragraph and science in the second body paragraph.

▶ **STEP 4** Write your essay. Make sure to elaborate on the supporting details from your T-chart with facts, examples, and explanations.

Connections to Life

Comparing Documentaries

Is truth stranger than fiction? Many filmmakers and writers would answer with a booming "Yes!" Filmmakers who want to show that truth is interesting will make a *documentary*. A **documentary** is a nonfiction film that creatively portrays an actual event, person, place, thing, or issue.

Filmmakers have the same reasons for producing documentaries as writers have for writing essays, articles, stories, or poems. Their purposes are *to inform, to entertain, to persuade,* and *to express themselves.* Like many writers, filmmakers may also have the purpose of *making money.* Every documentary will have at least one of these purposes. In fact, a documentary, like a written work, may have several purposes.

Two of a Kind? For this assignment, you will compare the purposes of two documentaries on the same topic. To do that, ask yourself the questions to the right.

- Does the filmmaker provide facts and explanations about a topic? If so, the purpose may be **to inform.**
- Does the filmmaker focus on a famous person, a funny event, or an attention-grabbing topic? Does the documentary contain flashy graphics, an appealing soundtrack, and eye-catching camerawork? If so, the purpose may be **to entertain.**
- Does the filmmaker appeal to viewers' emotions and try to get the viewers to think a certain way? If so, the purpose may be **to persuade.**
- Does the filmmaker explore a topic using a first-person narrator who reveals his or her inner thoughts about the topic? If so, the purpose may be **to express.**
- Does the filmmaker focus on a popular topic? If so, the purpose may be **to make money.** The larger the audience a documentary attracts, the more ads the network can sell.

YOUR TURN 13 Comparing Documentaries

View two documentaries on the same topic. As you watch, take notes on how information is presented in each, using the questions above as a guide. Then, write a paragraph or two comparing the two documentaries. Discuss how the documentaries' purposes are similar, and how they are different.

Focus on Viewing and Representing

Comparing Ideas in Photographs

When you look at a photograph of yourself, what do you see? You see yourself, right? The picture shows the color of your eyes and hair, the shape of your nose and mouth, and the style of clothing you wear. Actually, while the person in the picture certainly seems to look like you, it is not the *real* you.

WHAT'S AHEAD?

In this section you will compare ideas in photographs. You will also learn how to

- explain the difference between a photograph of an object and the real object
- analyze how photographs provide information

Photographs vs. Reality

Many people believe that photographs truly represent reality, but they do not. In truth, photographs, like all illustrations, only resemble an actual person, place, thing, or event. What you see in a photograph is not the same as what you see in real life because photographs have the following unique characteristics.

- **Photographs are two-dimensional and flat.** If you took a picture of the palm of your hand, could you turn the picture over and see the top of your hand? No. The photograph shows only one side. In real life, you can view all sides.

- **Photographs are easily reproduced and distributed.** It is easy to make copies of your birthday party pictures and send them to relatives and friends. Although it might be fun, it would be impossible to reproduce the real party over and over again.

- **Photographs contain a single point of view.** When you look at a head-on photograph of a baseball player hitting a baseball, you are looking at the action from the photographer's point of view. You do not see what the hitter sees. Photographers use the element of point of view to show how an image looks from a specific position.

Focus on Viewing and Representing 147

Photographs Provide Information

Even though looking at a photograph is not the same as actually seeing the real thing, photographs are helpful because they provide information in an easily accessible way. For example, if you want to know what a Tasmanian devil looks like, you could visit the nearest zoo, fly to Tasmania, or look at a photograph. The easiest choice, of course, would be to look at a photograph.

Photographs are also a powerful partner to the written and spoken word. In a newspaper, for instance, you might read about an erupting volcano. Not until you look at the picture that accompanies the article would you fully understand the massive destruction the volcano caused. Because photographs are so powerful and easy to reproduce, they are a popular form of media. Look in any magazine, newspaper, or textbook and you will find many photographs. You should be aware, however, that the information photographs provide can be changed by adjusting the *camera angle*, by *cropping* the photograph, and by using *captions*.

> **TIP** Photography is not the only media form that provides information.
> **?** Can you think of any others? **Hint:** The paragraph to the right can give you a few answers.

Up, Down, Sideways

A photographer can change the appearance of a person, place, thing, or event by changing the **camera angle.** Look at the examples below. In the picture on the left, the photographer stood on a ladder and shot the picture looking down. Do you see how the boy looks small and rather fragile? Now, look at the picture on the right taken of the same boy from a low angle. From this point of view, the boy looks big and powerful, even a little intimidating.

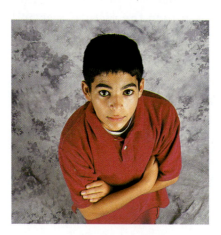 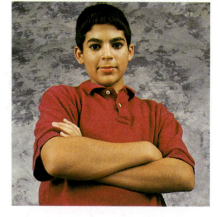

What's Missing? Photographs can be **cropped,** or cut, so background details do not distract the viewer from the main subject. However, cropping can change the meaning of a picture, as you can see below. In the picture on the left you see a spaceship hovering in the sky. In the picture on the right, though, you see what was cut from the first picture. Aliens are not landing; a girl is holding the spaceship by a string.

More Than Words Some photographs have **captions,** which are like titles. A caption provides viewers with a summary of what is shown in a picture. Captions can be neutral, giving only facts, or they can show a positive or negative attitude toward the subject. Look at the pictures and captions below and on the next page. You can see that the images are the same, but the captions show two very different attitudes toward grizzly bears.

TIP What attitude toward bears does this caption express?

Enjoying the spring weather, a mother bear and her young relax by the riverside.

Focus on Viewing and Representing **149**

TIP The purpose of any illustration is to illustrate an idea. Illustrators make choices about what style and medium will best suit their purpose. For example, the photograph to the right uses a realistic style, complementing the informative caption. The choice of photography as a medium also contributes to the informative purpose. Could a **?** different medium (such as a cartoon) or a different style (one using symbols to represent bears, for example) be as effective in complementing the caption text? Explain.

Here is the same picture with a different caption. Notice how the caption changes what you "see" in the photo.

Rangers warn park visitors not to approach mother grizzly bears. They will fiercely protect their cubs.

YOUR TURN 14 Comparing Ideas in Photographs

- Look at the photograph on the left below, while covering up the photo next to it. How do you feel about the subject? Write a caption for the photograph that summarizes what you see and expresses your feelings.

- Next, look at the photograph on the right. How do you feel about the subject now? Write a caption for the photograph that summarizes what you see and expresses your feelings.

- Finally, write a paragraph in which you compare the two photographs. Explain how the differences in the way each photo is presented may have affected the captions you wrote.

Chapter 4 **Exposition:** Comparing and Contrasting

CHAPTER

 Choices

Choose one of the following activities to complete.

▶ **CAREERS**

1. Tool Time Comparing and contrasting two subjects is a favorite tool of journalists, consumer advocates, scientists, sports commentators, and campaign managers for politicians. Find examples of how comparing and contrasting is used in these fields or in other fields. Then, write a **report** that describes examples of how people in their fields make comparisons.

▶ **VIEWING AND REPRESENTING**

2. News Views Give a short **oral report** comparing how two news sources—for example, a network TV newscast and an Internet news site—present the same story. Choose a recent situation or event that catches your interest, and look in two sources for reports about it. Compare and contrast the treatment of the story, including the story's focus, the amount of detail provided, and the viewpoints that are presented.

▶ **CREATIVE WRITING**

3. It's Like This Compose a **humorous poem** about a person, place, thing, or idea using similes. A simile is a comparison of two unlike things using *like* or *as*. For example, you could write a simile poem about happiness that begins, "Happiness is like a day without homework." In the rest of the poem, you would explain in a funny way the ways in which these two things are alike.

▶ **CROSSING THE CURRICULUM: MUSIC**

4. The Beat Goes On Does your favorite musician or band follow the same formula from one CD to the next? Find specific examples that show how the musician or band has changed or stayed the same over time. You might focus on lyrics, style, vocals, or other areas. Give a **multimedia presentation,** using audio or audio-visual clips to demonstrate your points.

 PORTFOLIO

Choices   151

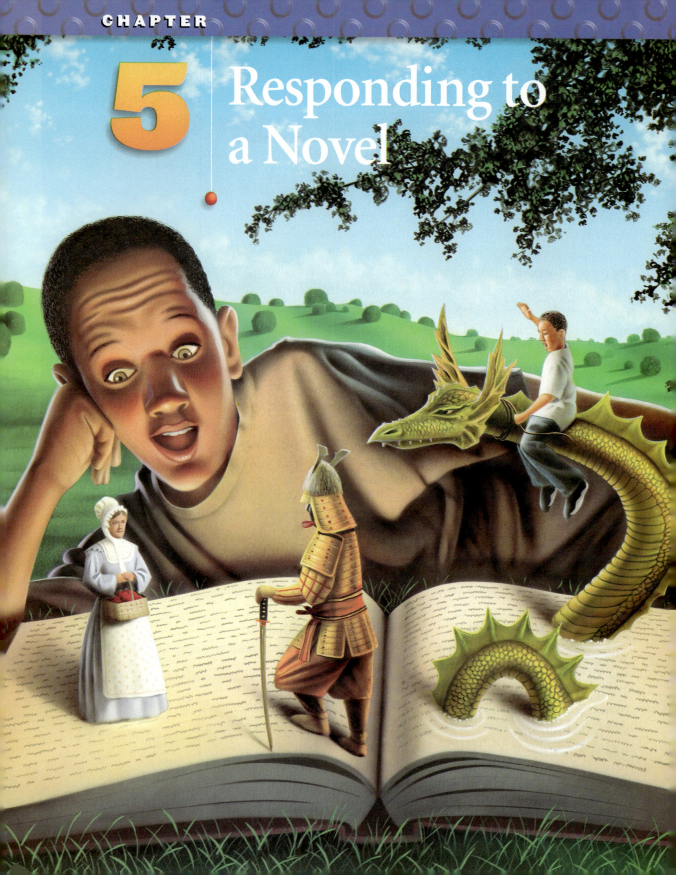

CHAPTER 5
Responding to a Novel

CONNECTING READING AND WRITING

Reading Workshop

Reading a Book Review

Writing Workshop

Writing a Book Review

Viewing and Representing

Comparing Media: Film, TV, and Literature

> **Informational Text**
>
> Exposition

You stand staring at the rows of bookshelves in your school library. You need to choose a book to read, but how can you? With so many books to choose from, it sometimes seems impossible to settle on just one.

One way to choose a book is to read a book review. A **book review** tells what a book is about and the reviewer's opinion of the book. You can find book reviews in many newspapers and magazines. Some sites on the World Wide Web are devoted entirely to book reviews.

Book reviewers help readers sort through the many choices they have when deciding what to read. Reviewers base their ideas about books on careful reading and on knowledge of what makes a book good. You can be a book reviewer, too. You can use your skills as a reader to judge a book. Then, by sharing your ideas, you will help others decide if a book might be good to read.

YOUR TURN 1 — Reviewing a Book

With a partner, think of a book that you liked and give two reasons why you liked it. Then, think of a book you disliked and give two reasons why you disliked it. Discuss your reasons.

internetconnect

go.hrw.com

GO TO: go.hrw.com
KEYWORD: EOLang 6-5

Reading Workshop

Reading a Book Review

WHAT'S AHEAD?

In this workshop you will read a book review. You will also learn how to

- identify the elements of a novel
- identify a writer's point of view

"**H**ilarious," "humorous," and "sarcastic" are words a reviewer uses in the review of the book *Catherine, Called Birdy*. Does this description make you interested in knowing more about the book? Read the following book review to see more of the reviewer's ideas about the book. Will it be a "thumbs up" or "thumbs down" review?

Preparing to Read

READING FOCUS

Elements of a Novel A novel does not just happen. A writer must put certain parts, or **elements,** into a book. Plot, character, setting, and a problem—a novel must have these elements, just as a baseball team needs a pitcher, a catcher, infielders, and outfielders. Reviewers focus on the elements of a novel when they read novels and when they write reviews about them. Notice which elements are mentioned in the review of *Catherine, Called Birdy* by Karen Cushman.

READING SKILL

Point of View We all have an attitude sometimes. Book reviewers specialize in having an attitude, and they will let you know what it is. The attitude of the reviewer (or of any writer) toward his or her topic is sometimes called the **point of view.** A book review will often end with a statement telling you whether the reviewer recommends reading the book. Long before you reach the end of a review, though, you will know how the reviewer feels. The reviewer's point of view will come across in the words he or she uses to talk about the book. What is the point of view of the reviewer of *Catherine, Called Birdy*?

154   Chapter 5   **Exposition:** Responding to a Novel

Read the following book review. In a notebook or on a separate sheet of paper, jot down answers to the numbered active-reading questions in the shaded boxes. The underlined words will be discussed in the Vocabulary Mini-Lesson on page 159.

from Great Books for Girls

Catherine, Called Birdy

BY KAREN CUSHMAN. 1994. CLARION. AGES 12–14.

Reviewed by Kathleen Odean

Catherine, daughter of a small-time nobleman in medieval England, is hilarious. In a diary format she records her daily life, the outrages she suffers as a girl, and her often humorous assessment of things. She longs to be outside frolicking instead of inside sewing, and she chafes at her lessons in ladylike behavior. Birdy is the sort of girl who organizes a spitting contest and starts a mud fight. She makes a list of all the things girls cannot do, such as go on a crusade,[1] be a horse trainer, laugh out loud, and "marry whom they will." She battles with her father, who wants to marry her off to the highest bidder, no matter how repulsive. Many of her best sarcastic remarks are reserved for him, and she irritates him whenever possible. She has a lively sense of humor and a palpable love of life. Few fictional characters are so vivid and funny—do not miss this one.

> **1. Who or what is the focus of the reviewer's comments?**

> **2. What does the reviewer think about the book?**

> **3. Does this review make you want to read the book? Why or why not?**

---

1. **crusade:** In the eleventh, twelfth, and thirteenth centuries, Christian nations repeatedly sent armies to the Holy Land, the region that is now made up of parts of Israel, Jordan, and Egypt. These armies repeatedly tried but failed to win back the Holy Land from the Muslims. These missions were called crusades.

First Thoughts on Your Reading

1. According to the review, what is the main character of *Catherine, Called Birdy* like?
2. What is the reviewer's main point?

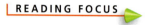

Elements of a Novel

A Recipe for Greatness When you cook, you must have certain ingredients for a dish to turn out well. A spaghetti dinner, for example, needs pasta and a good sauce.

Good stories and novels have several ingredients, or **elements**. A book reviewer will tell you about the elements of a particular novel. The reviewer will also let you know if he or she thinks the novelist got the recipe right. The chart below defines some elements of stories and novels and provides examples from a fairy tale you may know.

Elements of Stories and Novels	Examples from "Snow-White"
The **plot** is a series of related events that make up a story. The events revolve around a central problem, or **conflict**, which must be resolved before the story ends.	A jealous queen wants to kill her beautiful stepdaughter, Snow-White. Snow-White hides in the forest. She lives in a cottage with seven dwarfs. The queen tricks Snow-White into eating a poisoned apple that makes her appear dead. Snow-White is rescued by a prince.
The **main character** is the central person in the story.	Snow-White is the main character.
The **setting** is the time and place of a story.	The story is set a long time ago in a forest.

 Identifying Elements of a Novel in a Book Review

Re-read the review of *Catherine, Called Birdy* on page 155. Find the elements of the novel by answering the following questions.

- **Plot:** What does the reviewer tell you about what happens?
- **Character:** Who is the main character? What is she like?
- **Setting:** Where and when do the events take place?

Chapter 5 Exposition: Responding to a Novel

Point of View

READING SKILL

Grade "A" Quality   A book reviewer's job is to evaluate, or judge the quality of, a novel. A reviewer's **point of view** often comes through in the way he or she discusses the elements of the novel. Positive or negative words reveal the reviewer's attitude toward the book.

Read the following review of the fairy tale "Snow-White." Look for the reviewer's point of view by noting which elements the reviewer mentions and whether he or she uses positive or negative words. If you need help, the Thinking It Through that follows the review will guide you.

TIP   Reviewers use **positive words** (such as *powerful, exciting, fascinating,* and *funny*) to praise or compliment a novel. They use **negative words** (such as *weak, boring, unrealistic,* and *silly*) to criticize a novel.

> The character of Snow-White is unbelievably good and beautiful, but she is also much too trusting. Her beauty keeps the hunter and wild animals from harming her and provides her a charming home in the forest. However, her beauty does not hide her helplessness. She knows that the queen is trying to kill her, yet she continues to talk to strange women who come to the dwarfs' house. Three times she accepts deadly gifts from the disguised evil queen. Three times she survives. Anyone else would probably not be so lucky. Her character leaves the reader wondering how she manages to live happily ever after.

THINKING IT THROUGH   Identifying Point of View

▶ **STEP 1**   You can make a chart like the one on the next page to analyze a book review. In the middle column, note positive or negative words and phrases the reviewer uses to discuss each element. You may write *none* if the reviewer does not discuss a certain element.

▶ **STEP 2**   Based on the negative or positive words that the reviewer uses, decide what his or her point of view is. Write the point of view in the right-hand column of the chart. If the element is not discussed, you may leave the space blank.

Element	Positive or Negative Words and Phrases	Reviewer's Point of View
Plot	none describing plot	
Main Character	positive: good, beautiful, lucky negative: unbelievably, much too trusting, helplessness	Snow-White is beautiful, but that does not make her a great character.
Setting	positive: charming negative: none	There is not enough information to tell.

▶ **STEP 3** Put it all together. Look at the positive and negative words and phrases and decide what the reviewer thinks.

> The reviewer does not think "Snow-White" is a good story because the main character is too helpless and unbelievably lucky.

YOUR TURN 3 Identifying a Reviewer's Point of View

Re-read the review of *Catherine, Called Birdy* on page 155. Then, use the Thinking It Through steps to identify the reviewer's point of view. Be prepared to explain *why* you think the reviewer takes the point of view you have identified.

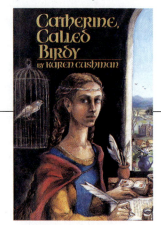

MINI-LESSON VOCABULARY

Wordbusting Strategy (CSSD)

A reviewer may use very specific words to communicate exactly what he or she thinks of a book. Often, the word *good* is just not good enough.

When you come across an unfamiliar word in a book review, you can use a four-part strategy called **Wordbusting**. The letters **CSSD** can help you remember the steps of the strategy. Use only as many steps as it takes to understand the word.

- **Context** Use clues from the words and sentences around the word.
- **Structure** Look for familiar roots, prefixes, or suffixes.
- **Sound** Say the word aloud. It may sound like a word you know.
- **Dictionary** Look up the word.

THINKING IT THROUGH — Using the Wordbusting Strategy

Here is an example of Wordbusting, using the word *outrages* from the review of *Catherine, Called Birdy*.

▸ **Context:** "In a diary format she records her daily life, the *outrages* she suffers as a girl, and her often humorous assessment of things."

In the sentence, outrages are something she suffers. Suffers tells me that outrages are bad.

▸ **Structure:** out + rage + s

Rage means "anger," so the word must have something to do with getting mad.

▸ **Sound:** out′ rāj′ iz

It sounds like out and rage. I think an outrage must be something that makes you mad.

▸ **Dictionary:** *Outrages* are acts that hurt someone or disregard a person's feelings.

My definition is pretty close.

PRACTICE

Use the Wordbusting strategy to figure out the meanings of the words to the right. The words are underlined in the review of *Catherine, Called Birdy* on page 155, so you can see the context of each word. After each definition, list the steps of CSSD that you used for that word.

1. assessment
2. frolicking
3. chafes
4. repulsive
5. palpable

MINI-LESSON TEST TAKING

Answering Questions About Unfamiliar Vocabulary

Reading tests may ask you to identify the meanings of new words. The words may be technical or specialized terms that you normally do not use. To figure out their meanings, you must find clues in the reading passage. Look at the reading passage below and the test question that follows it. Then, use the Thinking It Through steps to figure out the answer.

In the Middle Ages, books and other documents had to be copied by hand. Professional writers, called scribes, copied documents onto a kind of paper made from sheepskin. Often, many scribes sat together in a scriptorium, writing with ink and quill pens made from feathers. Scribes left wide margins on pages so that artists could draw colorful illustrations. When the handmade pages were complete, they were sewn together into a book.

You can tell from the passage that a scriptorium is

A. a person who copies documents
B. a pen made from feathers
C. a room where scribes work
D. a book made from sheepskin

THINKING IT THROUGH

Answering Questions About Unfamiliar Vocabulary

▶ **STEP 1** Read the whole passage and get a sense of what it is about.

The passage is about how scribes copied documents in the Middle Ages.

▶ **STEP 2** Look at the context of the word. Pay attention to words near the new term that may provide a clue to the word's meaning.

The passage tells me that scribes sat in a scriptorium. I can tell from the words "sat" and "in" that a scriptorium is a building or room.

▶ **STEP 3** Check your answer against the items in the test question.

A is wrong. The people who copied are scribes.

B does not match my answer.

C matches my answer. This is correct.

D is wrong. The scribes would not sit in a book.

Writing Workshop

Writing a Book Review

You have just taken a journey. Maybe you went back in time or visited a foreign land. Perhaps you fought dragons, danced with royalty, and conquered evil. How did you do these wonderful things? You read a book, of course.

You think that all your friends should visit the world in the book you have just read. You can show your friends this world by writing a **book review**. In this workshop you will write a book review about a young adult novel. You will summarize the book and tell whether you think it is worth reading.

WHAT'S AHEAD?

In this workshop you will write a book review. You will also learn how to

- preview and summarize a novel
- identify the elements of a plot
- replace clichés with your own words
- use appositives

Prewriting

Select a Novel

Plucky Heroines in the City   For this review, you will read a young adult novel. Think of the types of characters or settings you like to read about in novels. Then, look for a book with the type of character or setting that interests you most. To find a book, you might

- browse in bookstores—in person or online
- ask friends for recommendations
- go to the HRW Web site
- ask a librarian or media specialist for suggestions
- read some book reviews
- look for a new book by one of your favorite authors

TIP You can use a library's **card** or **online catalog** to find a book. These catalogs list books by their titles, by their authors' names, and by their subjects. For more on **libraries** and **catalogs** see page 277 and page 280 in the Quick Reference Handbook.

Preview of Coming Attractions

Once you have found several possible choices for your book review, **preview** each one to make your final decision. One student previewed *Tuck Everlasting* by Natalie Babbitt by following the steps in the Thinking it Through below.

THINKING IT THROUGH: Previewing a Novel

▶ **STEP 1 Look at the cover.** Is there something that makes you interested in the book?

The front cover has a mysterious pair of eyes on it. The back cover has a quotation that makes me curious about the book.

▶ **STEP 2 Read the book jacket summary.** What does the summary tell you?

The story is about a young girl who is kidnapped by a family who drank from a spring that lets them live forever.

▶ **STEP 3 Skim some pages.** Do you like the way the characters are shown? Do you see any interesting action taking place?

There are lots of examples of dialogue, and I like to hear the characters talking. Somebody escapes from jail.

▶ **STEP 4 Consider what you have found.** Does the book look interesting? Do you want to know more about the characters?

Yes, I want to know more about these characters. I think that this is a good choice for me.

Read Your Novel

KEY CONCEPT

TIP As you read, keep in mind the deadline for your review. Set aside time to read each day and set goals for how many pages you will read.

Please Note . . . As you read the book you have chosen, remember that you will be writing about it later. Keep nearby a sheet of paper divided into three columns. Label the columns *plot*, *setting*, and *main character*. Fill in the columns by answering the questions at the top of the next page as you read. Include page numbers next to important notes. The page numbers will help you if you need to go back and re-read some sections of the novel.

Chapter 5 **Exposition:** Responding to a Novel

Plot	Setting	Main Character
- What are the key events of each chapter? - What problem does the main character face? - How is the problem solved?	- Where does the story take place? - When does the story take place? - How much time passes in the story?	- Name: - Age: - What does the character look like? - What does the character like to do or play or eat?

 Selecting and Reading a Novel

Brainstorm a list of the types of novels you like to read. Follow the Thinking It Through steps on page 162 to preview a few novels and choose one that you think you will enjoy. Then, read your book and take notes in a three-column chart based on your answers to the questions above. Save your notes for later.

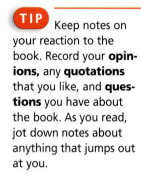 **TIP** Keep notes on your reaction to the book. Record your **opinions,** any **quotations** that you like, and **questions** you have about the book. As you read, jot down notes about anything that jumps out at you.

Think About Purpose and Audience

The Big Picture   You have read your book and are ready to tell people what you think. Before you begin, think about

- the **purpose** of your book review
- the people who will be reading it (your **audience**)

Your purpose for writing a book review will be closely linked to your audience and to *their* purpose for reading the review. Here are some questions and possible responses to help you think about your audience and their purpose.

Who is the audience for my book review?	Why might these people read my book review?	What types of information might interest my audience?
classmates	to decide whether to read a book	What is the book about?
community librarian	to decide whether to get a book for the library	What type of book is it? (mystery, fantasy, western, general fiction, and so on)
parents	to decide if a book is right for younger readers	How easy (or difficult) is it to read?
gift shoppers	to decide whether to buy a book as a gift	How much does it cost?

Writing Workshop   **163**

The audience for the review of *Tuck Everlasting* will be the student's classmates. Their purpose for reading will be to decide whether to read the book themselves. This audience will probably want to know what the book is about, but not how it ends. They might also be interested in knowing how easy or difficult the book is to read.

> **YOUR TURN 5** **Thinking About Purpose and Audience**
>
> Use the chart at the bottom of page 163 to help you consider your audience and their purpose for reading your review.

Gather and Organize Details

You Get the Idea   If you want people to read the book you have chosen, you need to say more about it than "It's good." You need to give them a *summary* of the book. A **summary** of a piece of writing includes only the key ideas of the piece. When you summarize a novel, you will briefly retell the important events. The notes that you took while you read your novel and the instructions on page 166 will help you write your summary.

There Is More to the Story   If a story were plot alone, it would not be much fun to read. Readers will be more interested in plot events if they know something about the people and places involved. When you write a summary, include a description of the characters and the setting. The chart below contains examples from *Tuck Everlasting*.

Character	Who is the main character? What is he or she like?	The main character is Winnie. She is a spoiled only child who is bored and tired of being told what to do.
Setting	Where and when does the story take place?	The novel is set in 1880 in the village of Treegap.
Plot	What problem does the main character face? How does he or she deal with the problem?	Winnie has to decide if she should keep the Tucks' secret—the fountain the Tucks drink from that gives them eternal life. She decides to help them. Helping them makes her brave.

MINI-LESSON CRITICAL THINKING

Identifying the Elements of a Plot

Once upon a Time Most fairy tales begin with "Once upon a time . . ." and end with ". . . happily ever after." The plot in between is usually easy to follow. Novels, on the other hand, usually have a more complicated plot. However, they, too, follow a plot pattern.

- Most stories begin with a **basic situation** in which you learn about the characters and the setting.
- The main character usually runs into a **conflict,** or problem, early in the story.
- This problem sets in motion a series of events, or **complications,** that make up the action of the story.
- All of these events build to a high point, the **climax.** The climax is the most exciting moment in the plot.
- Following the climax is the **resolution,** or outcome. In this part of the story, we see how everything works out for the main character.

A **plot line** helps you figure out all the important steps of a plot. Below is an example of a plot line for *Tuck Everlasting*.

PRACTICE

Create a plot line for the novel that you read.
(**Hint:** As you decide which events are the most important, think about what sticks out in your mind. What are the events that any reader would need to know for the story to make sense?)

Writing Workshop 165

Order! Order! You may want to begin your summary with details about character and setting. Then you can start summarizing the plot. Follow **chronological order,** telling what happens in the beginning and middle of the novel but do not tell how the novel ends, unless your audience is a group (such as librarians) who would prefer to know. **When you write your summary, use transitions like** *first,* *next,* **and** *last* **to link the details of the plot together.**

KEY CONCEPT

YOUR TURN 6 — Gathering and Organizing Details

Record details from your reading notes about plot, main character, and setting in a chart like the one on page 164. Put a number next to each detail in your chart to show the order in which you will present the details when you write your summary.

Designing Your Writing

Highlighting a Quotation Book reviews sometimes highlight a quotation from the book. The stand-alone quotation sparks the reader's curiosity. To include a quotation, follow these guidelines.

- Select a quotation by thinking about what the main character says or does at an important moment in the book.
- Set the quotation apart from the rest of your book review by placing it directly below your title and indenting it on both sides. List the title and author of the book beneath the quotation, indented on the left side. Here is an example.

> A Review of Natalie Babbitt's <u>Tuck Everlasting</u>
>
> She would try very hard not to think of it, but sometimes, as now, it would be forced upon her. She raged against it, helpless and insulted, and blurted at last, "I don't want to die."
>
> <u>Tuck Everlasting</u>, by Natalie Babbitt
>
> If you could live forever just by drinking water, would you do it? The Tuck family unknowingly does just that in Natalie Babbitt's fantasy novel <u>Tuck Everlasting</u>. . . .

166 Chapter 5 **Exposition:** Responding to a Novel

Preparing Your Evaluation

Four Stars ★★★★   After you have prepared notes for your book's summary, you should think about your *evaluation*. The evaluation is the last part of a book review. In an **evaluation,** you

- tell readers why you like or dislike the book
- include a recommendation to read or not to read the book

It is important to know whether or not you would recommend the book. After all, you want your **point of view,** or attitude, about the book to come across throughout your review. Also, remember who your audience is when you make your recommendation. For example, you might think a book is too easy to read, but if your audience is younger readers, the reading level might be just right for them.

Here are two example evaluations based on *Tuck Everlasting*.

> The question of whether Winnie would drink from the spring remained open through the whole book. I could tell she might go either way, so the suspense was great. I enjoyed watching Winnie discover a world beyond her sheltered life. I would recommend Tuck Everlasting to readers who wonder what it might be like to live forever and who like suspense and fantasy.

> Winnie's conflict over whether she would tell the Tucks' secret ended early in the book. From then on, I knew exactly how the book would end, and I found too many parts of the story unbelievable. I thought Winnie was weak and boring. She liked rules and order too much, and she hated getting dirty. I would not recommend the book except to big fans of fantasy.

TIP   Your **voice** shows your **point of view,** or attitude, about the book. Use positive words for characters and events that you like. Use negative words to describe characters you do not like and parts of the plot that do not work. For more on **point of view,** see page 157.

TIP   Many people know what types of books they like to read. If you tell your audience whether the book is a mystery, a western, a historical novel, a fantasy, or another type of book, it helps them decide whether to read it. Not all books fit into the above categories, so you may simply describe your book as "a novel for young adults."

YOUR TURN 7 Preparing Your Evaluation

Write an evaluation of the young adult novel you read for your book review. State clearly why you like or dislike the book and whether you think others should read the book or not.

Book Review

Framework	Directions and Explanations
Introduction ■ Attention grabber ■ Statement of author and title	Get your readers' attention by **introducing the topic of the book** in an interesting way. You may use a quotation, dialogue, a question, a metaphor or simile, or a slice of action to get your readers' attention. Be sure to identify the **author and title.** You might also tell readers what **type of book** it is: mystery, fantasy, historical fiction, and so on.
Body ■ Summary 　Details about setting 　Details about main character 　Details about plot	A **plot summary** should follow **chronological,** or time, **order.** Start with the beginning events, followed by the middle events, but do not reveal the novel's ending unless you think your audience would prefer to know it. 　Use **transition** words to give your paper *coherence.* In a **coherent** composition, one idea flows logically to the next.
Conclusion ■ Evaluation 　Reason 　Recommendation	Write your **evaluation.** Give readers at least one **reason** why you like or dislike the book. Finally, make a **recommendation** to your readers: Should they read the book or not?

YOUR TURN 8 — Drafting Your Book Review

Now it is your turn to draft a book review. As you write,
■ keep your audience in mind
■ refer to the framework above and the Writer's Model on the next page

A Writer's Model

The final draft below closely follows the framework for a book review.

TIP The highlighted words show the writer's point of view about the book's main character.

A Review of
Natalie Babbitt's *Tuck Everlasting*

If you could live forever just by drinking water, would you do it? The Tuck family unknowingly does just that in Natalie Babbitt's fantasy novel *Tuck Everlasting*. Living forever is complicated, though, especially when other people discover the secret.

Winnie, a ==lonely==, ==sheltered==, and ==spoiled== only child, lives in a house at the edge of a village called Treegap. One hot August day in 1880, she discovers the Tuck family and the magic spring that lets them live forever. The Tucks are kindhearted, but they do not want anyone to know their secret. To keep Winnie from telling what she has seen, the Tucks kidnap her and take her to their home. There, Mr. Tuck explains why no one else should know about the spring. He feels that living forever is a lonely and empty experience. No one has ever talked to Winnie about such important things before. Winnie begins to see the world a bit differently and becomes friends with the Tucks. The next day, however, an evil stranger threatens to tell the secret. Mrs. Tuck gets upset and accidentally kills the man when he tries to take Winnie away. The Treegap constable takes Mrs. Tuck to jail. Next, Winnie ==bravely== helps rescue Mrs. Tuck from jail. Winnie ==courageously== struggles with some tough decisions. For starters, she must decide whether to keep the Tucks' secret. She also faces the opportunity to drink from the spring and live forever with the Tucks.

Tuck Everlasting is excellent. It is full of suspense as Winnie makes choices, takes risks, and learns about life. Although it is a fantasy book, it contains some truths about life. I recommend it to anyone who has ever dreamed about living forever or has had to make a tough choice.

Attention grabber

Statement of author and title

Summary: Details about main character

Details about setting

Details about plot

Evaluation and reason

Recommendation

Writing Workshop **169**

A Student's Model

When you write a book review, you want your point of view about the book to be obvious. Diana DeGarmo, a sixth-grade student from Sand Springs, Oklahoma, makes her feelings known by clearly describing the main character and her situation in the following book review.

A Review of
Out of the Storm by Patricia Willis

Attention grabber

When single mother Vera lost her job in Garnet Creek, the family had to move to a new town. Patricia Willis, author of *Out of the Storm,* wrote this story from the viewpoint of Mandy, Vera's twelve-year-old daughter.

Statement of author and title

Summary

Mom and nine-year-old Ira adjusted to the new setting quickly, but Mandy resented everything about their new location. She held on to a dream that she and her deceased father had, and that dream prevented her from accepting her new life. She resented living with grumpy Aunt Bess and detested having to tend the sheep.

Mandy lived with her unhappiness and pitied herself until several incidents happened that made her realize that she was not the only kid who did not have a perfect life. She also found that others had dreams and perhaps by forgetting herself and helping someone else, she might find real happiness.

Evaluation

I think if a reader is looking for a book that tells of a family's struggle to live, *Out of the Storm* by Patricia Willis would be a good choice. I really liked this book because it showed characters learning to tough out bad situations. I also like the book's motto, "Sometimes it takes something Bad to make you see the Good."

Evaluate and Revise Content, Organization, and Style

A Second Look Once you have written a first draft, you need to think about how to improve it. Do this by taking a break from your review and then reading the draft twice. In the first reading, focus on your ideas. Do they make sense? Are they in the right order? The guidelines below will help you decide. In the second reading, look at your words and sentences. The Focus on Word Choice on page 173 will help you.

COMPUTER TIP

If you use a computer to write your review, you can use the underlining feature for Tips 1, 3, and 5. For Tip 2, highlight or color the text on your screen.

▶ **First Reading: Content and Organization** Use the following chart to evaluate and revise your book review.

Guidelines for Self-Evaluation and Peer Evaluation

Evaluation Questions	Tips	Revision Techniques
❶ Does the introduction grab the reader's attention and give the book's author and title?	**Put a check mark** next to any interesting statements. **Underline** the title and author of the book.	**Add** a quotation, question, or interesting statement to the introduction. **Add** the book's title and author if necessary.
❷ Does the summary include information about the book's setting and main character?	**Highlight** the book's setting. **Draw a wavy line** under information about the main character.	**Elaborate** with details about the book's setting and main character.
❸ Does the summary retell the book's major plot events? Does it give details that would interest readers?	**Put a star** next to each major plot event. **Underline** any information that would appeal to the review's audience.	**Delete** unimportant plot events and information. **Add** any important plot events missing from the summary.
❹ Does the summary show how the major events are connected?	**Draw a box around** each word that shows how the events are related.	**Add** transition words or **rearrange** events to make their order clearer.
❺ Does the conclusion include a clear evaluation with at least one reason? Does it include a recommendation?	**Underline** the evaluation. **Draw two lines** under the reason or reasons given for it. **Circle** the recommendation.	**Add** reasons to the evaluation, if necessary. **Add** a recommendation, if necessary.

Writing Workshop

ONE WRITER'S REVISIONS This revision is an early draft of the book review on page 169.

> Winnie⟨, a lonely, sheltered, and spoiled only child,⟩ lives in a house at the edge of a village called Treegap. One hot August day in 1880, she discovers the Tuck family and the magic spring that lets them live forever. ~~She had been following a frog into the forest.~~ The Tucks are kindhearted, but they do not want anyone to know their secret. ⟨To keep Winnie from telling what she has seen, the Tucks kidnap her and take her to their home.⟩

elaborate — *delete* — *add*

PEER REVIEW

If you are evaluating a peer's book review, ask yourself these questions:

- Do I understand what the book is about?
- Do I know what the writer thinks of the book?
- Does the book review make me want to read the book? Why or why not?

Responding to the Revision Process

1. Why do you think the writer elaborated by adding words to the first sentence?
2. Why do you think the writer deleted a sentence from the paragraph above?
3. Why do you think the writer added the last sentence?

▶ **Second Reading: Style** Now that you have looked at the big picture, it is time to focus on your sentences. There are many ways to edit sentences. One way is to eliminate *clichés*. **Clichés** are expressions that have been used so often they have lost their original meaning. When you hear or read a cliché, you probably do not even bother to picture the image in your mind. As a writer, the last thing you want is to have your readers ignore your ideas.

When you evaluate your book review for clarity and originality, ask yourself whether your writing contains any overused words or phrases—ones that you have heard so often that their original meanings seem lost. As you re-read your review, circle every word or phrase that you think is a cliché. Then, replace each cliché with your own words.

Clichés

Focus on Word Choice

When you are writing about a book you have read, you may want to use certain familiar expressions. However, clichés will weaken the punch of your writing. Here are some examples of clichés. See if you can think of others.

It is **raining cats and dogs.**   She is **as busy as a bee.**

Replacing clichés with more original wording will make your meaning clearer and your writing more interesting.

The rain is pummeling the ground.

She zips around from 7:00 A.M. until 7:00 P.M. each day.

ONE WRITER'S REVISIONS

There, Mr. Tuck explains why no one else should know about the spring. He feels that living forever is ~~no bowl of cherries~~ *a lonely and empty experience.*

Responding to the Revision Process
How did replacing the cliché "bowl of cherries" with another phrase improve the sentence above?

YOUR TURN 9 Evaluating and Revising Your Book Review

- First, evaluate and revise the content and organization of your review by using the guidelines on page 171.
- Next, replace any clichés in your writing. Use the guidelines on page 172 and the Focus on Word Choice above to help you.
- If a peer read your paper, think carefully about his or her comments before you revise.

Publishing

Proofread Your Book Review

Getting It Right Now you need to proofread, or **edit,** your book review. If you have too many errors in your book review, your readers may not take your recommendation seriously. To make sure you catch every error, also have a classmate proofread your review.

Grammar Link

Using Appositives

An **appositive** is a noun or pronoun that identifies or describes another noun or pronoun. An **appositive phrase** includes an appositive and its modifiers. Appositives and appositive phrases often answer the question *Who?* or *What?*

Appositive: My Spanish teacher, **Ms. Alvarez,** was born in Cuba. [*Ms. Alvarez identifies who the Spanish teacher is.*]

Appositive Phrase: I am interested in geology, **the study of the earth and rocks.** [*The study of the earth and rocks explains what geology is.*]

Appositives that are not essential to the sentence are set off with **commas.**

Our new gym teacher**, Mr. Samson,** trained as a gymnast. [*The name Mr. Samson is extra information. Commas must be used to set it off.*]

Commas are not needed if the appositive is essential to the meaning of the sentence.

My brother **Abdul** wants to be a gymnast. [*The speaker has more than one brother.*]

PRACTICE

Copy the sentences below on your own paper. Underline the appositive in each sentence, and insert commas where needed.

Example:
1. Last week I read *Tuck Everlasting* a novel about living forever.

1. Last week I read *Tuck Everlasting*<u>**,** a novel about living forever</u>.

1. The novel a fantasy for young adults is set a long time ago in a small village.
2. The main character Winnie Foster learns many things in the book.
3. Angus Tuck head of the Tuck family talks to Winnie about the loneliness of living forever.
4. Mae Tuck a character in the book accidentally kills a man.
5. The Tucks' son Jesse wants Winnie to drink from the spring. (They have two sons.)

Publish Your Book Review

Read All About It   Finally, your book review is finished. Your goal was to write a review that would inform others about a book. How will you get your audience to read your review? Here are some suggestions.

- Find a Web site or online bookstore that asks for reader reviews of young adult literature, and send in your review.
- Create a reading suggestion bulletin board in your classroom. Post a copy of your book review there. If you have access to a school Web site, help create a Web page for all the book reviews written by your classmates.
- Deliver your book review as an **oral response** to the novel. Summarize the book for your listeners, and then explain your evaluation. Be sure to provide clear reasons why you like or dislike the book.

Reflect on Your Book Review

PORTFOLIO

Building Your Portfolio   Take time to think about your book review now that it is finished. What did you learn from it? Good writers are always learning from their writing. You can, too, by answering the following questions.

- What did you find easy or difficult about writing a summary?
- When else could you use summary writing?
- Which evaluation guideline (page 171) was most helpful in evaluating and revising your book review? Why?

> **YOUR TURN 10**
> **Proofreading, Publishing, and Reflecting on Your Book Review**
>
> - Correct any punctuation, spelling, or grammar errors in your book review. Look closely at any appositives you used.
> - Publish your book review so that others can read it.
> - Answer the questions from Reflect on Your Book Review above. Record your responses in a learning log, or include them in your portfolio.

Connections to Literature

Writing a Short Story

Like a novel, a short story has characters, a setting, and a conflict. Because short stories are usually only a few pages long, they deal with just a few characters, a single setting, and a simple plot. As a result, short stories often seem more focused than novels. The challenge in writing a short story is getting the focus just right. Here is an opportunity to write your own short story.

Read All About It Read the beginning of the story "Ta-Na-E-Ka." Notice how the writer introduces the main character, setting, and conflict.

> As my birthday drew closer, I had awful nightmares about it. I was reaching the age at which all Kaw Indians had to participate in Ta-Na-E-Ka. Well, not all Kaws. Many of the younger families on the reservation were beginning to give up the old customs. But my grandfather, Amos Deer Leg, was devoted to tradition. He still wore handmade beaded moccasins instead of shoes and kept his iron-gray hair in tight braids. He could speak English, but he spoke it only with white men. With his family he used a Sioux dialect. . . .
>
> *Eleven* was a magic word among the Kaws. It was the time of Ta-Na-E-Ka, the "flowering of adulthood." It was the age, my grandfather informed us hundreds of times, "when a boy could prove himself to be a warrior and a girl took the first steps to womanhood."
>
> "I don't want to be a warrior," my cousin Roger Deer Leg confided to me. "I'm going to become an accountant."
>
> "None of the other tribes make girls go through the endurance ritual," I complained to my mother.
>
> — Mary Whitebird, "Ta-Na-E-Ka"

Plot a Course Every project needs a plan. Here is a plan to help you write your story.

1. **Brainstorm characters, settings, and conflicts.** Make a chart like the one below to generate ideas. For each column, think of all the possibilities you can imagine. One example is given.

Main Character	Setting	Conflict
Hector, an 11-year-old detective	a shopping mall	A storm knocks out all the electricity.

176 Chapter 5 **Exposition:** Responding to a Novel

2. **Choose a main character, a setting, and a conflict.** To create a story beginning, select one idea from each column in your chart. You can mix and match, choosing the character, setting, and conflict that give you the most interesting ideas.

3. **Generate details about character and setting.** To come up with details, answer the following questions.

Main Character	• What does he or she like to do? • How old is the character? • What does he or she look like?
Setting	• Where does the story take place? • When does the story take place? • What **sensory details** will help the reader imagine the setting?

4. **Map out the plot of your story.** Think of details for your plot, using the questions that follow. You may want to use a plot line like the one shown on page 165.

Questions:
- What events happen because of the conflict?
- How can you create **suspense,** keeping the reader wondering what will happen next?
- What happens first, second, or later?
- What event will be the climax?
- How will the conflict be settled?

Getting Started Once you map out your plot, start writing. If you need help getting started, look again at the first paragraphs of "Ta-Na-E-Ka." You may find it easier to begin in the middle of your story, and then write the beginning and the ending. Finally, remember that a good story has suspense, dialogue, description, and sensory details, and that its resolution ties up loose ends.

YOUR TURN 11 Writing a Short Story

Write a draft of a short story by following the steps you have just read. Exchange your draft with a partner. Read your partner's draft and look for the story elements of character, setting, and plot. Are any missing? Share your ideas with your partner. Then, revise your story as necessary.

After you have written the story, consider preparing a **dramatic interpretation** of it or a **play** based on it to present to your class. (For information on **dramatic interpretation,** see page 307 in the Quick Reference Handbook.)

Connections to Literature

Writing an Essay About a Poem's Sound Effects

Poets play with words to give their readers new ways of looking at the world. In just a few words, a poem can express a wealth of meanings. Many poems rely partly on the sounds of words to convey meaning. You can recognize and appreciate a poem's **sound effects** when you understand some of the special techniques poets use. In this section, you will choose a poem and write an essay analyzing its sound effects.

Sound Effect Check Poets often choose and arrange words to create sound effects. They may try to imitate a specific sound (such as the wind's howling or a bee's buzzing) or to create a mood (such as excitement or joy). Sound effects may provide a clue to a poem's meaning. Three kinds of sound effects are rhyme, rhythm, and repetition.

Rhyme is the repetition of vowel sounds and all sounds following them.

    shelf and *elf*   *comb* and *gnome*

Rhyme is used to emphasize ideas, organize the poem, and entertain the reader.

Rhythm is a musical quality created by the repetition of stressed (´) and unstressed (˘) syllables in a line or by the repetition of certain sounds.

You may notice the rhythm of words when you talk. Poets sometimes emphasize the rhythm and pattern of words to imitate actions described in the poem.

> How dŏth thĕ líttlĕ crócŏdíle
> Ĭmpróve hĭs shíning taíl,
> Ănd poúr thĕ wátĕrs ŏf thĕ Níle
> Ŏn évery góldĕn scále!
>
>   Lewis Carroll,
>   "How Doth the Little Crocodile"

Repetition is the effect of repeating a word, phrase, or line throughout a poem. Repetition creates rhythm, helps organize a poem, and emphasizes feelings or ideas. Notice the repetition in the following poem.

> Last night I dreamed of chickens,
> there were chickens everywhere,
> they were standing on my stomach,
> they were nesting in my hair,
> they were pecking at my pillow,
> they were hopping on my head,
> they were ruffling up their feathers
> as they raced about my bed.
>
>   Jack Prelutsky,
>   "Last Night I Dreamed of Chickens"

Jump In Read the poem on the next page. What sound effects can you find? (Hint: Read the poem aloud, and listen.)

> Whenever the moon and stars are set,
>   Whenever the wind is high,
> All night long in the dark and wet,
>   A man goes riding by.
> Late in the night when the fires are out,   5
> Why does he gallop and gallop about?
>
> Whenever the trees are crying aloud,
>   And ships are tossed at sea,
> By, on the highway, low and loud,
>   By at the gallop goes he.   10
> By at the gallop he goes, and then
> By he comes back at the gallop again.
>
> Robert Louis Stevenson, "Windy Nights"

First Impressions In order to analyze a poem's sound effects, you need to hear them. Read the poem aloud, and jot down your impressions or feelings about it. The following questions can help you identify your response to any poem. Sample responses to "Windy Nights" are provided.

- What did you think about when you read the poem? I thought about a windy night and the sounds that the wind makes.
- Do you like the poem? Why or why not? Yes, I like the way it repeats words.

A Closer Look Now, re-read the poem, listening more closely to its sound effects. Think about the following questions as you re-read the poem. Find examples in the poem to answer the questions. (Note the line numbers where you find your examples. You will need to use those examples for support in your essay.)

- Does the poem use rhyme?
- Does the poem have rhythm?
- Does the poem use repetition?
- What do the sound effects add to the poem? Would the poem be as effective without the sound effects?

What's the Plan? By now, you have a lot of information about the poem. You know what you think about it and the sound effects it uses. The next step is to organize your ideas before you draft your essay. Use the notes that you have taken on the poem, and put your ideas in a graphic organizer like the one below.

Introduction
- Mention the poem's title and author.
- Explain what the poem is about—summarize major events, ideas, or images.

↓

Body
- Explain your conclusion about how sound effects are used in the poem.
- Provide one quotation or example from the poem as evidence for each type of sound effect.

↓

Conclusion
- State whether you like the poem.
- Explain why you do or do not like it.

For Example Below is an analysis of the sound effects in "Windy Nights." Notice that the writer mentions the three kinds of sound effects in the poem and provides examples with their line numbers.

> "Windy Nights" by Robert Louis Stevenson is a poem about the noises of a windy night. The poet talks about a man riding a horse, but he is really talking about the wind. The sound effects in the poem help me hear and feel a windy night.
>
> The poem uses rhyme, rhythm, and repetition. The rhyming words are in a regular pattern. For example, the words at the ends of every other line rhyme ("set" and "wet" in lines 1 and 3). Then, there are two rhymes in the last two lines of each stanza ("out" and "about" in lines 5 and 6). This reminds me of the way the wind keeps coming back over and over. The rhythm of the poem also reminds me of the wind. Words like "whenever" (lines 1, 2, and 7) and "gallop" (lines 6, 10, 11, and 12) have the rhythm of a galloping horse. The repetition of these words makes the idea of the wind seem even stronger. The repetition of the word "by" in the last four lines makes me think of a night when the wind will not stop.
>
> I like the poem "Windy Nights." At first, I did not know why the poet talks about a man riding. Then, the repetition of the word "gallop" made me realize that the rider is the wind. I like the way the sound of the poem makes the meaning come alive.

 **Writing About a Poem's Sound Effects**

- Find a poem that contains sound effects. (Ask your teacher or librarian to help you.) Jot down your response to the poem. How do the sound effects help express the poem's meaning?
- Use the questions and the graphic organizer on page 179 to prepare a short essay that analyzes the sound effects in the poem.
- Revise your essay and check your final copy for spelling, punctuation, and grammar errors. (If you wish, present your ideas as an **oral response to literature** instead.)

Focus on Viewing and Representing

Comparing Media: Film, TV, and Literature

WHAT'S AHEAD?

In this section you will compare a book and a film or TV show of the same type. You will also learn how to

- identify the elements of a novel and techniques used in a film
- make generalizations about a genre

"I will wait until the movie comes out." So many books are made into films that you might be tempted to stop reading and only see movies. What would you lose if you did that? Books, movies, and television all tell stories, but they tell them in different ways.

Read the Book and Watch the Show

Use Your Critical Eye For this workshop you will work with a partner to compare the main characters in books and movies or TV shows of the same type or *genre*. **Genre** (zh än′rə) is a French word meaning "type" or "class." Works of the same genre share certain characteristics. For example, the main character in detective novels, films, and TV shows is often a private investigator who has one faithful friend but who tends to make other people angry. The investigator also shows great determination, especially if he or she gets injured while trying to solve the mystery.

Other genres include fantasy/science fiction, westerns, animal stories, war/spy stories, sports stories, and historical fiction. Can you think of an example for each of these genres?

Be Choosy With your partner, select a genre. From that genre, each of you should select a book that you have read before. Then, you should each watch a different film or TV show from the same genre. The following chart will give you some ideas.

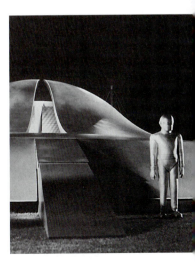

Focus on Viewing and Representing   **181**

Possible Book and Movie/TV Combinations by Genre

Genre	Books	Movies/TV Shows
Science Fiction Stories	*Fantastic Voyage* by Isaac Asimov *The Time Machine* by H. G. Wells	*The Day the Earth Stood Still* *Star Trek*
Animal Stories	*Call of the Wild* by Jack London *The Yearling* by Marjorie Kinnan Rawlings	*Wild America* *Fly Away Home*
War Stories	*Number the Stars* by Lois Lowry *Zlata's Diary* by Zlata Filipovic	*The Diary of Anne Frank* *Empire of the Sun*
Sports Stories	*Hoops* by Walter Dean Myers *The Contender* by Robert Lipsyte	*Brian's Song* *Wild Hearts Can't Be Broken*
Mysteries	*I Am the Cheese* by Robert Cormier *The A.I. Gang: Operation Sherlock* by Bruce Coville	*Fairy Tale: A True Story* *From the Mixed-Up Files of Mrs. Basil E. Frankweiler*
Westerns	*Jimmy Spoon and the Pony Express* by Kristiana Gregory *The Long Chance* by Max Brand	*Shane* *Gunsmoke*

> **TIP** Rent the video or check it out from the library. If you do not see a combination that you like in the chart above, talk to a librarian or your teacher to get suggestions.

Reading at the Movies Books, TV, and films have their own **media languages**—special ways of making meaning. The boldface terms below give you some of the language *you* will need to talk about the effects of these media.

How to Be a Character To create a believable character, a writer uses *characterization*. **Characterization** is the process of showing a character's personality. The writer can directly tell you what a character is like by using **description**. Writers can also indirectly show you what a character is like. When a writer uses **narration** (telling the events of a story) to tell us what a character is doing, for example, we get ideas about that character's personality. Another way that writers give us indirect information about character is through **dialogue**.

Like novelists, filmmakers and TV writers use narration and dialogue. Films and TV, though, have some additional techniques for showing character.

- **Facial expression and body movement:** Close-ups of actors' faces help reveal characters' feelings. A character may show confidence or fear by the way she walks. A nervous character might constantly wiggle a foot or play with a pen while he is talking.
- **Sound:** Music can be used to say something about characters. For example, the appearance of a threatening character may be accompanied by scary music. A filmmaker may also use different types of music to reflect a character's changing moods.

Tools of the Trade The Venn diagram below reviews some of the tools available to writers, TV show producers, and filmmakers. As you read the book and watch the TV show or movie you have chosen, think about how these tools are used to create character as well as other elements, such as setting and conflict.

writer	both	TV/filmmaker
description	narration dialogue	close-ups movement sound

Compare the Book and Movie or TV Show

What's the Difference? After you have read your book and watched your movie or TV show, you will compare the main characters in your two examples. The following charts compare the main characters in two fairy tales: a print version of "Sleeping Beauty" and a TV movie version of *Cinderella*. Make similar charts for the book and film or TV show you chose.

Story: "Sleeping Beauty" by Charles Perrault	
Main Character and Description	**Techniques Used to Create Element**
The princess: She is lovely, sweet tempered, and clever. She sings and dances. She doesn't do much in the story, but everyone loves her.	Description: The princess is described to us. Narration: The narrator explains what happens to the princess, who does not take any action. Dialogue: There are only a few lines of dialogue, and they don't tell us much.

Movie: *Cinderella*	
Main Character and Description	**Techniques Used to Create Element**
Cinderella: She is pretty, sweet, and kind, but her costumes are plain and tattered. She wants to be treated with respect.	Narration: The fairy godmother narrates what is happening. Facial expressions: Close-ups of Cinderella show her sadness when her family treats her badly and her joy when she dances with the prince. Sound: Cinderella sings happy songs when she is happy. She also sings songs that tell us about her dreams. Dialogue: The things she says tell us how she feels.

Reference Note

For more on **generalizations**, see page 287 in the Quick Reference Handbook.

Once you have completed your chart, get together with your partner to make a generalization about the main character in the genre you chose. To make a **generalization**—a statement about the general characteristics of something—use the equation below.

What you learned (about main character in that genre)
+ What you already know
_____
Generalization

Here is a generalization about the main character in a fairy tale.

> The main character in a fairy tale is often a girl who is sweet and beautiful and loves to sing.

This generalization can be supported by information in the chart, plus what the student's partner discovered, plus what both students know from hearing other fairy tales.

 ### Comparing Media and Making Generalizations

Choose a book and a movie or TV show from the same genre. Follow the steps on pages 181–184 to make a chart comparing the main characters in the book and the movie or TV show. Then, working with a partner, make a generalization about the main characters in that genre. Support your generalization with evidence from your partner's and your own charts.

CHAPTER 5 Choices

Choose one of the following activities to complete.

▶ **VIEWING AND REPRESENTING**

1. More than One Way
Respond to a movie that made a strong impression—good or bad—on you. Choose one of these options:

- Present an **oral review,** using the same strategies you used in your book review.
- Express your thoughts about the movie in a **poem** or a one-paragraph **reflection.**

▶ **WRITING**

2. That's What I Think
Share your thoughts about a novel by writing **e-mails** or **letters** to a pen pal. Discuss the main character, setting, and plot, as well as your reactions. Discuss your pen pal's book, too. Write at least two letters or e-mails each.

▶ **CONNECTING CULTURES**

3. It's a Small World The German "Aschenputtel," the Chinese "Yeh-Shen," and the English "Cinderella" are different versions of the same story. Read them, or read several versions of another story. Create **charts** comparing the stories' characters, settings, and plot events.

▶ **TECHNOLOGY**

4. Virtual Critic
Collaborate with a group to create a **database** of reports on educational computer games. As a group, decide which elements to evaluate or rank (sound effects, difficulty level, graphics, and so on). Then, create **forms** for evaluating the games. Each member should then choose a game, play it, and complete the form. Once you have all the information, the group will create a database **record** about each of those games.

▶ **CREATIVE WRITING**

5. All Together Now
Collaborate with a group of classmates in writing an original **short story** in response to a work you have all read. Each person in the group should write a paragraph. Discuss and revise the paragraphs as a group. Read your final version to the class, and discuss your experience of working as a group.

PORTFOLIO

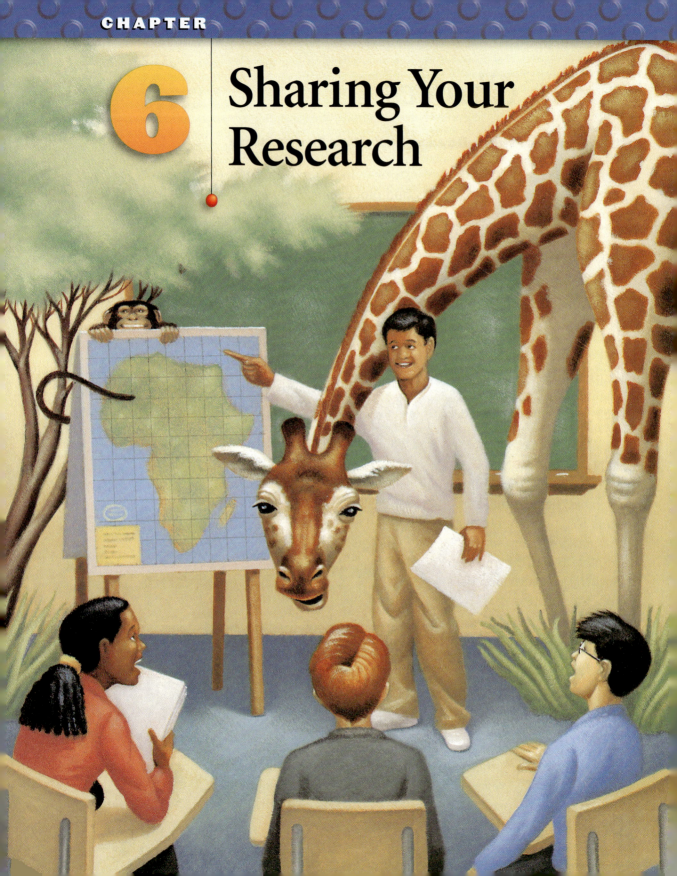

CHAPTER 6
Sharing Your Research

CONNECTING READING AND WRITING

Reading Workshop

Reading an Informative Article

Writing Workshop

Writing a Research Report

Speaking and Listening

Giving and Evaluating a Research Presentation

You just heard the greatest CD of all time. You want to know everything about the group—Where are they from? How do they get ideas for songs? What other recordings have they made? Finding answers to these questions requires research.

From sixth-graders to research scientists, people need to find and share information with others. One way for people to share this information is by writing a research report. Research reports are based on reliable sources—experts, informative books or articles, videotapes, or Internet sources. A research report writer pulls together information from different sources and presents it along with his or her own thoughts on a subject.

> **Informational Text**
>
> Exposition

YOUR TURN 1 — Seeking Information

With a few classmates, make a list of some subjects you have researched in the past, such as a hobby or sport, something in nature, or an interesting person. Then, discuss these questions:

- What sources did your group use to find information?
- Which sources were easy to use? Why? Which sources were difficult to use? Why?

internet connect

GO TO: go.hrw.com
KEYWORD: EOLang 6-6

Reading Workshop

Reading an Informative Article

WHAT'S AHEAD?

In this section you will read an informative article. You will also learn how to

- draw conclusions
- recognize an author's purpose for writing

What is a gold rush? Who were the original Forty-Niners? Why is California known as "the Golden State"? You will find the answers to these questions and more as you read "The California Gold Rush," the informative article on the next page.

Preparing to Read

READING SKILL

Making Inferences: Drawing Conclusions An **inference** is an idea a reader forms, based in part on what he or she has read, seen, or experienced. One type of inference is a *conclusion*. Readers draw **conclusions** by putting together the pieces of information a writer presents and adding their own knowledge to that information. For example, details such as an eye patch, a wooden leg, and a parrot perched on a person's shoulder are clues that can lead readers to conclude that the person being described is a pirate. As you read the following article, try to draw conclusions about the gold rush in California.

READING FOCUS

Author's Purpose An **author's purpose** is the reason the author writes a piece. In the following article, Kathy Wilmore answers questions like these about the California gold rush: *Who was involved? What did they do? Why? How did it start? How did it turn out?* The fact that the article answers such questions gives you a clue about why the author wrote it.

188   Chapter 6   **Exposition:** Sharing Your Research

Read the following selection. In a notebook, jot down answers to the numbered active-reading questions in the shaded boxes. Underlined words will be used in the Vocabulary Mini-Lesson on page 196.

from Junior Scholastic

THE CALIFORNIA GOLD RUSH

BY KATHY WILMORE

1 For seventeen years—ever since leaving his New Jersey home at age eighteen—James Wilson Marshall kept moving farther and farther west in search of a better life. In 1845, he went to California, which was part of Mexico then, and things finally seemed to turn around for him. A businessman named John A. Sutter gave him a job building a sawmill in a remote wilderness area in northern California. Build it, Sutter told him, and you can run the place for me. Sutter was looking to make a tidy profit; Marshall was just hoping to make a living. But on January 24, 1848, Marshall was <u>momentarily</u> distracted from his work. A glint of light caught his eye—and sleepy California was never the same again.

> **1.** Why do you think the author tells you so much about James Marshall?

"To See the Elephant"

In January 1848, California had a <u>population</u> of only 15,000 people. By the time December 1849 came around, the population was up to 100,000 and climbing. Why such a boom? Blame it on that glint that caught James Marshall's eye.

2

One cold and rainy day soon after, Marshall arrived at Sutter's house with "some important and interesting news." Sutter studied the stuff that Marshall had brought and

3

Reading Workshop 189

> **2. What was the glint that caught Marshall's eye?**

realized it was gold. He was not happy.

4 "I told [my employees] that I would consider it as a great favor if they would keep this discovery secret only for six weeks, so I could finish [building] my large flour mill at Brighton. . . . [I]nstead of feeling happy and contented, I was very unhappy, and could not see that it would benefit me much, and I was perfectly right in thinking so."[1]

5 Sutter's employees promised not to tell, but word leaked out. . . .

6 By 1849, the gold rush was on. People poured into California from all points of the compass. They arrived by ship or overland trails, crossing North America by wagon train, riding horses or mules, and even on foot.

7 These hopeful thousands, the first large wave of whom arrived in 1849, were known as Forty-Niners. Many had sold everything they owned to pay their way to California.

> **3. Why were the first miners called Forty-Niners?**

8 Ask a Forty-Niner why, and he or she was likely to reply, "I am going to see the elephant"—that is, to find something wonderful and rare.

---

1. From "The Discovery of Gold in California" by Gen. John A. Sutter, *Hutchings California Magazine* (November 1857).

"A Dog's Life"

9 Dreaming of gold was easy, but finding it was anything but. Miners faced hours of strenuous work. Some were able to reach out and pick up a gold-filled nugget, but that was rare.

10 Most miners spent hours slamming pickaxes into rocky soil, or scooping up panfuls of riverbed mud and rinsing it to find tiny grains of gold. They lived in rough, makeshift camps far from "civilization," with little shelter from cold mountain winds and rain. As William Swain described camp life in a letter sent home in 1850:

11 "George, I tell you this mining among the mountains is a dog's life. . . . [T]his climate in the mines requires a constitution like iron. Often for weeks during the rainy season it is damp, cold, and sunless, and the labor of getting gold is of the most laborious kind. Exposure causes sickness to a great extent for, in most of the mines, tents are all the habitation [home] miners have."[2]

> **4. Why do you think the author includes quotes such as this one in the article?**

Making a Go of It

12 Thousands of Forty-Niners made the trek to California with the idea

---

2. From a letter from California by William Swain, January 6 & 16, 1850.

of striking it rich, then returning home to spend their wealth. But for every Forty-Niner whose labor paid off handsomely, countless others had to find other ways of making a living.

13   Among those were thousands of Chinese. Word of "Gold Mountain"—the Chinese name for California—lit new hope among poverty-stricken peasants in China. In 1849, only 54 Chinese lived in California; by 1852, the number had risen to 14,000.

14   Chinese miners faced the resentment of many white Forty-Niners who saw them as unfair competition. . . . Looking for less risky ways of earning a living, many Chinese turned to service work: cooking meals, toting heavy loads, and washing clothes. Miners happily plunked down money for such services.

15   The Chinese were not the only Forty-Niners to make a go of things at something other than mining. One of the biggest success stories was that of a Bavarian <u>immigrant</u> named Levi Strauss. Strauss, a tailor, hoped to make his fortune by making and selling tents. But he found that another item he made was more popular: the heavy-duty work pants that became known as those "wonderful pants of Levi's." His blue jeans business prospered, and Strauss became one of the wealthiest men in California.

From Fortune to Misfortune

16   What of Sutter and Marshall, the men who started it all?

17   Sutter's workers all quit and poured their efforts into finding gold. When the first Forty-Niners arrived, they overran Sutter's land, wrecked his mills and farmlands, and even killed his cattle for food. . . .

> **5.** Do you think Sutter was right to be unhappy when Marshall first discovered gold? Why or why not?

18   Marshall's hope of earning a living by running the mill was destroyed when the workers quit and it was wrecked by treasure seekers. He became a drifter, then a poor farmer.

The Golden State

19   For California, however, the gold rush brought long-lasting benefits. California had become U.S. territory as a result of the treaty ending the Mexican War. That was signed on February 2, 1848—just eight days after Marshall spied that first glint of gold. California became the thirty-first state on September 9, 1850. In that short time, it grew from a place of scattered <u>settlements</u> to one of bustling seaports and boomtowns. Whether or not they ever had the thrill of "seeing the elephant," thousands of restless Forty-Niners found a place to call home. ■

First Thoughts on Your Reading

1. Why do you think the author wrote this article?
2. What qualities helped people succeed during the gold rush?

READING SKILL

Making Inferences: Drawing Conclusions

Add It Up Suppose you are watching a mystery on TV in which a character sneaks into a room, then races from the room carrying a small box. Another character enters the room and screams, "My jewelry has been stolen!" What happened? In order to understand the story, you will need to draw a *conclusion*.

A **conclusion** is a judgment a reader makes about a text based on details the author provides and on what the reader already knows about the subject. Here is an example.

> **What you read:** The Maximizer, the most powerful superhero, has captured the evil Dr. Z. Suddenly, Dr. Z throws a glowing liquid at the Maximizer, who collapses.
>
> + **What you know:** In other comic books, the superhero usually has one big weakness, which his or her enemy discovers at some point.
>
> ---
>
> **Conclusion:** Dr. Z has discovered the Maximizer's weakness. The glowing liquid makes the Maximizer helpless.

Read the following paragraph and try to draw a conclusion based on the details in it. If you have trouble reaching a conclusion, use the Thinking It Through steps on the next page.

> In 1901, the first cars were being mass-produced in the United States. They were popular and sold well. In that same year, a huge oil field was discovered at Spindletop, near Beaumont, Texas. Within three months, the population of Beaumont had grown from nine thousand to fifty thousand.

THINKING IT THROUGH

Drawing Conclusions

STEP 1 Identify the topic of the passage and look for the details about it.

Topic: cars and oil

Details: Cars were mass-produced, and a huge oil field was discovered in the same year. The town where oil was discovered grew.

STEP 2 Think about what you already know about the topic. How can you connect the details to your own knowledge or experiences?

I know cars use oil and gasoline. I also know people rush to places where big discoveries are made—the way the Forty-Niners rushed to California—because they hope to get rich.

STEP 3 Connect your knowledge or experiences you recalled from Step 2 with the details you identified in Step 1 to draw a conclusion about the subject.

Conclusion: People knew cars would need oil, so many people rushed to the place where it was discovered, hoping to get rich.

YOUR TURN 2 Drawing Conclusions

Use the Thinking It Through steps above to draw conclusions about the following parts of "The California Gold Rush." Read each passage listed and draw a conclusion by answering the question that follows each item on the list. Be prepared to support your conclusions with details from the reading selection.

- Paragraphs 3 and 4: Why did Sutter react as he did to the discovery of gold?
- Paragraph 15: What did the gold rush have to do with one businessman's making a fortune from the sale of work pants?
- The section titled "From Fortune to Misfortune": Was the gold rush lucky for Sutter? Why?

Author's Purpose

What's the Point?   When you read a comic book, you usually are reading to be entertained. The creator of that comic book most likely wrote it for exactly that purpose. Sometimes, though, writers use the comic-book form in order to express themselves—to tell about something meaningful that happened to them or to share their own feelings about something they think is important. Whether they write comic books or research reports, writers write for a **purpose,** or reason. Being aware of an author's purpose can help you set your own purpose for reading.

The following chart explains the four main purposes for writing. In the right-hand column, it gives clues that you can look for in a piece of writing to figure out an author's purpose.

Purpose	Explanation	Clues
to inform	Informative writing teaches something. It answers *Who? What? Where? When? Why?* and *How?* questions. It can explain the way bats navigate, how a firefighter made a daring rescue, or how to play a game.	• dates • names of real people and places • facts, maps, and charts • helpful headings • quotations from real people
to express a belief or feeling	Expressive writing shares a writer's beliefs or feelings about something. Poems and personal essays are examples of expressive writing.	• words about feelings • use of *I* • value words like *best, worst, great*
to be creative or entertain	Creative writing tells a story, uses drama or humor, or plays with language. Examples include novels, short stories, poems, and plays.	• a story with a beginning, middle, and end • dialogue • rhyme • humor • suspense
to influence or persuade	Persuasive writing tries to convince the reader to share the writer's opinion or to take some action. Examples include editorials, persuasive essays, reviews, and advertisements.	• opinions supported by reasons, facts, or examples • words like *should, must, have to* • value words like *best, worst, great*

Can you figure out the author's purpose in the following passage? You can if you look for clues from the chart on page 194.

> Although history tells about the taming of the American West, an important part of that story is often left out. History books should emphasize the contributions of Chinese immigrants. Chinese workers provided much of the labor for early railroads and took jobs that others considered too dangerous. They suffered from low pay, unfair laws, and frequent attacks by other groups. These people who helped to build the modern West should be honored.

Here is how one student identified clues in this paragraph to figure out the author's purpose.

Clues	What They Tell Me About Purpose
The paragraph includes facts about Chinese workers in the West.	The purpose could be to inform. These facts also seem to back up an opinion, though, so I think the purpose is probably to persuade.
The word <u>should</u> is used twice.	The purpose is definitely to persuade.

YOUR TURN 3 — Identifying the Author's Purpose

- Re-read "The California Gold Rush" on pages 189–191. Alone or with a partner, look for clues from the chart on page 194.
- List the clues you find and identify the purposes they point to, as in the above example.
- Finally, look over your list of the clues and purposes you have found in the article, and choose the purpose that you have listed most often.

MINI-LESSON VOCABULARY

Word Roots

An informative article on a subject you know little about may contain unfamiliar words. You can often figure out the meaning of a word if you recognize its *root*. A **root** is the main part of a word. For example, the words *personality* and *impersonal* have the same root—*person*. Word roots like *person* can stand alone, but some roots cannot. The chart to the right gives examples of such roots. These roots need word parts called *prefixes* and *suffixes* to become words. A **prefix** is a word part that may be added to the beginning of a root to change the root's meaning. A **suffix** may be added to the end of a root. (For more on **prefixes** and **suffixes,** see page 126.)

Word Root	Meaning	Examples
–civi–	relating to townspeople	uncivilized
–migr–	to move	migrate
–popul–	people	unpopular

THINKING IT THROUGH   Using Word Roots

Here is an example based on a word from the reading selection.

▶ **STEP 1** Peel off the prefixes and suffixes to identify the unfamiliar word's root.

The word is <u>population</u>. I can peel off the suffix <u>-ation</u>. That leaves <u>popul-</u>.

▶ **STEP 2** Use what you know about the root and the word's context to come up with a definition for the unfamiliar word.

I know <u>popul-</u> means "people." The words around <u>population</u> tell me how many people lived in California. <u>Population</u> must mean "the number of people."

▶ **STEP 3** Replace your definition in the original sentence to see if it makes sense.

"In January 1848, California had <u>a number</u> of only 15,000 people." That makes sense to me.

PRACTICE

Use the steps above to define the following words. They are underlined for you in the reading selection. For help with meanings of prefixes and suffixes, see pages 297–298.

1. momentarily (page 189)
2. civilization (page 190)
3. laborious (page 190)
4. immigrant (page 191)
5. settlements (page 191)

MINI-LESSON TEST TAKING

Answering Questions About Tables

Informative texts, including passages found on reading tests, often list factual information in table form. A table, which may have one or many columns, organizes facts into categories to help a reader quickly find information. The categories are usually listed as column headings. To read a table, read the column headings, and then look at the information in each column. When looking at information in the form of dates, notice the amount of time between dates.

The table to the right contains information about important discoveries in history. Study the information, and answer the question below the table.

Century	Discovery
16th	the fact that Earth circles the sun the existence of bacteria
17th	the power of gravity
19th	how to generate electrical current the existence of electrons
20th	bacteria-killing antibiotics the structure of DNA

According to the information in the chart, for how many centuries did people know about bacteria without knowing how to kill bacteria?

A. 20   **B.** 4   **C.** 2   **D.** 16

THINKING IT THROUGH   Answering Questions About Tables

▶ **STEP 1** Read the question, and identify the information you need to find in the chart.

I need to find when bacteria were discovered and when something that kills bacteria was discovered.

▶ **STEP 2** Identify the information in the chart that you can use to answer the question.

The chart says bacteria were discovered in the 16th century and antibiotics were discovered in the 20th century.

▶ **STEP 3** Decide what you need to do with the information to come up with an answer.

I need to figure out how long it was between these discoveries. If I count—16, 17, 18, 19, 20—I get five centuries.

▶ **STEP 4** If none of the choices matches your answer, cross out any choices you know are wrong. Then, review the question and chart to choose between the remaining answers.

Five centuries is not a choice. A and D are the centuries when the discoveries were made. Because 20 − 16 = 4, only four centuries passed between the discoveries. My choice is B.

Writing Workshop

Writing a Research Report

WHAT'S AHEAD?

In this workshop you will write a research report. You will also learn how to

- ask questions to guide your research
- find and list reliable sources
- take organized notes
- use precise nouns
- capitalize and punctuate titles correctly

Have you heard about a snake that grows to be thirty feet long? Did you know that some gladiators in ancient Rome were women? When you find out an unusual fact, the first thing you want to do is tell someone else about it. Writers of research reports feel exactly the same way. They dig into subjects they are curious about, and then, through writing, they share what they have learned. In this workshop you will have the opportunity to exercise your curiosity about a topic that interests you and tell others about what you discover.

Prewriting

Choose and Narrow a Subject

What Grabs You? How did the Grand Canyon get there? Why do chipmunks hibernate? Asking questions like these can help you choose an interesting subject for your research report. Here are more strategies to help you brainstorm subjects.

- Take a survey of your classmates' hobbies *(in-line skating, coin collecting, building model boats . . .)*
- Make an "I wonder" log *(I wonder why cats purr . . . , how helicopters fly . . . , who discovered electricity . . .)*
- Browse a television guide or magazine or newspaper for interesting subjects *(people in the news, medical marvels, strange animals, space technology . . .)*

198   Chapter 6   Exposition: Sharing Your Research

Pin It Down   Once you have listed several possible subjects, you can choose the most interesting one. **You will need to focus on a part of the subject small enough to cover in one report.** For example, suppose that volcanoes fascinate you. Can you imagine the amount of research it would take to cover everything there is to know about volcanoes? To make it easier on yourself, you need to narrow that subject down to a focused topic. Your focused topic might be an active volcano in Hawaii. Here are more examples of narrowing a broad subject to a focused topic:

KEY CONCEPT

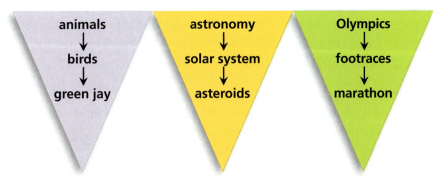

Here is how one writer narrowed a subject to a focused topic.

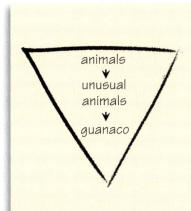

I like animals, but "animals" is too much to write about in a research report. I need to narrow this subject.

I want to write about an animal that most people have never heard of.

In an article about a wild animal ranch, I read about guanacos. I had never heard of a guanaco, and I doubt many other people have either.

TIP   Once you have your focused topic, make a plan to be sure you have enough time to complete your report. Divide the total time you are given among these activities:

- finding information (1/8 of total time)
- taking notes (1/4)
- organizing your notes (1/8)
- writing the first draft (1/4)
- revising (1/8)
- proofreading and publishing your report (1/8)

YOUR TURN 4   Choosing and Narrowing a Subject

Brainstorm some subjects that interest you, and choose one you want to research. Then, use an upside-down triangle to find a focused topic. Record your thoughts as you narrow your topic.

Writing Workshop   **199**

Think About Purpose, Audience, and Voice

The *Why* of It   Your **purpose** is your reason for writing. You have two purposes for writing a research report: to discover information for yourself, and to share what you learn with others.

The *Who* of It   The **audience** for your report will be people who share your interest in the topic but do not already know a great deal about it. In most cases, that audience will include your classmates and teacher. You need to think about your audience before you begin doing your research. Ask yourself the questions in the left-hand column of the chart below. One student's responses appear in the right-hand column.

1. What does my audience already know about my topic?	They probably know nothing more about the guanaco than I do.
2. What does my audience need to know?	what it is, where it lives, what it looks like, what it does
3. What kind of information would my audience find interesting?	any unusual or surprising facts that I discover

The *How* of It   The sound of your writing is your **voice**. When your purpose is to inform, you should select a voice that sounds knowledgeable and interesting. Express your ideas in a clear, direct way, without using slang or clichés.

Confusing and slangy   I bet you never heard of a humpless camel-like thing.

Clear and interesting   Visitors to the Andes Mountains may spot a creature resembling a tiny camel without a hump.

YOUR TURN 5 — Thinking About Purpose, Audience, and Voice

Your purpose is to discover information and share it with others. Answer the questions in the chart above to consider how you might communicate what you learn with your readers.

Ask Questions

The K-W-L Method   When you think about your topic, you are probably full of questions such as: *What does it look like? Where does it come from? What does it do?* Research begins with questions like these. Of course, there are some things you already know about your topic.

You can use a K-W-L chart to list what you already **K**now about a topic, what you **W**ant to know about it, and what you **L**earned about it through research. Look at how one student organized his ideas about the topic of guanacos. As he finds answers to his questions, he will list them in the right-hand column.

What I Know	What I Want to Know	What I Learned
A guanaco is part of the camel family. It lives in South America.	What does a guanaco look like? What do guanacos do? Do humans and guanacos get along?	

TIP   You might discover new questions once you begin doing research. Add them to your chart only if they really fit your topic. As one student researched his topic, he came up with and evaluated these questions:

Where do other members of the camel family live?	Other camels are not part of my topic. I won't add this question.
Why are there fewer guanacos now than there used to be?	This fits my topic. I'll add it to my K-W-L chart.

YOUR TURN 6   Asking Questions

Create a K-W-L chart like the one above on your own paper. In the left column, list everything that you already know about your topic. In the middle column, list the questions you have about your topic. Leave the right column of your chart blank. You will fill it out as you do your research.

TIP   Another way to organize what you already know about a topic and what you would like to know is to create a cluster diagram. For more on **clustering**, see page 345 in the Quick Reference Handbook.

Find Sources

Who Has the Answers?
The best place to start your research is in the library, but that is just the beginning. You will look in several places to find answers to your questions. Some of the resources you can use include

- **primary sources,** such as letters, diaries, journals, narratives, interviews, guest speakers, autobiographies, oral histories, and research notes
- **secondary sources,** such as encyclopedia articles, biographical sketches, and books, Web pages, and documentaries that compile researched information

Keep in mind that information does not always have to come from print sources. You can also find answers to your questions by watching a documentary; listening to an informative program on the radio; or reading charts, maps, and other graphics.

You will not find all of the information you need in a single source. You should plan to use at least three different kinds of sources in order to investigate all aspects of your topic, including various viewpoints on it. For example, you could find information on your topic in a book, in a magazine article, and on the Internet. Using a variety of sources will help you find complete answers to your research questions. If you have trouble finding sources **relevant,** or related, to your topic, go to the media center or ask your school's media specialist for help.

Make a List of Sources

Who Said That?
When everyone talks at once, it is hard to remember who said what. You may have the same problem when you do research. When you find information about your topic in several different places, you may not remember where you found a particular fact. You will need to keep track of where you find the answers to your questions. **Make a numbered list of all of the sources you find that might be helpful in your research.** In your list, include information about each source. The chart on the next page tells you what information you need for each type of source you might use. The listings in the chart follow the style of the Modern Language Association (MLA).

 **TIP** Some sources are better than others for research. Look for nonfiction sources created by people or organizations likely to know a great deal about the topic. In other words, look for **authoritative** sources—ones that are credible, accurate, and unbiased. For example, you would get better information on African snakes from a *National Geographic* article than from a movie about the adventures of a fictional explorer.

KEY CONCEPT

Reference Note
For more on using the **media center,** see page 276 in the Quick Reference Handbook.

KEY CONCEPT

202 Chapter 6 Exposition: Sharing Your Research

Information on Sources

Books: Author. Title. City where book was published: Name of Publisher, copyright year.

Ricciuti, Edward R. What on Earth Is a Guanaco? Woodbridge, CT: Blackbirch Press, 1994.

Magazine and Newspaper Articles: Author (if known). "Title of Article." Name of Magazine or Newspaper Date article was published: page numbers.

Lambeth, Ellen. "Here Comes Paco Guanaco: In the Hilly Grasslands of South America, a Camel Is Born." Ranger Rick Nov. 1996: 4-8.

Encyclopedia Articles: Author (if known). "Title of Article." Encyclopedia Name. Edition number (if known) and year published.

Goodwin, George G. "Guanaco." Collier's Encyclopedia. 1997.

Television or Radio Programs: "Title of Episode." Title of Program. Name of host (if known). Network. Station Call Letters, City. Date of broadcast.

"In the Land of the Llamas." NOVA. PBS. WNPB, Morgantown. 4 Dec. 1990.

Movie or Video Recordings: Title. Name of Director or Producer (if known). Format (videocassette or videodisc). Name of Distributor, year.

The Living Edens: Patagonia. Videocassette. PBS Home Video, 1997.

Internet Sources: Author. "Title." Name of Web site. Date of electronic publication. Name of Sponsoring Institution. Date you accessed information <Internet address>.

Note: Some sites may not list all of the above information. Include what the site does list and skip the items it does not list.

"Gwen the Guanaco." Victory Ranch. 26 Jan. 1999 <http://www.victoryranch.com/gwen.htm>.

Other Electronic Sources: Author (if known). "Title." Title of Database or CD-ROM. Medium (CD-ROM or Database). Copyright date.

Sentman, Everett. "Guanaco." Grolier 1998 Multimedia Encyclopedia. CD-ROM. 1997.

TIP Why should you keep track of your sources?

- You may need to find a source again if you come up with another interesting question later in your research.
- Your readers may want to go to your sources to learn more about your topic.
- Your teacher may expect you to include a list of sources to show the research you did.

MINI-LESSON CRITICAL THINKING

Searching the World Wide Web for Information

The World Wide Web contains enormous amounts of information. One way you can find what you need is to use a *search engine*. A **search engine** is a Web site that allows you to hunt for information. By typing a **keyword**—a word related to your topic—into the search engine, you will get a list of possible sites.

Another way to find information from a search engine is to use a *directory*. A **directory** lists categories of information. Each category is divided into smaller and smaller subcategories that you can follow until you find a site that relates to your topic.

Below is a path a student took through categories and subcategories in a directory. The main menu, where he began his search, is on the left. The highlighted choice shows the category the student chose. His choice leads to the next list of subcategories and finally to a list of sites with information about guanacos and other mammals.

TIP Remember, not all Web sites are equal. For your research report, choose sources such as universities, government sites, and major newspapers and broadcast networks. When you get a list of sites, look first at those that have URLs (addresses) ending in *.org* (nonprofit organizations), *.edu* (educational institutions), and *.gov* (U.S. government agencies). (For more on **evaluating Web sites,** see page 285.)

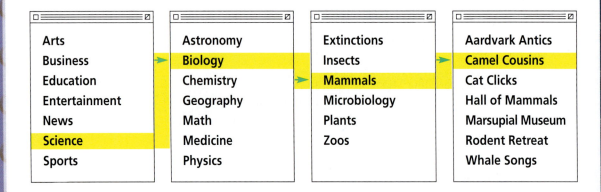

PRACTICE

Search the Internet two different ways for Web sites on the topic of your research report. In your first search, type a keyword into a search engine. In your second search, go through the categories and subcategories in a directory. Which search proved to be more successful? Compare your results with those of your classmates.

YOUR TURN 7 **Finding and Listing Sources**

Find at least five sources you might use for researching your focused topic. Follow the instructions on page 203 to list important information about these sources. Give each source a number to help you identify sources when you take notes later. For now, do not worry about the order of items in your list. You will alphabetize your source list later (by author's last name or by title, if no author is given).

COMPUTER TIP

Write down the address of any Web site you come across that looks helpful, even if you are not using it right away. You will be able to find the site again quickly by calling up the exact address.

Take Notes

Getting the Facts Now, begin looking for answers to your research questions. Remember, you are looking for answers to the questions in your K-W-L chart. **Your questions will guide your research process.** Record each fact, description, or expert opinion you find, along with information about where you found it. The guidelines below will help you take notes.

- Use a separate note card or a sheet of paper for each new note.
- At the top of each note card, write the question that the notes on the card answer.
- Write the number of the source at the top of each note, so you will always be able to tell exactly where you found the information.
- **Summarize** information explained in a long passage. Even with shorter passages, **paraphrase,** or write the ideas in your own words. If you copy exact words from a source, put them in quotation marks.
- If the information is from a printed book or article, put the page number at the end of your note.

KEY CONCEPT

TIP While you research, keep your K-W-L chart handy. In the "What I Learned" column, write in the authors or titles of the sources where you found your answers. This will help you focus on using a variety of sources. It will also help you see quickly which of your questions still need answers.

Reference Note

For more on **paraphrasing** and **summarizing,** see pages 288 and 291 in the Quick Reference Handbook.

Source number — ③
Question — What is a guanaco?
Notes in your own words — - member of the camel family
- small and South American
Page number — page 127

Writing Workshop   **205**

MINI-LESSON WRITING

Paraphrasing

Paraphrasing means putting information from a source into your own words. Copying an author's words and presenting them as your own is **plagiarizing.** Plagiarizing is the same as stealing another writer's work. If you want to use a writer's exact words, put them in quotation marks and identify the source.

The passages below show the difference between paraphrasing and plagiarizing. The paraphrase on the left tells the ideas of the source passage in different words. The plagiarized passage on the right copies long strings of words which are printed in boldface.

> **Source Passage:** Guanacos, South American members of the camel family, lack the familiar humps of Asian and African camels. Slim and long-legged, guanacos move quickly and gracefully over the rugged terrain of their native Andes Mountains.
>
> **Paraphrase:** Although it is part of the camel family, the South American guanaco does not have a hump like its cousins in Asia and Africa do. It is slim, has long legs, and can run fast in its habitat, the Andes Mountains.
>
> **Plagiarism:** As **members of the camel family,** guanacos **lack the familiar humps of Asian and African camels.** They are able to **move quickly and gracefully over rugged terrain.** They live in the Andes Mountains.

PRACTICE

Read each source passage below, then the passage to its right. Tell whether the passage paraphrases or plagiarizes the source. Explain your answer in a sentence or two.

Source Passage

1. Manifest Destiny was the belief in the nineteenth century that the United States would eventually stretch across the entire continent, from the Atlantic Ocean to the Pacific Ocean.

2. The first settlers from the United States reached northeastern Texas in 1815, encouraged by the Mexican government, which controlled the territory at that time.

Paraphrase or Plagiarism?

1. People believed in the nineteenth century that the United States would eventually reach from the Atlantic Ocean to the Pacific Ocean. This belief was called Manifest Destiny.

2. The government of Mexico encouraged people from the United States to move to its territory of Texas. The first settlers moved to the northeast part of the state in 1815.

YOUR TURN 8 | Researching Your Topic and Taking Notes

Using the sources you found earlier, locate answers for your research questions. Take notes from each source, being careful to put the information in your own words. Note the source of each piece of information you find by putting its source number on your note card.

TIP To make the most of your time, skim long passages looking for key words, ones that relate to your topic. Then, read only the sections that contain the key words.

Organize Your Information

Getting It Together   A pile of notes will be about as useful to your readers as a box full of bicycle parts. Both need to be put together in a logical way to be of any use. Once you have gathered information from your sources, organize those ideas into categories. The questions you wrote on the top of your note cards will help you. Group together note cards that answer the same question so you can compare your findings and get a complete picture. Each group of cards will become a paragraph in your report. If some note cards do not seem to belong to any group, set them aside for now.

Outline Your Report

Planning It Out   An **outline** is a plan for your report. It shows how you are grouping the information you have gathered and the order in which you will present the information in your report. One type of outline you can make is an *informal outline*. An **informal outline** lists a report's major **subtopics,** or categories of information related to your topic. It also lists the specific facts that make up each subtopic.

To identify the subtopics for your informal outline, first change the questions from your K-W-L chart into headings. A **heading** is a phrase that covers all the items listed below it. For example, the question "Where do guanacos live?" could be turned into the heading "Where guanacos live." As you turn your questions into headings, write each heading on a piece of paper, leaving several lines after it blank. Then, under each heading, write facts from your note cards or jot down a few words that will remind you what to include when you write your report.

Reference Note

For more on **outlines,** both informal and formal, see page 347 in the Quick Reference Handbook.

Writing Workshop   **207**

The partial informal outline below shows the information the student writing about guanacos will use in his research report.

> **TIP** Review your outline to make sure you have at least two pieces of information under each body heading. If you don't, you may need to do a bit more research. You can also check any note cards you set aside to see if they fit under one of the headings. If not, you will not use those cards for this report.

Body: Where guanacos live
           Andes Mountains of South America
           how guanacos handle their habitat
           protected reserves
What guanacos look like
           similarities to camels—legs, hoofs, neck, lips
           differences—ears, no hump, height, fur color
What guanacos do
           spit cud accurately
           run fast and early in life
           swim across streams and between islands
How guanacos get along with people
           carrying loads
           wool used for coats and robes
           hunted for meat

Reference Note
For help in making **graphic organizers** like conceptual maps and time lines, see pages 347 and 348 in the Quick Reference Handbook.

> **TIP** Instead of an informal outline, you might create a **conceptual map** to organize your information. At the top of a conceptual map is a circle containing the topic. Extending out from the topic circle are circles containing subtopics. Circles containing facts and other information connect to the subtopics that they explain. Another useful tool for organizing information from various sources is a **time line.** You can use a time line to show the time order of events in history.

YOUR TURN 9 Organizing Your Notes and Creating an Informal Outline

Group your notes based on the questions they answer. Then, create an informal outline by following these steps:

- Turn questions into headings.
- List your headings on a sheet of paper, leaving several blank lines after each.
- Write notes under each heading telling which information you will include from your note cards. You do not need to use complete sentences.

Designing Your Writing

Creating Headings To help readers see how your ideas are organized, include a descriptive heading before each section of your report. If you are writing on a computer, put your headings in boldface print or underline them using word-processing features. If you are typing or hand-writing your report, print the headings in capital letters or underline them.

Write a Main Idea Statement

Tell It Like It Is To make sure your readers remember the major points you make about your topic, include a *main idea statement* in your introduction. A **main idea statement,** or **thesis,** tells readers the topic of a piece of writing and the main points the writer will make about the topic. Here is how you can develop a main idea statement for your report.

THINKING IT THROUGH — Writing a Main Idea Statement

STEP 1 Identify the major points in your outline.
strange looking, unusual talents, useful to humans, threatened by hunting

STEP 2 Combine the major points in a single sentence.
Guanacos are strange-looking animals with unusual talents, and they are useful to humans but threatened by hunting.

STEP 3 If your step 2 sentence is long, condense the ideas into a more compact main idea statement.
Guanacos are unusual animals that are useful to humans but threatened by hunting.

YOUR TURN 10 Writing a Main Idea Statement

Use the Thinking It Through steps above to develop a clear and compact main idea statement for your research report.

Research Report

Framework	Directions and Explanations
Introduction ■ Attention-getting beginning ■ Main idea statement	One way to grab your readers' attention is to begin with a colorful description of something related to your topic. Your **main idea statement** should clearly identify your topic and the major points in your report.
Body ■ Heading 1 facts ■ Heading 2 facts and so on	The headings in your informal outline represent subtopics. **Each subtopic will be covered in its own paragraph. Support** each subtopic with facts and explanations from your research, and **elaborate** on your support by explaining each fact or example. Clearly distinguish your own ideas from those of your sources' authors.
Conclusion ■ Restatement of main idea	In addition to restating your main idea, your conclusion may be a good place to share information that did not fit in the body of your report. The Writer's Model, for example, tells what is being done to solve the problem discussed in the report.
List of Sources ■ Alphabetized by author	A list of sources is also called a **Works Cited list** or **bibliography.** List only the sources you actually used for your report. See the chart on page 203 for how to list different kinds of sources.

 Drafting Your Report

Write the first draft of your report. Use the framework above and the following Writer's Model to guide you.

Chapter 6   **Exposition:** Sharing Your Research

A Writer's Model

The final draft below closely follows the framework for a research report on the previous page.

The South American Guanaco

Visitors to the Andes Mountains may spot a creature resembling a tiny camel without a hump. This animal is the guanaco, a South American member of the camel family. Guanacos are unusual animals that are useful to humans but threatened by hunting.

For thousands of years guanacos have grazed on tough grasses in the high plains and hills of the Andes Mountains. They can be found from southern Peru to the tip of South America. Their blood can handle the thin mountain air. Steep, rocky paths are no problem for guanacos because they are nimble like mountain goats and have thick, padded soles that protect their feet. Their only wild enemy is the mountain lion, but people have hunted the guanaco so much that the species is in danger. Some herds live in protected reserves in Argentina and Chile.

Like other camels, the guanaco has long legs, two-toed hoofs, a long neck, and floppy lips. It can survive without water for long periods of time, just like a desert camel. The guanaco looks different from the humped camel. It has pointed ears and a slender body, and it stands less than four feet high. In some ways it looks more like a deer or an antelope than a camel. It is reddish brown with a dark gray head and a pale belly.

The guanaco has some strange talents. Like other kinds of camels, the guanaco helps its stomach digest grass by chewing it up again after it has been in the stomach for a while. This rechewed grass, or cud, comes in handy when another animal bothers the guanaco. It can accurately hit whatever is annoying it with smelly green spit, with no warning at all. The guanaco

(continued)

Attention grabber

Main idea statement

Heading 1:
Where guanacos live

Heading 2:
What guanacos look like

Heading 3:
What guanacos do

(continued)

can also run fast and swim well. Almost as soon as they are born, guanacos can race to safety if their mothers spot danger. Adult guanacos can run as fast as thirty-five miles an hour. Guanacos swim almost as well as they run. They easily cross cold, fast-running mountain streams. Believe it or not, they even swim in the ocean. They have been seen swimming from island to island off the coast of Chile in the Pacific Ocean.

Heading 4: How guanacos get along with people

Guanacos are helpful to people and are in trouble because of them. People use guanacos to carry loads on the prairies and in the mountains of South America. Their wool is also used for making coats. Newborn guanacos are often killed so that their silky wool can be made into beautiful robes called *capas*. The number of guanacos has also been reduced by hunters, who kill them for their meat.

Restatement of main idea

To help the guanaco survive the threat of people hunting it for meat and hides, this unusual little camel will need to be protected. Some South American countries are already taking steps that may help guanacos to be plentiful again.

TIP A research report and its *List of Sources* are normally double-spaced. Because of limited space on these pages, A Writer's Model and A Student's Model are single-spaced. The *Elements of Language* Internet site provides a model of a research report in the double-spaced format. To see this interactive model, go to **go.hrw.com** and enter the keyword **EOLang 6-6**.

List of Sources

Burton, John A. <u>The Collins Guide to the Rare Mammals of the World</u>. Lexington: The Stephen Greene Press, 1987.

Goodwin, George G. "Guanaco." <u>Collier's Encyclopedia</u>. 1997.

"Guanaco." <u>Wildlife Gallery</u>. Fota Wildlife Park. 26 Jan. 1999 <http://www.zenith.ie/fota/wildlife/guanaco.html>.

Lambeth, Ellen. "Here Comes Paco Guanaco: In the Hilly Grasslands of South America, a Camel Is Born." <u>Ranger Rick</u> Nov. 1996: 4-8.

A Student's Model

Genna Offerman, a sixth-grader from Marshall Middle School in Beaumont, Texas, wrote about a game many people enjoy—billiards. Below is an excerpt of her research report.

Billiards

. . . Billiard games are played on a rectangular table. This table has rubber cushions around its inside upper edge and is covered with a felt cloth. A billiard table has six holes, called pockets, where the balls go. Many billiard games require fifteen numbered balls. Balls one through eight are all solid colors, and balls nine through fifteen are white with a colored stripe. Also, for some billiard games, a white cue ball is used. A player uses a cue stick, which is made of wood, to hit the white cue ball into a numbered ball. The goal is to get the numbered ball into a pocket.

Subtopic 1: Equipment needed to play billiards

The game of billiards has been around since the 1400s. It was developed in Europe from the game croquet, which is played on the lawn with mallets and balls. When croquet was moved indoors, people began playing it on a table that was made green to resemble grass. By the 1600s, the game of billiards had become so popular that Shakespeare mentioned it in the play *Antony and Cleopatra*.

Subtopic 2: History of billiards

No one knows when billiards came to the United States, but from an early date the game was popular. American woodworkers were producing billiard tables by the 1700s, and George Washington was said to have won a game in 1748. In 1850, Michael Phelan wrote the first American book on the game. . . .

Subtopic 3: History of billiards in the United States

List of Sources

<u>Billiards: The Official Rules and Records Book</u>. Iowa
    City: Billiard Congress of America, 1966.
"Billiards." <u>1997 Grolier Multimedia Encyclopedia</u>. CD-
    ROM. 1997.

Revising

Evaluate and Revise Content, Organization, and Style

Double Duty To make the information in your research report as clear as possible for your readers, you will need to read it at least twice. First, evaluate the content and organization, using the guidelines below. Then, check your writing style using the guidelines on page 215.

▶ **First Reading: Content and Organization** Use the following chart to evaluate the content and organization of your report. The tips in the middle column will help you decide how to answer the questions in the left column. If you answer *no* to any question, use the Revision Technique to improve that part of your writing.

Guidelines for Self-Evaluation and Peer Evaluation		
Evaluation Questions	**Tips**	**Revision Techniques**
❶ Does the introduction contain a main idea statement that identifies the topic and major points of the report?	**Highlight** the main idea statement.	**Add** a main idea statement or **revise** the main idea statement to give complete information about the topic, if needed.
❷ Does each paragraph in the body explain only one part of the topic?	**Label** each body paragraph with the type of information it provides about the topic.	**Rearrange** ideas so each paragraph covers only one part of the topic, or **delete** ideas that do not belong.
❸ Does each paragraph contain facts that give clear information about the topic?	**Put a check mark** above each fact that explains the topic.	**Add** facts to any paragraph with fewer than two check marks.
❹ Does the conclusion restate the report's main idea?	**Circle** the sentence that puts the main idea statement in different words.	If needed, **add** a sentence that states the main idea in another way.
❺ Does the report include information from at least three sources?	**Number** the items on the list of sources.	**Elaborate** on the ideas in your report by using information from another source as needed.

ONE WRITER'S REVISIONS These are revisions of an early draft of the research report on pages 211–212.

> The guanaco can also run fast and swim well. Almost as soon as they are born, guanacos can race to safety if their mothers spot danger. Adult guanacos can run as fast as thirty-five miles an hour. ~~This is another way that they are like antelopes and deer.~~ [delete] Guanacos swim almost as well as they run. They easily cross cold, fast-running mountain streams. Believe it or not, they even swim in the ocean. *They have been seen swimming from island to island off the coast of Chile in the Pacific Ocean.* [elaborate]

Responding to the Revision Process

1. How did deleting a sentence improve the passage above?
2. Why was it important for the writer to add the final sentence?

PEER REVIEW

When you are reviewing another student's report, ask yourself these questions:

- Does this report explain information clearly enough for me to tell someone else about this topic?
- What part of this report caught my interest the most? Why?

▶ **Second Reading: Style** When sharing information with others, you should communicate your ideas as clearly as possible. One way to do this is to use *precise nouns* in your writing. **Precise nouns** name a person, place, thing, or idea in a specific way. Look for places in your writing where you can be more precise by changing a vague noun to one that is more specific.

When you evaluate your research report for style, ask yourself whether your writing uses specific words to name people, places, things, and ideas. As you re-read your report, put an asterisk above each vague, non-specific noun (especially look for ones like *thing, stuff, animal,* and *person*). Then, replace vague nouns with more precise ones (for instance, *boulder, DVDs, giraffe,* and *landlord*). (You may find more specific nouns in your notes.) The Focus on Word Choice on the next page can help you learn more about using precise nouns.

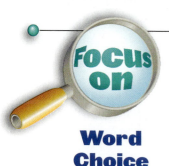

Focus on Word Choice

Using Precise Nouns

When you read the word *flower*, what image comes to mind? You might picture a daisy, while another reader might think of a buttercup or a daffodil. *Flower* is a vague noun because it lets the reader choose what to picture. When you write, give your readers the right picture by using *precise nouns* such as *honeysuckle* or *violet*. **Precise nouns** name people, places, things, or ideas in a specific way. Look at the sentences below. Which one tells you exactly what the writer had in mind?

Vague The author Luis Valdez created a *program* for *people*.

Precise The author Luis Valdez created a *theater company* for *farm workers*.

Replace vague nouns in your writing with more precise ones that will get your picture across. Precise nouns will help your readers learn about your topic.

TIP If you have trouble coming up with a precise noun, look up the vague noun in a **thesaurus.** Among the synonyms for the vague noun, you will often find more specific ones that you might use to revise your writing.

ONE WRITER'S REVISIONS

For thousands of years, the animals have grazed on tough plants in the high plains and hills of the mountains.
(guanacos / grasses / Andes)

Responding to the Revision Process
How do you think the changes the writer made improve the sentence above?

YOUR TURN 12 Evaluating and Revising Content, Organization, and Style

Review the first draft of your report. Then, improve your report by using the Content and Organization Guidelines on page 214, the Focus on Word Choice above, and peer comments.

Publishing

Proofread Your Report

Polish It   You want your readers to focus on learning about your topic, not on finding errors. Look over your report carefully and correct any mistakes. Use the following Grammar Link to make sure your sources are written correctly.

> **TIP** You can use other **resources** to help you proofread your report, such as a dictionary or a spellchecker.

Grammar Link

Capitalizing and Punctuating Titles

Sources of information for research reports are listed in a certain way. You may see the title of a source listed inside quotation marks, written in italics, or underlined. Some words are capitalized, and others are not. Here are three rules about how to write titles.

Titles of major works should be underlined or typed in *italics*. Major works include books, encyclopedias, magazines, newspapers, databases, Web sites, movies, and television series. Underline these titles when you type or hand-write your report. If you are using a computer, you can use the *italics* function.

Put titles of short works inside quotation marks. These include chapters of books; articles from encyclopedias, magazines, and newspapers; individual pages from Web sites; and titles of single episodes in a TV series.

Capitalize the important words in a title. The only words you will not capitalize in a title are articles (*a, an, the*), conjunctions (*and, but, or*), and prepositions with fewer than five letters (*to, for, with, in,* and so on). However, capitalize the first and last words of a title, no matter what they are.

PRACTICE

Rewrite the following titles. Capitalize each correctly and place it inside quotation marks or underline it.

Example:

1. Newspaper article: students stop disaster on playground
1. "Students Stop Disaster on Playground"

1. Magazine article: with a song in his heart
2. Book: the giant guide to the internet
3. Movie: the iron giant
4. Whole Web site: the science of lightning
5. Episode in a TV program: the perfect pearl

Writing Workshop   217

TIP Your teacher may ask you to create a title page for your report. If so, neatly include on a separate sheet of paper all of the required information—usually the title of your report, your name and your teacher's name, your class period, and the date.

Publish Your Report

Share the Wealth Now you can share what you have learned with an audience. Here are some ideas for presenting your findings in a variety of formats.

- With other students who wrote on similar topics, create and illustrate a book of research reports. This book might be kept in the classroom for independent reading or placed in the library for all students to enjoy.
- Make a display that includes your report and helpful illustrations. Place it in a hallway display case or the library, or share it with other classes.
- Try adapting your report into a children's book. Retell the most interesting facts and details in language children can understand. Work with a partner to illustrate your book.

Reflect on Your Report

Building Your Portfolio Take some time to think about how you researched your topic and wrote your report. Did you achieve your purpose? What would you do differently next time? Consider these questions:

- Where in your report do you think you did the best job of clearly answering a research question? Why do you think this was the best part?
- What kinds of information sources were useful? Would you use these types of sources for a future report?

YOUR TURN 13 Proofreading, Publishing, and Reflecting on Your Report

- Correct any errors in spelling, punctuation, and sentence structure. Be particularly careful about writing titles of sources correctly.
- Publish your report for an audience of interested readers. You might use one of the suggestions above.
- Answer the Reflect on Your Report questions above. Record your responses in a learning log, or include them in your portfolio.

218   Chapter 6   **Exposition:** Sharing Your Research

MINI-LESSON TEST TAKING

Writing an Informative Essay

In a research report you explain what you have learned about a topic. Some writing tests, though, will ask you to explain something about *yourself*. You may be asked to explain something that is important or enjoyable to you. Because these essays clarify, or make clear, your relationship to a topic, they are sometimes called **clarification essays.**

You can organize your ideas for a clarification essay just as you organized the information in your research report by using an informal outline. You will also elaborate on your ideas by using explanations. Read the following prompt, and think about how you would respond.

Everyone has a place that is important to him or her. It may be a place with special memories or a place that makes a person feel comfortable. Choose a place that is important to you, and write an essay about it. Explain three things that make this place special or tell three reasons why the place is special to you.

THINKING IT THROUGH — Responding to an Informative Prompt

▶ **STEP 1** Read the prompt to see what you must do. Identify the topic, audience, and format.

I'm going to write an essay that tells three reasons why a place is special to me. A specific audience was not named so I'll write to my teacher.

▶ **STEP 2** Choose a topic for your answer.

My grandfather's workshop is special to me.

▶ **STEP 3** Brainstorm ideas about your connection to the topic.

Things that make his workshop special:
1. good smells—oil, wood, sawdust
2. the furniture Grandpa makes
3. the jewelry box I made for Mom

▶ **STEP 4** Write your essay. In each body paragraph, elaborate on your connection to the topic.

1. smells—linseed oil & turpentine, fresh-cut pine, nose-tickling sawdust
2. furniture—high chair in progress, repairing Grandma's rocker, refinishing dresser
3. jewelry box—carved top, smooth finish

Connections to Life

Creating Visuals to Share Information

Showing Them Think back to the time when you were first learning to read. Remember how the books had pictures? You used the pictures to figure out what was being said. **Visuals** help readers and listeners of all ages understand the topic better. In this section you will learn how you can boost your audience's understanding by creating or finding a visual to include in your report.

The most obvious kind of visual is a **photograph** or **drawing**. The writer of the research report on guanacos, for example, found this photograph in a book. He photocopied it and included it in his report.

Make a Choice Before you create a visual, you must first decide two things: what information you are going to show and how you are going to show it. To decide what information to show, read your report and find anything your audience may need help understanding. Then, decide how you can put that information in a visual. The chart on the next page gives you some examples.

Get the Picture Once you have made your decision about what kind of visual will be most helpful for your audience, you will need to create or find it. You might use one of the following ideas.

- Draw it freehand.
- Trace it, using tracing paper or a projector.
- Photocopy it if you have access to a copier.
- Cut it out of a magazine or newspaper if you have permission.
- Create it in a computer program.
- Download it from an Internet source if you have permission to do so.

When you create your own graphic, use color carefully. In general, use no more than three colors in a graph, chart, or time line. Color attracts attention, but too many colors distract the reader and make information hard to find. A map, however, may need more than three colors to contrast all adjoining states and countries.

> **TIP** If you will use your visual in a **multimedia presentation,** have a friend hold your visual at the front of the room while you look at it from the back of the room. Make sure the visual is easy to read and understand even from across the room. Do some lines need to be bolder? Do some words need to be bigger? Would color help?

Type of Information and Examples	Best Visual to Use and Example
a series of events or a schedule Examples: • series of events in a historical period • schedule for a bus route	time line Jan. 24, 1848 — Gold discovered at Sutter's Mill Feb. 2, 1848 — California becomes a U.S. territory 1849 — Miners rush to California Sept. 9, 1850 — California becomes 31st U.S. state
statistics: facts that involve numbers Examples: • the percentage of people who ride bicycles • number of votes received by each student council candidate	chart such as a pie chart 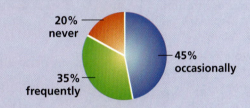
an area's physical features, political divisions, or other geography-related topics Examples: • The mountains, valleys, lakes, and rivers of Utah • The location of one of Canada's provinces—Prince Edward Island	map 

YOUR TURN 14 Using Visuals

Use these steps to create a visual for your research report.

- Decide what information to show and the best visual to use.
- Create or find your visual, making sure it is large and clear.
- List the source if you have copied, cut out, or downloaded the visual. For a reminder about how to list sources, see page 203.

Focus on Speaking and Listening

Giving and Evaluating a Research Presentation

WHAT'S AHEAD?

In this section you will give and evaluate a research presentation. You will also learn how to

- turn your research report into notes for a speech
- practice formal speaking skills
- identify important parts of a presentation
- evaluate a speech

Researchers sometimes present their findings in a formal presentation or speech. A research presentation tells an audience the important points a researcher has discovered. Here is your chance to share your research findings through oral presentations and to discover what your classmates learned.

Giving a Research Presentation

Even the most interesting report can sound dull if a speaker reads it word for word. A good speaker looks at the audience while presenting information. To make this possible, speakers use note cards to remind themselves of the points they want to make. They also practice their speeches until they are comfortable with what they are saying. To turn your research report into a research presentation, follow these guidelines.

TIP Have a partner help you practice by answering these questions about your presentation.

- Are there any points in the speech that are not clear?
- Does the visual (if one is used) help me better understand the information?

- Look back at the informal outline you created for your research report. Each heading in your outline can be a separate note card.
- On each note card, neatly write words or phrases from your notes, outline, or report that will help you remember the points you want to share with your audience. Write major ideas only (including key evidence and examples), but plan to elaborate or clarify your ideas as you speak.

Chapter 6   **Exposition:** Sharing Your Research

- Number the note cards in the order that you will present them.
- Practice your speech out loud. Because the occasion for giving your speech is fairly formal, use standard English and avoid using slang or clichés. Consider your volume and rate, speaking loudly and slowly. Everyone in your audience—including people at the back of the room—should be able to understand you.
- If you use a visual or prop, practice holding it up or pointing to it while facing the audience.
- Practice making eye contact by having a friend listen to you or by looking at yourself in a mirror.
- Refine your speech as you practice. Evaluate yourself, or collaborate or confer with a peer, using the criteria below.

TIP You can add a note to your cards to remind you when to use your visual during your speech.

> **YOUR TURN 15**
>
> **Giving an Oral Research Presentation**
>
> Follow the guidelines on page 222 and above to present the information in your research report to your class.

Reference Note

For more on **formal speaking,** see page 301 in the Quick Reference Handbook.

Evaluating a Research Presentation When you evaluate a presentation, you will look at the content of the speech and the speaker's delivery. **Content** is the ideas a speaker presents. **Delivery** includes how the speaker talks, uses gestures, and makes eye contact with the audience.

Get the Message To evaluate content, consider how clear and organized the speaker's information is. Here is how one student evaluated the content of a classmate's speech.

TIP Monitor your understanding as you listen to the speech. If you are confused about something the speaker said, wait until he or she is finished to raise your hand and ask a question for clarification.

Content	Comments
- Can you understand the main ideas in the speaker's verbal message?	- He says guanacos are unusual animals that are in trouble.
- Can you identify support for the speaker's main ideas?	- He describes what guanacos look like and what they do. He also talks about how they are being hunted.
- Does the speaker seem to understand the topic well?	- He really knows about guanacos. I wish he would explain how they swim. Overall content: great

Special Delivery   A speaker who mumbles or says "um" frequently draws attention to his or her delivery. When you listen to a speech, you may only notice a speaker's delivery if there are problems such as these. When a speaker's delivery is good, you can focus on the content of the speech. To identify good delivery, answer these questions as you listen.

Delivery	Comments
• Does the speaker talk loudly and clearly enough?	• He was easy to understand except when he turned to point at the map.
• Does the speaker look at the audience?	• He is mostly looking at his notes.
• Do the speaker's nonverbal signals (gestures or voice) emphasize important ideas in the verbal message?	• He emphasizes things with his voice, but not with gestures.
• If visuals are used, are they helpful?	• The map and picture both help me understand the topic better. Overall delivery: good

TIP   Many speakers use technology to incorporate visuals into their presentations. They might use a VCR, a monitor, an overhead projector, or presentation software to present and enhance their ideas. To evaluate whether a presenter has used technology effectively, think about whether the technology helps the presenter achieve his or her purpose—to inform. Does the technology contribute to the presentation, or does it distract from the presenter's ideas?

Put It All Together   As you listen to a speech, use charts like the one on page 223 and the one above to make notes about content and delivery. Considering both the content and the delivery of a presentation takes concentration, so try to limit your distractions. You may want to sit closer to the speaker and put away everything except your evaluation charts and a pen or pencil.

Reference Note
For more on **eliminating barriers to effective listening,** see page 309 in the Quick Reference Handbook.

YOUR TURN 16   **Evaluating an Oral Presentation**

Evaluate a research presentation by one or more of your classmates. Create charts like those on page 223 and this page to evaluate both the content and delivery of the speech.

Chapter 6   **Exposition:** Sharing Your Research

CHAPTER 6 Choices

Choose one of the following activities to complete.

▶ CAREERS

1. Expert Guidance When you see someone doing an exciting job on television, you might wonder how you might someday get that job. Choose a career that interests you. Then, ask classmates or adults you know to refer you to someone with that job. Interview this person, and ask what education and training are needed to get into that career. Present your findings by creating a **career guide** with other students who choose this activity.

▶ LISTENING

2. My Kind of Tune Do you enjoy hip-hop, country, or some other kind of music? Research the important elements of a particular style of music, and choose a recording of that style of music. Then, write a **review** that evaluates how well the recording uses the elements of its musical style. Give a **multimedia presentation** in which you share your review and play the recording.

▶ CROSSING THE CURRICULUM: PHYSICAL EDUCATION

3. Hall of Fame Make a **trading card** for a famous athlete of the past. Include a picture of the athlete, important dates, records, and other interesting facts you uncover in your research. You might consider choosing one of these athletes: Jim Thorpe, Jackie Joyner-Kersee, Sonja Henie, or Satchel Paige.

▶ CREATIVE WRITING

4. A Fresh Angle Try one of the following ideas to share information about your research topic: Write an entertaining **letter** about your topic to someone you think might be interested in it, or write a **short story** that uses the information you learned researching your topic. You could also write a **poem** about your topic, describing or explaining it in a creative way. Share your writing with others by mailing it, reading it aloud, or posting it on a bulletin board.

PORTFOLIO

CHAPTER 7

Making a Difference

CONNECTING READING AND WRITING

Reading Workshop

Reading a Persuasive Essay

Writing Workshop

Writing a Persuasive Letter

Focus on Listening

Evaluating a Persuasive Speech

> **Informational Text**
>
> Persuasion

"Pleasepleasepleasepleaseplease?!" This may be how young children attempt to get their way, but by now you probably know that whining and repetition are not effective when you are older. You are more likely to get what you want through the art of **persuasion**—convincing others by giving reasons that make sense. Whether you are trying to persuade others or others are trying to persuade you, good reasons make all the difference.

Persuasion comes in many forms. A spoken request from a friend is usually casual and unplanned. The kind of persuasion you read or write is more carefully structured. It includes an opinion and specific reasons to support the opinion. The kind of persuasion you view, including TV ads and billboards, adds pictures and even jingles that appeal to your emotions as well as to your mind.

YOUR TURN 1 — Discovering Persuasion

In a small group, discuss the following questions.

- What makes a spoken request convincing? a TV ad? a billboard?
- Is one of these types of persuasion usually more persuasive than the others? Which one? Why?

internet connect

GO TO: go.hrw.com
KEYWORD: EOLang 6-7

Connecting Reading and Writing

Reading Workshop

Reading a Persuasive Essay

WHAT'S AHEAD?

In this section you will read a persuasive essay. You will also learn how to

- **identify facts and opinions**
- **recognize the reasons and evidence writers use to persuade readers**

You finish your lunch, and then you throw away the wrapper and bag. You pry a new computer game out of layers of plastic and cardboard, tossing the packaging away before you play the game. You even drag your broken desk chair out to the curb to be picked up on trash day. Think about the amount of stuff you throw away every day, and multiply that amount by 300 million, the estimated population of the United States. That is a lot of garbage! The author of the following essay will try to persuade you to change your ways. Will you be convinced?

Preparing to Read

READING SKILL

Fact and Opinion Strong *opinions* often inspire people to write persuasive essays. To be effective, though, a writer must support opinions with **facts,** or statements that can be proved true. As you read the following essay, watch out for statements of **opinion,** which cannot be proved.

READING FOCUS

Reasons and Evidence In the courtroom dramas you see in movies and on TV, do jurors accept a lawyer's argument without question? Of course not. Even TV lawyers provide *reasons* and *evidence* to convince juries of their cases. Writers have the same duty to their readers. They must support their opinions with enough reasons and evidence to persuade their readers. See if William Dudley, the writer of the following essay, has done a convincing job.

Read the following essay. In a notebook, jot down answers to the numbered active-reading questions in the shaded boxes. Underlined words will be used in the Vocabulary Mini-Lesson on page 235.

from The Environment:
Distinguishing Between Fact and Opinion

The U.S. Has a GARBAGE CRISIS

BY WILLIAM DUDLEY

1 America is a "throwaway" society. Each year Americans throw away 16 billion disposable diapers, 1.6 billion pens, and 220 million tires. For the sake of convenience, we tend to throw these and other used goods away rather than repair or recycle them. The average American household generates 350 bags, or 4,550 gallons, of garbage per year. This comes out to a total of 160 million tons of garbage a year. We have to change our throwaway lifestyle before we are buried in it.

1. What opinion does the writer express in this paragraph?

2 We are running out of places to put all the garbage we produce. About 80 percent of it is now buried in landfills. There are 6,000 landfills currently operating, but many of them are becoming full. The Environmental Protection Agency estimates that one-half of the remaining landfills will run out of space and close within the next five to ten years.

2. What reason does the writer give in this paragraph?

3 Can we simply build new landfills to replace the old ones? The answer is no. For one thing, we are running out of space. We cannot afford to use up land that is needed for farms, parks, and homes.

4 In addition, many landfills contain toxic chemicals that can leak into and pollute underground water supplies. In New York City, over seventy-five wells had to be closed because of such toxic waste poisoning.

3. Which statements in paragraph 4 can be proved? How?

5 One suggested alternative to landfills is to burn the trash. In some states, large incinerators are used to burn garbage, and the heat that is generated is used to produce electricity. But this solution

4. What evidence supports the writer's reason that there are problems with burning trash?

has drawbacks. Burning trash pollutes the air with dioxin and mercury, which are highly poisonous. Furthermore, burning does not completely solve the landfill problem. Leftover ash produced by burning is often highly toxic, and it still has to be buried somewhere.

6   The only real solution to the garbage crisis is for Americans to reduce the amount of trash they throw away. There are two methods of doing this. One is recycling—reusing garbage. Bottles can be washed and reused. Aluminum cans can be melted down and remade. Currently in the U.S., only 11 percent of solid waste is used again as something else. . . .

7   We must also reduce the amount of garbage we produce in the first place. We should use less plastic, which is hard to recycle and does not <u>decompose</u> in landfills. Much garbage is useless packaging. Consumers should buy foods and goods that use less packaging. We also should buy reusable products rather than things that are used once and thrown away. . . .

8   A woman in California was asked about garbage. She replied, "Why do we need to change anything? I put my garbage out on the sidewalk and they take it away." Attitudes like hers must be changed. We have to face the inevitable question posed by Ed Repa, manager of the solid waste <u>disposal</u> program at the National Solid Waste Management Association: "How do you throw something away when there is no 'away'?"

5. How does this example help the writer make his point?

230   Chapter 7   **Persuasion:** Making a Difference

> **First Thoughts on Your Reading**
>
> **1.** What is the author trying to convince the reader to do?
>
> **2.** Which parts of the essay were convincing to you? Why?

Fact and Opinion

READING SKILL

Is That a Fact?   Maybe you have seen a TV show in which a detective asks witnesses for "just the facts." *Facts,* not opinions, will help the detective solve the case. Facts also help writers persuade readers because **facts** are statements that can be proved true. Facts may include numbers, dates, or measurements.

Opinions, on the other hand, are impossible to prove. An **opinion** is a person's judgment. Phrases such as "I believe," "I feel," or "I think" indicate an opinion. Telling readers what *should* be done is another sure clue that an opinion is being expressed. Judgment words such as *best, worst, greatest,* and *prettiest* may be clues that a statement is an opinion. The following pairs of statements show the difference between facts and opinions.

Fact	The city council passed the proposal **five to one**.
Opinion	**I think** the city council made a **smart** decision.
Fact	Our school buses were made in **1995**.
Opinion	The school board **should** buy newer buses.
Fact	Jefferson was the **third** president.
Opinion	Jefferson was the country's **best** president.

Try identifying facts and opinions in the paragraph below. If you have trouble, follow the steps on the next page.

> The city should encourage people to ride bicycles for short trips. Bicycles do not pollute. Taking several short car trips can create more pollution than a longer drive. If people tried bicycling for these short trips, they would enjoy it. Cyclists travel at slower speeds, which allows them to take in nature's sights and sounds. I think an ad campaign could convince people to stop depending on cars for all of their transportation.

Reading Workshop

THINKING IT THROUGH: Identifying Fact and Opinion

▶ **STEP 1** Read the paragraph. Look for clues, such as *should, good, bad,* or *I believe,* that signal an opinion.

Sentences with opinion clues: "The city <u>should</u> encourage people to ride bicycles for short trips." "If people tried bicycling for these short trips, they would <u>enjoy</u> it." "<u>I think</u> an ad campaign could convince people to stop depending on cars for all of their transportation."

▶ **STEP 2** Read the paragraph again to identify facts. Look for numbers, measurements, or things that can be proved.

Sentences with fact clues: "Bicycles <u>do not pollute</u>." "Taking several short car trips can create <u>more pollution</u> than a longer drive." "Cyclists travel at <u>slower speeds</u>. . . ."

TIP Quiz a classmate by writing five sentences on your paper from the essay. Then, have your partner identify each sentence as either a fact or an opinion. Your partner should also explain his or her answers.

YOUR TURN 2: Identifying Fact and Opinion

Re-read the essay on pages 229–230, and look for fact and opinion clues. Identify three sentences that contain facts and three sentences that contain opinions, and explain how you can tell.

| READING FOCUS ▶

Reasons and Evidence

Building a Case Have you ever tried to build a human pyramid? The base of the pyramid needs to have more people, and stronger people, than the top does. Look at the following diagram of a persuasive essay. Notice how it looks like a pyramid.

A lot of this in his notes.

232 Chapter 7 Persuasion: Making a Difference

The opinion in a persuasive essay is like the person at the top of a human pyramid. The *reasons* are like the people in the middle row who support the person on top. The *evidence* in a persuasive essay is like the group of people who form the base of a human pyramid. Persuasive writing must have support to be strong, just as a human pyramid needs strong supporters.

Reasons A **reason** explains *why* the writer holds a particular opinion. In a persuasive essay the writer will usually write one or two paragraphs explaining each reason. For example, in the paragraph on page 231, the writer who wanted the city to encourage bike riding gave the reason that it would help reduce air pollution.

Evidence Just saying that bicycling reduces air pollution is not convincing. The city council or mayor would need evidence before believing the reason. **Evidence** is the support for a reason, the specific *facts* and *examples* that illustrate the reason. You already know that a **fact** is a statement that can be proved true. An **example** is an event or illustration that shows one specific instance of a reason. Here is evidence a writer used to support a reason in an essay about creating more community bike trails. Would this reason be as convincing without the evidence?

> **Reason:** Many people enjoy bike riding.
>
> **Fact:** 80% of the students at my school own bicycles.
>
> **Example:** When I ride my bike in my neighborhood, I always see lots of other people riding bikes, too.

> **TIP** In paragraph 3 on page 229, the writer addresses a *counter-argument*. A **counter-argument** is a reader's **objection** to the writer's opinion. A writer can address a counterargument by presenting a reason that explains why the objection is either incorrect or unimportant.

> **TIP** Using reasons and evidence to support an opinion is called making a *logical appeal*. A **logical appeal** persuades because it makes sense. There are two other ways persuasive writers appeal to readers. While logical appeals try to persuade your head, **emotional appeals** try to persuade your heart. Humane Society ads showing adorable puppies and kittens up for adoption are examples of emotional appeals. Finally, **ethical appeals** try to persuade you by making the presenter seem trustworthy. One example of an ethical appeal would be a public service announcement featuring a respected celebrity speaking sincerely about a serious issue.

See if you can spot the reasons and evidence in the paragraph on the next page. The graphic organizer below it will help you check your answers.

> People should donate supplies to the Helping Hands Community Assistance Program now. The supplies of clothing, shoes, and blankets are very low. There are only four coats, six blankets, and one pair of shoes now available. The director says that they need enough clothing for twenty adults and ten children. Also, winter is coming soon. Winter always brings a higher demand for warm clothing. Last winter some families left empty-handed because supplies were gone.

TIP The sentence that identifies the issue and the writer's opinion on the issue is called the **opinion statement.**

The writer of the paragraph above used reasons and evidence to be as persuasive as possible. Here is a graphic organizer showing how she built her case. Notice how the graphic organizer is shaped like a pyramid. The reasons and evidence hold up the opinion.

YOUR TURN 3 — Identifying Reasons and Evidence

Re-read "The U.S. Has a Garbage Crisis" on pages 229–230. Then, create a graphic organizer like the one above. Fill in your boxes with the writer's opinion, his reasons for that opinion, and the evidence that supports each of his reasons. (Hint: You will find this information in paragraphs 1–5 of the reading selection.)

MINI-LESSON VOCABULARY

Dictionary and Thesaurus

Persuasive writing asks you to take a side on an issue. To make an intelligent decision, you need to be sure you understand all of the words you read. You can use reference books to find an unfamiliar word's meaning. Here are two examples.

- **Dictionary**   In a dictionary you will find the word's definition, its pronunciation, its part of speech, examples of how it is used, and its history.

- **Thesaurus**   In a thesaurus you will find other words that are *synonyms* of the unfamiliar word. **Synonyms** are words that have almost the same meaning, such as *happy* and *glad*.

Dictionaries can sometimes be confusing when they list several definitions for one word. To find the right definition of a word, use the following steps.

THINKING IT THROUGH   Choosing the Right Definition

Here is an example based on the word *convenience* from the reading selection on page 229.

▶ **STEP 1** Look up the word in a dictionary. Read the entire definition.

Convenience means: 1. personal comfort 2. a favorable condition

▶ **STEP 2** Use each of the meanings in the context of the reading selection. Decide which meaning makes the most sense in the sentence.

"For the sake of personal comfort we tend to throw things away." That sounds good.

"For the sake of a favorable condition we tend to throw things away." That sounds strange. I think the first definition is correct in this context.

PRACTICE

Look up the words to the right in a dictionary. Use the steps above if the word has more than one definition. Write the correct definition of the word. Then, look the word up in a thesaurus and find a synonym that is familiar to you. Write that word next to the definition.

1. generates (page 229)
2. toxic (page 229)
3. incinerators (page 229)
4. decompose (page 230)
5. disposal (page 230)

MINI-LESSON TEST TAKING

Answering Questions About Fact and Opinion

When you take a reading test, you may be asked to identify statements of fact or opinion. Suppose the following paragraph and question were in a reading test. How would you approach them?

> New equipment should be purchased for Esperanza Park. The existing playground equipment is old and dangerous. Three children have received serious cuts from the jagged metal edges of the swing set. The equipment is seventeen years old and cannot be repaired. The city should make Esperanza Park a fun, safe place to play for children and families in the city.

Which of the following is an OPINION expressed in this passage?

A. Children have gotten hurt on the playground.

B. The playground equipment should be repaired.

C. The playground equipment contains jagged metal edges.

D. Esperanza Park should be made safer for children.

THINKING IT THROUGH — Identifying Fact and Opinion

▶ **STEP 1** Determine what the question is asking you to do.

The question asks me to find an opinion in the passage. An opinion is a statement that makes a judgment and can't be proved.

▶ **STEP 2** Eliminate choices that do not answer the question. If the question asks for a fact, eliminate opinions. If it asks for an opinion, eliminate facts.

Choice A says "children have gotten hurt." This is a fact because you could ask parents whether their children have been hurt. C says the equipment has "jagged metal edges." This could be proved by looking at the equipment.

▶ **STEP 3** Look at the remaining choices to make sure that each is the kind of statement the question asks for. Then, choose the answer that is stated in the passage. (If the question asks you to identify an opinion, look for opinion clue words.)

The remaining choices are B and D. Choice B is an opinion because it uses the word should, but the passage says the equipment "cannot be repaired." Choice D also uses the word should, so it is an opinion, too. The last sentence of the passage says this in different words. I'll choose D.

Writing Workshop

Writing a Persuasive Letter

WHAT'S AHEAD?

In this workshop you will write a persuasive letter. You will also learn how to

- develop reasons and evidence
- predict and answer objections
- choose and focus a call to action
- revise stringy sentences
- use possessives correctly

When you were younger, did you write letters to ask someone for a special toy? Maybe you wanted a certain doll or a new bicycle, so you described the toy and explained why you wanted it. Were you later thrilled to discover that your wish had been granted?

Now that you are older, you may know that letters can achieve results more important than toys. Here is your opportunity to use the power of persuasive writing to make a difference in the world around you. This workshop will teach you how to write a persuasive letter that will help make a positive change in your school, neighborhood, or town. The thrill of making a difference can be even more satisfying than receiving a new toy!

Prewriting

Choose an Issue

Dare to Care Given a choice between soup or sandwiches for lunch, you might answer, "I don't care." For you, the kind of food is not an issue. In persuasive writing, though, *issues* are important. An **issue** is a topic with at least two sides about which people disagree. **In a persuasive letter the writer tries to make the reader agree with his or her opinion on an issue.** Persuasive letters also may ask readers to take action on an issue.

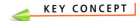

TIP Make sure you choose an issue that gets people fired up, not just a topic. For example, "school hours" is a topic that can be explained, while "making the school day longer" is an issue about which many people disagree.

Take Your Pick The issue you choose should be one that is important to you. If you do not feel strongly about an issue, how can you convince your readers to care about it? Ask yourself what issues most affect your world. Completing the following sentence starters will help you identify issues that matter to you.

My school would be a better place if ____.

I become upset when I see ____.

Little by Little You should also choose an issue that is small enough for one person or group to have an effect. For example, one student chose the issue of littering. Although she also felt strongly about the issue of homelessness, she felt that by taking on a smaller issue, she would be better able to make a difference. She also knew that an anti-littering campaign for her soccer league would be an issue she could tackle in a letter.

Write Your Opinion Statement

Take a Stand If you have chosen an issue that is important to you, you probably already know what your opinion on it is. You simply need to put that opinion into words. **An opinion statement should clearly state what the issue is and where the writer stands on it.** Here is how the writer who chose the issue of recycling came up with her opinion statement.

KEY CONCEPT

TIP An opinion statement may also be called a **thesis statement**.

> **issue:** litter at soccer games
> **+ how I feel about it:** soccer fields should be kept free of litter
>
> **opinion statement:** We need to start an anti-littering campaign to keep the soccer fields clean.

YOUR TURN 4

Choosing an Issue and Writing an Opinion Statement

Brainstorm issues that might make your community or the world a better place. Choose an issue that is both important to you and small enough to tackle in a letter. Write down your opinion about the issue. Then, put the issue and your opinion together into a single clear sentence—your opinion statement.

238 Chapter 7 **Persuasion:** Making a Difference

Consider Audience and Purpose

Dear Sir or Madam . . .   You would not ask the President of the United States to shorten the school day. Yes, the President can do many things, but your request is likely to get lost in the shuffle of national issues. Because your **purpose** is to persuade your reader, it is important to write to someone who cares about the issue and can do something about it. **Contacting the right audience to consider your request is an important part of your letter's effectiveness.** Identify local people who have the power to do what you want. Your audience may be one person or a group of people. Notice how one student used the following questions to help identify her specific audience.

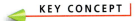
KEY CONCEPT

What part of your community does the issue involve?	Starting an anti-littering campaign at the soccer fields would involve my soccer league.
What is the specific name of the person or group you need to contact?	My league handbook says the president of the Eastside Soccer League is Jake Matsuo.
What do you know about this person or these people? (How old are they? What interests or concerns them? Why might they disagree with you, or object to your opinion?)	I know he's an adult, and he is interested in soccer. I think he is interested in keeping things running smoothly and in keeping fees low for players. He might object to my opinion if he thinks an anti-littering campaign would be time-consuming or expensive.

TIP In writing, **voice** reflects your tone and attitude. To persuade readers, you need to use a believable voice. In other words, you should sound as if you know what you are talking about and you take the issue seriously. You should also appeal to your audience by making it clear that you understand and care about their interests.

YOUR TURN 5 Considering Audience and Purpose

Your purpose is to persuade someone who has the power to grant your request. Use the questions above to figure out who that person or group of people is and think about what you know about them.

MINI-LESSON: CRITICAL THINKING

Understanding Your Audience

Imagine sweltering under the hot summer sun at the beach when a vendor selling mugs of steaming hot chocolate comes along. Are you tempted to buy? Of course not. The vendor has forgotten the basic rule of persuasion: Appeal to your audience's interests. Once you know your audience's interests, you can predict their main **objection,** or reason why they might disagree with you. Objections often revolve around how much time or effort a proposed change would take, or how much the change would cost. By appealing to your audience's interests, you can make objections such as these seem less important.

> **TIP** An objection is also called a **counterargument.**

THINKING IT THROUGH: Addressing Objections

You want to persuade the city council to support a Latino cultural festival. Here's how to address their objection.

▶ **STEP 1** Identify the main reason your audience might disagree with you.

The city council might say that having a Latino cultural festival would be expensive.

▶ **STEP 2** Consider what is important to this audience.

- saving money
- bringing people together

▶ **STEP 3** Based on your audience's interests, identify a reason for your opinion that makes the audience's objection seem less important.

The festival can be a fun activity for the community, and it can be inexpensive. To save money, volunteers can organize the festival, and vendors can pay a fee to sell food and crafts.

PRACTICE

Suppose that you want to organize a tutoring program at your school. Older students would tutor younger students for one hour after school. Using the Thinking It Through steps above, identify a possible objection each of the audiences to the right might have. Then, list reasons that would address each audience's objection. Explain each reason.

1. the school principal
2. parents
3. students who would serve as tutors

Develop Reasons and Evidence

Answering the Big Question Understanding your audience's interests will help you to answer their main question—"Why should I care?" **Your audience will want to know the reasons why they should accept your opinion.** You can begin developing solid reasons by asking why your opinion makes sense.

Your opinion needs more support than reasons alone, though. Evidence—from research and your experience—must support each reason for the reasons to be believable. **Facts,** which can be proved true, and **examples,** which illustrate a point, can provide support for reasons. See how the following reason is supported by a fact and an example.

KEY CONCEPT

TIP The facts and examples should also provide **logical support** for your reasons. If they are not **relevant,** or clearly connected to the reason, your audience may become confused.

> **Reason:** Volunteers help people.
>
> **Fact:** Since 1961, Peace Corps volunteers have helped people in 134 countries around the world.
>
> **Example:** My older sister volunteers by helping two fourth-graders with their math homework.

In the chart below, a student lists several reasons to begin an anti-littering campaign. In the middle column, the student gives facts and examples to support each of her reasons. In the right-hand column, she decides whether each reason and its supporting evidence will appeal to her audience.

Reasons	Supporting Evidence	Appealing to Audience?
An anti-littering campaign will make people aware of the trash problem.	My parents had to pick up trash left by others. That made them be more careful not to litter.	Yes. Most people want to enjoy the games and not worry about litter.
An anti-littering program will earn money.	By recycling, we can earn 32 cents for each pound of cans. This money can help pay for clinics to train new coaches.	Yes. If we pay for clinics with recycling money, the league won't have to raise fees to cover these things.
Participating in an anti-littering program helps players earn badges in Scouts.	I can earn 2 badges. Several players I know participate in Scouts.	No. This will help a few of us, but not the president of the soccer league.

Writing Workshop **241**

Reference Note

For more on **facts** and **examples**, see page 233.

From the chart on the previous page, you can tell that this student realized that the last reason might not appeal to her audience. The president of a soccer league is probably more interested in soccer than in scouting. The student thought about possible objections the president might have to the project. Then, she came up with a reason that would take his objection into account. See her revision in the chart below.

New Reason	Supporting Evidence	Appealing to Audience?
This project will not take very much time or effort.	Teams will make posters and rotate collecting the recycling containers. Parents and players do all the work.	Yes. He won't have to find people to do the work. This reason will also show that picking up trash and recycling is not too much trouble, which I think might be his objection.

TIP It is not enough just to give evidence. You also need to explain why your evidence is convincing. In the chart on page 241, the student explained in the Supporting Evidence column the meaning of each piece of evidence. ("This money can help pay for clinics to train new coaches.") This kind of explanation is called **elaboration**.

 Developing Reasons and Evidence

- Create a chart like the one on page 241, listing reasons and evidence to support your opinion. (Use the library to find facts to support your reasons.) Use the right-hand column to decide whether each reason will appeal to your audience.

- Replace any reasons that will not appeal to most of your audience. You should have at least two good reasons, each supported by facts or examples.

Choose and Focus a Call to Action

911 Means Action! When you dial 911, the operator knows instantly that you are asking for help. In a way, your persuasive letter is also a 911 call because it includes a *call to action*. **A call to action tells readers how they can respond to your ideas.** To get your readers to take action, your call to action must be both *reasonable* and *specific*.

A **reasonable** request is financially possible and within the audience's power. There is no point in asking a local audience to spend billions of dollars to end all wars or to house all homeless people. Instead, your call to action should focus on smaller actions. Suggesting that your audience sign a petition or volunteer a few hours of time is not too much to ask.

A **specific** request is clear and tells exactly what you want readers to do about an issue. How can a reader tell whether "Please do more for our children" is a call for more sidewalks or for a new playground? The specific call to action, "Start a tutoring program for elementary students," would be more effective.

THINKING IT THROUGH

Writing a Call to Action

Here is how to write a reasonable and specific call to action.

▶ **STEP 1** Decide exactly what action you want to take place.

I want to see trash picked up and recycled at our soccer games.

▶ **STEP 2** State the call to action in concrete terms so there is no confusion about what you are asking.

Maybe my call to action is too vague. I can ask the league to get recycling containers and put them at the soccer fields.

▶ **STEP 3** Address your call to action directly to the audience.

"Please buy and place recycling bins for aluminum cans at the soccer fields. Then, ask teams to participate in the anti-littering campaign."

YOUR TURN 7

Choosing and Focusing a Call to Action

Decide what you want to ask your readers to do about the issue you have chosen. Then, use the steps above to write a **call to action** that is reasonable, clear, and specific. Be direct, but remember a call to action is a request. Therefore, be polite, too.

Writing Workshop   243

Persuasive Letter

Framework	Directions and Explanations

Introduction
- Attention-grabbing opening
- Opinion statement

Grab your readers' interest right away with an **interesting beginning.** For example, you could begin your letter with an anecdote (a brief story), or a question. Next, include a clear **opinion statement** that tells your audience exactly what you think about the issue you have chosen.

Body
- Reason #1
  Evidence supporting reason #1
- Reason #2
  Evidence supporting reason #2
  and so on

- Support your opinion with at least two good reasons. Write a **paragraph for each reason.** You can arrange your body paragraphs in **order of importance,** starting with the most important reason, or in **climactic order,** ending with the most important reason.
- Support each of your reasons with at least one specific **fact** or **example** each.
- **Elaborate** support by explaining the meaning of each fact or example or by summing up your point.

Conclusion
- Summary of reasons
- Call to action

Remind your audience why this issue is important by **summarizing** your reasons in a single sentence. Next, tell your audience what they should do about the issue with a reasonable and specific **call to action.**

YOUR TURN 8 Drafting Your Persuasive Letter

Now, it is your chance to write a first draft of a persuasive letter. As you write, refer to the framework above and the Writer's Model on the next page.

244   Chapter 7   **Persuasion:** Making a Difference

A Writer's Model

The final draft below closely follows the framework for a persuasive letter on the previous page.

Dear Mr. Matsuo:

    My soccer team won its game last Saturday. I was happy and excited until I started walking toward the parking lot. I passed cups and candy wrappers left in the stands and six trash cans overflowing with aluminum cans. Seeing all the trash that people did not throw away and the cans that could be recycled bothered me. With your help, we can improve the Eastside Soccer League. We need to start an anti-littering campaign to keep the soccer fields clean.

    An anti-littering campaign would help people become aware of the trash problem. Since I talked to my family about the problem, they have noticed how bad the trash is, too. After last Saturday's game, they made sure they picked up their trash so that they were not contributing to the problem. Letting people know there is a problem is the first step to solving it.

    If we make recycling part of the plan, the anti-littering campaign can earn money. By recycling aluminum cans, the Eastside Soccer League can earn 32 cents per pound. Since there are twelve trash cans at the soccer fields that each can hold about two pounds of cans, and there are fifteen games in the season, we could earn as much as $115.20. This money could be used to pay for clinics to train new coaches. That way, more people could get involved in the league because training would be available.

    Finally, this project will take little time and effort. This can be a project for the parents and the players. Each team will make posters encouraging people to be responsible for their trash. Also, the two teams playing the last game on a field will pick up trash left in the stands and empty the two recycling containers on their field. Once all twelve

(continued)

Attention-grabbing opening

Opinion statement

Reason #1: Help people become aware

Evidence (example)

Elaboration

Reason #2: Earn money

Evidence (facts)

Elaboration

Reason #3: Easy to do

Evidence (examples)

(continued)

Elaboration

containers are emptied, one parent can drive the cans to the recycling center. This work will take just a few minutes of time. Since the teams already rotate playing times, no one team will be stuck with this chore every week.

Summary of reasons

An anti-littering campaign will help people become aware of the trash problem and earn money for the league without becoming a time-consuming or expensive project. Please buy and place recycling bins for aluminum cans at the soccer fields. Then, ask teams to participate in the anti-littering campaign.

Call to action

Sincerely,

LaVonne Barton

LaVonne Barton

Designing Your Writing

Reference Note

For more on **business letters**, see page 340 in the Quick Reference Handbook.

TIP If you have access to a computer, show your reader that you are serious about your issue by typing your letter. If you do not have access to a computer, write your letter using your best cursive or printing.

Business Letter Format To add to your persuasive letter's impact, use a business letter format like the one below.

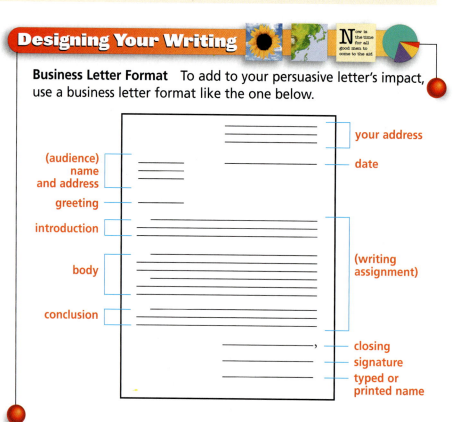

246 Chapter 7 **Persuasion:** Making a Difference

A Student's Model

Concern for the global, rather than local, environment prompted sixth-grader Tyler Duckworth to write a letter to the President of the United States.

My name is Tyler Duckworth, and I am a sixth-grade student at Liberty Middle School in Morganton, North Carolina. I think the first thing you should do, Mr. President, is take specific action to protect our environment. As an avid reader of books about science, I am concerned about the natural wonders of our nation and of the world being preserved both for my generation and for future generations.

Opinion statement

First of all, the pollution of our earth seems to be on the increase; factories, cars, and people continue to pollute. Statistics show that acid rain is on the increase, and the hole in the ozone layer is widening at an alarming rate. I feel action must be taken now, before it is too late. . . .

Reason #1: Increasing pollution

Evidence (facts)

Also, the land in the rain forests is essential to our survival. Each year, more and more land in the rain forests is destroyed. If man continues to destroy the rain forests, the species present in them and the plant life present in them can never be replaced. The action taken must be firm and bound by law.

Reason #2: Losing rain forests

Evidence (facts)

I believe that you, Mr. President, care about our country. You have stated in many speeches that I have listened to and in many articles that I have read that you care about our environment. It is essential that you, as our leader, do what is necessary to preserve the earth for future generations.

Reason #3: President's record

Evidence (facts)

In my dad's office, he has a quote that reads, "We do not inherit the earth from our ancestors; we borrow it from our children." That, too, is my belief as a twelve-year-old citizen of the greatest country in the world. Mr. President, I ask you to please act now to save our country and our world.

Call to action

Writing Workshop

Revising

Evaluate and Revise Content, Organization, and Style

COMPUTER TIP
You can find many reference materials on CD-ROM, and you can use the Internet as a resource. For example, if you need additional support for a reason, you can look up facts on reliable Web sites or on a CD-ROM version of an encyclopedia.

Twice Is Nice Double the persuasive power of your letter by giving it at least two readings. In the first reading, focus on the content and organization of your first draft. The guidelines below can help. In the second reading, look at the individual sentences using the Focus on Sentences on page 250.

▶ **First Reading: Content and Organization** When you **edit** your letter, you evaluate what you have written and revise it to make it better. Use the following guidelines to make your letter more persuasive. First, answer the questions in the left-hand column. If you need help answering the questions, use the tips in the middle column. Then, use the revision techniques in the right-hand column to make necessary changes.

Guidelines for Self-Evaluation and Peer Evaluation

Evaluation Questions	Tips	Revision Techniques
❶ Does the introduction have a clear opinion statement?	**Underline** the opinion statement.	**Add** an opinion statement, or **revise** a sentence to state your opinion clearly.
❷ Does the letter give at least two reasons to support the opinion?	**Put stars** next to the reasons that support the opinion.	If necessary, **add** reasons that support the opinion.
❸ Does at least one piece of evidence support each of the reasons?	**Circle** evidence that supports each reason. **Draw a line** to the reason each piece of evidence supports.	If necessary, **add** facts or examples to support each reason. **Rearrange** evidence so it is close to the reason it supports.
❹ Does the letter explain each fact and example?	**Put a check mark** next to each explanation.	**Elaborate** by adding explanations for each fact and example.
❺ Does the conclusion include a specific and reasonable call to action?	**Draw a wavy line** under the call to action.	**Add** a call to action, or **revise** the call to action to make it more specific and reasonable.

248   Chapter 7   **Persuasion:** Making a Difference

ONE WRITER'S REVISIONS This revision is an early draft of the letter on page 245.

> With your help, we can improve the Eastside Soccer
> *We need to start*   *to keep the soccer fields clean*
> League. ∧An anti-littering campaign∧ ~~would help~~.
>
>   An anti-littering campaign would help people become aware of the trash problem. Since I talked to my family about the problem, they have noticed how bad the trash is, too. After last Saturday's game, they made sure they picked up their trash so that they were not contributing to the problem.∧ *Letting people know there is a problem is the first step to solving it.*

revise

elaborate

Responding to the Revision Process

1. Why did the writer revise the sentence at the end of the first paragraph?
2. Why did the writer add a sentence to the end of the second paragraph?

▶ **Second Reading: Style** You have taken a look at the big picture of your letter. In your second reading, you will look at the pieces of that picture by focusing on the sentences. One way to improve your writing is to make stringy sentences more compact.

    When you evaluate your letter for style, ask yourself whether your writing avoids using long sentences made up of strings of ideas. As you re-read your letter, highlight long sentences that use *and, but,* or *so* to join two or more complete thoughts—ideas that can stand alone. Then, break one or more stringy sentences into two shorter sentences. The Focus on Sentences on the next page can help you learn more about eliminating stringy sentences.

PEER REVIEW

As you read a peer's persuasive letter, ask yourself these questions:

- Who is the target audience for this letter? Does the writer appeal to their interests?
- What is the strongest piece of support? What makes it stand out?

Writing Workshop

Focus on Sentences

Eliminating Stringy Sentences

When your purpose is to persuade, your style should also be persuasive. Avoid using stringy sentences. Reading long, stringy sentences is like listening to a person who goes on and on. They bore readers, and a bored reader is an unconvinced reader. To eliminate stringy sentences, follow these steps.

- First, find the conjunctions *and, but,* or *so* in a very long sentence. Put a slash mark before each conjunction.
- Then, see if each part has a subject and a verb. If each part of the sentence has both a subject and a verb and expresses a complete thought, then it can stand alone.
- Revise a stringy sentence by breaking it into two or more separate sentences. Each complete thought may have its own sentence.

TIP If part of the sentence does not express a complete thought, that part will not be able to stand alone in its own sentence.

ONE WRITER'S REVISIONS

My soccer team won its game last Saturday, ~~so~~ I was happy and excited until I started walking toward the parking lot ~~and~~ I passed cups and candy wrappers left in the stands and six trash cans overflowing with aluminum cans.

Responding to the Revision Process

How did breaking the sentence above into three sentences improve it?

YOUR TURN 9 Evaluating and Revising Your Persuasive Letter

Use the guidelines on page 248 and page 249 to evaluate and revise the content, organization, and style of your letter. If a peer read your letter, consider his or her comments as you revise.

Publishing

Proofread Your Letter

Edit for Oomph Careless mistakes decrease the persuasive power of your letter. Proofread your letter for mistakes in grammar, spelling, and punctuation.

Grammar Link

Punctuating Possessives Correctly

The **possessive** form of a noun or pronoun shows ownership. Using possessives helps writers make their points more concisely. Read the example below.

the playground equipment at our school
our school's playground equipment

Here are four rules to remember about possessives.

To form the possessive case of a singular noun, add an apostrophe and an *s.*

girl's sweatshirt   car's bumper

To form the possessive case of a plural noun ending in *s,* **add only the apostrophe.**

books' pages   stores' signs

Do not use an apostrophe to make a noun plural. If you are not sure when to use an apostrophe, ask yourself, "Does the noun possess what follows?" If you answer *yes,* you need an apostrophe.

Do not use an apostrophe with possessive personal pronouns. These pronouns include *its, yours, theirs, his, hers,* and *ours.*

The dog missed **its** owner.

PRACTICE

Write the following sentences on your own paper, adding apostrophes where they are needed. If a sentence is correct, write C next to the sentence on your paper.

Example:
1. In visitors eyes, our towns trash is its biggest problem.
1. *In visitors' eyes, our town's trash is its biggest problem.*

1. Recycling helps meet the citys goals as outlined in its long-range plan.
2. Other towns have recycling programs.
3. Theirs are successful. Ours still needs the councils approval.
4. The countys landfill is quickly filling up from the four towns trash.
5. Voters signatures filled page after page of one groups petition.

Writing Workshop 251

Publish Your Letter

Post It! Publishing a persuasive letter is simple. It requires an envelope, a correct address, and a stamp. Just mail it to the person or the individual people in your target audience. Here are two other ways to reach your readers.

- Even if you will not be mailing your letter, but handing it to someone you know well, use a business envelope to show that you mean business.
- If you have access to e-mail, you can send the letter electronically. Make sure you carefully type the message to avoid introducing mistakes. Be sure to confirm your readers' addresses before sending your letter.

PORTFOLIO

Reflect on Your Letter

Building Your Portfolio The best way to judge your letter's effectiveness is to see what response you get. You may have to wait a while. Factors you may not know about may lead to a "No," a vague response such as "We will consider your request," or no response at all. However, you can judge your letter in the context of your entire portfolio by answering the following questions.

- What are my strengths as a writer? What did I do well in this piece and in other pieces in my portfolio? Which piece was my best or favorite? Why?
- What writing skills do I need to work on? If I had the chance, what would I do differently in this piece or in other pieces in my portfolio? Why?
- What are my goals as a writer now? What kinds of writing does my portfolio seem to be missing? What would I like to try next?

Proofreading, Publishing, and Reflecting on Your Persuasive Letter

- Correct mistakes in punctuation, spelling, capitalization, and grammar. Pay particular attention to possessives.
- Publish your letter to your target audience.
- Answer the Reflect on Your Letter questions above. Record your responses in a learning log, or include them in your portfolio.

MINI-LESSON: TEST TAKING

Answering Questions That Ask You to Persuade

Some writing tests ask you to choose and support an opinion on an issue. Your response may be a persuasive letter or essay. If the following prompt were on a test, how would you approach it?

> The city council has a limited budget for a new park. It is trying to decide between spending money for large shade trees or for an in-line skating path. Decide how you think the money should be spent. Then, write a letter convincing the city council to vote in favor of your decision. Give three reasons for your opinion.

THINKING IT THROUGH — Writing a Persuasive Essay

▶ **STEP 1 Identify the task the prompt is asking you to do.**

The prompt asks me to decide how the council should spend the money. I have to write a letter stating my opinion and give three reasons to support it.

▶ **STEP 2 Decide on your opinion.**

I like in-line skating, but I think trees are more important.

▶ **STEP 3 Develop three reasons to support your opinion.**

1. More people will enjoy trees.
2. Trees give shade, which makes the park more comfortable.
3. Trees take time to grow, so we need to plant them now. A skating path can be added any time.

▶ **STEP 4 Develop evidence (facts and examples) to support your reasons.**

1. All people appreciate trees. I only know people my age who skate.
2. Summer temperatures are in the 90s. Shade will keep the playground and picnic tables cool even in hot weather.
3. We planted a tree when I was six, and it is still not as tall as our house.

▶ **STEP 5** Write your essay. Include your opinion in the introduction, make each reason a paragraph—with support—and give a call to action in your conclusion.

▶ **STEP 6** Edit (evaluate, revise, proofread) your essay.

Connections to Life

Writing a Humorous Advertisement

Is all persuasive writing serious? Not at all. Many people, in fact, find humor more persuasive than logic. Advertisers often rely on humor to persuade their audiences to buy their products. Humorous advertisements usually include these elements: a specific **product** being sold; a **reason** for buying the product, and funny **sounds** or **visuals**. Here is an example of a humorous print ad. Can you identify the elements?

Must be the **Grow Strong Vitamins** you gave her...

Grow Strong Vitamins give your children the boost they need to grow strong bones and healthy bodies. Who knows what your child could do with **Grow Strong Vitamins**? Try them and see!

A Little Imagination To come up with an idea for a humorous ad, begin by identifying a product you would like to advertise. Next, think of a brand name for your product. Brainstorm a list of reasons why people should buy your product. Then, choose a humorous way to get one of those reasons across to an audience. Consider these techniques.

- **Exaggeration** Exaggerate one of the claims of your product. This is the technique the ad on page 254 uses, exaggerating how strong and healthy children who use Grow Strong Vitamins become.
- **Irony** To create humor, say or show the opposite of what readers expect. You might show a family riding in a car. The dad says, "How much longer?" Then, the mom says, "Are we there yet?" The slogan would read, "Kids aren't the only ones who look forward to the fun at Giggles Amusement Park."
- **Silliness** Use silly sounds, voices, words, or visuals, or create a silly character to pitch your product. Talking animals, aliens, and cartoon characters are all used to sell products. For example, a cartoon version of a computer virus might complain about an antivirus software that keeps killing him off.

Sell It Once you have a good idea of what will be in your ad, you can produce it. Create one of these types of ads.

- **Radio Ad** You can turn your idea into a radio ad if the humor is in the words and sounds you include. To do this, you will need to write a script, create sound effects, and record the ad.
- **Print Ad** If the words and pictures are the funny parts of your idea, you can create a print ad like the one on page 254. You may create your ad by cutting and arranging pictures and words, or you might try creating it on a computer with copyright-free pictures.
- **Television Ad** If both sounds and visuals are important in your ad, turn your idea into a television commercial. You should write a script for the ad and find a good location to shoot, as well as any costumes or props that are important for your idea. Cast classmates to act in your ad if you wish, and videotape it using your school's video equipment.

(For information about **speaking,** see page 301. For information about **graphics,** see page 269. For information about **video production,** see page 79.)

YOUR TURN 11 Writing a Humorous Advertisement

Using the guidelines above, develop an idea for a humorous advertisement. Then, produce the ad as a radio ad, print ad, or television ad, and share it with your class.

Focus on Listening

Evaluating a Persuasive Speech

WHAT'S AHEAD?

In this section you will evaluate a persuasive speech. You will also learn how to

- identify your purpose for listening
- develop criteria for evaluating persuasive messages
- analyze a speaker's delivery and persuasive techniques

If you think you lack experience in evaluating persuasive speeches, think again. If you read magazines, watch TV commercials, or notice billboards, you are highly qualified. Any time you laugh at a clever advertisement or roll your eyes at a weak one, you are evaluating persuasion.

Listen with a Purpose

All persuasive messages, including advertisements, are created for the purpose of convincing people to do something or to believe something. When you listen to an ad or a persuasive speech, you may want to get information. However, your *main* purpose for listening will probably be to see whether you agree with the speaker's opinion. To do that, you must evaluate the speaker's message. Here are the elements to evaluate in a persuasive speech.

- **Content** is driven by the speaker's purpose. Since the speaker's purpose is to persuade, you can expect the content to include opinions, reasons, and evidence.
- **Delivery** refers to how the speaker delivers the message.
- **Believability** refers to whether or not you can believe the speaker.

Not all persuasive messages try to convince through solid evidence. Many persuasive speakers (and advertisers) also draw from a grab bag of *persuasive techniques*. **Persuasive techniques** rely on

Reference Note

For more on **evaluating a speech**, see page 312 in the Quick Reference Handbook.

emotional impact to "sell" an idea or product. Here are four of the most common persuasive techniques.

- **Bandwagon** A speaker may use this method to make you feel that everyone else is doing something, so you should do it, too. The statement "Everyone agrees that recycling is important" is an example of the bandwagon approach.
- **Testimonial** A speaker may try to persuade you with an example from his or her own experience, or a **testimonial.** For example, the speaker might say, "Volunteering at our local animal shelter has been a great experience for me."
- **"Plain Folks"** A speaker may try to show that he or she shares the concerns of the audience members. "Like you, I'm concerned about the cost of school supplies. Getting the supplies we need can be difficult when prices keep going up."
- **Emotional Appeals** This technique uses the audience's own emotions to get them on the speaker's side. An emotional appeal might tap into listeners' concern for others by telling sad stories about young refugees. Other appeals might spur the audience's school spirit or their anger about animal cruelty through words with positive or negative **connotations** (meanings beyond a dictionary definition).

TIP Persuasive techniques are sometimes called **propaganda** techniques. They are used not only to sell products, but also to convince others to share an opinion. Listeners should be careful not to be convinced by propaganda alone. They should demand that a persuasive speaker also give solid support for his or her opinions.

Develop Criteria

Use the elements of a persuasive speech to develop **criteria** for evaluation. To develop criteria for a persuasive speech, first identify and interpret (or understand) these parts of each element.

- **Content** Consider the **verbal elements:** major ideas and supporting reasons and evidence, facts and opinions, persuasive techniques.
- **Delivery** Consider the **nonverbal elements:** posture, gestures, eye contact, voice, facial expressions.
- **Believability** Consider the speaker's **perspective,** or attitude. For example, believable speakers are considerate of their audiences. They think about what their audiences will find persuasive. In contrast, speakers who try to force their opinions on their audiences without considering their audiences' views will be less believable.

Ask yourself what each item above would be like in a successful speech. The Thinking It Through steps on the next page can help.

THINKING IT THROUGH — Developing Criteria

▶ **STEP 1** Choose one item of a persuasive speech to evaluate, and ask yourself, "What should this be like in a persuasive speech?"

What should <u>eye contact</u> be like in a persuasive speech?

▶ **STEP 2** Brainstorm an answer to your question.

A speaker should try to look at various audience members, not just one or two people. This will make the speaker seem more honest and believable.

▶ **STEP 3** Turn your answer into a statement that says what a speaker should do when giving a persuasive speech. Then, develop criteria for the rest of the items listed on page 257.

A speaker should make eye contact with the audience often.

Reference Note
For more on **telling fact from opinion,** see page 231.

Evaluate a Speech

Once you have a list of criteria, you are ready to evaluate a persuasive speech. You may want to make a chart with your criteria in one column and space for notes in another. As you listen, remember your purpose. Do you agree with the speaker's opinion? To convince, speakers should support opinions with facts. Be sure you distinguish between facts and the speaker's opinions.

TIP As you listen to any speech, monitor your understanding, or make sure that everything the speaker is saying makes sense to you. Is anything confusing? If the situation allows, ask clarification questions to have any confusing points explained more clearly. After the speech, you might also look up in a dictionary or thesaurus any unfamiliar word the speaker uses.

YOUR TURN 12 — Evaluating a Persuasive Speech

- Follow the steps in the Thinking It Through above to develop criteria for evaluating a speech. Make sure your criteria cover content, delivery, and believability items.

- Listen to a persuasive speech and make notes about how the speaker does or does not meet each of your criteria. Does the speaker convince through evidence or "sell" through emotion? Afterward, rewrite any illegible notes, and add explanations for any short or confusing notes.

- Write a brief evaluation of the speech using the information in your notes. If other students evaluate the same speech, compare your impressions in a small group. Was the speaker effective? Why or why not?

CHAPTER 7 Choices

Choose one of the following activities to complete.

▶ **EDITORIAL CARTOONS**

1. The Politics of Art An editorial cartoon is a humorous drawing that tries to persuade readers to believe something. Editorial cartoons are usually located on the opinion page of the newspaper. Find an editorial cartoon and analyze it. Answer questions such as these: What is the artist trying to convince readers to believe? How does the drawing help the cartoonist make his or her persuasive point? Were you persuaded by the cartoon? Why or why not? Create a **bulletin board display** that includes the cartoon and a one-paragraph analysis.

▶ **CAREERS**

2. Persuasion in Practice Lawyers, advertisers, and newspaper columnists use persuasion every day. Research one of these careers. How do people in these professions get others to think a certain way? Do they use logical, emotional, or ethical appeals? (See tip on page 233.) Summarize what you learn about the career in a short **essay**.

▶ **CROSSING THE CURRICULUM: SOCIAL STUDIES**

3. On the Go What place would you propose to visit as a class field trip? In a small group, create a petition with specific educational reasons for your selection. Your petition should begin with a short **letter** explaining where you want to go and why. The letter should be followed by a **form** with spaces for students to sign their names and list their grade level.

▶ **SPEAKING**

4. Talk Them into It Make a **persuasive speech** to your class, either on the issue you chose for your letter or on another issue that is important to you. Make sure your opinion and call to action are clear. Support your opinion with reasons and evidence, and organize them in a way that will make sense to your listeners.

PORTFOLIO

PART 2
Quick Reference Handbook

- The Dictionary 262
- Document Design 264
- The History of English 272
- The Library/Media Center 276
- Reading and Vocabulary 286
- Speaking and Listening 301
- Studying and Test Taking 315
- Viewing and Representing 325
- Writing 337

Quick Reference Handbook

Quick Reference Handbook

The Dictionary

Types and Contents

Types of Dictionaries Different types of dictionaries provide different kinds of information. You should choose a dictionary that will have the kind of information you need. The following chart shows the types of dictionaries.

Types of Dictionaries
An **abridged** dictionary is the most common type of dictionary. The word *abridged* means shortened or condensed, so an abridged dictionary contains most of the words you are likely to use or encounter in your writing or reading. **Example** *Merriam-Webster's Collegiate Dictionary, Tenth Edition*
A **specialized** dictionary defines words or terms that are used in a particular profession, field, or area of interest. **Example** *Stedman's Medical Dictionary*
An **unabridged** dictionary contains nearly all the words in use in a language. **Example** *Webster's Third International Unabridged Dictionary*

Dictionary Entry

When you look up a word in the dictionary, the entry gives the word and other information about it. Look at the dictionary entry on the next page. The following explanations of the parts of the entry will help you get the most out of your dictionary.

1. **Entry word** The entry word is printed in boldface (thick) letters. It shows the way the word should be spelled and how to divide the word into syllables. It may also show whether a word should be capitalized or if the word can be spelled in other ways.
2. **Pronunciation** The pronunciation of a word is shown with symbols. These

cloud (kloud) *n.* ⟦ME *cloude, clude,* orig., mass of rock, hence, mass of cloud < OE *clud,* mass of rock: for IE base see CLIMB⟧ **1** a visible mass of tiny, condensed water droplets or ice crystals suspended in the atmosphere: clouds are commonly classified in four groups: *A* (high clouds above 6,096 m or 20,000 ft.) CIRRUS, CIRROSTRATUS, CIRROCUMULUS; *B* (intermediate clouds 1,981 m to 6,096 or 6,500 ft. to 20,000 ft.) ALTOSTRATUS, ALTOCUMULUS; *C* (low clouds, below 1,981 m or 6,500 ft.) STRATUS, STRATOCUMULUS, NIMBOSTRATUS; *D* (clouds of great vertical continuity) CUMULUS, CUMULONIMBUS **2** a mass of smoke, dust, steam, etc. **3** a great number of things close together and in motion [a *cloud* of locusts] **4** an appearance of murkiness or dimness, as in a liquid **5** a dark marking, as in marble **6** anything that darkens, obscures, threatens, or makes gloomy —*vt.* **1** to cover or make dark as with clouds **2** to make muddy or foggy **3** to darken; obscure; threaten **4** to make gloomy or troubled **5** to cast slurs on; sully (a reputation, etc.) —*vi.* **1** to become cloudy **2** to become gloomy or troubled —**in the clouds 1** high up in the sky **2** fanciful; impractical **3** in a reverie or daydream —**under a cloud 1** under suspicion of wrongdoing **2** in a depressed or troubled state of mind

symbols help you pronounce the word correctly. In the sample entry, look at the *k* symbol. It shows you that the *c* in *cloud* sounds like the *c* in *can,* not like the *c* in *ice.* Special letters or markings that are used with letters to show a certain sound are called **phonetic symbols.** **Accent marks** show which syllables of the word are said more forcefully. Look in the front of a dictionary for an explanation of the symbols and marks it uses.

3. **Part-of-speech labels**   These labels are abbreviated and show how you may use the word in a sentence. Some words may be used as more than one part of speech. For each meaning of a word, the dictionary shows the part of speech. In the sample entry, *cloud* can be used as a noun or as a verb, depending on the meaning.

4. **Etymology**   The *etymology* tells how a word entered the English language. The etymology also shows how the word has changed over time. In the sample entry, the abbreviations *ME* and *OE* trace the history of the word *cloud* from Middle English back to Old English. The final abbreviation *IE* tells the word's parent language, which is Indo-European. (See also **History of English** on page 272.)

5. **Definitions**   If the word has more than one meaning, the different definitions are numbered. To help you understand the different meanings, dictionaries often include a sample phrase or sentence after a numbered definition. (See also **Examples** below.)

6. **Examples**   A dictionary may show how the entry word is used. The examples are often in the form of phrases or sentences using the word in context.

7. **Idioms**   A dictionary entry may sometimes give examples and definitions of *idioms* that include the word. An *idiom* is a phrase that means something different from the literal meanings of the words. Dictionaries provide definitions because you cannot always define idioms using the usual meanings of the words.

Document Design

Manuscript Style

Whether you write your paper by hand or use a word-processing program, you should always submit a paper that is neat and easy to read. The guidelines in the chart below can help. You should also ask your teacher for help. He or she may have additional guidelines for you to follow.

Guidelines for Manuscript Style

1. Use only one side of each sheet of paper.

2. Type your paper using a word processor, or write it neatly in blue or black ink.

3. For handwritten papers, ask your teacher if you should skip lines. For typed papers, many teachers prefer that you double-space your assignment.

4. Leave one-inch margins at the top, bottom, and sides of your paper.

5. The first line of every paragraph should be indented five spaces (letter lengths), or half an inch. You can set a **tab** on a word processor to indent five spaces automatically.

6. Number all pages in the top right-hand corner. Do not number the first page.

7. Make sure your pages look neat and clean. For handwritten papers, use correction fluid to correct your mistakes. However, if you have several mistakes on one page, write out the page again. For papers typed on a computer, you can make corrections and print out a clean copy.

8. Use the heading your teacher prefers for your name, your class, the date, and the title of your paper.

9. Include graphics if they will make your ideas clearer to the reader. (See also **Graphics** on page 269.)

Desktop Publishing

To produce professional-looking reports, newsletters, and other documents, writers use *desktop publishing.* **Desktop publishing** describes all of the techniques involved in using a computer to make attractive documents. A computer's desktop publishing program contains many features. These features help a writer create eye-catching documents that contain text (words) and graphics (images and pictures). You can also apply many of the following desktop publishing techniques to handwritten papers.

The following section explains how you can effectively arrange, or lay out, the text of your document. For information about how graphics can make your ideas clearer to readers, see page 269.

Page Layout

Page layout refers to the design, or appearance, of each page in a document. As you plan the design of your page, consider each of the following elements.

Alignment   The word *alignment* refers to how lines of text are arranged on the page. Aligning your text the right way can give your page a neat, attractive look.

- **Center-aligned**   Text that is *center-aligned* is centered on an imaginary line that runs down the middle of the page or column. You may have used center-alignment for titles of papers or reports. You might also find centered text on posters, advertisements, and invitations.

  EXAMPLE
  These lines are center-aligned.
  The text is centered on
  an imaginary line that runs down
  the middle of this column.

- **Left-aligned**   When text is *left-aligned,* each line begins on the left margin of the page or column. Because English is read from left to right, most blocks of text are left-aligned.

  EXAMPLE
  These lines of text are left-aligned.
  Each line in this column starts at
  the same place on the left margin.

- **Right-aligned**   Text that is *right-aligned* is lined up on the right side of the page or column. Right alignment makes short, important bits of information stand out. For instance, when you write reports, you may right-align your name, the date, and the page numbers so that the teacher can find them.

  EXAMPLE
  These lines are right-aligned.
  Each line in this column
  ends at the same place
  on the right margin.

- **Justified**   Text that is *justified* forms a straight edge along the right and the left margins. Spaces may be added to the lines so that the lines are the same length. (The last line in justified text may be shorter than the other lines if it contains only a few words.) You often see justified text in books, newspapers, and magazines.

> **EXAMPLE**
> This text is justified. The text forms a straight edge along the right and left margins of this column.

- **Ragged**   Text that is *ragged* lines up along only one margin. Use ragged text for your reports.

> **EXAMPLE**
> This text is ragged. The text lines up along the left margin but not along the right.

Bullet   A *bullet* (•) is a large dot or other symbol used to separate items in a list. Bullets attract the reader's eyes and make information easier to read and remember. Consider these guidelines when using bullets.

- A bulleted list should contain at least two items.
- Each item in your list should begin with the same type of wording. For example, each item in this bulleted list begins with a declarative sentence, or a sentence that makes a statement.

Contrast   The balance of light and dark areas on a page is called *contrast.* Light areas have very little text and few, if any, pictures or graphics. Dark areas contain lots of text and perhaps pictures or graphics. Pages of high contrast—or a good mix of both light and dark areas—are easier to read than pages with low contrast.

Emphasis   *Emphasis* is a way of showing readers the most important information on a page. In a newspaper, a headline in large and heavy type can create emphasis. Color, graphics, and boxes around the text can also create emphasis.

> **EXAMPLE**
> **Sunken Treasure Discovered**
> SUNNY SEA—Diving students made an amazing discovery Saturday one mile off the Texas coast. . . .

Gutter   A *gutter* is the inner margin of space from the printed area of a page to the binding.

Headers and Footers   A writer uses *headers* and *footers* to provide information about the document. Headers are lines of information that appear at the top of each page in a document. *Footers* are lines of information that appear at the bottom of each page in a document. Headers and footers frequently contain the following information.

- author's name
- name of magazine, newspaper, or document
- publication date
- chapter or section title
- page numbers

Headings and Subheadings   Titles within a document are called *headings* and *subheadings* (also called *heads* and *subheads*). Headings and subheadings show readers how information in a document is organized.

- *Headings* tell readers the title or topic of a major section of text. A heading appears at the beginning of a section of text and is usually in bold or capital letters. (See also **Type** on this page.)

- *Subheadings* are more descriptive headings within a major section. Subheadings break a section into smaller sections. Subheadings help readers find the information they need. To separate the subhead from the main text, subheadings may be in a different size or style of type than that of the main text.

EXAMPLE

Keeping Our Parks Clean —— (heading)

Weekend Cleanups Give Parks a Whole New Look —— (subheading)

The biggest commitment Girl —— (text) Scout Troop #912 is making to the city this year is a program called Weekend Cleanups. Every Saturday, five girls from the troop pick an area park and clean up trash that people have left behind.

Indentation When you *indent* a line, you move the first word a few spaces to the right of the left margin. Always indent five spaces or half an inch at the beginning of a new paragraph.

Margins The *margin* on a page is the blank space that surrounds the text on the sides, top, and bottom. Some word-processing programs automatically set margins at 1.25 inches for the sides and 1 inch for the top and bottom. You can change the margins, however, to be larger or smaller. Changing the margins will allow you to fit more or less text on a page. Check with your teacher before changing your margins on an assignment.

Rules *Rules* are vertical or horizontal lines in a document. Rules can be used to separate columns of text or to set off text from other elements, such as headlines or graphics.

Title and Subtitle The *title* of a document is its name. A *subtitle* is a secondary, more descriptive title. Subtitles are sometimes joined to titles with a colon. However, if the subtitle is on its own line, no colon is needed. A title and subtitle appear on a separate page at the beginning of a book.

EXAMPLE

The 5 in 10 Pasta and Noodle Cookbook (title)
5 Ingredients in 10 Minutes or Less (subtitle)

Type

Type refers to the characters (letters and other symbols) in a printed text. Thanks to computer programs, a writer can experiment with the size and design of type in a document until the right look is achieved. When you create a document, there are many different aspects of type that you should consider.

Fonts A *font* is a set of characters (such as numbers, letters, and punctuation marks) of a certain size and design. For example, 12-point Courier is a font. The font size is 12 points (see below); the font design is called Courier. A computer program will let you use many different fonts. A font design is also called a *typeface*.

Font Size   The size of type in a document is called the *font size* or *point size*. The size of type is measured in points, which are $\frac{1}{72}$ of an inch. School assignments are usually printed in 10- or 12-point type. Captions for pictures are usually printed in smaller point sizes than the main text is. Titles may be printed in larger point sizes.

EXAMPLE

Title —————— 24 point
Text text text text ———— 12 point
Caption caption caption ——— 9 point

Font Style   The *font style* of type refers to the way the type is printed. You may use a font style, such as italic, to show that you are typing a book title. You may also use a different font style, such as boldface, to call attention to important words in your writing. Look at the examples of font styles below and in the next column.

- **Boldface**   A *boldface* word is written in thick, heavy type. You can use boldface to show important information.

  EXAMPLE

  This entire sentence is written in boldface type.

- **Capital letters**   A *capital* (or **uppercase**) *letter* usually signals a proper name, the beginning of a sentence, or a title. You can put titles and headings in all capital letters. To make an idea stand out, you can put a word or a sentence in text in all capital letters. However, if you put too many words in all capital letters, the idea may not stand out as much.

- **Condensed**   When type is *condensed,* the letters in a word will have less space between them. A writer uses condensed type to save space.

  EXAMPLE

  This sentence is written in condensed type.

- **Expanded**   When type is *expanded,* the letters in a word will have more space between them. Writers use expanded type to fill up space.

  EXAMPLE

  This sentence is written in expanded type.

- **Italics**   Type that is *italic* has a slanted style. Like boldface, italic type can be used to call attention to information. Italic type is also used in text to signal titles.

  EXAMPLE

  This sentence is written in italic type.

- **Lowercase letters**   A *lowercase letter* is not a capital or a small capital. (See **Small capitals** below.) Lowercase letters are the letters we use most often.

- **Shadow** A word written in **shadow** style appears to cast shadows. Shadow style may be used for titles and headings.

  EXAMPLE
  This sentence is written in shadow style.

- **Small capitals** Use **small capitals** when writing abbreviations referring to time. For example, when typing the time 5:45 P.M. and the year A.D. 1812, you should use small capitals.

Leading Another word for *line spacing* is *leading* (rhymes with *wedding*). **Leading** is the distance between each pair of lines of text. When a text is single-spaced, there is no extra space between lines. Books, magazines, and newspapers are usually single-spaced. Assignments for your teacher are usually double-spaced. Double-spacing your papers makes it easier for your teacher to read your assignment and make corrections or comments on the page.

Legibility A document is *legible* when its text and graphics are clearly readable. A document with high legibility uses a simple, easy-to-read font size and design for the main text. Well-designed graphics are another key to legibility.

Typeface See **Font** on page 267.

Graphics

Graphics can often communicate information more quickly and effectively than words. Graphics you can use in your document include *charts, graphs, tables, diagrams,* and *illustrations.* They can

- show information
- explain how to do something
- show how something looks, works, or is organized
- show what happens over a period of time

The main purpose of a graphic is to support or explain the text of your document. Whether you create graphics by hand or by computer, make sure that they are informative and easy to read.

Arrangement and Design

Use the following ideas to create informative and effective graphics.

Accuracy Make sure all of your graphics contain *accurate* information. In other words, the information in your graphics should be true and from reliable sources.

Color Readers are attracted to colorful graphics, especially when colorful graphics appear on a page of black-and-white text. You can use *color* to do the following:

- get a reader's attention
- call attention to certain information
- group items on a page
- help organize a page or even an entire document

Keep these tips in mind when you choose colors for your graphics.

- **Use warm colors sparingly.** Red, orange, yellow, and other warm tones seem to jump off the page. Overusing warm tones will decrease their dramatic effect.
- **Use cool colors to create a calming effect.** Cool colors, such as blue and green, make readers feel calmer. Use them as background colors.

Labels, Captions, and Titles You can explain your graphics by adding *labels* and *captions*. **Labels** appear within the graphic or are connected to specific areas of the graphic by thin lines called *rules*. Labels identify different parts of graphics, charts, tables, and diagrams. **Captions** are phrases or sentences that describe a graphic. Many photographs and illustrations have captions. Captions appear directly beside, above, or under the graphic. If your graphic has no labels or captions, give it a descriptive *title*.

Types of Graphics

Use the definitions and examples below to help you decide which graphics to use in your document.

Chart A *chart* helps show how pieces of information relate to each other. Two of the most common types of charts are flowcharts and pie charts.

- **Flowcharts** show an order of events. The boxes in a flowchart contain text, and appear in order from left to right or from top to bottom. Flowcharts usually contain arrows to direct readers from one box to the next.

EXAMPLE

- **Pie charts** show percentages, or how parts of a whole relate to each other. (See also **Charts** on page 293.)

Diagram A *diagram* uses symbols, such as arrows, to show how to do something or how something works. As with the other graphics in this section, diagrams can be drawn by hand or by using a computer program.

EXAMPLE

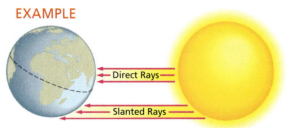

Graph A *graph* can show changes over time in a way that allows readers to understand the changes at a glance. The horizontal axis (the line that runs across the page) of a line or bar graph usually shows periods or points in time. The vertical axis (the line that runs up and down) shows quantities. (See also **Line graphs** and **Bar graphs** on page 294.)

Illustration An *illustration* is a drawing or photograph that can show readers items or events that are unfamiliar, new, or hard to describe. It can also show how something works, how to do something, or what someone or something looks like. (See also **Diagrams** on page 294 and **Illustration** on page 330.)

Storyboard *Storyboards* illustrate the different moments, or scenes, of an event or story. Storyboards are frequently used to map out a story or to plan a video segment. Storyboards contain boxes that each represent one scene in the sequence. The boxes contain drawings and text to be spoken by a narrator or actors within the scene. Example storyboards appear below.

Table A *table* contains information such as numbers and statistics, but it does not show trends the way a graph does. While a reader of a graph can immediately see an increase or decrease, readers of tables must look at all of the information and draw their own conclusions. For example, after studying the following table, a reader could conclude that membership in the Park Hills Computer Club rose for three years in a row.

EXAMPLE

Number of Middle School Students in the Park Hills Computer Club	
Year	Number of Members
1999	10
2000	19
2001	21

Time Line A *time line* shows events that happen over a period of time. The points along a time line show years or groups of years. The events that happen during a given year or period of years are described above, below, or to the side of the time line. (See also **Time Lines** on page 295.)

EXAMPLE

Clarissa finds a nest of baby sea turtles on the beach. They head toward the ocean.

One of the turtles cannot walk to the ocean with its brothers and sisters. It struggles on its back.

Clarissa turns the baby sea turtle over so it can walk toward the ocean.

The History of English

Origins and Uses

A Changing Language

No one knows exactly when or how English got started. We do know that English and many other modern-day languages come from an early language that was spoken thousands of years ago. The related languages still resemble that parent language, just as you resemble your parents. For example, notice how similar the words for *mother* are in the following modern-day languages.

ENGLISH mother	FRENCH mère
SPANISH madre	ITALIAN madre
SWEDISH moder	

Over 1,500 years ago, a few small tribes of people invaded the island that is now Britain. These tribes, called the Angles and Saxons, spoke the earliest known form of English, called **Old English**. Old English was very different from ours.

English continued to evolve through a form known as **Middle English**. While our language has always changed and grown, some of our most basic words have been around since the very beginning.

EARLY WORD
hand   dohtor   andswaru   hleapan

PRESENT-DAY WORD
hand   daughter   answer   leap

Changes in Meaning It may be hard to believe that the word *bead* once meant "prayer." Many English words have changed meaning over time. Some of these changes have been slight. Others have been more obvious. Below are a few examples of words that have changed their meanings.

naughty—In the 1300s, *naughty* meant "poor or needy." In the 1600s, the meaning changed to "poorly behaved."

lunch—In the 1500s, a *lunch* was a large chunk of something, such as bread or meat.

caboose—*Caboose* entered the English language in the 1700s when it meant "the kitchen of a ship."

Even today the meanings of words may vary depending on where they are used. For example, in America a *boot* is a type of shoe, but in Great Britain, a *boot* may refer to the trunk of a car.

Changes in Pronunciation and Spelling

If you traveled back in time a few hundred years, you would probably have a hard time understanding spoken and written English.

■ **Changes in pronunciation** English words used to be pronounced differently from the way they are pronounced today. For example, in the 1200s, people pronounced *bite* like *beet* and *feet* like *fate*. They also pronounced the vowel sound in the word *load* like our word *awe*.

You may have wondered why English words are not always spelled as they sound. Changes in pronunciation help account for many strange spellings in English. For example, the *w* that starts the word *write* was not always silent. Even after the *w* sound that started the word *write* was dropped, the spelling stayed the same. The *g* in *gnat* and the *k* in *knee* were once part of the pronunciations of the words, too.

■ **Changes in spelling** The spellings of many words have changed over time. Some changes in spelling have been accidental. For example, *apron* used to be spelled *napron*. People mistakenly attached the *n* to the article *a*, and *a napron* became *an apron*. Here are some more examples of present-day English words and their early spellings.

EARLY SPELLING

| jaile | locian | slæp | tima |

PRESENT-DAY SPELLING

| jail | look | sleep | time |

■ **British vs. American spelling and pronunciation** Pronunciations and spellings still vary today. For instance, the English used in Great Britain differs from the English used in the United States. In Great Britain, people pronounce *bath* with the vowel sound of *father* instead of the vowel sound of *cat*. The British also tend to drop the *r* sound at the end of words like *copper*. In addition, the British spell some words differently from the way people in the United States do.

AMERICAN

| theater | pajamas | labor |

BRITISH

| theatre | pyjamas | labour |

Word Origins

English grows and changes along with the people who use it. New words must be created for new inventions, places, or ideas. Sometimes, people borrow words from other languages to create a new English word. Other times, people use the names of people or places as new words.

■ **Borrowed words** As English-speaking people came into contact with people from other cultures and lands, they began to borrow words. English has borrowed hundreds of thousands of words from French, Hindi, Spanish, African languages, and many other

Origins and Uses

languages spoken around the world. In many cases, the borrowed words have taken new forms.

FRENCH ange
ENGLISH angel

HINDI champo
ENGLISH shampoo

AFRICAN banjo
ENGLISH banjo

SPANISH patata
ENGLISH potato

- **Words from names** Many things get their names from the names of people or places. For example, in the 1920s, someone in Bridgeport, Connecticut, discovered a new use for the pie plates from the Frisbie Bakery. He turned one upside down and sent it floating through the air. The new game sparked the idea for the flying plastic disk of today.

Dialects of American English

You probably know some people who speak English differently than you do. Different groups of people use different varieties of English. The kind of English you speak may sound unusual to someone else. The form of English a particular group of people speaks is called a *dialect*. Everyone uses a dialect, and no dialect is better or worse than another.

Ethnic Dialects Your cultural background can make a difference in the way you speak. A dialect shared by people from the same cultural group is called an *ethnic dialect*. Because Americans come from many cultures, American English includes many ethnic dialects. One of the largest ethnic dialects is the English spoken by many African Americans (called African American Vernacular English). Another is the Hispanic English of many people whose families come from places such as Mexico, Central America, or Cuba.

Regional Dialects Do you *make* the bed or *make up* the bed? Would you order a *sub* with the *woiks* or a *hero* with the *werks*? In the evening, do you eat *supper* or *dinner*? How you answer these questions is probably influenced by where you live. A dialect shared by people from the same area is called a ***regional dialect***. Your regional dialect helps determine what words you use, how you pronounce words, and how you put words together.

Not everyone from a particular group speaks that group's dialect. Also, an ethnic or regional dialect may vary depending on the speaker's individual background and place of origin.

Standard American English

Every dialect is useful and helps keep the English language colorful and interesting. However, sometimes it is confusing to try to communicate using two different dialects. Therefore, it is important to be familiar with **standard American English**. Standard English is the most commonly understood variety of English. Language that does not follow these rules and guidelines is called **nonstandard English**. Nonstandard English is inappropriate in situations where standard English is expected.

NONSTANDARD   I don't want *no* more spinach.

STANDARD   I don't want *any* more spinach.

NONSTANDARD   Jimmy was *fixing* to go hiking with us.

STANDARD   Jimmy was *about* to go hiking with us.

Formal and Informal   Read the following sentences.

Many of my friends are excited about the game.

A bunch of my friends are psyched about the game.

Both sentences mean the same thing, but they have different effects. The first sentence is an example of **formal English,** and the second sentence is an example of **informal English.**

Formal and informal English are each appropriate for different situations. For instance, you would probably use the formal example if you were talking to a teacher about the game. If you were talking to a friend, however, the second sentence would sound natural. Formal English is frequently used in news reports and in schools and businesses.

■ **Colloquialisms**   Informal English includes many words and expressions that are not appropriate in more formal situations. The most widely used informal expressions are *colloquialisms.* **Colloquialisms** are colorful words and phrases of everyday conversation. Many colloquialisms have meanings that are different from the basic meanings of words.

EXAMPLES
I wish Gerald would *get off my case.*
Don't get *all bent out of shape* about it.
We were about to *bust* with laughter.

■ **Slang**   *Slang* words are made-up words or old words used in new ways. Slang is highly informal language. It is usually created by a particular group of people, such as students or people who hold a particular job, like computer technicians or artists. Often, slang is familiar only to the groups that invent it.

Sometimes slang words become a lasting part of the English language. Usually, though, slang falls out of style quickly. The slang words in the sentences below will probably seem out of date to you.

That was a really *far-out flick.*
Those are some *groovy duds* you're wearing.
I don't have enough *dough* to buy a movie ticket.

Origins and Uses   275

The Library/Media Center

Using Print and Electronic Sources

Libraries contain huge amounts of information. In a library you can read about your favorite celebrities in the latest magazine, research breeds of dogs to choose a family pet, or find tips to help you in a sport. Whatever information you are looking for, your library has the tools to help you find it. Knowing how to use the library can bring you hours of enjoyment.

The information in a library takes many forms. The resource you use depends on the type of information you need. The following chart shows ways that information is classified.

Print Sources	
Fiction	Stories (novels, short stories, and plays)
Nonfiction	Factual information about real people, events, and things; includes biographies and "how-to" books
Reference books	General information about many subjects
Magazines and newspapers	Current events, commentaries, and important discoveries
Maps, globes, atlases, and almanacs	Geographic information, facts, dates, and statistics
Pamphlets	Brief summaries of facts about specific subjects
Nonprint Sources	
Audiotapes, records, films, filmstrips, slides, videotapes, CD-ROMs	Stories (narrated, illustrated, or acted out), music, instructions and educational material, facts and information about many specific subjects
Computers	Information stored electronically, allowing for easy access and frequent updates

Books Many books that you can use as sources are packed full of information. The specific information that you might need can sometimes be hard to find. You will find information more easily if you know how to use every part of a book. The following chart shows the types of information you will find in a book.

Information Found in Parts of a Book

The **title page** gives the full title, the name of the author (or authors), the publisher, and the place of publication.

The **copyright page** gives the date of the first publication of the book and the date of any revisions.

The **table of contents** lists titles of chapters or sections of the book and their starting page numbers.

The **appendix** provides additional information about subjects found in the book; it sometimes contains tables, maps, and charts.

The **glossary** defines, in alphabetical order, various difficult terms or important technical words used frequently in the book.

The **bibliography** lists sources used to write the book and provides names of books about related topics.

The **index** lists topics mentioned in the book, along with the page or pages on which they can be found; it sometimes lists the page where a certain illustration may be found.

Call Number When you need to find a book in the library, first find its **call number**. A call number is a code using letters and numbers that is assigned to a source in a library. Call numbers indicate the category a book is in and where it is located. Books in school and community libraries use the *Dewey Decimal Classification system*. (See also **Card Catalog** below.)

The *Dewey Decimal Classification system* assigns a number to each nonfiction book. These numbers are assigned according to the book's subject. Using this system of arrangement, books that contain factual information about similar subjects are placed near each other on the library shelves. **Biographies** are arranged differently from other nonfiction books. Most libraries arrange biographies alphabetically by the name of the subject in a separate section. **Fiction** books are arranged alphabetically by author in their own section of the library.

Card Catalog The easiest way to locate a book in the library is to look up the call number in the library's card catalog. There are two kinds of card catalogs: the traditional card catalog and the online catalog.

The traditional *card catalog* is a cabinet of small drawers. Each drawer holds many small file cards. There are cards in this file for every book in the library. The cards are arranged in alphabetical order by title, author, or subject. Each fiction book has a *title card* and an *author card*. A nonfiction book will also have a *subject card*. The graphic on the next page shows the information contained in the card catalog.

Using Print and Electronic Sources

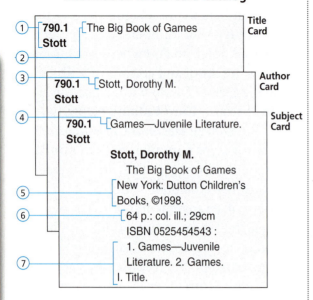

1. The **call number** assigned to a book by the Library of Congress or the Dewey Decimal Classification system
2. The full **title** of a book
3. The **author's full name,** last name first
4. The general **subject** of a book; a subject card may show specific headings
5. The place and date of **publication**
6. A **description** of the book, such as its size and number of pages, and whether it is illustrated
7. **Cross-references** to other headings or related topics under which you can find additional books

Many libraries now use electronic or online card catalogs instead of traditional card catalogs. (See also **Online Catalog** on page 280.)

CD-ROMs

CD-ROM stands for **C**ompact **D**isc-**R**ead **O**nly **M**emory. A CD-ROM is a computer disc that holds visual and audio information. "Read Only" tells you that you can get information from the disc, but you cannot make changes to the disc. In order to use a CD-ROM, you must have a computer with a CD-ROM disc drive. CD-ROMs are popular because they can hold as much as 100,000 pages of information per disc. CD-ROMs can also perform searches, provide interactive graphics, and supply sound. You might use an encyclopedia, dictionary, or other programs on CD-ROM.

Indexes

When researching a topic, you might start by consulting an *index,* which lists topics, sources, or authors. The *Readers' Guide to Periodical Literature,* for example, helps readers find articles, poems, and stories from more than two hundred magazines and journals. The guide lists articles alphabetically both by author and by subject. Each entry has a heading printed in boldface capital letters. In the front of the *Readers' Guide* is a guide to abbreviations that appear in the entries. Below is an example of an online *Readers' Guide* entry. The next page shows an example from the printed version.

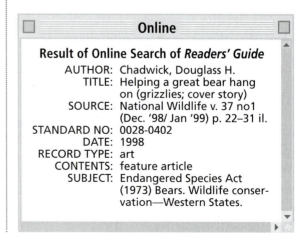

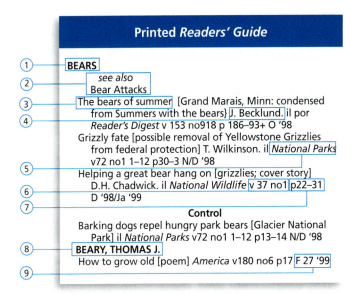

Internet The *Internet* does not exist in one place. Instead, it is a network, or web of connections, among computers all over the world. While the Internet was originally created to share science information, it has expanded today to include sites on virtually any topic. Many libraries have computers that you can use to connect to the Internet. The most popular way to view information on the Internet is through a World Wide Web browser. (See also **World Wide Web** on page 281.)

Microforms *Microforms* are photographs of articles from newspapers and magazines that have been reduced to take up less space. Two types of microforms are *microfilm,* a continuous roll of film, and *microfiche,* small cards of film. To use microforms, you must also use machines that magnify the information and project it onto a screen for you to read.

Newspapers Newspapers include different types of reading materials that are often contained in several separate sections. As a reader, you probably read the various parts of a newspaper for different reasons.

If you are reading to learn about differing viewpoints or opinions on an issue, read the editorial section. The editorial section is also a good place to get ideas for persuasive papers. As you read an editorial, identify points with which you agree or disagree. Also, try to identify the reasons and evidence the writer uses.

If you want to find information or gain knowledge, try reading the city, state, or national news sections. For each news story you read, ask yourself the *5W–How?* questions (see page 60). If you use the news story as a source for one of your papers, be sure to put the information into your own words.

If you want to be entertained, you might want to read the comics or the entertainment section.

Online Catalog

The *online catalog* is stored on a computer. To find the call number for a book, type in the title, the author, or the subject of the book. The computer will show the results of your search. The results are a little different in each library, but the search results that follow are typical.

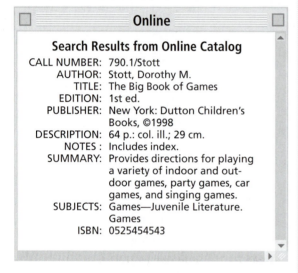

Online Databases

Online databases are collections of information stored on a computer. You can use online databases to search for information. They are usually created for specific groups or organizations. Many databases require users to pay a fee, but other databases are free. You can use the World Wide Web to access some databases.

Once you have accessed a database, search for specific topics by typing in a *keyword* or key phrase. You can print out the information you find. The results of the search for articles about bears in the *Online Readers' Guide* on page 278 is an example of an online database.

Online Sources

An *online source* is a source of information that can be accessed only by computer. You can find and access online information through computer networks. A network is a group of computers connected by telephone lines, by fiber-optic cables, or via satellite. Computer networks make the Internet and the World Wide Web possible.

Radio, Television, Film, and Video

Some of the most common sources of information today are *radio* and *television*. You can find news broadcasts, newsmagazines, and documentaries on radio and television stations every day. Additional educational programs are available on *film* or *video*. To find shows that might have information you need, consult magazines or newspaper listings that contain descriptions of radio and television programs. If you want to rent or borrow a video, check out books that have descriptions of educational videos. You might find several books of video listings at your local library. Before using a film or video as a source of information, check the ratings to make sure it is appropriate. (See also **Critical Viewing** on page 328 and **Media Messages** on page 314.)

Reference Sources

Type	Description	Examples
Encyclopedias	• many volumes • articles arranged alphabetically by subject • good source for general information	*Collier's Encyclopedia* *Compton's Encyclopedia* *The World Book Multimedia Encyclopedia*™
General Biographical References	• information about birth, nationality, and major accomplishments of outstanding people	*Current Biography* *Dictionary of American Biography* *The International Who's Who* *World Biographical Index on CD-ROM*
Atlases	• maps and geographical information	*Atlas of World Cultures* *National Geographic Atlas of the World*
Almanacs	• up-to-date information about current events, facts, statistics, and dates	*The Information Please Almanac, Atlas and Yearbook* *The World Almanac and Book of Facts*
Books of Synonyms	• lists of more interesting or more exact words to express ideas	*Roget's International Thesaurus* *Webster's New Dictionary of Synonyms*

Reference Sources There are many different kinds of reference sources, print and nonprint, that you can use to find specific kinds of information. Most libraries devote an entire section to reference works. The chart above lists some of the reference sources you might use.

Vertical File Many libraries have a ***vertical file,*** a filing cabinet containing up-to-date materials such as newspaper clippings, booklets, and pamphlets.

World Wide Web (***WWW*** or the ***Web***) The ***World Wide Web*** is part of the Internet. It is a system of connected documents, called ***Web pages*** or ***Web sites.*** These pages or sites contain text, graphics, and multimedia presentations such as video and audio. The documents on the Web are connected by *hyperlinks.* By clicking on a **hyperlink** you can navigate from one Web site to another. To use the World Wide Web, you must use a computer that has Internet software installed. The following terms will help you.

Using Print and Electronic Sources

- **Browser**   A *browser* is software that allows you to find and view Web pages. A browser also allows you to download, or get and save, software or files. Using a browser to read your way around the Web is called *browsing*. (See also **Web site** on this page.)

- **Hyperlink**   A *hyperlink* is a connection from one place on the Web to another. Hyperlinks, also known as *links,* might appear as words or icons. By clicking on them, you can move to another place on the same Web page or to a different Web page or site. Hyperlinks are usually a different color from the other text and underlined.

- **Search engine**   A search engine is a program used for searching for information on the World Wide Web. (See also **World Wide Web, Searching** on page 283.)

- **URL**   (*U*niform *R*esource *L*ocator) A *URL* is the specific address of a Web page. URLs may include words, abbreviations, numbers, and punctuation. Below is a URL with its parts labeled.

1	2	3

    http://www.go.hrw.com/programs/science

    1. The language used by the Internet service
    2. The *hostname.* The hostname is made up of a series of domains. Reading from right to left, each domain gives your computer more and more specific information when you send it out to look for a Web site. In the example above, *com* tells your computer that the Web site you want is a part of a commercial network. In the same example, *hrw* is the name of the company whose computer contains the Web site, and *go* is the specific machine within *hrw* that contains the Web site.

    Here are the abbreviations of the most common networks.

Common Networks on the World Wide Web	
com	commercial or individual
edu	educational
gov	governmental
org	usually nonprofit organization

    3. The specific address of the page requested. Not all URLs contain this last part.

- **Web site** (or **Web page**) A Web site or Web page is a location on the World Wide Web. The *home page* is the first page on a Web site. A typical home page gives you an overview of the Web site's contents. It also contains hyperlinks to pages within the Web site and sometimes hyperlinks to other Web sites. (See also **Hyperlink** on this page.) Other information on a home page includes information about the site's author or sponsor as well as the date the site was last updated. On the next page is an example of a Web page viewed with a browser program.

1. **Toolbar** The buttons on the toolbar let you move back to previous pages, move forward, print a page, search for information, or see or hide images.
2. **Location indicator** This box shows you the address (URL) of the site you are currently viewing.
3. **Content area** The area of the screen where the Web page appears.
4. **Hyperlink** Click on these buttons to find information and other Web sites available through the browser.
5. **Scroll bar** Clicking along the horizontal or vertical scroll bar (or on the arrows at either end) allows you to move left to right or up and down in the image area.

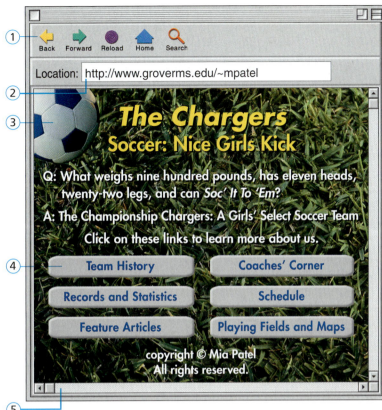

World Wide Web, Searching

The World Wide Web is full of information, but you must find it before you can use it. Luckily, there are tools to help you find what you need. You can search the Internet by using a *search engine* or a *directory*.

- **Search engines** When you use a search engine, you look for Web sites by doing a *keyword search*. A **keyword search** lets you look for Web sites that contain specific words or phrases. Type important words about your topic in the space provided on the search engine screen. Then press the Return key or click on the Search or Find button. The search engine will provide a list of sites that fit your search. Sites that contain all of your keywords will be at the top of the list.

Sometimes your keyword search will list too many Web sites to look at, or sometimes it may not find any sites at all. When this happens, you need to narrow your keyword search. Try the following strategies to narrow your searches, or consult the Help section of your search engine for other ideas.

Refining a Key Word Search	
Tip	**How It Works**
Use specific terms.	Words have many different, and sometimes unexpected, meanings. Using more specific words can help you get just the right results.
	EXAMPLE To find information on making videos, enter *video production* instead of *movies*.
Put words that go together as a phrase into quotation marks.	If you are searching for a phrase, type it in quotation marks. The search engine will find sites that use the words exactly as they are typed.
	EXAMPLE Type in "computer games" to find information on the latest gaming software instead of information on types of computers or board games.
Use *AND* and *NOT*.	You can narrow your search by using the words *AND* and *NOT*. Placing *AND* between two words will narrow your results to pages that contain both words. Putting *NOT* between two words will help exclude sites with information you do not want.
	EXAMPLE Type in "Brooklyn Bridge" AND "Golden Gate Bridge" to find sites on both the Brooklyn and Golden Gate bridges.
	To find sites about the human heart, but not romance, enter "heart NOT love."
Use *OR*.	Using *OR* can make your search broader. The results list will include sites that contain any of your important words.
	EXAMPLE Type in "Brooklyn Bridge" OR "Golden Gate Bridge" to find sites that discuss either the Brooklyn Bridge or Golden Gate Bridge.

■ **Directories**   A directory is an organized list of Web sites. Directories organize sites into categories, such as *sports*. Each category is broken down into smaller and smaller categories, helping you narrow your search. Most search engine sites include directories.

World Wide Web, Web Site Evaluation   The World Wide Web is full of information because anyone can post sites there. Since no one supervises the Web, you are much more likely to find false information there than you are in a newspaper or book. Follow the tips on the next page to **evaluate** Web sites you use.

Evaluating Web Sites	
Questions to Ask	**Why You Should Ask**
Who created the Web site? Who is the Web site's sponsor?	The creator or sponsor of a Web site chooses its content. Look on the site's home page to find the author or sponsor. Make sure you use only Web sites that are sponsored by trustworthy organizations, such as government agencies, universities, and museums. To help identify these sites, look for URLs containing *edu, gov,* or *org*. National news organizations are also good sources of information.
When was the page first posted? Has it been updated?	Look for this information at the end of the home page. It sometimes includes the copyright notice, date last updated, and a link to the creator's e-mail. Make sure you use only up-to-date information.
What links to other Web pages does the site include?	The most trustworthy Web sites will usually provide links to other trusted sites. Look at the links provided to get hints about the quality of this site.
Is the Web site objective?	Objective sites present ideas from both sides and focus on facts rather than opinions. Avoid sites that appear to use fictional support for ideas or claims.
Is the Web site well designed?	Look for easy-to-read type, clear graphics, and working links. Well-designed and well-maintained Web sites are easy to read and navigate. Sites should also have correct spelling, punctuation, and grammar.

You can avoid spending a lot of time evaluating a Web site—not only for accuracy but also for relevance to your needs—if you learn to make **predictions.** When you see a list of search results, consider the title of each site to predict the content and the viewpoint of the Web site. If the title sounds appropriate, look at the home page. Professional-looking design, relevant photos, and clear organization may lead you to predict that the site will be useful to you. On the other hand, if you see misspelled words, cluttered graphics, or other unprofessional signs, you might instead try a different site from your list of search results.

Quick Reference Handbook

Reading and Vocabulary

Reading

Skills and Strategies

You can become a better reader by using the following skills and strategies.

Author's Point of View, Determining
The opinion or attitude an author expresses is called **point of view,** or **bias.** Figuring out the author's point of view can help you evaluate what you are reading. (See also page 157.)

EXAMPLE   Philately (fə•lat′′l•ē), or the study of postage stamps, is an interesting way to learn about the world. When you examine stamps from around the world, you learn about history, different cultures, and art all at the same time.

Author's point of view: Collecting stamps is interesting and educational.

Author's Purpose, Determining
An author has a reason, or **purpose,** for writing. An author may write to inform, to persuade, to express feelings, or to entertain. Determining an author's purpose will help you decide if his or her conclusions are fair.

EXAMPLE   Skateboarding is an exciting and athletic sport. It combines speed with control and is safe as long as it is done in a properly designed park with safety pads and helmets. If you want a fun way to stay fit, pick up your skateboard!

Author's purpose: To persuade people that skateboarding is a good form of exercise.

Cause-and-Effect Relationships, Analyzing
A **cause** makes something happen, and an **effect** is what happens as a result of that cause. Ask "Why?" and "What are the effects?" as you read to examine causes and effects. (See also page 65.)

EXAMPLE   Many traditional medicines of Asia use the bones and body parts of tigers. Local people can make a large amount of money by poaching, or illegally hunting, and selling parts of tigers. Because their parts are so valuable, tigers are close to extinction.

Analysis: The *cause* is killing tigers to sell their parts for medicines. The *effect* is that tigers are threatened with extinction.

Clue Words, Using Writers often use certain *clue words* to connect their ideas. The type of clue words a writer uses can help readers understand what type of organization the author is using. (See also **Text Structures** on page 291.)

Clue Words	
Cause-Effect Pattern	
as a result	since
because	so that
if . . . then	therefore
nevertheless	this led to
Chronological Order	
after	first, second
as	now
before	then
finally	when
Comparison-Contrast Pattern	
although	however
as well as	on the other hand
but	unless
either . . . or	yet
Listing Pattern	
also	most important
for example	to begin with
in fact	
Problem-Solution Pattern	
as a result	this led to
nevertheless	thus
therefore	

Conclusions, Drawing You draw *conclusions* about a text by combining information that you read with information you already know. (See also page 192.)

EXAMPLE   The ancient Egyptian process of mummification was expensive and time-consuming. The entire process took seventy days and involved various ceremonies. Tombs where the mummies were laid to rest were sometimes crowded with furniture and models of other everyday items.

Conclusion: Most ancient Egyptians who were mummified were wealthy people in life.

Fact and Opinion, Distinguishing
A *fact* is a statement you can prove with an outside source. An **opinion** gives a personal belief or attitude, so it cannot be proved true or false. Writers often support their opinions with facts. Distinguishing facts from opinions can help you be a better reader. (See also page 231.)

EXAMPLE

Fact: The earliest armor of European knights of the Middle Ages was a short leather or cloth tunic known as a *hauberk*. [You could look this up in an encyclopedia or dictionary and find that it is true.]

Opinion: Knights of the Middle Ages were kindhearted soldiers. [This is what one writer thinks or believes. The statement cannot be proved true in every case.]

Generalizations, Forming
Generalizations are formed by gathering information as you read and connecting it to your own experiences to make a

Reading

judgment or statement about the world in general. (See also page 21.)

EXAMPLE Students at Jordan Middle School are now eating healthier meals at lunch. Inspired by student requests, cafeteria workers have stopped cooking fried, greasy foods and have created new recipes using fresh fruits and vegetables. While some school officials worried that students would not like the new menu, cafeteria sales have actually gone up. It seems that healthy food is the newest trend at Jordan Middle School.

Generalization: Many young people prefer healthy choices for lunch to fatty, fried foods.

Implied Main Idea, Identifying

Sometimes the main idea of a piece of writing is not directly stated but only suggested or *implied*. To identify an implied main idea, read the text and think about the details in it. Then, create a statement that expresses the text's overall meaning. (See also page 53 and **Stated Main Idea** on page 291.)

EXAMPLE Many students sleep less than seven hours a night. In a school survey, sixty percent of the students complained of being tired during the school day. Fifteen percent of the students admitted that they had fallen asleep during class. This sleepiness makes it difficult to pay attention and learn at school.

Implied main idea: Students should get more than seven hours of sleep.

Inferences, Making

Making an *inference* is making a guess based on what you read and what you already know about the topic. *Conclusions*, *generalizations*, and *predictions* are types of inferences. Making inferences helps you to understand ideas about the situation in the text even though the author does not directly state them. (See also **Conclusions** and **Generalizations** on page 287 and **Predicting** on page 289.)

EXAMPLE Aruna sprang out of bed and quickly put on her soccer uniform, making sure she had her lucky socks. She ate a nutritious breakfast and tried not to be worried. As her dad drove her to the field she rehearsed the plays in her mind. When she met her team, each girl had an air of nervous determination about her.

Inference: Aruna is about to play in an important soccer game.

Paraphrasing

To *paraphrase* is to express an author's ideas in your own words. Paraphrasing helps you understand complicated readings. *Plagiarism* is copying someone else's words and ideas and claiming that they are your own. Since a paraphrase is a rewording of another piece of writing, a paraphrased passage is usually around the same length as the original. A brief rewording that explains the key ideas of the original passage is called a *summary*. (See the chart on page 317 for **Paraphrasing Guidelines**.)

EXAMPLE A well-known French marine scientist and filmmaker, Jacques Cousteau spent much of his life exploring underwater. He contributed to the invention of the Aqua-Lung™, a breathing apparatus that allowed divers to stay underwater longer. Cousteau made films about his ocean explorations and won Academy Awards for *The Silent World* in 1956 and *World Without Sun* in 1966.

Paraphrase: Jacques Cousteau was a French filmmaker who explored the ocean as a diver and marine scientist. He contributed to the creation of the Aqua-Lung™, a breathing device for divers. Two of Cousteau's films about the ocean, *The Silent World* and *World Without Sun,* won Academy Awards.

Persuasive Techniques, Analyzing

When writers want to convince readers to think or act in a certain way, they may use *persuasive techniques.* Some persuasive techniques include using facts, reasons, and evidence. Other persuasive techniques use words and ideas that create an emotional reaction. Watch out for persuasive arguments that use only *emotional appeals.* (See also page 257.)

EXAMPLE Homelessness is a problem that will not be solved until more people get involved in the solution. Many programs exist to help homeless citizens, including programs that build houses, distribute food, and give temporary shelter. The government recognized the importance of caring for the homeless with the passage of the McKinney Homeless Assistance Act in 1987. If you want to make a difference, you should get involved with solving the problem of homelessness. After all, not everyone is fortunate enough to have a place to call home.

Analysis: The second and third sentences use facts to support the opinion in the first sentence. The last sentence is an emotional appeal aimed at readers' sympathy. It may not be persuasive because it assumes that the readers probably have homes.

Predicting

Predicting is deciding what will happen next. To make predictions, read the passage and use your past experiences to help you guess what will happen next. The point of predicting is to get involved with what you are reading, not to be correct every time. Therefore, it is all right to make a wrong guess. (See also page 86.)

EXAMPLE Jackie Joyner-Kersee approached the starting line at the 1992 Olympics in Barcelona. She had won track competitions since she was fourteen years old. At the 1984 Olympics, Joyner-Kersee won a silver medal in the heptathlon. She won two gold medals in the 1988 Olympics in Seoul, Korea. As Joyner-Kersee took her stance for this latest race, she was once again ready to run for gold.

Prediction: Jackie Joyner-Kersee is about to win another Olympic gold medal.

Problem-Solution Relationships, Analyzing

A *problem* is an unanswered question, while a *solution* is a suggested answer. Authors who write about problems often also write about one or two solutions and try to explain what effects the solutions will have. When you read, ask "What is the problem?" and "Who has the problem?" Then, identify the solutions that the writer suggests.

EXAMPLE A vacant lot in the west side neighborhood of Journeyville had become a dumping area filled with trash. Tired of this eyesore, several neighbors approached the city council about creating a community center building. While the council was in favor of the proposal, they did not have the budget to build the center. Another group of neighbors got together on weekends and began to move the trash. As the land was cleared, they built swing sets and even started a community garden. Now the lot is a bustling center of the community.

Analysis: The problem was that the west Journeyville neighborhood had a vacant lot with too much trash in it. This problem disturbed the neighbors. One possible solution was to have the city create a community center there. Another solution was to create a community park and garden.

Reading Log, Using a When you write informally about what you read, you are keeping a *reading log.* In a reading log, you can write down questions, write about personal connections you make with the reading, or make note of important sections. In addition to writing down your thoughts during reading, you can use your reading log to write down ideas you have before reading (prereading), or after reading (postreading).

Reading Rate, Adjusting *Reading rate* is the speed at which you read something. Readers adjust their reading rates based on their purpose for reading, the difficulty of the reading material, and their knowledge about the subject. The chart at the bottom of this page shows how you can adjust your reading rate for different purposes.

SQ3R SQ3R is a study strategy that you can use when you read. SQ3R is an abbreviation of the five steps in this process:

S *Survey* the passage. Look over the headings, titles, illustrations, charts, and any words in boldface or italics.

Q *Question* yourself about the passage. Make headings, subtitles, and boldface words into questions that you can answer after you read.

R *Read* the entire passage. Answer your questions as you read.

R *Recite,* or say out loud, the answers to your questions.

R *Review,* or look back over, the passage. Read it again quickly and quiz yourself with the questions.

Reading Rates According to Purpose		
Reading Rate	**Purpose**	**Example**
Scanning	Quickly reading for specific details	Finding the last name of a character in a novel
Skimming	Quickly reading for main points	Previewing a chapter from your science textbook by reading the headings before you read the text
Reading for mastery (reading to learn)	Reading to understand and remember	Reading and taking notes from a book for a research report
Reading at a comfortable speed	Reading for enjoyment	Reading a novel by your favorite writer

Stated Main Idea and Supporting Details, Identifying The *main idea* of any piece of writing is its most important idea. Sometimes main ideas are found at the beginning of a paragraph in a topic sentence. Other times, the main idea may be found at the end of the passage, as a conclusion. Main ideas are backed up by *supporting details* that explain and give more information about the main idea. When a main idea is directly stated, it is called an *explicit main idea*. (See also page 53 and **Implied Main Idea** on page 288.)

EXAMPLE Even though they are known as disease-causing organisms, today viruses are being used to fight illnesses. Scientists are using the organisms to produce proteins for research and industry. Also, since viruses carry genetic information, they are being used to carry correct genetic information to defective cells.

Stated main idea: Viruses are being used to combat illnesses.

Supporting details: Viruses are used to produce proteins for research and industry, and they carry correct genetic information to defective cells.

Summarizing A *summary* is a brief restatement of the main points expressed in a piece of writing. Summarizing can help you understand a difficult reading passage. Summaries are similar to paraphrases since summaries restate someone else's ideas in your own words. Summaries, however, are usually much shorter than the original passage because they do not include every detail. (See also **Paraphrasing** on page 288. See the chart on page 318 for **Summarizing Guidelines**.)

EXAMPLE Virtual reality lets even the most couch-bound television watcher feel like he or she is skiing in the Swiss Alps. Virtual reality combines computer-created worlds with a headset that enables a person to see images in three dimensions. By using data gloves that transmit hand motions, a person can seem to be inside the computer environment.

Summary: Virtual reality is a system combining computers, headsets, and data gloves to make a person feel that he or she is within a different setting.

Text Structures, Analyzing *Text structures* are patterns of organization that a writer uses. There are five common patterns: *cause-effect, chronological order, comparison-contrast, listing,* and *problem-solution*. Sometimes a writer may use one pattern, and other times a writer may combine two or more patterns. By understanding the way a piece of writing is organized, you can better understand the information you are reading. These guidelines can help you analyze a text structure:

1. Look for clue words that might hint at a specific pattern of organization. (See also **Clue Words** on page 287.)
2. Look for important ideas and connections between those ideas. Is there an obvious pattern?
3. Draw a graphic organizer to help you understand the text structure. Your graphic organizer may look like one of the five common text structures illustrated on the next two pages.

- *Cause-effect pattern* focuses on the relationship between causes and their effects or results. (See also page 65.) The following chain shows how nutritional education can lead to health and energy.

Causal Chain

learning about nutrition
↓
identifying poor food choices
↓
making better eating choices
↓
feeling healthy and energetic

- *Chronological order* shows events or ideas in the order in which they happen. (See also page 23.) The sequence chain in the next column lists the steps for blowing up a balloon.

Sequence Chain

stretch the balloon
↓
blow air into the balloon
↓
repeat until balloon is full
↓
hold neck of balloon between finger and thumb
↓
use other hand to tie knot in balloon

- *Comparison-contrast pattern* focuses on how two or three ideas or events are alike or different. (See also page 124.) The Venn diagram at the bottom of the page compares a human brain and a computer.
- *Listing pattern* organizes information in a list form using classifications such

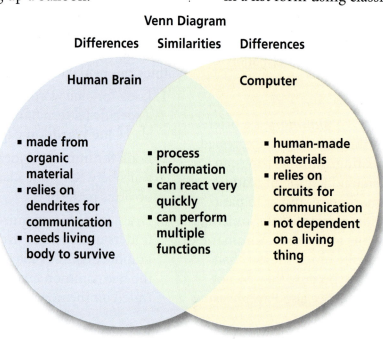

Venn Diagram

Differences — Similarities — Differences

Human Brain

- made from organic material
- relies on dendrites for communication
- needs living body to survive

- process information
- can react very quickly
- can perform multiple functions

Computer

- human-made materials
- relies on circuits for communication
- not dependent on a living thing

as importance, size, location, or other important criteria. The list below organizes dogs by size.

List
Dogs of Different Sizes
1. Chihuahua (small)
2. cocker spaniel (medium)
3. Saint Bernard (large)

- *Problem-solution pattern* focuses on one or more problems and solutions to the problem. The pattern also explains the outcomes of each solution and the final results of the problem and solution. (See also page 74.) The following example shows a problem and some possible solutions.

Cluster

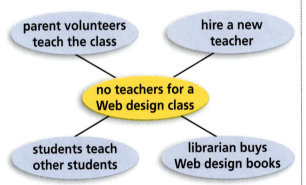

Transitional Words and Phrases, Identifying
Transitions are words and phrases writers use to connect ideas and to make writing read more smoothly. By identifying transitions, you can understand how the ideas in a piece of writing fit together.

Visuals and Graphics, Interpreting
Visuals and *graphics* communicate information with pictures or symbols. Visuals and graphics can communicate very complex information in a simple way. When you read writing that contains visuals or graphics, examine the information and draw your own conclusions.

- **Elements** Effective visuals and graphics contain the following elements. (See also page 269.)
    1. A *title* identifies the subject or main idea of the graphic.
    2. The *body* of the visual gives information in the form of a graph, chart, time line, diagram, or table.
    3. *Labels* identify and explain the information shown in the visual or graphic.
    4. A box called a *legend* may be included to identify symbols, colors, or scales to help the reader interpret the graphic.
    5. The *source* tells where the information in the graphic was found; knowing the source helps readers evaluate the accuracy of the graphic.

- **Types** Several common types of visuals are *charts, diagrams, graphs, tables,* and *time lines.*
    1. **Charts** show how the parts of something relate to the whole thing. In the *pie chart* on the next page, notice how all of the segments contribute to the whole picture. Pie charts often do not show specific numbers but focus on percentages instead.

Reading 293

Types of Volunteers

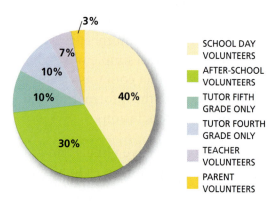

- SCHOOL DAY VOLUNTEERS
- AFTER-SCHOOL VOLUNTEERS
- TUTOR FIFTH GRADE ONLY
- TUTOR FOURTH GRADE ONLY
- TEACHER VOLUNTEERS
- PARENT VOLUNTEERS

Number of Students Tutored Through Volunteer Program

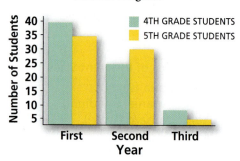

2. **Diagrams** use symbols (such as circles or arrows) or pictures to compare ideas, show a process, or show how an object is built. The following diagram shows how to make a "valley fold," a typical starting step in the Japanese art of origami.

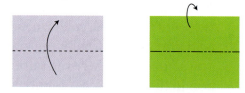

3. **Graphs,** including bar graphs and line graphs, show changes or trends over time. In a graph, the horizontal line, called an axis, represents points in time such as hours, days, or years. The vertical axis shows quantities or amounts. When you read graphs, check to see that the amounts on the axes are clearly marked. Also, look at the starting points of both axes to help you read the graph correctly. Notice that the same information is presented in the following bar graph and line graph.

Number of Students Tutored Through Volunteer Program

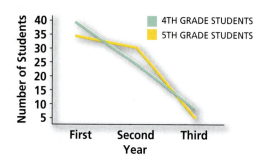

4. **Tables** give information in a simple way. Tables do not include symbols or graphics that show patterns in the information. Instead, readers must think carefully about the information found in a table and draw their own conclusions. For example, a reader might conclude based on the following table that the number of volunteer tutors increases every year.

Number of Volunteers in the Peer Tutoring Program	
First year	8
Second year	10
Third year	15

5. **Time lines** place events in order as they take place over a period of time. In the example below, the events are identified below the time line, while segments of time are shown above it.

Development of the Tutoring Program

Fall of first year	Spring of first year	Second year	Third year
Tutored only during school day		Began recruiting parent volunteers	
	Expanded to after-school tutoring		Nearly doubled number of volunteers

■ **Viewing tips** When you come across graphics or visuals, stop and examine the information. Use the tips below to help you understand graphics.

1. Read the title, labels, and legend of a graphic before you try to analyze the information.
2. Draw your own conclusions from the graphic and compare them to the writer's conclusions.
3. Ask yourself if the graphic might be leaving out information. Sometimes, an author leaves out information that does not agree with his or her conclusions.

Vocabulary

Skills and Strategies

You can use the following skills and strategies to become a more effective reader.

Context Clues One way to figure out the meaning of an unfamiliar word is by finding clues in its **context,** the words and sentences surrounding it. This chart shows some of the most common types of context clues. (See also page 25.)

How to Use Context Clues
Type of Clue
Definitions and Restatements: Look for the meaning of the unfamiliar word restated in other words somewhere in the sentence. *Dionne's little brother continued to **aggravate** her, doing all the things that bother her.* [Aggravate must mean "bother."]
Examples: Look for an example that gives you clues to the meaning of the unfamiliar word. *Malik had many **aspirations**, such as his dream of being a doctor.* [Aspirations must be "dreams."]
Synonyms: Look for a word that has a similar meaning used in the context. *The **faculty** of our school is well-educated. Most of the teachers have advanced degrees.* [Faculty must mean "teachers."]

(continued)

(continued)

How to Use Context Clues
Type of Clue
Antonyms or Contrasts: Look for words that have an opposite meaning of the unfamiliar word. *My favorite aunt is **eccentric**. Her attitudes are anything but typical.* [*Eccentric* must mean "not typical."]
Cause and Effect: Look for clues that an unfamiliar word is related to the cause or is the result of a cause. *When Jaime **ridiculed** my hat, I felt embarrassed and took it off.* [*Ridicule* must mean "make fun of."]

Word Bank You can create a *word bank* by making a list of unfamiliar words you encounter. Creating your own word bank can help you improve your vocabulary. When you add a word to your bank, look up its definition in the dictionary. You might keep your word bank in a notebook or in a computer file.

Word Meanings The meanings of words change over time or in the situations in which they are used. You always want your words to say exactly what you mean. The following definitions and examples can help.

- **Clichés and tired words** A *cliché* is an overused expression. These expressions were once fresh and expressive, but their overuse has made them seem dull and tired. Clichés weaken your writing.

  EXAMPLES *fresh as a daisy, easy as pie, so hungry I could eat a horse*

  A *tired word* has been used so often and so carelessly that it has become worn out and almost meaningless.

  EXAMPLES *nice, fine, pretty, terrific*

- **Denotation and connotation** A word's direct, "dictionary" definition is called its **denotation.** Words also have a **connotation,** the emotional meanings a word suggests. Connotations can have powerful effects on readers and listeners.

  EXAMPLES The words *firm* and *strict* have very similar denotations. However, *firm* has the positive connotation of being stable. *Strict* has more a negative connotation of being harsh and severe.

- **Figurative language** *Figurative language* is the imaginative use of words and phrases to describe one thing by comparing it to something else. Figurative language requires the reader to look beyond the literal, or usual, meaning of the words.

Type of Figurative Language	Example
A **metaphor** directly compares one thing to another.	Daisies are little suns shining in a field.
Personification uses human characteristics to describe non-human things.	The plants stretched their arms toward the sun.
A **simile** compares two different things using the words *like* or *as*.	The dancers floated across the floor like leaves blowing in the wind.

■ **Idioms**   *Idioms* are phrases with a different meaning than each word's literal, or usual, meaning. Idioms are frequently common to a particular region, culture, or time period. They cannot be explained grammatically or translated word-for-word.

EXAMPLES
She was *sitting on pins and needles* as she waited.
Jim went *out on a limb* and asked another question.
Last night Sarah and Javier went out and *cut a rug*.

■ **Loaded words**   *Loaded words* are terms that are used to have a strong positive or negative impact on the reader or listener. Loaded words can be very persuasive since they appeal to the reader's or listener's emotions.

EXAMPLES
Leah *frowned* at her dog's *misbehavior*.
Leah *scowled* at her dog's *disobedience*.

■ **Multiple meanings**   Many words have several different meanings. To determine which meaning is being used, look at the word's context. If you still have difficulty figuring out the meaning, look up the word in the dictionary and read each meaning. Then, try each meaning in the sentence to pick the correct one. (See also page 56.)

EXAMPLE   As we sailed out on the choppy waves of the lake, my brother looked *green*.
green (grēn) *adj.* **1.** relating to the color found in grass and plants; **2.** naive and inexperienced; **3.** sickly and nauseated [The third definition best fits the context.]

Word Origins   See **The History of English** on page 272.

Word Parts   Many words in English are made up of smaller *word parts.* These word parts are known as *roots, prefixes,* and *suffixes.* Knowing the meanings of word parts can help you understand the meanings of unfamiliar words.

■ **Roots**   The *root* is the foundation on which a word is built. The root contains the word's basic meaning. Prefixes and suffixes are added to the root. (See also page 196.)

Commonly Used Roots		
Root	**Meaning**	**Example**
–audio–	hearing, sound	audience
–bibli–, –biblio–	book	bibliography
–log(ue)–, –logy–	study, word	geology
–magni–	large	magnificent
–micro–	small	microscope
–ped–	foot	pedestrian
–phon–	sound	telephone

■ **Prefixes**   A *prefix* is a word part that is added before a root. When a prefix is added to a root, the word it forms is a combination of the prefix and the root meaning. (See also page 126.)

Vocabulary   297

Commonly Used Prefixes

Prefix	Meaning	Example
anti–	against, opposing	antiwar
bi–	two	bicycle
dis–	away, opposing	disagree
mis–	wrong	mistake
non–	not	nonfat
over–	above, too much	overdone
pre–	before	preread
re–	again	replace
semi–	half	semicircle
sub–	under	submarine
un–	not	unhappy

■ **Suffixes** A *suffix* is a word part that is added after a root. Adding a suffix may change both a word's meaning and its part of speech, as in *joy/joyful*. (See also page 126.)

Commonly Used Suffixes

Suffix	Meaning	Example
–able	can, will	respectable
–dom	state, condition	kingdom
–en	make	weaken
–ful	full of	stressful
–hood	state, condition	neighborhood
–ish	suggesting, like	feverish
–less	without	penniless
–ly	characteristic of	quickly
–ment	result, act of	commitment
–ness	quality, state	goodness, sadness
–ous	characterized by	luxurious

Words to Learn You can study the 300 words below to improve your vocabulary this year. Try to learn as many unfamiliar words from this list as you can.

abdomen
absorb
abundant
acquire
adjust
amateur
ambitious
analyze
anthem
apologize
applaud
application
appreciate
appropriate
architect
arid
associate
assume
astonish
aviation

ballot
barrier
benefit
betray
biography
boast
bombard
Braille
bureau

campaign
candidate
captivity
career
caution
ceremony
characteristic
collapse
collide
commotion
competition
complaint
complex
compliment
conceal
conduct
conference
congratulate
conscience
consent
contrast
contribute
conviction

cooperate
corporation
counterfeit
courteous
cultivate

dainty
debate
debt
decrease
definite
demonstration
deny
departure
descendant
descriptive
desirable
desperate
destination
detect
determination
disadvantage
disastrous
discomfort
discourage
disguise
disgust
dissolve
district
disturb
document
doubtful
doubtless
dramatic
dread
duplicate

earnest
eavesdrop
eliminate
employer
engage
entertain
envy

error
escort
essential
establish
eternal
exception
exclaim
exert
export
extraordinary

fatal
feat
flammable
flexible
flourish
foe
foul
foundation
fragrant
frantic
furious

gasp
generation
generous
genuine
glimpse
gorgeous
gossip
gratitude
guidance

hazard
hearty
heir
heroic
hesitate
hibernate
hoist
honorable

identical
ignite
imitate

impatience
import
impostor
inaccurate
incident
inexpensive
inform
inhale
innumerable
inspiration
instinct
interrupt
interview
intrusion
investment
inviting
involve
irregular
issue

jeopardy
journalism
justify
juvenile

keen
knapsack

legend
leisure
license
linger
locally
lunar
luscious
luxurious

majority
mammoth
management
marvel
maximum
merchandise
migrate
miraculous

mobile
mourning

navigator
nominate
notion
nuisance
numerous

oath
obvious
occasion
offense
offspring
omit
ordinary
ornamental

paralysis
particle
persuade
pharmacy
pierce
plead
plot
pollute
portion
possess
precipitation
predict
prehistoric
previous
prey
privacy
profession
prohibit
promotion
protest
portrait
provoke
pry
publicity

qualify
quantity

Vocabulary 299

quarantine
quote

ransom
rash
reaction
realm
rebel
receipt
reckless
reduction
reference
regret
regulate
rehearsal
reign
relate
reliable
remedy
request
requirement
resemble

reservoir
resident
resign
respectable
responsibility
revolution
routine

sacrifice
satisfy
scheme
scholar
security
self-confidence
self-respect
separation
session
severe
simplify
solitary
specify
static

stray
suburbs
summarize
superior
surgery
survey
survival
suspicion
symbol
sympathy

temporary
tension
terminal
terrain
text
theme
thorough
threat
toll
toxic
tradition

tragedy
transparent
twilight

unexpectedly
unfavorable
unfortunate
unite
urge

vacuum
vault
vicinity
victim
victorious
villain
visual
vivid
vocal

wardrobe
widespread

yacht

Speaking and Listening

Speaking

You probably enjoy having conversations with your friends. You can build on the skills you use in conversations to develop new speaking skills for different situations. Use the strategies in this section to become a more effective speaker.

Formal Speaking

In formal speaking, a specific time and place are set aside for someone to give a presentation to a group. The purpose of this presentation may be to inform, to persuade, to discuss problems and solutions, or to entertain.

Content and Organization of a Presentation
The following steps can help you create an effective presentation.

1. **Choose a topic.** Sometimes, your topic will be assigned. However, when you are free to choose your own topic, try one or more of these ideas.
   - Consider turning a piece you have written into a presentation.
   - Brainstorm a list of topics.
   - Re-read your journal to find ideas.
   - Ask friends, family members and teachers for ideas.
   - Look through magazines and newspapers.

2. **Identify the purpose and occasion of your presentation.** Your *purpose* is why you are speaking—what you want your presentation to accomplish. The purpose of your presentation will help you determine your word choice and usage (formal or informal). Here are some common purposes for presentations.

Purposes for Presentations	
Purpose	**Examples of Presentation Titles**
To inform give facts, explain how to do something, or present a problem and propose a solution	• Life Aboard a Covered Wagon • How to Choose a Bike Helmet • How We Can Protect Coral Reefs

(continued)

(continued)

Purposes for Presentations	
Purpose	Examples of Presentation Titles
To persuade attempt to change opinions or get listeners to take action	• Where's Our School Spirit? • Hidden Dangers on the Playground
To entertain share a funny or interesting story or event	• A Birthday to Remember • My First Home Run

The *occasion* is the event or situation that prompts you to speak. Often, the occasion may be a class assignment. At other times it may be a meeting of a club you belong to or an awards ceremony. Reviewing what you know about the occasion will help you prepare a presentation. For example, think about the date, the time of day, the place, and how much time you will have.

3. **Think about your audience.** Knowing the occasion will give you a general idea of who your audience will be. Consider your listeners' needs and interests and use words they will understand. The questions in the following chart can help you. Your answers may also help you decide on your **point of view,** or the way you will approach your topic.

Analyzing Your Audience		
Question	If your answer is . . .	Your presentation should . . .
How much does the audience already know about the topic?	not much	provide background information about the topic
	some	connect information the audience may not know to what they already know
	a lot	share new and interesting information
How interested in the topic do you think the audience will be?	very interested	keep the audience interested by spacing out surprising ideas or information
	a little interested	get the audience more interested by beginning with a question or a surprising fact
	not interested	show the audience how the topic affects them personally

4. **Gather information.** For some topics, you can draw information from your own experience or papers you have already written. For others, you may need to do research. You can read newspapers and magazines, check the Internet, or talk to people who know the topic well. (See also **Library/Media Center** on page 276.)

5. **Organize your information.** Organizing your ideas for a presentation is like arranging information for a written paper. You will include an introduction that states your main idea, support your main idea with evidence, examples, and elaboration, and summarize your main points in a conclusion. Below is an example of a plan for a specific kind of presentation, one that explores a problem and a possible solution.
   - Define the problem.
   - Support your definition with evidence (reasons, facts, and the opinions of experts).
   - Present your ideas about the problem's causes (*Why is this happening?*) and effects (*What are the results?*).
   - Suggest a solution, and show how it is connected to the problem.
   - Present evidence showing why your solution is a good one.

   See the Writing Workshops in this book for ways to arrange information for other purposes.

6. **Make note cards.** Each note card for your speech should have notes on only one major point and include supporting details that elaborate on that point. Make a special note on the card to remind you when to show or refer to a visual in your speech. Number your note cards to help you keep them in order.

7. **Use media.** Consider including media such as visuals or sounds in your speech if they will make your ideas clearer or help listeners remember an important point. Media should be easy for you to use and easy for your audience to see, hear, and understand. Otherwise, you may lose your train of thought or confuse your listeners. Here are forms of media you might consider using.
   - electronic media, including Web pages
   - audio recordings such as CDs or cassettes
   - audiovisual recordings, including videotapes, videodiscs, and short films
   - slides or filmstrips
   - traditional visuals such as charts, graphs, illustrations, and diagrams

   (See also **Creating Visuals to Share Information** on pages 220–221.)

Delivery of a Presentation

These steps will help you give your presentation.

1. **Practice.** Practice your presentation until you are sure you know it well. Ask friends or family members to listen to your speech and suggest ways to make it better. If you plan to use visuals or other media, be sure to include them in your practice.

2. Deliver your presentation. Use these tips to help you deliver your presentation effectively.

- *Stay calm and confident.* Before you begin speaking, take a deep breath. Stand up straight, look alert, and pay attention to what you are saying.
- *Use body language.* The chart below lists nonverbal signals, or body language, that will add to your message.

Nonverbal Signals

Eye contact
Look into the eyes of your audience members
Purposes
- Shows that you are honest or sincere
- Keeps audience's attention

Facial expression
Smile, frown, raise an eyebrow
Purposes
- Shows your feelings
- Emphasizes parts of your message

Gestures
Give thumbs up, shrug, nod, or shake your head
Purposes
- Emphasizes your point
- Adds meaning to the speech

Posture
Stand tall and straight
Purpose
- Shows that you are sure of yourself

- *Use your voice effectively.* Here are verbal elements to consider as you practice and deliver your speech. You may adjust these elements depending on your **audience** and the **setting**. For example, you might use a soothing tone with children. If you are giving a morning talk, you might vary your pitch to capture your audience's attention.

Verbal Element	Definition
Diction	Pronounce words clearly, or *enunciate*. Speak carefully so that your listeners can understand you.
Mood (or tone)	Your speech or oral interpretation may make your listeners feel a certain emotion. Making listeners feel happy, angry, or sad about what you are saying can help them remember your points better.
Pitch	Your voice rises and falls naturally when you speak. If you are nervous, your voice may get higher. To control your pitch, take deep breaths and stay calm as you give your speech.
Rate (or tempo)	In conversations you may speak at a fast rate, or speed. When you make a speech, you should talk more slowly to help listeners understand you.
Volume	Even if you normally speak quietly, you will need to speak loudly in a formal speech. Listeners at the back of the room should be able to hear you clearly.

- *Use standard English.* Pronounce words correctly, and use correct grammar. You should avoid using slang or jargon. If you use any technical terms in your speech, define them for your listeners.

Other Formal Speaking Situations

Here are two other types of formal speeches and strategies you might use to give each type of speech.

- **Making an announcement** An *announcement* is a short speech that provides information to a group of listeners. Often, it includes instructions about a current situation or an upcoming event. Write out your message ahead of time, and use the following tips.

How to Make an Announcement

1. Include all the important facts. Most announcements provide the following information:
- the kind of event or situation
- who is involved in the event or situation
- the time and location of the event or situation
- why the event is important
- any special information, such as the cost of admission

2. Add interesting details that will catch your listeners' attention.

3. Announce your message slowly, clearly, and briefly.

4. If necessary, repeat the most important facts.

- **Introducing a speaker** To introduce a speaker to an audience, identify the speaker and tell listeners a little about his or her background. Your introduction should also prepare the audience to hear what the speaker has to say. Make the speaker feel welcome, but keep your comments brief.

Informal Speaking

When you speak informally, you do not plan in advance what you will say. The guidelines that follow will help you to speak more effectively in discussions and in social situations.

Group Discussion Group discussions are an important part of many clubs and classes. To get the most from such discussions, follow these tips.

1. **Set a purpose.** Setting a purpose will help your group identify what you need to accomplish in the time you have. This purpose may be
   - to connect ideas, insights, and experiences with others
   - to cooperate in gaining information
   - to solve a problem
   - to reach a decision or recommend a course of action

2. **Assign roles.** Each person in the group has a role to play. For example, your group may choose a chairperson, whose role is to keep the discussion moving smoothly. Another person may be named the recorder. This person's role is to take notes of what is said during

the discussion. No matter what your role is, use the guidelines below to contribute effectively to the discussion.

Guidelines for Group Discussions

1. Prepare for the discussion. If you know what topic your group will discuss, find out some information about the topic ahead of time.

2. Listen to what others say. Be willing to learn from the other members of your group. Do not interrupt when someone is speaking. Instead, listen and wait until it is your turn to speak.

3. Do your part. Contribute to the discussion by sharing your ideas and knowledge. Encourage other members of the group to do the same, and express your agreement or disagreement with their points in an appropriate way.

4. Stay on the discussion topic. If the discussion gives you other, related ideas, keep your group's purpose in mind. Make a note for yourself about an idea, but only discuss ideas that fit your group's topic and purpose.

5. Ask questions. If you are not sure you understand the point a member of your group is making, summarize it and ask him or her to explain it more clearly. Others in the group may also be confused.

Speaking Socially
In any social situation, remember to speak politely and clearly. The following strategies will help.

■ **Giving directions or instructions** When you need to give directions or explain how to do something, make sure your directions or instructions are clear and complete. Here are some pointers.

How to Give Directions or Instructions

1. Before you give information, plan what you want to say. Think of the information as a series of steps.

2. Explain the steps in order. Be sure you have not skipped any steps or left out important details.

3. If necessary, repeat all of the steps to be sure your listener understands them.

■ **Making introductions** Use these tips to introduce people who do not know each other or to introduce yourself to someone new.

How to Make Introductions

1. You can use first names if you are introducing people your own age. ("Mirha, this is Josh.")

2. Speak first to the older person of the people you are introducing. ("Dad, this is my friend Keisha.")

3. Introduce yourself to others if no one introduces you first. Start a conversation by asking a question.

4. When you need to introduce someone to a large group of people, introduce him or her to just a few people at a time. ("Class, this is Gordon Delgado. Gordon, meet Letrice, Michael, and Bao.")

5. If someone you are meeting offers to shake your hand, do so. You may offer to shake hands with someone your own age.

6. Mention something the two people you are introducing to each other have in common. ("Trey, meet my cousin Li. Li runs as much as you do.")

■ **Speaking on the telephone** It is important to use the telephone courteously. Here are some suggestions.

Guidelines for Telephoning
1. Call at a time that is convenient for the person you are calling.
2. Be sure to dial the correct number. If you reach a wrong number, apologize for the error.
3. Speak clearly. Say who you are when the phone is answered. If the person you are calling is not there, you may want to leave your name, phone number, and a short message.
4. Do not stay on the telephone too long.

Oral Interpretation

An *oral interpretation* is a dramatic reading of a written piece. The purpose of the reading is to entertain.

1. **Choose a selection.** Poems, short stories, and plays can provide you with good material for an oral interpretation.

Type of Literature	Characteristics of a Good Selection
Poem	■ tells a story (an epic or a narrative poem)
	■ has a speaker (uses the word *I*) or has dialogue (a conversation between characters)
	■ expresses a particular emotion
Short story	■ has a beginning, middle, and end
	■ has characters whose words you can act out (a narrator who tells the story or characters who talk to one another)
Play	■ has a beginning, middle, and end
	■ has one or more characters with dialogue

When you choose a selection, think about the occasion. Should you be serious, or can you have some fun? How much time will you have? Also, consider your audience. Will your listeners find the selection interesting? Will they understand its meaning?

2. **Adapt the material.** Sometimes, you may need to shorten a story, poem, or play to make it work as an oral interpretation. To make a shortened version, or *cutting,* follow these suggestions.

How to Make a Cutting
1. Decide where the part of the selection you want to use should begin and end. Follow that part of the story in time order.
2. Cut dialogue tags, such as *she said.*
3. Cut out parts that do not have anything to do with the part of the story you are telling.

3. **Present your interpretation.** Once you have chosen a selection, you can use the following guidelines to help you present it.

- *Prepare a reading script.* A *reading script* is a neatly typed or handwritten copy of the selection marked to show exactly how you will present it.

> **How to Mark a Reading Script**
>
> **1.** Underline words or phrases you plan to stress.
>
> **2.** Use a slash (/) to show each pause.
>
> **3.** Make notes in the margin about when you will raise or lower your voice, use gestures, or create a particular mood. Also, note where to use your voice to show juncture, or connect related ideas.

- *Write an introduction.* You may need to introduce your interpretation to your audience. In your introduction, you can tell what happened before your scene in the story, describe the characters involved, or tell listeners from whose point of view the story is being told (one of the characters, for example).
- *Practice.* Rehearse your selection carefully. Practice reading the material aloud, using voice tone, movements, and emphasis, or stress. Think about how you can make the meaning and mood of the selection clear to your audience. Practice in front of a friend or family member or in front of a mirror until you feel confident about your presentation.

Self-Evaluation

Evaluating means judging. Evaluating your formal speaking is a good way to improve your speaking skills. When you can judge what went well and what did not, you can focus on the areas that need work. After you give a speech or present an oral interpretation, take some time to review your performance. Coming up with a set of **evaluation criteria,** or standards, will help you cover all the bases. In general, evaluation criteria for speaking should look at

- content (what you say—"Did I state a main idea and support it with evidence? Were the media I used easy to see, hear, and understand? Did I handle them well?")
- organization (how you group and order your ideas—"Did I explain my ideas in a clear and logical way?")
- delivery (how you use language and present your ideas)

To come up with specific criteria for delivery, look at the charts on page 304. Ask a question about each of the important ideas covered. For the term *rate,* for example, you might ask "Did I speak at a steady rate?"

You can use these criteria during practice sessions as well as after you speak. They will help you to measure your progress during the year and judge for yourself just how far you have come as a speaker. (See also the **Points to Evaluate** chart on page 313.)

Listening

Active listening means making sense of the information you hear. Becoming an active listener will help you understand and evaluate a speaker's ideas.

Basics of the Listening Process

Like reading, listening is a process. Here are strategies you can use before, during, and after listening to get the most from a spoken message.

Before Listening Take these steps before you begin to listen.

1. **Know why you are listening.** You will be a more effective listener if you remember your purpose for listening. The amount of attention you give to a speaker depends on your purpose for listening. For example, you would probably pay closer attention to your teacher giving directions than to friends discussing a topic that does not interest you. Some common purposes for listening are
   - for enjoyment, entertainment, or appreciation
   - for information or explanation
   - for forming opinions or evaluating ideas
2. **Limit distractions.** Listening is not always easy. The room you are in may be too hot or too cold or too stuffy. You may have other things on your mind. These guidelines will help you make the best of the situation.

Eliminating Barriers to Effective Listening

Stay positive, and focus on the speaker. As you sit down, clear your mind to help you concentrate on what the speaker will say.

Adjust to your surroundings. Be sure to sit where you can see and hear the speaker well.

Prepare to think about the message. Focus on what the speaker is saying, not on how he or she looks, talks, stands, or moves.

Listening to a Speaker Follow these guidelines to be a courteous and effective listener.

- Look at the speaker, and pay attention.
- Do not interrupt the speaker. Do not whisper, fidget, or make distracting noises or movements.
- Respect the speaker's race, accent, clothing, customs, and religion.
- Try to understand the speaker's point of view. Remember that your own point of view or attitude toward the topic affects your judgment.
- Listen to the entire message before you form an opinion about it.
- Take notes. Do not try to write down every word. Instead, focus on the speaker's most important details. (See also **Notes** on page 316.)

Responding to a Speaker Your role as a listener does not end when a presentation is over. Here are some ways to respond to the speaker and add to your understanding of the topic.

- Ask questions. If you did not understand something the speaker said, ask about it. The speaker's response to your question can clear up any confusion, which can help you and others.
- Give positive feedback. Point out one or two things the speaker did well. If you disagree with the speaker's message, find something else to praise, such as the use of media.
- Give constructive criticism. Politely point out something the speaker could do even better the next time.
- Use body language to give positive feedback. Listen to the questions and answers that follow the presentation. Stay seated until the speaker turns to leave.
- Compare your response to the presentation with the responses of others. You may gain a new insight or help someone else gain one.

Listening with a Purpose

Different strategies can help you achieve different purposes for listening. The strategies that follow will help you listen more effectively to appreciate (or be entertained), to comprehend (or understand), and to evaluate a speech.

Listening to Appreciate When you listen to appreciate, you are listening to enjoy what you hear. Usually, you listen to literature or oral tradition for appreciation.

- **Listening to literature** In a way, listening to literature is like reading it yourself. In both situations, you carry out a process, or series of steps.

Listening to Literature

Before you listen

- Preview the work by asking questions. What kind of literature is it—a story, a poem, a play? What is the title? Who wrote it? What is it about?
- Make **predictions** about what you will hear. (A prediction is a guess based on what you already know.) Do not worry about whether your predictions are correct. Making them is a way of sharpening your focus, not a test you must pass.

As you listen

- Picture the characters, actions, and scenes the writer describes.
- Identify the **tone** (the writer's attitude toward the topic) and the **mood** (the emotions, or feelings, the work creates in the listener).
- Connect the work with your own life. Which experiences or feelings seem similar to ones you have had?
- Jot down questions or comments the work brings to mind. Are there any parts you do not understand? What would you like to ask the writer?

Listening to Literature

After you listen

- Respond personally to the work. What did you like or dislike about it? How did it make you feel? What did you learn from it?
- Summarize the selection. What happened in the selection? What did you learn about life from listening to this work?
- Confirm or adjust your predictions. Which ones were right on target? Which ones did you need to change and in what ways?
- Identify how the writer uses elements of literature, such as rhyme, suspense, and imagery. How did these elements help shape the work?

■ **Listening to oral tradition** *Oral traditions* are messages that are passed down from older people to younger people through the spoken word. These messages often take the form of folk tales and songs that use stories to teach a moral—a lesson for living—or to pass down history or culture. The following tips will help you be an active listener when you have the chance to hear such stories.

Strategies for Listening to Oral Tradition

1. Compare the elements of literature in different stories. Many folk tales and folk songs have similar characters, settings, plots, and themes. As you listen, recall stories you know that have similar elements. How are the stories alike, and how are they different?

2. Compare how storytellers use language. A storyteller sometimes uses labels (names for objects or ideas) or sayings that reflect his or her culture or region. For example, depending on a storyteller's region, he or she might use the label *stoop* or *porch* to mean a covered entrance to a house. As you listen to a speaker from a different region or culture, compare his or her sayings and labels with your own.

3. Compare the way the story is told in different regions. Among Native Americans, for example, trickster tales appear widely. Depending on the region, though, the main character—the trickster—could be a raven, a coyote, a mink, a blue jay, a rabbit, a spider, or a human. Often, the geography, wildlife, or weather patterns mentioned are clues to where the story (or the storyteller) is originally from.

Listening to Comprehend Use the steps in the chart below and the strategies on the next page to help you get information from a message you hear.

How to Listen for Information

Find the major ideas.

Identify the most important points the speaker makes. Listen for clue words, such as *major* or *most important*.

Identify supporting evidence.

How does the speaker support the main idea? What details does the speaker emphasize with gestures, visuals, or verbal cues, like "for example"?

(continued)

(continued)

How to Listen for Information

Distinguish between facts and opinions.

A fact is a statement that can be proved to be true. An opinion is a belief or judgment about something. It cannot be proved to be true.

Listen for comparisons and contrasts.

The speaker may emphasize a point or explain an idea by comparing or contrasting it to something familiar to you.

Pay attention to causes and effects.

Does the speaker say or hint that some events cause others to happen? Does the speaker suggest that some events are the results of other events?

Predict outcomes and draw conclusions.

Connect the speaker's words and ideas to your own experiences. What conclusions can you draw about the topic? What might happen as a result of events the speaker discusses?

- **LQ2R** The LQ2R study method is especially helpful when you are listening to a speaker who is giving information.

  L *Listen* carefully to information as it is presented.

  Q *Question* yourself as you listen. Make a list of your questions as you think of them.

  R *Recite* to yourself, in your own words, the answers to your questions as the speaker presents them. Summarize the information in your mind, or jot down notes as you listen.

  R *Relisten* as the speaker concludes the presentation. The speaker may repeat the major points of the speech.

- *5W-How? questions* When you are listening for details, try to sort out information that answers the basic *5W-How?* questions: *Who? What? When? Where? Why?* and *How?* For example, when you are introduced to someone new, you may want to listen for the person's name (*Who?*) and their hometown (*Where?*).

- **Listening to instructions and directions** Instructions and directions are usually made up of a series of steps. To understand the steps, follow these guidelines.

How to Listen to Instructions

1. Listen to each step. Listen for words that tell you when each step ends and the next one begins—for example, *first, second, next, then,* and *last.*

2. Listen for the number of steps required and the order you should follow. Take notes if necessary.

3. In your mind, make an outline of the steps you should follow. Then, picture yourself completing each step in order.

4. Make sure you have all the information you need and understand the instructions. Ask questions if you are not sure about a particular step.

5. If the situation allows, repeat the instructions back to the speaker. Listen to any further corrections or comments the speaker makes.

Listening to Interpret and Evaluate
Evaluating a presentation involves judging its content, organization, delivery, and believability. The questions in the chart on the next page will help you.

Points to Interpret and Evaluate

Content and Organization

Interpret the speaker's message and purpose
- Can you sum up the main idea?
- Why is the speaker giving the presentation?

Evaluate how clearly the content was organized
- Does the speaker explain ideas in a clear and logical order?
- Can you list each of the main points?

Delivery

Evaluate the speaker's use of verbal and visual elements
- Did the speaker speak loudly and clearly?
- Did the speaker use visuals? If so, did the speaker handle them well? Were the visuals clear and easy to understand?

Evaluate the use of nonverbal elements
- Did the speaker use body language—posture, gestures, facial expressions?
- Did the nonverbal elements match the speaker's words? For example, did the speaker use hand gestures or a raised voice when making an important point?

Believability (Content + Delivery = Believability)

Interpret the speaker's perspective or point of view
- What is the speaker's attitude toward the topic?

Analyze the speaker's techniques
- Did the speaker try to *convince* by using reasons and evidence or *sell* his or her point by appealing to listeners' emotions? Did the speaker use propaganda? (See page 333.)

Special Listening Situations

Group Discussion See page 305.

Interviews An *interview* is a good way to gather firsthand information for a project or a report. The suggestions that follow can help when you interview.

How to Conduct an Interview

Before the interview
- Make an appointment with the person you would like to interview. Make sure you arrive on time.
- Decide what you want to know.
- Make a list of questions. Avoid questions that require only yes or no answers.

During the interview
- Listen carefully. Be respectful, even if you disagree with the person.
- Take notes. If you do not understand something, ask questions about it.
- Thank the person before you leave.

After the interview
- Make sure your notes are clear.
- Write a summary as soon as you can.

Media Messages The *media* are communication forms that you read and hear. Media include newspapers, magazines, radio, television, and the Internet. They are sometimes called the *mass media* because they reach masses, or large numbers, of people. Much of the information we receive comes to us by listening to the media. For that reason, it is important to be a critical listener.

- **Analyzing media messages** *Analyzing* means identifying the parts of something and understanding how those parts work together. To analyze a media message, use the following questions.

Analyzing Media Messages

What is the purpose of the message? Many media messages have more than one purpose. For example, most news programs give information. To make money, though, a program will sell time to advertisers, who pay according to how many viewers will see their ads. Therefore, the program will also try to entertain so it can attract more viewers.

Is the information correct and up-to-date? What is the source of the information? If no sources are given, you have no way of knowing whether the information can be trusted.

How does the message use language? Does it include persuasive words, such as *you should*? Does it use persuasive techniques (see page 289)? Are you being given straight information, or are you being sold a product, service, or idea?

What ideas does the message take for granted? What is left out is as important as what is included. For example, a program on teens that tells only about the problems they cause presents a one-sided message.

What is your opinion of the message? Based on your answers to the questions in this chart, form your own opinion about the message. If you think the message may not be accurate, you may want to find more information on your own.

- **Identifying lack of objectivity in the media** The following chart lists some signs to watch for in media messages. Seeing any of these signs in a message is a clue that the message may be unfair or unbalanced.

Evaluating Media Messages

Bias—leaning toward one side of an issue. A biased speaker may not give opposing views equal time or may not mention them at all.

Misleading Information—bending facts or statistics to support an idea. A speaker may bend facts to move an audience to take action or to win over an undecided audience.

Prejudice—judging people or situations, most often in a negative way, before the facts are known. Prejudiced speakers may ignore facts that do not agree with their views.

Studying and Test Taking

Studying

Skills and Strategies

One purpose of studying is to learn information a little bit at a time so you can do well on tests and earn good grades. However, studying also helps you remember important information you may need later in life. (See also **Test Taking** on page 319.)

Making a Study Plan Set up a study schedule that will help you succeed. Follow the suggestions below to make effective use of your study time.

1. **Know your assignments.** Write down your assignments for each class and the date when each one is due. Make sure you understand the instructions for each assignment.
2. **Plan to finish your work on time.** Break larger assignments into smaller steps. Use a calendar to set deadlines and keep track of when you should be finished with each step.
3. **Study.** Set aside a time and a place where you can work on your assignments without becoming distracted.

Organizing and Remembering Information There are many different ways you can study because there are many different ways to handle information. The strategies listed on the following pages can help you organize and remember information as you study.

- **Classifying** When you *classify* items, you sort them into groups, or categories, with other items that are related to them. The name of the category describes the relationship between the items in the group. If you break your notes into categories, you will have an easier time learning the information.

  EXAMPLE In what category do the following things fit?
  dolphin, shark, whale, octopus
  Answer: ocean animals

■ **Graphic organizers**   New information is sometimes easier to understand if you organize it visually. The process of classifying and organizing information in a *graphic organizer* will help you learn the information. Studying information in a ***graphic organizer,*** such as a map, chart, or diagram, is often more effective than studying the same information in a paragraph. (See also **Text Structures** on page 291).

■ **Memorization**   Sometimes you need to *memorize* information. To develop memorization skills, follow the tips below. Information is easier to memorize if you practice in frequent, short, focused sessions. You may also find that working with another person who can quiz you helps you commit information to memory.

How to Memorize

Memorize only the most important information. Whenever possible, shorten the material you need to remember.

Practice the material in different ways. For example, write the material by hand onto a sheet of paper. Read the paper aloud. Put it away. Then, write out the material again from memory.

Invent memory games. Find words that have the same first letters as the important terms and string them together into a sentence, or make up poems or songs that help you remember facts and details.

■ **Notes on reading or lectures**   Taking accurate ***notes*** is worth the extra effort. As you read at home or listen in class, you should record detailed information in your notebook. Then, you will be ready to study for even the most challenging tests.

How to Take Study Notes

1. Identify and write down the main ideas presented in class or your reading. These main ideas should be headings in your notes. In class, listen for key words and phrases, such as *first, most important,* or *therefore.* These words often introduce main ideas and tell you how ideas are related. In a textbook, look for chapter headings and subheadings. They usually contain key ideas.

2. Keep your notes brief. Use abbreviations, and sum up source material in your own words.

3. Include brief examples or details from the source material. Important examples or details can help you recall the key ideas more easily.

4. Look over your notes as soon as you write them. Be sure you have included the most important information.

At the top of the next page is an example of careful study notes one student wrote after reading a passage about the Cherokee Nation. The notes show the main ideas as headings. Underneath each main heading, you will find a group of important details that relate to that heading. Notice that the notes are brief.

Background information
  Cherokee leaders wanted to modernize
  1827—formed a legislature, wrote a constitution, started a judicial system
  built a capital—New Echota in Georgia

Causes for removal
  New settlers of European descent did not want to share land in the Southeast with Indians
  1828—gold discovered on edge of Cherokee territory and Andrew Jackson was elected president. Jackson believed Indians should not have nations within the U.S.

Effects
  1830—Indian Removal Act passed
  Jackson gives the Five Civilized Tribes (Cherokee, Chickasaw, Choctaw, Creek, Seminole) land in Indian Territory (Oklahoma)
  Cherokees must leave their lands in Georgia and Tennessee

■ **Outlines** An *outline* can help you organize ideas. When you write an outline, you group ideas in a pattern that shows their relationship to one another. (See also **Prewriting Techniques** on page 343.)

■ **Paraphrasing** When you *paraphrase,* you explain someone else's idea in your own words. When you put an idea in your own words, you will understand it better and remember it longer. (See also **Paraphrasing** on page 288.)

How to Paraphrase

1. Read the selection carefully before you begin.

2. Be sure you understand the main idea of the selection. Look up any unfamiliar words in a dictionary.

3. Determine the tone of the selection. (What is the attitude of the writer toward the subject of the selection?)

4. Identify the speaker in fictional material. (Is the poet or author speaking, or is a character speaking?)

5. Write your paraphrase in your own words. Shorten long sentences or stanzas. Use your own, familiar vocabulary, and keep the ideas in the same order as they are in the selection.

6. Be sure that the ideas in your paraphrase match the ideas expressed in the original text.

■ **SQ3R** *SQ3R* stands for *Survey, Question, Read, Recite,* and *Review.* It is a reading strategy that helps you learn information from a book. (See also **SQ3R** on page 290.)

■ **Summarizing** A *summary* is a brief restatement of the main ideas expressed in a piece of writing. A summary is similar to a paraphrase because you express another person's ideas in your own words. However, a summary is usually shorter than a paraphrase because you only note the most important points. (See also **Summarizing** on page 291.)

How to Summarize
1. Skim the selection you wish to summarize.
2. Read the passage again closely. Look for main ideas and supporting details.
3. Write your summary in your own words. Include only the main ideas and the most important supporting points.
4. Evaluate and revise your summary. Check that you have covered the most important points. Make sure that the information is clearly expressed and that the reader can follow your ideas.

- **Writing to learn**   *Writing* is a valuable study tool. Writing helps you organize your thoughts, solve problems, make plans, and get your mind ready to learn. The chart below contains some kinds of writing that can help you learn about yourself and your world.

Types of *Writing to Learn*
Freewriting helps you focus your thoughts.
Example writing for five minutes to brainstorm everything you know about a subject you are studying
Autobiographies help you examine the meaning of important events in your life.
Example writing about a personal event that showed you the importance of learning
Diaries help you recall thoughts, express feelings, and clear your mind.
Example expressing the feelings you have about a subject about which you are learning
Journals help you record observations and descriptions or explore answers to questions.
Example recording questions that you develop about a topic, and exploring possible answers to them
Learning logs help you define or analyze information or propose a solution.
Example listing and defining words you learned in Spanish class

Test Taking

Studying for Tests

There are two common tests you are likely to take in school: essay tests and objective tests. The information in this section will help you prepare for both kinds of tests.

Essay Tests   An *essay test* measures your understanding of the material you have learned in class by asking you to explain your answers. Essay answers are usually a paragraph or more in length.

How to Study for Essay Tests

1. Read the assigned material carefully.
2. Make an outline of the main points and important details.
3. Invent your own essay questions, and practice writing out the answers.
4. Evaluate and revise your practice answers by checking your work against your notes and textbook. You can also use the **Writing Workshops** in this book to help you write an essay answer.

Objective Tests   *Objective tests* measure your ability to remember specific information, such as names, terms, dates, or definitions. Most objective test questions have only one correct answer.

How to Study for Objective Tests

1. Identify important terms or facts in your textbook and class notes.
2. Review the information in more than one way. For example, for a science test, you may need to learn the definitions for scientific terms. Make flashcards. Practice identifying the definition from the term, then the term from the definition.
3. Practice and repeat information to remember it. Go over difficult information more than once.
4. If possible, briefly review all the information shortly before the actual test.

Types of Test Questions

The following section describes the different types of questions you may find on tests you take in school. Read about these questions to find tips and strategies for answering them.

- **Essay questions**   To answer an *essay question,* you usually write a paragraph or several paragraphs. Your essay should have a topic sentence, supporting details, and a conclusion. The following steps can help you answer essay questions. (See also the **Key Verbs That Appear in Essay Questions** chart on page 320.)

1. **Scan the directions on the test.** How many questions are you required to answer? Select the ones you think you can answer best. Plan how much time you can afford to spend on each answer. Then, stick with your plan.

2. Read each question carefully. Be sure you understand exactly what the question is asking before you plan your response. If a question contains several parts, your answer should contain several parts as well.

3. Pay attention to important terms in the question. Identify the task that the essay question asks you to complete. You can tell what the task is by looking at the key verb that appears in the essay question. Refer to the chart below.

Key Verbs That Appear in Essay Questions		
Key Verb	**Task**	**Sample Question**
analyze	Take something apart to see how each part works.	Analyze the effects that a balanced diet has on a growing body.
compare	Point out ways that things are alike.	Compare cross-country skiing to water skiing.
contrast	Point out ways that things are different.	Contrast the schools in Japan and the United States.
define	Give specific details that make something unique.	Define the term *personification*.
demonstrate	Give examples to support a point.	Demonstrate how the Internet helps people communicate.
describe	Give a picture in words.	Describe the appearance of a test tube of water after another substance is added.
explain	Give reasons.	Explain why the moon looks different at various times each month.
identify	Point out specific characteristics.	Identify the types of figurative language.
list	Give all steps in order or all details about a subject.	List the countries that make up the United Kingdom.
persuade	Give your opinion on an issue and provide reasons to support it.	Persuade your science teacher that your science class should or should not start a vegetable garden.
summarize	Give a brief overview of the main points.	Summarize the story told in "Raymond's Run."

4. **Use prewriting strategies.** After you identify the key verbs in the question, make notes and an outline to help you decide what you want to say. Write your notes or a rough outline on a piece of scratch paper.
5. **Evaluate and revise as you write.** You may not have time to write your whole essay over, but you can edit your essay to strengthen it. Correct any spelling, punctuation, or grammatical errors, and make sure you have answered every part of the question.

Qualities of a Good Essay Answer
The essay is well organized.
The main ideas and supporting points are clearly presented.
The sentences are complete and well written.
There are no distracting errors in spelling, punctuation, or grammar.

■ **Matching questions** *Matching questions* ask you to match the items in one list to items in another list.

EXAMPLE

Directions: Match the animals in the left-hand column to the correct kind of animal in the right-hand column.

_B_	1. Greyhound	**A.**	Amphibian
_D_	2. Sparrow	**B.**	Mammal
_A_	3. Bullfrog	**C.**	Reptile
_C_	4. Crocodile	**D.**	Bird
_E_	5. Sea Bass	**E.**	Fish

How to Answer Matching Questions

1. Read the directions carefully. Some items may be used more than once. Others might not be used at all.

2. Scan the columns. Match the items you know first. That way you can spend more time thinking about more difficult items you are less sure about.

3. Complete the rest of the matching. Make your best guess on the remaining items.

■ **Multiple-choice questions** A *multiple-choice question* provides a number of possible answers and asks you to select the one that is correct.

EXAMPLE

1. Which of the following items is *not* a characteristic of poison ivy?
    - **A.** Its oil causes people to itch.
    - **B.** Each leaf has three leaflets.
    - **C.** It produces white berries.
    - (**D.**) It grows into a tall tree.

How to Answer Multiple-Choice Questions

1. Read the question or statement carefully. Before you look at answer choices, make sure you understand the question or statement. Watch for words such as *not* and *only*. These words limit your choice of possible answers.

2. Read all the choices before answering. If you know an answer choice is incorrect, rule it out. Think carefully about the remaining choices, and select the one that makes the most sense.

■ On-demand reading questions

On-demand questions are ones you cannot study in advance. *On-demand reading questions* ask you about a reading passage. In some cases, you will find answers to the questions in the passage. Other times, you may need to draw from your own experiences or understanding of the passage.

EXAMPLE

Directions: Read the passage below, and answer the question that follows.

   Julia threw her roller skates down on the sofa. She plopped down next to them and pouted. Didn't anyone remember that it was her birthday? No one in her family had said "Happy birthday" to her before she went skating this morning. She walked into the kitchen to get lunch, and her face brightened. Her family was there and so were all her friends! On the table, there was a cake with twelve candles. It was surrounded by presents.

1. Why does Julia pout?
   A. She thinks her family has forgotten that it is her birthday.
   B. She fell while roller-skating.
   C. Her friends did not come to her birthday party.
   D. Her family forgot her presents.

> **How to Answer On-Demand Reading Questions**
>
> **1. Read the passage carefully.** Make sure you know the main idea and important details.
>
> **2. Read the questions that follow the reading passage.** Usually the questions are multiple-choice. (See also **Multiple-Choice Questions** on page 321.) Sometimes you will be asked to write short, precise answers to questions. (See also **Short-Answer Questions** on page 324.)
>
> **3. Notice which words from the passage are repeated in the questions.** In the example above, the question includes the word *pout*, which is part of the word *pouted* from the second sentence of the reading passage. That clue tells you that the answer is in the second sentence of the reading passage or somewhere near it.
>
> **4. If the language of the passage does not appear in the question, you must draw your own conclusions.** Your conclusion may be based on your own experiences and knowledge.

■ On-demand writing questions

On-demand writing questions are the core of many state writing tests. They are essay questions that ask you to write a persuasive, informative, narrative, or descriptive essay. Since these questions are broad and related to your experience, you cannot study for the content of an on-demand writing question. However, you can prepare by writing a practice essay and asking for feedback from your teacher or classmates.

EXAMPLE

   Your principal is thinking about requiring all students to take a class about career selection. Persuade your principal that such a class is or is not a good idea.

How to Answer On-Demand Writing Questions

1. Read the question and decide what it is asking. Look for the key verbs in the question. These verbs will tell you whether your answer should be persuasive, informative, narrative, or descriptive. (See also the **Key Verbs That Appear in Essay Questions** chart on page 320.)

2. Plan your answer. Use prewriting strategies to help you plan before you begin writing. (See also **Prewriting Techniques** on page 343.)

3. Evaluate and revise your answer as you write. Make sure your answer has a clear topic sentence, supporting details, transitions between ideas, and a conclusion.

■ Reasoning or logic questions

Reasoning or *logic questions* test your reasoning skills rather than your knowledge of a specific subject. Reasoning or logic questions may ask you to identify the relationship among several items, to identify a pattern in a sequence of numbers, or to predict the next item in a sequence.

EXAMPLE

What comes next?

1 2 3 4

In this sequence of drawings, the hour hand on the clock starts at noon and moves three hours forward in each picture. In the fourth position, the hour hand will have reached the nine o'clock position.

How to Answer Reasoning or Logic Questions

1. Make sure you understand the instructions. Reasoning or logic questions are often multiple-choice. On some tests, however, you may need to write a word or phrase, complete a number sequence, or draw a picture for your answer.

2. Analyze the relationship implied in the question. Look carefully at the question to gather information about the relationship of the items.

3. Draw reasonable conclusions. Evaluate the relationship of the items to decide your answer.

■ Sentence-completion questions

Sentence-completion questions test your knowledge of vocabulary words. These types of questions ask you to choose an answer that correctly completes the meaning of a sentence.

EXAMPLE

1. On stage the two performers seemed like good friends. In reality, however, the two were ____ who were always competing for the same roles.
   A. cousins
   B. pals
   C. rivals
   D. equals

How to Answer Sentence-Completion Questions

1. Read the sentence carefully. Make sure you understand the words in the sentence. Some sentences may contain

(continued)

(continued)

How to Answer Sentence-Completion Questions

clues to the meaning of the word or words that go in the blanks. In the example on the previous page, *however* is a clue that the two performers were not friends offstage. Therefore, the correct answer is *rivals*.

2. Rule out incorrect answer choices. If you can immediately rule out an answer choice, mark through it.

3. Fill in the blank with the remaining choices, and choose the best answer. If you are not sure which choice is correct, use each one in the blank of the sentence and choose the answer that makes the most sense.

■ **Short-answer questions** *Short-answer questions* ask you to write brief, precise responses. Short-answer questions vary in length. You may be asked to fill in a blank, label a map, or write one or two sentences.

EXAMPLE Why do whales frequently rise to the surface of the sea?

Answer: Whales cannot breathe underwater. They come up to the surface to get air through their blowholes.

How to Answer Short-Answer Questions

1. Read the question carefully. Some questions have more than one part. Be sure to answer the entire question.

2. Plan your answer. Briefly decide what ideas and details you need to include in the answer.

3. Be as specific as possible. Write a full, exact answer.

4. Budget your time. Answer the questions you know first. Save time for more difficult questions.

■ **True-false questions** *True-false questions* ask you to determine whether the statement you are given is a true statement or a false statement.

EXAMPLE
1. T (F) Cockroaches never fly.

How to Answer True-False Questions

1. Read the statement carefully. If any part of the statement is false, then the whole statement is false. A statement is true only if it is entirely and always true.

2. Look for word clues. Words such as *always* or *never* limit a statement's meaning.

Viewing and Representing

Understanding Media Terms

People who work in and write about the media often use special terms. Learning some of those terms will help you evaluate or judge the media messages you see and hear. It will also help you create your own media messages.

The terms in this section are divided into three lists: **Electronic Media Terms, General Media Terms,** and **Print Media Terms.** If a term is used in both print media and electronic media, it is defined under **Print Media Terms** only. For information on the Internet and the World Wide Web, see the **Library/Media Center** section beginning on page 276. For more on using type and graphics, see **Document Design** beginning on page 264.

Electronic Media Terms

Advertising See **Advertising** on page 333.

Animation *Animation* is a way of making photographs of drawings appear to move. Each drawing in an animated film is only slightly different from the ones before and after it. When the photographs of these drawings are projected very quickly (at 24 images per second), the figures in them seem to move.

Broadcasting *Broadcasting* is sending television or radio signals through the airwaves over a wide area. *Commercial broadcasting* is sending these signals to make money. Commercial broadcasters are paid by advertisers to air commercials along with the broadcasters' programs. *Public broadcasting* refers to nonprofit radio and television. The Public Broadcasting Service (PBS) in the United States has more than three hundred member TV stations. Companies, viewers, and listeners pay most of the cost of public broadcasting. Some money comes from the federal government.

Cable Television *Cable television* uses powerful antennas to pick up television signals and then delivers the signals to homes and businesses through cables. Some cable companies only provide the signals to viewers. Others create original programs as well. (See also **Broadcasting** on page 325.)

Camera Angle The *camera angle* is the angle at which a camera points toward a subject. Placing the camera at a high angle above the subject makes the subject look small. Placing the camera at a low angle makes the subject look tall and powerful. Tilting the camera makes the subject seem off-balance.

Camera Shot A *camera shot* is the way an image in a film or video is presented to viewers. The following are the three most common shots used in film production.

- **Close-up shot**   a shot made from very close to the subject, for example, a shot of a person's eyes
- **Medium shot**   a shot made from a midrange distance, for example, a shot of a person from the waist up
- **Long shot**   a shot made from far away, for example, a shot of a football field from a blimp

Commercial Broadcasting   See **Broadcasting** on page 325.

Copy   See **Copy** on page 333.

Credits   *Credits* list the people who worked on a presentation. Credits are usually listed at the end of a television program, film, or video.

Documentary   A *documentary* is a film or television program that explores the meaning of an actual event. Most documentaries include a combination of interviews and footage of actual events. Some documentaries include reenactments of events by actors and an offscreen narrator. A documentary's main purpose may be to inform, to persuade, or to entertain. In addition, some documentaries are intended to make money for their producers. A documentary may have more than one purpose. For example, a filmmaker might create a documentary that both informs viewers about the problem of pet overpopulation and tries to persuade them to take actions to help solve that problem.

Editor   See **Editor** on page 333.

Feature News   See **Feature News** on page 334.

Film   *Film* is a medium for recording sounds and images. Message makers who need sounds and images to be crisp and clear, to last a long time, or to be presented on a large screen will film their messages. Filmed images can appear more sophisticated than images recorded on videotape, but film is more expensive to buy and develop than videotape is. (See also **Videotape** on page 328.)

Hard News   See **Hard News** on page 334.

Internet   The *Internet* is a network of computers that lets computer users communicate with each other. Using the Internet requires a computer with a modem and Internet software. The modem links the computer with a telephone or cable line. For a monthly fee, Internet service providers (ISPs) provide access to the Internet. (See also **World Wide Web** on page 281.)

Lead   See **Lead** on page 334.

Medium   See **Medium** on page 334.

Message   See **Message** on page 332.

News   See **News** on page 335.

Newsmagazine   See **Newsmagazine** on page 335.

Photography   See **Photography** on page 335.

Producer   A *producer* is the person who oversees the production of a movie or a radio or TV program. He or she decides what overall message to present. The producer also gathers a crew or staff, raises and manages the money needed to create the film or program, and keeps the production on schedule. (See also **Production** on page 335.)

Public Broadcasting   See **Broadcasting** on page 325.

Reporter   See **Reporter** on page 336.

Script   A *script* is the words to be spoken during a play, a film, or a TV or radio program. TV, film, and play scripts also include notes about the images to be shown and the movements or emotions that actors will perform. The script for a news broadcast is called *copy*. (See also **Copy** on page 333.)

Soft News   See **Soft News** on page 336.

Sound   In film and video, sound is all of the recorded material that you hear, including dialogue, music, sound effects, and so on. In addition to getting the spoken words across to viewers, producers and filmmakers use sound to achieve the following goals.

- **Create an illusion**   You might see two actors in a film rushing to get farm animals into a barn. Sound effects, such as wind noise and thunder, can signal to you as a viewer that these characters want to protect their livestock from an approaching storm. It is unlikely that the scene was shot on a stormy day, though.

- **Create a mood**   The music that a producer chooses to play while certain images are on screen can guide the audience to feel a certain way about those images. For example, music with a strong rhythm played during a chase scene can make viewers feel tense, as if they are moving quickly, too.

Understanding Media Terms

Source   See **Source** on page 336.

Storyboard   A *storyboard* is a set of drawings that show the order of shots and scenes in a script. A storyboard may also include dialogue, narration, and audio and visual cues. For an example of a storyboard, see page 271.

Target Audience   See **Target Audience** on page 336.

Text   See **Text** on page 336. (See also **Script** on page 327.)

Videotape   *Videotape* is a medium used to record sounds and images. Message makers may use videotape because the medium and equipment needed are relatively inexpensive when compared with film. Videotape equipment may also be more accessible and easier to use than film equipment. When using videotape, message makers must consider that images and sounds recorded on videotape tend to have less *resolution*, or clarity, than filmed images. They must also keep in mind that videotape does not last as long as film. (See also **Film** on page 326.)

General Media Terms

Audience   An *audience* is a group of people who see or hear a media message. Advertisers aim their messages at the audiences they think will buy their products or services. (See also **Advertising** on page 333 and **Target Audience** on page 336.)

Authority   The term *authority* means how well the source of a message seems to know the subject. If a message appears to come from an expert source, you will think it has authority.

Bias   A *bias* is a slanted point of view, either in favor of an issue or against it. A biased message maker may not even mention information that supports views other than his or her own. (See also **Point of View** on page 333.)

Context   *Context* is the material that surrounds a media message. For example, the context of an ad on a children's TV program is the other ads on the program and the program itself. Context may affect the way people respond to a message.

Credibility   *Credibility* means being believable. Whether or not a speaker or writer seems believable is up to the audience to decide. (See also **Message** on page 332.)

Critical Viewing   *Critical viewing* means analyzing visual messages to understand them and evaluate or judge them. Visual messages include photographs, editorial cartoons, films, and television programs, to name just a few.

Keeping the five key ideas on the next page in mind as you view messages will help you become a more critical viewer.

Key Ideas for Critical Viewing

Key Idea 1: All messages are put together by people.

People who create visual messages must make many choices. They must decide which elements (words, images, sounds) to include and how to arrange them. One of the most important decisions the creator of a visual message makes is what to leave out. When you understand that visual messages are constructed, you can analyze how the elements work together. You can also recognize the skill that went into creating the message.

Key Idea 2: Messages are one person's version of reality.

When you see something in a visual message, remember that the reality may be quite different. For a TV ad for a theme park, for example, everything from the actors to the camera angles to the background music is carefully chosen and arranged to make the park seem even more fun than it is. When you understand that a visual message is a version of reality, you can evaluate how authentic (true-to-life) the message seems.

Key Idea 3: People make their own meanings from messages.

The meaning you draw from a visual message depends on your prior knowledge (what you already know) and on your experience. Everyone's prior knowledge and experience are different, so different viewers may draw different meanings from the same message. When you connect the message to your own knowledge and experience, you can form your own ideas about what the message means.

Key Idea 4: Messages have a wide range of purposes.

Every message has a purpose. Usually, that purpose is to inform, to persuade, to entertain, or to express thoughts and feelings. Most mass-media messages also have another purpose: to make money for the message makers and for the people who own and run the media. Knowing that a visual message might be presented to make money can help you decide for yourself whether you will let it influence you.

Key Idea 5: The medium shapes the message.

Different visual media have different strengths and weaknesses. For example, a still photograph shows just one moment in time, but it can be studied over and over. Film has movement and sound, but the images flash by quickly. The people who create visual messages must choose the medium that will best help them achieve their purpose. Understanding how the medium shapes the message can help you see why a message affects you in a certain way.

Evaluating Media Messages

The following questions will help you analyze and evaluate media messages.

- Who created the message?
- What elements (words, images, or sounds) does the message include?
- How are the elements arranged?

Understanding Media Terms

- How well are the elements used?
- What may have been left out of the message?
- How is this version of reality similar to and different from what I know from my own experience or from other sources?
- How authentic (true-to-life) does the message seem? Why?
- Of what does the message make me think? How does it make me feel about the world? about myself? about other people?
- What seems to be the main purpose of the message? Is there also another purpose? If so, what is it?
- What medium carries the message?
- How do the characteristics of the medium (image, sound, motion) shape the message?

Formula   A *formula* is a set way of doing something. In television and film, it refers to a common way of presenting material or combining characters. For example, situation comedies often use this formula: A character gets into an uncomfortable situation, which is usually caused by a misunderstanding or by one of the character's own faults. The situation gets sillier and sillier until finally, someone or something comes along and solves the character's problem. By the end of the show, the character is out of trouble and everything is back to normal.

Genre   A *genre* is a category of art forms or media products that share certain common ways of doing things. Genres found on television include

- children's programming
- documentary
- drama
- game show
- infomercial
- music video
- news broadcast
- sitcom (situation comedy)
- soap opera
- talk show

Illustration   An *illustration* is a picture created as a decoration or to explain something. Drawings, paintings, photographs, and computer-generated artwork can all be illustrations. The following are some elements of illustration.

- **Color**   Color creates a certain mood or draws attention to a certain part of an illustration.
- **Form**   Form refers to the three-dimensional look of an illustration. Depth and weight make an illustration more effective. Illustrators can create shadows and bright spots to make an illustration look three-dimensional.
- **Line**   Everything you see around you has some sort of line. Some lines are obvious, like the vertical line made by walls meeting in a corner. However, you might not notice other lines, for example, the lines made by the fur of a cat. Illustrators use line to show depth in

a drawing and to show viewers where the horizon in a drawing is.

- **Shape** Shape is the two-dimensional outline of something. Lines come together to make a shape, and all of the shapes in an illustration are connected.

Images An *image* is a visual representation of something. It may be a painting, a photograph, a sculpture, or a moving picture, among other things. An image may be *still* or *moving*.

- A *still image,* such as a photograph, allows viewers to notice detail and spend time considering the meaning of the image. Still images may also be easier than moving images for message makers to manipulate through cropping or using computer programs.

- A *moving image* is a series of still images projected quickly onto a television or film screen. A moving image may show an actual event (called *documentary footage*), or it may show an event arranged by the message maker (a *dramatization*). Documentary footage includes scenes shown on the evening news; dramatizations include fictional movies. Both kinds of moving images are the message maker's version of an event and may be incomplete or altered in some way.

To analyze how message makers create certain effects using images, consider the points in the chart below.

\multicolumn{2}{c}{**Creating Effects with Images**}	
Technique	**Definition/Effects**
Color	Color can emphasize certain parts of an image or guide viewers to feel a certain way about an image. When a spot of color suddenly appears in a black-and-white movie, the director wants viewers to pay special attention to that part of the image. Photographing an image through a yellow filter can create a happy mood in the image.
Juxtaposition	This technique involves putting two or more images next to each other to create meaning. For example, a comedy show that cuts between images of a person happily walking down a city street and a piano dangling from an apartment window tells its viewers that the person's walk will be rudely interrupted by the piano. Editing moving images together or placing still images side by side can sometimes communicate more meaning than an individual image.
Slow or Fast Motion	A message maker may speed up or slow down a moving image to create a certain effect. Making an image move faster than normal can create a comic effect, while slowing an image down can create a tense, dramatic effect.

Media Law The First Amendment of the U.S. Constitution states that Congress shall pass no law that limits the freedom of the press. One effect of this amendment is that, except during wartime, the United States government seldom uses *censorship*. *Censorship* is any attempt by a government or other group to limit the amount or type of information people receive. However, there are laws that regulate, or control, the media. The Federal Communications Commission (FCC) enforces U.S. laws dealing with electronic media, including radio, television, and the Internet. A person whose reputation has been hurt by lies that were printed or broadcast about him or her may sue the people responsible for the false statements. The creator of a media message may *copyright* that message to stop anyone from *plagiarizing*, or stealing his or her work.

Media Literacy *Media literacy* is the ability to find, analyze, evaluate, and communicate messages in many different forms. (See also **Critical Viewing** on page 328.)

Message A *message* is an idea communicated using symbols (things that stand for ideas). Symbols may be language, gestures, images, or sounds. The *content* of a message is the information it presents. (See also **Credibility** on page 328, **Realism** on page 333, and **Source** on page 336.)

Multimedia Presentation A *multimedia presentation* is any presentation that uses two or more forms of media. For example, when you give an oral presentation including visuals (such as slides, transparencies, or posters), you are giving a multimedia presentation. One medium is your voice, and the other is the visuals you use to support your presentation. A multimedia presentation that involves the use of presentation software or Web sites is sometimes called a **technology presentation.**

Newsworthiness *Newsworthiness* is the quality that makes a news event seem worth reporting. An event may be considered newsworthy if it meets any of the following criteria, or standards.

Criteria	Definitions
Timeliness	events or issues that are happening now or that people are interested in right now
Impact	events or issues that have a direct effect on people's lives
Human Interest	stories about people's basic needs or stories that affect the audience's emotions
Celebrity Angle	stories about famous people

Persuasion See **Propaganda** on page 333.

Point of View A message maker's *point of view* is the way he or she approaches a topic. The message maker's background and beliefs often affect his or her point of view. For example, in a newspaper story about a local zoo, one reporter might focus on how the zookeepers are helping save endangered species. Another reporter with different experiences might focus on what the animals are missing by not being in the wild. (See also **Bias** on page 328 and **Propaganda** below.)

In photography, point of view refers to the photographer's approach to his or her subject. Choices that affect the photographer's point of view include selecting the subject and the camera angle. (See also **Photography** on page 335.)

Propaganda *Propaganda* is the use of certain techniques to make a message as persuasive as possible. The word *propaganda* has a negative connotation as it originally referred to messages that lied or distorted the truth in order to influence public opinion. However, the practice of using some propaganda techniques—such as the celebrity testimonial—is widely accepted in the field of advertising. Many of these techniques work by leading you to make a generalization about the ad. Suppose, for example, a company uses a basketball star to advertise its shoes. The company wants you to generalize that anyone who wears those shoes will play as well as the basketball star does. (See also **Advertising** on this page, **Bias** on page 328, and **Point of View** above.)

Realism *Realism* means showing people and events just the way they appear, without making them seem better or worse in any way.

Stereotypes *Stereotypes* are beliefs (usually negative ones) about a whole group of people. For example, some adults do not trust teenagers even though relatively few teenagers ever cause problems. Such beliefs are usually based on too little evidence or on false or misleading information.

Visual Literacy *Visual literacy* is the ability to understand how the visual media communicate meaning. (See also **Critical Viewing** on page 328.)

Print Media Terms

Advertising *Advertising* is using images or words to persuade an audience to buy, use, or accept a product, service, or idea. Advertisers pay the media for time or space in which to run their ads.

Byline A *byline* lists the name of the reporter or writer of a print article or a broadcast presentation.

Copy *Copy* is the text in a media message. (See also **Script** on page 327.)

Editor An *editor* oversees the work of reporters. Editors decide what news stories will appear, check facts, and correct mistakes.

Understanding Media Terms 333

Editorial Cartoon An *editorial cartoon* is a cartoon, usually found in the editorial section of a newspaper, that shows the cartoonist's opinion about a current event or issue. An editorial cartoonist may make his or her point in the following ways.

- exaggerating the impact of an event or issue
- drawing people involved in the event as *caricatures,* or giving them exaggerated features that make it obvious to readers who is being represented
- connecting the event to another event or story with which readers will be more familiar

Feature News The primary purpose of *feature news* (or soft news) is to entertain. These stories may or may not be timely. They may be about ordinary people or celebrities or about animals, events, places, or products. A profile of a neighborhood volunteer who brings food to homeless people is an example of a feature-news story. (See also **Hard News** below and **Soft News** on page 336.)

Font A *font* is a style of lettering used for printing. (See also **Font** on page 267.)

Hard News *Hard news* is reporting based on facts. It covers important current events and issues such as politics. Usually, it answers the basic *5W-How?* questions. A hard-news story might provide information about a flood that occurred today or about the problem of overcrowded classrooms in local schools. (See also **Feature News** on this page and **Soft News** on page 336.)

Headline A *headline* is the title of a newspaper article. Headlines are usually set in large, bold type. They have two purposes: to hook the reader's attention and to tell the reader the topic of the article.

EXAMPLE: **Fido Fetches Family from Flames**

Lead A *lead* is the first few words or the first paragraph of a news story. It answers some or all of the *5W-How?* questions and tries to hook the audience's attention with a surprising fact or idea.

EXAMPLE: (HOBBS, NM) A family pet proved himself a hero early yesterday when he alerted the sleeping occupants of a burning home here. Even though he could have easily escaped through his doggie door, Fido the terrier chose to stay and bark until the Yellowbird family had all woken up and fled the house.

Medium The *medium* of a message is the means by which it is sent. (*Medium* is the singular form of *media.*) **Print media** include newspapers and magazines. **Electronic media** include radio and television, audio and video recordings, film, and the Internet. The *mass media* are the media that reach a very large audience.

Message See **Message** on page 332.

News *News* is the presentation of current information. The people who own and run *media outlets,* such as newspapers or television stations, decide which stories to cover. They try to choose stories that will interest or affect their audience. Local news outlets present stories about their region of the country. National news outlets cover national and world issues and events.

Newsmagazine A *newsmagazine* is a publication that discusses recent events and issues. Most print newsmagazines appear once a week. In television the term refers to a news program that airs one or more times a week. Such programs usually analyze and explore the meanings of events.

Photography *Photography* is the process of recording a still image on film with a camera. Like any other visual message, a photograph records only the parts of an image that the message maker chooses to include. The choices a photographer can make about an image include the following.

- **Camera angle** By placing the camera at different angles relative to the subject, a photographer can guide viewers to feel a certain way about the subject. (See also **Camera Angle** on page 326.)
- **Film type** A photographer may choose color or black-and-white film depending on what he or she wants viewers to get from the image. Black-and-white film can emphasize shapes or create a dramatic effect, while color images appear more realistic.
- **Lighting** A photographer may have control over the light available when the photo is taken. If so, he or she can use just a few lights set at dramatic angles for effect, or use full light for a more natural-looking image.
- **Subject** When taking a photo of a scene, a photographer may position the camera to get only the most important part of the scene or to eliminate images that take away from his or her message. Even after the photo has been taken, *cropping* can be used to cut out an unwanted part of the scene. Message makers can also add *captions* that guide viewers to draw a conclusion about the photo. (See also **Message** on page 332.)

Political Cartoon See **Editorial Cartoon** on page 334.

Production *Production* is the process of creating a publication, a film, a video, or a radio or television program. Production takes place in three stages.

- **Preproduction** Copy or scripts are gathered and fine-tuned. Money is raised, and plans are made for how it will be spent. Staff and crew are hired, and schedules are planned.
- **Production** The work is filmed, recorded, or printed.
- **Postproduction** Finishing touches are added. Books and newspapers are bound or gathered. Films and tapes

are edited, soundtracks are recorded, and sound and special effects are added.

Reporter A *reporter* is a journalist who gathers information. Reporters work with editors to create print or electronic reports.

Soft News *Soft news* is general-interest material, such as information on fashion trends, presented in a news format. The purpose of soft news is to entertain. For example, a soft-news story might explain how the special effects for a new science fiction movie were created. (See also **Feature News** and **Hard News** on page 334.)

Source A *source* is a person or publication that gives a journalist information or ideas. Journalists try to use sources that have authority and seem credible. (See also **Authority** and **Credibility** on page 328, and **Message** on page 332.)

Target Audience A *target audience* is a group of people for whom a message or product is designed. For example, the target audience of advertisements for acne medications is teenagers.

Text The term *text* refers to the words, printed or spoken, that are used to create a message. (See also **Message** on page 332.)

Writing

Skills, Structures, and Techniques

Good writing does not just happen. A writer must work at his or her writing. You can use the following ideas and information to become a more effective writer.

Applications See **Forms** on page 339.

Composition A *composition* is a piece of writing that has several paragraphs. Compositions have three main parts: *introduction*, *body*, and *conclusion*. All three parts work together to communicate the author's main idea or point.

- **Introduction** The *introduction* is the first paragraph of your composition. An introduction should do two things: Get your readers' attention and tell them the main idea of the composition.
  1. **Grab the readers' attention.** Your introduction should make your readers want to read more. The chart in the next column gives some strategies for drawing in your reader.

> **How to Catch Your Readers' Attention**
>
> **Begin by asking a question.**
> *Do you wonder what to do with all of your free time after school and on the weekends?*
>
> **Begin with an anecdote or a funny story.**
> *House painting has always been something I do well, so when I showed up at the volunteer building site, I was ready to paint. Little did I know that my friend Joaquin was ready to paint me.*
>
> **Begin with a startling fact.**
> *You may not think that you can help to build a house, but with the teamwork of young people and adults, a house can be quickly built, painted, landscaped, and prepared for a family to move in.*

2. **Present the main idea statement, or thesis.** The *main idea statement,* or *thesis,* is a sentence or two that tells your topic and your main idea about it. Use your main idea as a guide as you plan, write, and revise your paper. Here are some strategies for writing a main idea statement.

How to Write a Main Idea Statement

1. Ask yourself, "What is my topic?"
volunteering

2. Review your prewriting notes. Think about how the facts and details fit together. Identify the idea that connects the details to one another.
Volunteering is good, hard work.

3. Use specific details to make the main idea clear. Zooming in on specific details will make the main idea more focused.
Volunteering to build homes taught me to respect all kinds of people, to work hard, and to challenge myself.

■ **Body** The main idea is supported and developed in the *body* of the composition. The body usually contains several paragraphs with supporting statements, facts, and details. Each paragraph has its own main idea, called a *topic sentence,* and all of the topic sentences support the main idea statement. As you write the body of a composition, keep the following tips in mind.

1. Make sure that you arrange the information in your composition in a way that will make sense to your reader.
2. Do not include details that distract from your main idea.
3. Show how your ideas are connected by using *transitional words and phrases.*

■ **Conclusion** The *conclusion* of your paper sums up your information and makes your final points. Your conclusion should do the following things.

1. **Give the readers a sense of completion.** Good conclusions leave the readers feeling satisfied, not as if they have been left hanging.
2. **Restate the main idea.** The conclusion is your last chance to make your point. In addition to summing up your main points, restate your main idea in different words.

How to Write a Conclusion

Refer to your introduction.
When I thought that I was in for an easy day of fun and painting, I was only partly right. I had fun with my friends. We even had a paint fight. However, I also learned how to work with others to help others.

Restate your main idea.
I now know that by giving up a Saturday, I did not miss out on fun. I had a great time and felt that my day was spent in an important way.

Close with a final idea or example.
I enjoyed my Saturday of painting so much that I have decided to spend one day each month volunteering in some way.

E-mail Electronic mail, or *e-mail,* is a way of sending messages over the Internet rather than through the post office. E-mail is used for both personal and business correspondence. Since e-mail messages are instant, people sometimes write casually. Casual messages are fine for informal e-mail with friends. When e-mailing teachers or businesses, however, you should follow the guidelines below.

E-Mail Guidelines

- Keep your message short, since reading through long e-mails can be difficult and confusing.

- When you have several questions or points, use a bulleted list or indentations to make your e-mail easier to read.

- Use correct spelling, grammar, punctuation, and standard English.

- Include salutations (or greetings) and closings, especially if you are writing to someone for the first time.

- Do not send angry or rude messages. E-mail is easily forwarded. Therefore, someone other than the person you originally wrote to may end up receiving your message.

- Avoid using all capital letters in your messages. Writing in capitals in e-mail is similar to shouting. If you need to emphasize a word or phrase, place an asterisk (*) before and after it.

- Double-check the address in the address line of your message to make sure you are sending your message to the right person.

- Fill in the subject line in your message. Giving your readers an idea of the topic of your message allows them to read the most important messages first.

- Do not forward e-mails to others unless you have the original author's permission.

Forms You will be called upon to fill out forms many times throughout your life. You fill out forms or applications for library cards, savings accounts, even school club memberships. Below is an example of a simple information form.

Information Form

Date 7/26/01

Name Bliss Winston

Address 705 E. Oak St.

City Oakland   State CA   ZIP 90821

Home Phone 555-0141

Date of Birth 12/21/90

Parent or Guardian Joseph Winston

The following tips will help you fill out forms correctly.
1. Read all instructions before you begin. Look for special instructions to see whether you should use a pen or pencil.
2. Read each item carefully.
3. Print neatly all the information that is requested.
4. Proofread the form to make sure you did not leave anything blank. Also, check for errors and correct them neatly.
5. Mail the form to the correct address or give it to the correct person.

Letters   Most people like to receive mail. To get letters, though, you need to write letters. That is why it is important to develop good writing skills for social and business letters. There are several different kinds of letters. All of them have a purpose and an audience. The chart at the bottom of this page lists some common types, purposes, and audiences for letters.

Letters, Business   *Business letters* have specific purposes. People write business letters to apply for a job or communicate about a business. Make sure your business letters look professional. Type or use your best handwriting, and use standard, formal English.

■ **Envelopes**   To make sure that your letter goes where you want it to go, address the envelope neatly and correctly. Follow these tips.
1. Place your return address in the top left-hand corner of the envelope.
2. Write the name and address of the person to whom the letter is being sent in the center of the envelope.
3. Use the standard two-letter postal abbreviation for the state name, followed by the ZIP Code.

Return address

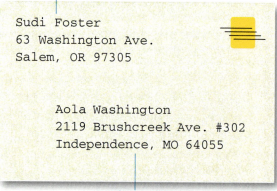

Mailing address

Letters

Type of Letter	Purpose for Writing	Probable Audience
Business	to inform a business about a service you need or how a service was performed	a business or organization
Informal or Personal	to tell about your ideas or feelings, to be polite, to thank someone, or to tell someone about a planned event	close friends, relatives, or social acquaintances

■ **Forms for business letters** The six parts of a business letter are usually arranged in one of the two following styles.
1. **Block form** In the block form, every part of the letter begins at the left margin of the page. A blank line is left between paragraphs, which are not indented.
2. **Modified block form** In the modified block form, the heading, the closing, and your signature are placed to the right of an imaginary line down the center of the page. The middle parts of the letter begin at the left margin. Paragraphs are indented.

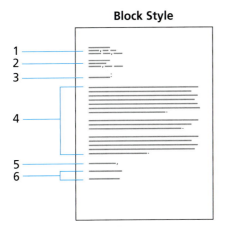
Block Style

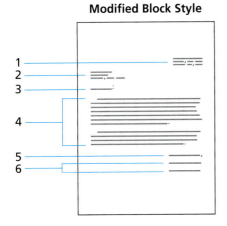
Modified Block Style

■ **Parts of a business letter** There are six parts to a business letter.
1. The *heading* of a business letter has three lines: your street address; your city, state, and ZIP Code; and the date you are writing the letter.
2. The *inside address* gives the name and address of the person to whom you are writing. If you are directing your letter to someone by name, use a courtesy title (such as *Mr., Ms., Mrs.,* or *Miss*) or a professional title (such as *Dr.* or *Professor*) in front of the person's name. After the person's name, include the person's business title (such as *Principal* or *Business Manager*). If you do not have a person's name, use a business title or position title (such as *Refunds Department* or *Editor in Chief*).
3. Your *salutation* is your greeting to the person to whom you are writing. In a business letter, the salutation usually ends with a colon (such as in *Dear Professor García:*).
   If you are writing to a specific person, you can use the person's name (such as *Dear Ms. Lyon*). If you do not have a specific name, use a general greeting (such as *Dear Sir or Madam:* or *Ladies and Gentlemen:*). You can also use a business or position title instead (*Dear Committee Leader:*).
4. The *body* contains the message of your letter. Leave a blank line between paragraphs in the body of the letter.
5. Conclude your letter politely. The *closing* of a business letter often uses one of several common phrases (such as *Sincerely, Yours truly,* or *Respectfully*

Skills, Structures, and Techniques

yours). Capitalize only the first word. End the closing with a comma.

6. Your *signature* should be written in ink directly below the closing. Your name should be typed or printed neatly just below your signature.

■ **Types of business letters**   Types of business letters include the following.

1. **Adjustment or complaint letters**   When you write an *adjustment* or *complaint letter,* you state a problem and explain how you think it should be solved. For example, if you are unhappy with a product you bought, you might write a letter like the one below.

```
5208 Range Drive
St. Louis, MO 63117
June 15, 2001

Gadgets Mail Order
1992 Highland Road
Albany, NY 12212

Dear Sir or Madam:

I am returning science kit #609
that was delivered yesterday. It
arrived with a broken microscope.

Please replace the kit or refund
my purchase price of $69.95 plus
$4.30 that I paid for postage
and handling.

Sincerely,
Ramiro Sanchez
Ramiro Sanchez
```

2. **Appreciation letters**   When you write an *appreciation letter,* you tell people in a business or organization that they did a good job. Give details about what they did that you liked. For example, perhaps you want to tell the manager of a restaurant that you appreciate the good service you received there.

3. **Request or order letters**   In a *request letter,* you ask for specific information about a product service. An *order letter* tells a business about a product or service you want such as a free brochure (an excerpt is shown below). Be sure to include all important information, such as the item number, size, color, brand name, and price.

```
I would like to order three back
issues of Zip! magazine. Please
send the issues from March,
April, and May 2001. In the mag-
azine, you state that back
issues are $3 each, including
postage. I have enclosed a money
order for $9. Thank you for
sending the issues as soon as
possible.
```

Letters, Informal or Personal   An *informal* or *personal letter* is a good way to communicate with a friend or relative. A personal letter is like a conversation, only much better. Conversations may be interrupted or forgotten, but a letter is often treasured and read many times.

A personal letter is a token of friendship. It usually contains a personal message from you, the sender, to the person you are writing to, the receiver. For example, you might write a friend to congratulate him or her for receiving a school award. You might write to tell a friend about the new school you attend.

When you are sending a personal letter, remember to write about a subject that interests you and the person you are writing.

■ Types of informal or personal letters

There are three common types of informal or personal letters. Each of these types is meant for a particular purpose.

1. **Invitations**   You write an invitation to ask someone to an event. Include specific information about the occasion, such as the type of event, time, and place, and any other information your guests might need to know (such as how to dress and what to bring, if anything).

2. **Letters of regret**   You will need to write a letter of regret when you receive an invitation to an event that you will not be able to attend. You should always respond in writing to invitations that include the letters *RSVP*. (These letters are an abbreviation for the French words that mean "please reply.")

3. **Thank-you letters**   When you receive a gift or a favor, you should write a thank-you letter. The purpose of a thank-you letter is to express your appreciation when someone has spent time, trouble, or money to do something for your benefit. In addition to thanking the person, you might include a paragraph or so of personal news or friendly, chatty information. Try to think of something about the person's effort or gift that made it special to you. In the following example, the writer explains why she enjoys a gift from her grandfather.

> 9300 Leon St.
> Burlington, VT 05401
> October 6, 2001
>
> Dear Grandpa,
>   Thank you so much for the wonderful beagle puppy you brought down from the farm. She must have been the smartest one in the litter. She already knows her name after only two days. We named her Waggles because her tail wags all the time. She's the greatest gift. Thanks!
>
>   Love,
>   Rita

Prewriting Techniques   One of the hardest parts of writing is getting started. The following prewriting techniques can help you find topics for writing. They can also help you gather information and ideas about a topic. As you try the different techniques, you may find some are more helpful to you than others. You might even use more than one technique when writing a composition.

Prewriting techniques often include the use of a *graphic organizer*. A **graphic organizer** is a visual way of representing thoughts or ideas. Graphic organizers can help you "see" what you are thinking. You can use graphic organizers to find a subject to write about, to gather information, and to organize your information.

1. **Finding ideas**   Use the following techniques to find ideas for writing.

- **Asking 5W-How? questions**   To gather information, news reporters often ask the **5W-How? questions:** *Who? What? Where? When? Why?* and *How?* You can do the same for any topic. Some questions may not apply to your topic. For other topics, there may be many answers to one question. Here are some *5W-How?* questions about Native American cliff dwellings.

WHO?	*Who* lived in cliff dwellings?
WHAT?	*What* was their daily life like?
WHERE?	*Where* are cliff dwellings found?
WHEN?	*When* did people live in cliff dwellings?
	When did they leave them?
WHY?	*Why* did they build their villages on or into cliffs?
	Why did they leave their villages?
HOW?	*How* did they get food and water?

- **Asking "What if?" questions**
    "What if?" questions can help you think creatively. Let your imagination wander to find as many answers as you can.

    What if I could change one thing in my life? (What if I could make myself invisible? What if I had a car and a driver's license?)

    What if some everyday thing did not exist? (What if the earth had no moon? What if radios had not been invented?)

    What if I could change one thing about the world? (What if everyone in the world had enough food and a home? What if animals could talk with people?)

- **Brainstorming**   When you **brainstorm,** your thoughts fly in all directions. Start with a broad subject, then quickly list everything you can think of about the subject. You can brainstorm alone or with a group.

Guidelines for Brainstorming
Write any subject at the top of a piece of paper or on a chalkboard.
Write down every idea that occurs to you. If you are brainstorming in a group, one person should record all the ideas.
Do not stop to judge what is listed.
Do not stop until you run out of ideas.

    Here are some brainstorming notes on the subject *astronauts*. When you are brainstorming, it is fine to list unusual ideas. Unusual ideas may lead to the perfect topic.

    <u>Astronauts</u>

Sally Ride	space explorers
Neil Armstrong walking on the moon	floating without gravity
space shuttle	cramped space, food in tubes
spacesuits	man in the moon
diving suits	woman in the moon
lunar rover	Astrodome

- **Clustering** *Clustering* is sometimes called *mapping* or *webbing*. It is a visual kind of brainstorming.

Guidelines for Clustering
Write your subject in the center of your paper and then circle it.
Around the subject, write related ideas that come to you. Circle these, and draw lines to connect them with the subject or with other ideas.
Keep going. Write new ideas, circle them, and draw lines to show connections.

The following is a cluster diagram on the topic of Hispanic grocery stores, or *bodegas*.

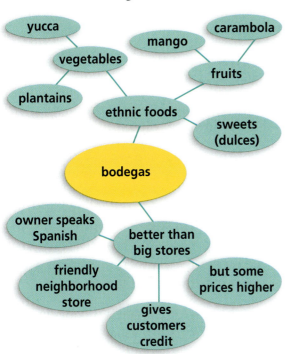

- **Freewriting** *Freewriting* means just that—writing freely. Begin with a word or phrase, and then write whatever comes to mind.

Guidelines for Freewriting
Time yourself for three to five minutes, and keep writing until the time is up.
Write your topic first. Then, write down the ideas your topic gives you.
Do not stop or pause. If you can't think of anything to write, keep writing the same word or phrase until something else pops into your head.
Do not worry about spelling, punctuation, or complete sentences.

EXAMPLE

Bicycling. I like pedaling pedaling pedaling. Aching muscles, biking in the rain. Ride everywhere—school, soccer, down to lake. Never without my helmet, remember Travis's accident. Dangerous at night—reflectors, headlight, reflective tape on jacket. Safety, safety rules—driver's license for bike riders?

In *focused freewriting* (or *looping*), you begin with a word or phrase from freewriting you have already done. You might choose "biking in the rain" and do three minutes of freewriting on this limited topic.

Skills, Structures, and Techniques   **345**

- **Writer's notebook or journal**
  Fill your *writer's journal* with experiences, feelings, and thoughts. You can put in cartoons, quotations, song lyrics, and poems that have special meaning for you. When you need a writing topic, look through your journal to find an idea you want to expand. You can also have a section called a *learning log,* where you write about things you learn. Keep your journal in a notebook, file folder, or computer file.

Writer's Notebook Guidelines
Write every day, and date your entries.
Write as much or as little as you want. Do not worry about spelling, punctuation, or grammar.
Give your imagination some space. Write about dreams, daydreams, and far-out fantasies.

EXAMPLE

July 12, 2001. Saw people doing strange exercise in the park Sat. morning. They moved SO slowly like in a dream. A slow-motion dance. Seven people following movements of an old Chinese woman, few old, mostly young, all moving together. We watched a long time. They call it tai chi—it made me feel good.

2. **Gathering information** When you run out of ideas from your imagination or you need facts, you can turn to other sources. Use the following strategies to find more information on a topic.

- **Listening with a focus** You can find information by listening to radio and TV programs and tapes or by interviewing someone who knows something about your topic. Before you listen, write out some questions about your topic. Then, listen for answers and take notes. (See also **Listening** on page 309.)

- **Reading with a focus** When you look for information in print, follow the guidelines in the chart below.

Reading Guidelines
Find your topic in a book's table of contents or index. Turn to the pages listed.
Do not read every word. Skim pages quickly, looking for your topic.
When you find information on your topic, slow down and read carefully.
Note main ideas and key details.

3. **Arranging ideas** The following strategies will help you to organize and summarize your ideas. These strategies can be especially helpful for organizing ideas from a number of different sources.

- **Charts** A *chart* is a way of classifying information. Charts help you begin to gather and organize your facts and details before you write. One type of chart is a table like the one below made by a student who is researching types of armor worn by knights in the Middle Ages.

Armor in the Middle Ages	
Type of Armor	Description
hauberk	a tunic made from chain mail with a hood
surcoat	a coat worn over the chain mail suits to protect them from the sun; the coats are decorated with identifying emblems
plate armor	plates of solid metal designed to deflect arrows

- **Conceptual mapping** *Mapping,* or *conceptual mapping,* is similar to clustering. The difference is that it is used to organize information that you have gathered rather than to find ideas. You can use conceptual mapping to group your main ideas and supporting details before you write your paragraphs. An example of a conceptual map is shown at the bottom of the page.

- **Outlines** An *outline* is another way to organize important information. When you make an outline, you arrange the ideas to show the main ideas and the supporting details. You can use the outline as a guide to writing.

    You may need to use different types of outlines. For a report, your teacher might require you to write a *formal outline,* like the one at the top of the next page, with Roman numerals for headings and capital letters for subheadings.

Conceptual Map

Rainforest Animals in Peru

Tree Sloth
- lives in trees
- slow
- eats leaves, flowers, and twigs

Howler Monkey
- eats leaves
- lives in groups
- howls at dawn and dusk

Jaguar
- top predator
- hunts alone at night
- largest and most powerful cat in Americas

Skills, Structures, and Techniques   **347**

Formal Outline

```
Title: Kids About Town
Main Idea: After-school activi-
  ties are good, but you should
  limit how many you do.
I. Benefits
   A. Group Activities (soccer
      team)
      1. learn teamwork
      2. make friends
      3. physical fitness
   B. Individual Activities
      (violin lessons)
      1. develop self-discipline
      2. learn a skill
II. Drawbacks
   A. Less Study Time
   B. Stress
```

To organize your writing quickly, you can use an *informal outline* like the one below.

Informal Outline

Topic: After-School Activities

Benefits	Drawbacks
group activities (soccer): learn teamwork	sometimes too busy to study
make friends	stress caused by worrying about my grades and when I will have time for everything
physical fitness	
individual activities (violin lessons): develop self-discipline	
learn a skill	

■ **Sequence chain** See **Text Structures, Analyzing** on page 291.

■ **Time line** A *time line* organizes information by the date it happened. The time line below shows one student's progress in learning to use a personal computer.

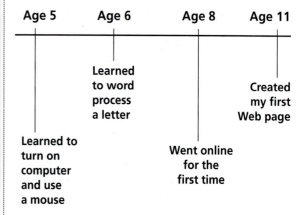

■ **Venn diagram** A *Venn diagram* uses circles to show how two subjects are alike and different. Each subject has its own circle, but the circles overlap. In the overlapping part, you write details that are the same for both subjects. In the parts that do not overlap, you write details that make these subjects different. (See also page 132.)

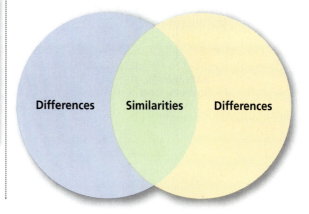

Symbols for Revising and Proofreading

Symbol	Example	Meaning of Symbol
≡	I will see you on saturday morning.	Capitalize a lowercase letter.
/	My Dog's name is Spot.	Lowercase a capital letter.
∧	Do not walk ^away^ from me.	Insert a missing word, letter, or punctuation mark.
℘	After you go go home, give me a call.	Leave out a word, letter, or punctuation mark.
∽	peice	Change the order of letters.
¶	¶ After you finish the first steps, continue on to the next.	Begin a new paragraph.
⊙	Dr. Chavez	Add a period.
∧	Yes, I like strawberry smoothies.	Add a comma.

Revising and Proofreading Symbols When you are revising and proofreading, indicate any changes by using the symbols in the chart above.

Style When you act a certain way or dress a certain way, you are creating your personal style. When you write, you decide what words you are going to use and how you are going to arrange those words in sentences. The choices you make create your *style* of writing. Your writing style is personal because you are the one who created it.

Transitions *Transitions,* or *transitional expressions,* are words and phrases that show the connections between ideas in a piece of writing. Transitions make your writing *coherent,* or smooth and easy to read.

Voice The way a piece of writing "sounds" is its *voice.* As you write, try to express your ideas clearly and naturally. Although some writing requires a formal voice because of its audience and purpose, the writing should still sound like you. Your writing voice also reveals your attitude about your topic and your audience. Treat both with respect by choosing your words carefully.

INDEX

Abridged dictionary, 262
Accent marks, in dictionary entry, 263
Accuracy, 202, 314
Accurate information, in graphics, 269
Action details, 30
Action verbs, in headline, 73
Actors, feelings expressed by, 183
Adding (as revision technique) 12, 36, 69, 103, 104, 139, 171, 214, 248
Adjective(s), comparative form of, 142
Adjustment letter, 342
Adverb(s), comparative form of, 142
Advertising
    humorous, 254–55
    in media, 333
    in print, 255
    on radio, 255
    relationship, documentary filmmakers and advertisers, 146
    on television, 255
Advice column, 74
Affixes. *See* Prefixes; Suffixes.
African American Vernacular English, 274
Alignment, of page, 265–66
Alliteration, 42
Almanacs, 281
Alphabetization, of source list, 205
American English. *See also* Standard English.
    dialects of, 274
    spelling and pronunciations, 273
Analyzing
    of cause and effect, 65
    media messages, 314
    sound effects in poetry, 179
Anchor, for television news segment, 79, 80, 82
And. *See* Conjunctions.
Anecdotes, 337
Animation, in electronic media, 325
Announcements, 305
Apostrophes, and possessive personal pronouns, 251
Appendix, in a book, 277
Appositive(s), 174
Appreciation letter, 342
Arguments. *See also* Facts; Opinions; Persuasion; Persuasive essay (reading); Persuasive essay (writing).
    counterarguments and, 233
Arranging ideas, 31

Art and artwork. *See also* Graphic(s); Illustrations; Visuals.
    designing a newspaper, 77
    editorial cartoons, 76, 83, 259
Articles, capitalizing in titles, 217
Atlases, 281
Audience, media and, 328
Audience (speaking)
    adapting word choice for, 45
    analyzing for presentation, 302
    and verbal elements of speech, 304
Audience (writing). *See also* Advertising; Target audience.
    for autobiographical incident, 29
    for book review, 163–64
    for business letters, 340
    for comparison-contrast essay, 130–31
    for "how-to" paper, 95
    for informal or personal letters, 340
    for news article, 60
    for persuasive letter, 239, 240, 241–42
    for research report, 200
Audio. *See* Television.
Author(s)
    bias of, 286
    of book, 168
    point of view, 286
    purpose of, 188, 194–95, 286
Authoritative sources, 202
Authority, in media, 328
Autobiographical incident (reading)
    chronological order, 18, 23–24
    making inferences (forming generalizations), 18, 21–22
    reading selection, 19–20
Autobiographical incident (writing)
    prewriting, 27–31
    proofreading/publishing, 39–40
    revising, 36–38
    Student's Model, 35
    Writer's Model, 33–34
    writing, 32
Autobiographies, writing to learn and, 318

Babbitt, Natalie, 169
Background information for telling a story, 29, 45
Background knowledge. *See* Prior knowledge.
Bandwagon technique, 257
Banta, Natalie, 68
Bar graphs, 143, 294
Barriers to effective listening, eliminating, 309. *See also* Listening.

Basic situation, 165
Believability
    evaluation and, 313
    of persuasive speaker, 256
Beowulf, 272
Bias, 202, 314. *See also* Point of view.
    of author, 286
    media and, 328
Bibliographic references, 210
    in a book, 277
Biography. *See also* Autobiographical incident; Autobiographies.
    in the library, 277
Block style (of business letter), 341
Block style (of comparison-contrast essay), 124
Body
    of book review, 168
    of business letter, 341
    of comparison-contrast essay, 136
    of composition, 338
    of "how-to" paper, 98
    of news article, 66
    of persuasive letter, 244
    of research report, 210
    of visual and graphic, 293
Body language
    movement and feelings, 183
    as positive feedback, 310
    in presentation, 304
Boldface fonts, 268
Book(s)
    call number of, 277, 278
    comparing with film and television, 181–84
    information found in parts of, 277
    information in card catalog, 277–78
    as sources, 132, 202, 203
Book jacket, 162
Book review (reading)
    elements of a novel, 154, 156
    point of view, 154, 157
    reading selection, 155
Book review (writing)
    gathering and organizing details, 164–66
    identifying plot elements, 165
    preparing your evaluation, 167
    prewriting, 161–67
    proofreading and publishing, 174–75
    purpose and audience for, 163–64
    revising, 171–73
    Student's Model, 170
    Writer's Model, 169
    writing, 168–70
Borrowed words, 273–74
Brainstorming. *See also* Prewriting.
    for clarification essays, 219
    for comparison-contrast essay, 129
    for "how-to" paper, 94
    for humorous advertisement, 255
    for presentation topic, 301
    prewriting and, 344
    for research report, 199
    for short story, 176
British English, spelling and pronunciations, 273
Broadcasting, 325
Brochures, 225
Browser, World Wide Web, 279, 282
Bullet, in page layout, 266
Bulletin board display, 259
Business letters. *See also* Letters (correspondence).
    envelopes for, 340
    format of, 246
    forms of, 341
    parts of, 341–42
    purposes for, 340
    types of, 342
Byline, 333

C

Cable television, 326
"California Gold Rush, The" (Wilmore), 189–91
Call number, 277, 278. *See also* Card catalog.
Call to action, in persuasive letter, 242–43
Camera person, for television news segment, 79, 82
Cameras, 335
    camera angle, 148, 326
Camera shot, 326
Capitalization
    of proper nouns, 39
    of titles and subtitles of works, 217
Capital letters, 268
Captions
    in graphics, 270
    in photography, 149–50, 335
Card catalog, 162, 277–78. *See also* Online catalog.
Career development activities
    comparing and contrasting by journalists, 151
    expert guidance, 225
    in journalism, 83
    letter writing, 117
    persuasion and, 259
    writing journal entry about person who interests you, 47
Career guide, 225
Carroll, Lewis, 178
Cartoons. *See* Editorial cartoons.
Categories, for ideas in research, 207. *See also* Organizing ideas.
Catherine, Called Birdy (Cushman), 155
Cause, definition of, 286

Cause-and-effect pattern, 287, 292
Cause-and-effect relationships
    analysis of, 65, 286
    as context clues, 295
CD-ROM, as source, 202, 278
Censorship, 332
Center-aligned text, 265
Central idea. *See* Main idea.
Characterization, 182–83
Characters
    main character, 162, 163
    in novel, 156
    in short story, 176–77
    in *Tuck Everlasting,* 164
Charts, 197, 221, 711–13, 346–47. *See also* Diagrams; Graphic(s).
    answering questions about, 197
    flowcharts, 112–13, 270
    learning "how-to" from graphics and, 112–13
    pie chart, 270, 294
    T-chart, 145
Choppy sentences, combining, 141
Chronological order, 166
    analysis of text pattern of, 292
    for autobiographical incident, 31
    chart of, 24
    clue words, 287
    in "how-to" paper, 96, 98
    plot summary in, 168
    for story, 45
Clarification, of speech, 224, 258
Clarification essay, 219
Classification
    of information as study skill, 315
Classification essay, 145
Clichés, 172, 173, 296. *See also* Tired words.
Closing, of business letter, 341
Clue words, 287. *See also* Context clues; Text structures.
Clustering, prewriting and, 345
Coherence. *See also* Organizing ideas; Rearranging (as revision technique); Specific language; Transitional words and phrases.
    in book review, 168
    in "how-to" paper, 98
Collaborative writing
    database records, 185
    forms, 185, 259
    short story, 185
Collection of written works. *See* Portfolio building.
"Collection Question, A" (Hester), 138
Colloquialisms, 275
Colors
    cool colors and warm colors, 270
    creating effects with images, 331
    in graphics, 269–70
    illustrations and, 330
    in visuals, 221

Columns, in newspaper article, 73
Combining (as revision technique), 12, 70, 140
Combining sentences, 71, 141
Comic book form, 192, 194
Commas
    and appositives, 174
    with conjunctions connecting sentences, 71
    for items in a series, 106
Commercial broadcasting, 325
Common nouns, 39
Community, sharing information with, 240
Comparative form
    of adjectives, 142
    of adverbs, 142
Comparing and contrasting
    comparative adjectives and adverbs, 142
    of film and book in same genre, 183–84
    of film, TV, and literature, 181–84
    of ideas in photography, 147–50
    oral traditions, 47, 311
    perception of spoken message with others, 258, 310
Comparison-contrast essay (reading)
    comparison-contrast structure, 120, 124–25
    points of comparison, 120, 123–24
    reading selection, 121–22
Comparison-contrast essay (writing), 128–45
    choose and narrow two subjects, 128–30
    main idea statement for, 133
    organizing information for, 132–33
    prewriting, 128–35
    proofreading and publishing, 142–44
    purpose and audience for, 130–31
    revising, 139–41
    Student's Model, 138
    support for, 132–33
    Writer's Model, 137
    writing, 136–38
Comparison-contrast pattern, 287, 292
Comparison-contrast structure, 120, 124–25
Complaint letter, 342
Complications, in plot, 165
Composition
    body of, 338
    conclusion of, 338–39
    introduction of, 337–38
Compound sentences, run-on sentences changed to, 72
Compound words, 92
Comprehension, listening and, 311–12
Computers. *See also* Internet; World Wide Web.
    desktop publishing, 265–69
    editing with, 38, 107
    evaluating writing, 248
    headings, 209
    networks, 280
    online card catalog, 280
    online databases, 280
    online sources, 280

revising with, 141, 171
spellchecker on, 107
thesaurus for replacing dull verbs, 38
Computer software
learning "how-to" from, 112, 114–15
presentation software, 224
Conceptual maps, 208, 347
Conclusion of written work
book review, 168
comparison-contrast essay, 136
composition, 338–39
"how-to" paper, 98
persuasive letter, 244
research report, 210
Conclusions. *See* Drawing conclusions.
Condensed type, 268
Conferencing. *See* Peer review.
Conflict, in short story, 176–77
Conjunctions
combining sentences, 71, 72
stringy sentences and, 250
Connecting cultures, 46
comparing folk tales, 47
ethnic dialect, 274
Connecting with others through speaking and listening, 17, 85, 119, 187, 305–306. *See also* Making connections.
Connections to life, 74–75, 146, 220–21, 254–55
Connections to literature. *See* Literature connections.
Connotation, definition of, 296
Constructive criticism, 310
Content and Organization Guidelines for Self-Evaluation and Peer Evaluation
autobiographical incident, 36
book review, 171
comparison-contrast essay, 139
"how-to" paper, 103
news article, 69
persuasive letter, 248
research report, 214
Content (speaking), evaluating, 256
Context, 25, 159, 160
of media message, 328
Context clues, 25, 160, 194, 195
identifying meanings of words with, 295–96
Contrasting. *See* Comparing and contrasting.
Conversation. *See* Dialogue; Speaking.
Convincing, in persuasive speech, 256, 258, 313
Copy. *See also* Script.
media, 333
Copyright page, of a book, 277
Corresponding with others. *See* E-mail; Letters (correspondence).
Counterargument, 233
Cover of novel, 162
Creative writing

as author's purpose, 194
humorous poem, 151
about research topic, 225
story writing with group of classmates, 185
Credibility, 202. *See also* Believability.
media definition of, 328
Credits, in electronic media, 326
Criteria (speaking)
developing, to evaluate persuasive speech, 257–58
developing, to evaluate self, 308
Criteria (writing). *See* Content and Organization Guidelines for Self-Evaluation and Peer Evaluation; Style Guidelines.
Critical thinking. *See* Mini-lesson (critical thinking).
Critical viewing, of visual messages, 328–30
"Critter Crew" (Mearns), 7
Cropping, of photographs, 149, 335
Cross-curricular activities (art)
editorial cartoons, 83
Cross-curricular activities (music), multimedia presentation, 151
Cross-curricular activities (physical education), trading cards, 225
Cross-curricular activities (science)
articles about, 83
flowchart or graphic for process in, 117
Cross-curricular activities (social studies), letters and forms for field trips, 259
Cross-curricular activities (speech), class "how-to" demonstration, 117
Cross-references, in card catalog, 278
CSSD (context, structure, sound, dictionary), 159
Culture. *See* Connecting cultures.
Cursive writing, 41
Cushman, Karen, 155
Cutting, 307

Database
online, 280
of reports on educational computer games (creating), 185
Definitions
as context clues, 295
in dictionary entry, 263
Deleting (as revision technique), 139, 171
Delivery, of presentation, 223, 224, 256, 303–304
Denotation, definition of, 296
Description
details in, 30
as literary technique, 177, 182
in short story, 177
writing, 41, 109–11

Designing your writing
   bar graph, 143
   business letter format, 246
   headings, 209
   illustrating steps in a process, 101
   for newspaper production, 77
   quotations in book reviews, 166
Desktop publishing
   definition of, 265
   page layout, 265–67
   type, 267–69
Details. *See also* Evidence.
   action details, 30
   arranging and organizing, 63–64, 134, 164–66
   evaluation of, 63–64, 135
   gathering, 60–63, 164, 166
   in news article, 66
   organizing in spatial order, 110
   relevant, 135
   sensory details, 10, 30, 46, 109
   supporting details, 6, 127
Dewey Decimal classification system, 277, 278
Diagrams, 113, 270, 294
   Venn diagram, 132, 348
Dialects, of American English, 274
Dialogue, 182
   informal English for, 45
   in short story, 177
Diaries, studying and, 318
Diction, 304
Dictionary, 159, 235
   parts of entry, 262–63
   types of, 262
Differences, 129, 131, 145. *See also* Comparing and contrasting.
Directions (instructions). *See also* Instructions.
   for demonstration to class, 117
   guidelines for giving, 306
   listening to, 312
Directory, for Internet search, 204, 283, 284
Direct quotations, 66
Discover, writing to. *See* Writing to discover.
Discussion. *See* Group discussion.
Distractions, listening and, 309
"Do Animals Think?" (Lambeth), 4
Documentaries, 326. *See also* Producer.
   comparing documentaries, 146
   definition of, 146
   footage, 331
   as research source, 202
Document design
   desktop publishing and, 265–68
   graphics in, 269–71
   manuscript style, 264
   page layout, 265–67
   type, 267–69

Documenting sources, 202–203, 210
Dorling Kindersley Nature Encyclopedia, The, 14
Double-spaced text, 269
Drafting. *See* Writing (first draft).
Dramatic interpretation. *See also* Oral interpretation.
   of experience (telling a story), 45–46
   of play, 47
   of poem, 44
   of story, 177
Drawing conclusions, 188, 192–93, 287
Dudley, William, 229–30

Editing, 251. *See also* Grammar Links; Revising (writing); Proofreading.
   for appropriate word choice, 38, 173, 216
   of book review, 171
   of news article, 55, 69
   of persuasive essay, 253
   for sentence variety, 71, 141
Editor, in media, 333
Editorial cartoons, 76, 83, 259, 334
Editorials (writing), 76
Effect, definition of, 286
Effects, of media messages, 182, 224, 329–30
Elaboration
   of description, 110
   in persuasive letter, 244
   as revision technique, 36, 69, 103, 139, 171, 214, 248
   with specific language, 97
   supporting evidence and, 242
   to support spoken ideas, 222, 303
   in writing, 97, 110, 210, 244
Electronic mail. *See* E-mail.
Electronic media terms, 325–28
Elements
   of novels, 154, 156
   of plot, 165
Eliminating barriers to effective listening. *See* Barriers to effective listening, eliminating.
E-mail, 47
   guidelines for, 339
   persuasive letter and, 252
   response to novel in, 185
Emotional appeals, 233
   as persuasive technique in speech, 257
Emotions. *See* Feelings.
Emphasis, in page layout, 266
Encyclopedias, 202, 281
English language
   American English dialects, 274
   changes in, 272–73

colloquialisms in, 275
formal, 45, 275
history of, 272–75
informal, 45, 275
Middle English, 272
nonstandard, 274–75
Old English, 272
slang in, 275
standard English, 274–75
word origins, 273–74

Entertaining
as author's purpose, 194
documentary for, 146

Entry word, in dictionary entry, 262

Envelopes, addressing, 340

Essay
proofreading of, 39
publishing, 40
reflecting on, 40

Essay tests
evaluating and revising, 321
key verbs in, 320
prewriting, 321
qualities of good answer, 321
questions, 12–13, 319–21
studying for, 319

Ethical appeals, 233

Ethnic dialect, 274

Etymology, in dictionary entry, 263

Evaluation. *See also* Content and Organization Guidelines for Self-Evaluation and Peer Evaluation; Peer review; Revising (writing); Style Guidelines.
of book, 167
of details in a news article, 63–64
of event in a news story, 58–59
of oral presentation, 311
of persuasive speech, 256–58
of research presentation, 223–24
of self, in formal speaking, 308
of Web sites, 284–85
of writing, 248

Evaluation criteria, 308

Events, newsworthy, 58–59

Evidence, 228, 232–34
to clarify and support spoken ideas, 222, 303
elaboration and, 242
in persuasive essay, 253
for persuasive letter, 241, 242

Exact verbs, 37, 38

Exaggeration, in humorous advertisement, 255

Examples
in dictionary entry, 263
for persuasive letter, 241
to support spoken ideas, 222

Expanded type, 268

Experience, personal. *See* Life experience.

Experts, career guidance from, 225

Explanations
in comparison-contrast essay, 136
in "how-to" paper, 98

Expository writing, 58
book review, 161–75
comparison-contrast essay, 128–44
"how-to" paper, 94–107
informative essay, 219
newspaper article, 58–73
research report, 198–218

Expressing, as author's purpose, 194

Expressive writing, 15, 17, 27–40. *See also* Autobiographical incident.

Eye contact, 304

Facial expressions, 183, 304
of Cinderella, 184

Facts, 228, 231–32, 233. *See also* Opinions.
distinguishing from opinions, 287
in news article, 60–61
in persuasive letter, 241
test on, 236

Faulty generalizations, 22

Feature news, 334. *See also* Soft news.

Feedback, 310

Feelings, expressed by actors, 183

Fiction books, 277

Figurative language, 42, 43, 109, 296
metaphor, 109
simile, 109

Films. *See also* Documentaries; Videos and videotapes.
comparing with TV and literature, 181–84
definition of, 326
documentary, 146
as information source, 280

First impressions, of poems, 179

5W-How? questions, 279
listening to comprehend and, 312
news article and, 50, 54–55, 60–62, 63, 66
prewriting and, 344

Flowcharts, 23–24, 31, 112–13, 270
diagrams and, 113

Focused topic, 199

Focused writing, 345

Fonts (typefaces), 248, 267–69, 268. *See also* Underlining (italics).
boldface, 268
in print media, 334
size of, 268
style of, 268–69

Footers, 266

Index 355

Formal English, 45, 275
Formal outlines, 347–48
Formal speaking, 301–305
    announcements, 305
    introductions to presentations, 305
    presentations, 301–305
Format, of business letter, 246
Forming generalizations. *See* Generalizations.
Forms
    for evaluating, 185
    for field trips, 259
    filling out, 339–40
Formula, in media, 330
Foul Shot (Hoey), 43
Four *W's* *(What? When? Who? Where?),* 29
Freewriting
    focused, 345
    guidelines for, 345
    studying and, 318
Friendly letters. *See* Personal letters.
Functional print, reading, 112–15, 293–95

G

Games, writing instructions for, 117
Generalizations, 18, 21–22, 184, 287–88
Genres in media, 330
Genres of literature, 181
Glossary, in a book, 277
Goals, for writing improvement, 107
Grammar Links
    capitalizing and punctuating titles, 217
    capitalizing proper nouns, 39
    correcting run-on sentences, 72
    punctuating possessives correctly, 251
    using appositives, 174
    using commas in a series, 106
    using comparatives correctly, 142
Graphic(s), 264. *See also* Illustrations.
    arrangement and design of, 269–70
    charts, 112–13, 197
    cool colors and warm colors in, 270
    creating, 221
    diagrams, 113
    elements of effective graphics, 293
    functions of, 269
    interpreting, 293–95
    for science process, 117
    for television advertisements, 255
    types of, 270–71, 293–95
Graphic organizers
    for comparison-contrast essay, 130
    for conceptual maps and time lines, 208
    flowcharts, 23–24, 31
    prewriting and, 343
    of reasons and evidence, 234
    studying and, 316
    time line, 31, 208, 211
Graphs, 221, 294
    bar graph, 143
    using in documents, 270–71
Group activities, story writing as, 185
Group discussion
    guidelines for, 306
    of persuasive speech, 258
    purpose of, 305
    role assignment in, 305–306
    summarizing, 306
Gutter, 266

H

Handwriting, 41
Handwritten papers, 264
Hard news, 334
Headers, 266
Headings, 209, 266–67
    of business letter, 341
    of document, 264
    in outline, 207
    in outlining research report, 207
Headline, of news article, 73, 334
Hoey, Edwin A., 43
Home page, 282
"How Doth the Little Crocodile" (Carroll), 178
"How-to" article (reading)
    forming mental images and, 86, 91
    making predictions and, 86, 87–88
    reading selection, 89–90
"How-to" instructions (viewing)
    in charts and graphics, 112–13
    in computer software, 114–15
    in TV and video programs, 115–16
"How-to" paper (writing)
    audience for, 95–96
    elaborating, 97
    illustrating steps in a process, 101
    planning of, 96
    prewriting, 94–96
    proofreading and publishing, 106–107
    purpose of, 95
    revising, 103–105
    Student's Model, 102
    for test, 108
    transitional words and phrases in, 104, 105
    Writer's Model, 99–100
    writing of, 98–102
"How-to" videos, 112, 115–16

Humor
    poem, 151
    writing humorous advertisement, 254–55
Hyperlinks, 281, 282

I

Ideas, prewriting and organizing, 346–48
Idioms
    definition of, 297
    in dictionary entry, 263
Illustrations. *See also* Diagrams; Graphic(s); Photographs and photography.
    of autobiographical incident, 34
    elements of, 330–31
    media choice in, 150
    photographs, 147–50
    of steps in a process, 101
    style of, 150
    using in documents, 271
Images
    moving, 331
    still, 331
Implied main idea, 50. *See also* Main idea.
    identifying, 288
Indentation
    in page layout, 267
    for paragraphs, 264
Indexes
    in a book, 277
    as information sources, 278–79
Inferences, 26, 288
    forming generalizations and, 18, 21–22
Influencing, as author's purpose, 194
Informal English, 45, 275
Informal or personal letters. *See* Personal letters.
Informal outlines, 207–208, 348
    subtopics in, 207, 210
Informal speaking, 305–307
Information. *See also* Sources.
    in card catalog, 278
    in graphics, 269
    listening for, 311–12
    organizing for presentation, 303
    in photographs, 148–50
    for presentation, 303
    prewriting and gathering, 346
    print and electronic sources, 276–85
    on World Wide Web, 204
Informational sources. *See* Sources, reference.
Informative article (reading)
    author's purpose, 188, 194–95
    drawing conclusions, 188, 192–93
    making inferences, 188, 192–93
    reading selection, 189–91
Informative essay, 219
Informative writing. *See* Expository writing.
Informing
    as author's purpose, 194
    documentary for, 146
Inside address, of business letter, 341
Instructions. *See also* Directions (instructions); "How-to" paper.
    in charts, 112–13
    in chronological order, 96
    for computer software, 114–15
    demonstrations to class, 117
    for games, 117
    guidelines for giving, 306
    for "how-to" paper, 95
    listening to, 312
    writing, 108
Intent. *See* Purpose.
Interesting beginning, of persuasive letter, 244
Internet, 132. *See also* World Wide Web.
    definition of, 327
    as information source, 279
    online catalog, 162
    as source, 202
Interviews
    conducting, 225, 313
    for news article, 61
    as sources, 202
Introduction
    to book review, 168
    of comparison-contrast essay, 136
    of composition, 337–38
    to "how-to" paper, 98
    to persuasive letter, 244
    to presentations, 305
    to research report, 210
Inverted pyramid structure, 50, 54–55, 63, 66
Invitations, 343
Irony, in humorous advertisement, 255
Italics, 268. *See also* Underlining (italics).

J

Journal
    career interests, 47
    entry-writing activities, 47
    studying and, 318
    writer's, 346
Journalism, careers in, 83
Judgment words, 231
Justified text, 265–66
Juxtaposition, creating effects with images, 331

Key words
    in skimming, 207
    in Web search, 204, 280, 283, 284
K-W-L chart for researching, 201, 205

Labels (for graphics)
    on diagrams, 113
    on flowcharts, 112–13
    for graphics and visuals, 270, 293
Labels (regional or cultural), 274, 311
Lambeth, Ellen, 4
Language. *See also* English language.
    figurative, 296
"Last Night I Dreamed of Chickens" (Prelutsky), 178
Lead, in news story, 63, 66, 334
Leading, 269
Learning log, 346
    comparison-contrast essay and, 144
    news article and, 73
    studying and, 318
Left-aligned text, 265
Legend, for visuals and graphics, 143, 293
Legible handwriting, 41
Letters (correspondence). *See also* Personal letters.
    adjustment or complaint letter, 342
    appreciation letter, 342
    book review in, 185
    business, 246, 340–42
    for career development, 117
    for class field trip, 259
    envelopes for, 340
    informal or personal, 340, 342–43
    invitation, 343
    persuasive letter, 237–53
    of regret, 343
    request or order letter, 342
    about research topic, 225
    thank-you letter, 343
Library/Media center, print and electronic sources of, 276–85
Life experience, writing about. *See* Autobiographical incident (writing).
Line graphs, 294
Line spacing. *See* Leading.
Listening
    analyzing persuasive techniques, 257
    to appreciate, 309–310
    asking questions (for clarification), 223, 258, 310
    comparing perceptions, 116, 258, 310
    to comprehend, 311–12
    connecting with others through, 17, 85, 119, 187, 305–306
    distinguishing between fact and opinion, 256, 257, 312
    distractions in, 309
    eliminating barriers to, 224, 309
    to evaluate, 312–13
    evaluating a persuasive speech, 256–58
    evaluating a research presentation, 223–24
    5W-How? questions and, 312
    with a focus, 346
    guidelines for, 309
    to "how-to" TV programs and videos, 115–16
    for information, 311–12
    to instructions and directions, 312
    interpreting speaker's message, 223–24, 257, 258, 313
    interpreting speaker's purpose and perspective, 256, 258, 313
    interviews and, 313
    to literature, 310–11
    LQ2R study method and, 312
    for major ideas and supporting evidence, 223, 257, 311
    to media messages, 314
    monitoring understanding, 223, 258
    for nonverbal-message elements, 224, 257, 313
    to oral tradition, 311
    organizing spoken ideas, 116
    preparing to listen, 309
    purpose for, 256, 309, 310–13
    researching music and, 225
    and responding to speaker, 310
    summarizing spoken ideas, 116
    taking notes and, 116, 224, 309
Listing pattern, 287, 292–93
List of sources, of research report, 202–203, 210
Lists
    bulleted, 266
    of sources, 202–203, 205
Literature connections. *See also* Genres of literature.
    comparing with film and television, 181–84
    listening to, 310–11
    narrative poem, 42–44
    poetry, 178–80
    short story, 176–77
    writing a descriptive paragraph, 109–11
Loaded words, 297
Location words, 109
Log. *See* Learning log.
Logical order, 134
Logical progression, 63
Logical support, 135, 139, 241. *See also* Support.
Logic questions, 323
Looping. *See* Freewriting.

Lowercase letters, 268
LQ2R study method, and listening for information, 312

M

Magazines, 202
    as sources, 132
Mail. *See also* E-mail.
    persuasive letter and, 252
Main character, 162, 163
Main idea
    answering questions about, 57
    in composition, 338
    implied main idea, 50, 53, 288
    stated main idea, 50, 53–54, 291
Main idea statement, 133, 136, 210
    for research report, 209
"Make It Grow" (Thompson), 102
Making connections
    in storytelling, 46
Making inferences, drawing conclusions and, 188, 192–93
Making predictions. *See* Predicting.
Manuscript style, guidelines for, 264
Maps. *See* Clustering; Conceptual maps.
Maps (source of information), 202
Margins, 264. *See also* Alignment.
    page layout and, 267
Mass media, 314. *See also* Media; Media messages.
Matching questions, 321
Meaning(s)
    changes in English and, 273
    multiple, 297
    word, 296–97
Mearns, Anna, 7
Media. *See also* Films; Internet; Multimedia presentations; Videos and videotapes.
    comparing film, TV, and literature, 181–84
    definition of, 314
    producing a television news segment, 79–82
    using in presentation, 303
Media center. *See* Library/Media center.
Media law, 332
Media literacy, 332. *See also* Critical viewing.
Media messages, 314
    analyzing, 314
    evaluating, 329–30
    objectivity in, 314
Media terms
    electronic media terms, 325–28
    general media terms, 328–33
    print media terms, 333–36
Medium, 334

Memorization, as study skill, 316
Mental images, forming, 86, 91, 111
Messages, 332. *See also* Media messages.
    critical viewing of visual messages, 328–30
Metaphors, 42, 109, 296
Microfiche, 279
Microfilm, 279
Microforms, 279
Middle English, 272
Mini-lesson (critical thinking)
    arranging ideas, 31
    cause and effect, 65
    elements of a plot, 165
    evaluating details, 135
    searching World Wide Web, 204
    understanding your audience, 240
Mini-lesson (test taking), 26, 41, 57
    answering main idea questions, 57
    answering questions about charts, 197
    clarification essay, 219
    classification essay, 145
    fact and opinion, 236
    informative essay, 219
    making inferences, 26
    making predictions, 93
    persuasive essay, 253
    supporting details, 127
    unfamiliar vocabulary and, 160
    writing description for tests, 41
    writing instructions, 108
Mini-lesson (vocabulary). *See also* Vocabulary.
    compound words, 92
    context clues, 25
    dictionary and thesaurus, 235
    multiple-meaning words, 56
    prefixes and suffixes, 126
    wordbusting strategy (CSSD), 159
    word roots, 196
Mini-lesson (writing)
    elaboration with specific language, 97
    paraphrasing, 206
Modified block style (of business letters), 341
Modified block style (of comparison-contrast essay), 134
Modifiers. *See* Comparative form.
Money making, documentary for, 146
Monitor, for oral research presentation, 224
Monitoring understanding, 223, 258. *See also* Listening.
Mood, 304, 310
    creating with sound, 327
Movies. *See* Films.
Moving image, 331
"Mr. Sagers Moves to Cyprus High" (Banta and Tidwell), 68
Multimedia presentations, 332. *See also* Media.
    music activity and, 151
    visuals in, 220–21

Multiple-choice questions, 321
Multiple-meaning words, 56
Musical works
multimedia presentation and, 151
researching, 225

Names. *See* Capitalization; Titles (works).
Narration, in film and literature, 182
Narrative (writing)
autobiographical incident, 27–40
narrative poem, 42–44
short story, 176–77
Negative words, 157–58
Networks, computer, 280
News, 335
feature news, 334
hard news, 334
producing a TV news segment, 79–82
reporting, 49
soft news, 336
Newsmagazine, 335
Newspaper
production of, 76–78
school newspaper, 59
as source, 202, 279
Newspaper article (reading)
inverted pyramid structure for, 50, 54–55, 63, 66
main idea, 50, 53–54
reading selection, 51–52
Newspaper article (writing), 58–73
advice column, 74–75
audience, 60
columns in, 73
prewriting, 58–64
proofreading and publishing, 72–73
revising, 69–71
Student's Model, 68
varying sentences, 71
Writer's Model, 67
writing, 66–68
Newsworthiness, criteria for, 332
"Nixon-Kennedy Presidential Debates, The" (Wakin), 121–22
Nonstandard English, 274–75
Nonverbal signals, 304
Notebook, writer's, 346
Note cards, for presentation, 303
Note taking. *See* Taking notes.
Noun(s)
common nouns, 39
precise nouns, 215, 216
proper nouns, 39

Novels
elements of, 154, 156
previewing, 162
writing a review of, 161–75

Objections
addressing, 240–42
to arguments, 233
by audience, 240
Objective tests, 319, 321–24
Objective voice, 61
Objectivity, in media messages, 314
Occasion, of presentation, 223, 302
Offerman, Genna, 213
Old English, 272
On-demand reading questions, 322
On-demand writing questions, 322–23. *See also*
Multiple-choice questions; Short-answer questions.
Online catalog, 162, 277, 280
Online databases, 280
Online Readers' Guide, 280
Online sources, 280
Opinions, 163, 228, 231–32. *See also* Persuasive essay (reading); Persuasive letter (writing).
distinguishing from facts, 236, 287
persuasion and, 237
in persuasive essay, 253
Opinion statement, 234
in persuasive letter, 238, 244
Oral interpretation. *See also* Dramatic interpretation.
choosing selection for, 307
cutting for, 307
definition of, 307
presenting, 308
Oral response, book review as, 175
Oral traditions, 45. *See also* Storytelling.
comparing folk tales in different cultures, 47
listening to, 311
Order letter, 342
Order of ideas. *See also* Chronological order; Organization.
logical order, 134
spatial order, 110
Organization, patterns of. *See* Text structures.
Organizing ideas. *See also* Arranging ideas; Content and Organization Guidelines for Self-Evaluation and Peer Evaluation; Plan (writing).
for book review, 164, 166
for comparison-contrast essay, 132–33
during listening, 116
of news article, 63–64
for presentation, 303

for research report, 207
Outlining
    formal, 347–48
    informal, 207–208, 210, 348
    prewriting and, 347–48
    of research report, 207
    studying and, 317
Out of the Storm (Willis), 170
Overhead projector, for oral research presentation, 224

Page alignment, 265–66
Page layout, 265–67
Paper(s). *See* Document design.
Paragraphs
    descriptive, 109–11
    indentation of, 264
    in long pieces of writing, 32, 98, 136, 210, 244
    in persuasive letter, 244
Paraphrasing, 206, 288–89
    studying and, 317
Parks, Rosa, 19–20
Peer evaluation. *See* Content and Organization Guidelines for Self-Evaluation and Peer Evaluation; Peer review.
Peer review, 37, 70, 104, 140, 172, 215, 249
Perrault, Charles, 183
Personal letters
    purpose for, 340, 342–43
    types of, 343
Personification, 42, 296
Perspective (of a speaker). *See* Bias; Point of view.
Persuasion. *See also* Advertising; Persuasive essay (reading); Persuasive letter (writing); Propaganda.
    analyzing techniques of, 289
    as author's purpose, 194
    and careers, 259
    documentary for, 146
Persuasive essay (reading)
    preparing to read, 228
    reading selection, 229–30
Persuasive essay (writing), 253
Persuasive letter (writing), 237–53
    audience and purpose for, 239
    call to action in, 242–43
    choosing an issue, 237–38
    opinion statement for, 238
    prewriting, 237–43
    proofreading and publishing, 251–52
    reasons and evidence for, 241–42
    revising, 248–49
    Student's Model, 247
    Writer's Model, 245–46
    writing, 244–47
Persuasive letter, call to action in, 242–43
Persuasive speech, 259
    evaluating, 256–58
Persuasive techniques, in speech, 257
    convincing, 256, 257, 258
    propaganda, 257, 314
    selling, 257, 258
Phonetic symbols, in dictionary entry, 263
Photographs and photography
    comparing ideas in photographs, 147–50
    information in, 148–50
    media and, 335
    vs. reality, 147
Phrases, transitional, 293
Pie chart, 221, 270, 293–94
Pitch, as verbal element
    speaking in a different voice, in storytelling, 46
    in speech presentation, 304
Plagiarism, 206, 288
Plan (study plan), 315
Plan (writing). *See also* Order of ideas; Organizing ideas.
    of "how-to" paper, 96
    writing essay about poem, 179
Plot, 156, 162, 163
    elements of, 165
Plot line, 165
Poem
    humorous (writing), 151
    narrative (writing), 42–44
    about research topic (writing), 225
    writing essay on sound effects, 178–80
Point-by-point style, 124, 125
Point of view. *See also* Bias; Propaganda.
    in book review writing, 167
    determining author's point of view, 154, 157–58, 286
    media and, 333
    in presentation, 302
    voice and, 167
Points of comparison, 120, 123–24, 136
    choosing, 131–32
Political cartoons. *See* Editorial cartoons.
Portfolio building. *See also* Writing portfolio.
    autobiographical incident and, 40
    book review and, 175
    comparison-contrast essay and, 144
    "how-to" paper and, 107
    to identify strengths and weaknesses, 252
    news article and, 73
    persuasive letter and, 252
    research report and, 218
    to set goals, 107, 252
Positive feedback, 310
Positive words, 157–58

Possessives, punctuation of, 251
Precise nouns, 215, 216
Predicting, 86, 93, 285
    as reading skill, 289
Prefixes, 126, 196
    definition of, 126, 297–98
    list of, 298
Prelutsky, Jack, 178
Preposition(s), capitalization in titles with, 217
Prereading, xxviii–xix, 290
Presentation. *See also* Technology presentation.
    content and organization of, 301–303
    delivery of, 303–304
    multimedia, 151, 220–21, 332
    purposes for, 301–302
    research, 222–24
Presentation software, for oral research presentation, 224
Previewing, 162
Prewriting. *See also* Text structures; Writing applications.
    arranging ideas, 346–48
    autobiographical incident, 27–31
    book review, 161–67
    brainstorming, 344
    charts and, 346–47
    clustering, 345
    comparison-contrast essay, 128–35
    conceptual mapping and, 347
    essay tests and, 321
    5W-How? questions and, 344
    freewriting and, 345
    graphic organizer and, 341
    "how-to" paper, 94–97
    listening and, 346
    news article, 58–65
    on-demand writing questions and, 322–23
    outlining and, 347–48
    persuasive letter, 237–43
    reading and, 346
    research report, 198–209
    time line and, 348
    Venn diagram and, 348
    "What if?" questions and, 344
    writer's notebook or journal, 346
Print, advertisements in, 255
Print media terms, 333–36
Printed handwriting (manuscript), 41
Prior knowledge, xxviii–xix
    drawing conclusions and, 193
Problem solution
    in advice column, 74–75
    analyzing relationships, 289–90
    pattern, 287, 293
Process. *See also* "How-to" article (reading); "How-to" instructions; "How-to" paper (writing).
    flowchart or graphic for, in science, 117

Producer, 327
    of TV news segment, 79, 81
Product(s), humorous advertisement for, 254–55
Production, stages of media, 335–36
Progression (order of details) 63–64, 96, 164–66. *See also* Arranging ideas; Organizing ideas; Rearranging (as revision technique).
Pronunciation
    British *vs.* American, 273
    changes in English and, 273
    in dictionary, 262–63
Proofreading. *See also* Publishing (writing); Revising (writing).
    autobiographical incident, 39
    book review, 174
    compare-contrast essay, 142
    "how-to" paper, 106
    news article, 72
    by a peer, 39, 72, 106, 142, 174
    persuasive letter, 251
    research report, 217
    symbols for, 349
Propaganda, 257, 333
Proper nouns, capitalization of, 39
Proposal. *See* Persuasive letter (writing).
Public broadcasting, 325
Publishing for various audiences. *See also* Writing applications.
    of book review, 174–75
    of comparison-contrast essay, 142–44
    of "how-to" paper, 106–108
    news article, 72–73
    of persuasive letter, 251–52
    of research report, 217–18
Punctuation
    of appositives, 174
    of possessives, 251
    of titles of works, 217
"Puppy Love or Hamster Heaven," 137
Purpose (of media messages)
    of informative video, 116, 146, 224, 329–30
Purpose (reading) xviii–xix
    author's purpose, identifying, 188, 194–95
Purpose (speaking and listening)
    adapting word choice in speech to, 301
    for formal speaking, 301–302
    interpreting speaker's purpose, 256, 313
    listening with a, 256, 309, 310–13
Purpose (writing)
    of autobiographical incident, 29
    of book review, 163–64
    of comparison-contrast essay, 130–31
    evaluating achievement of, 107, 218
    of "how-to" paper, 95
    of persuasive letter, 239
    of research report, 200

Questioning
    in interviews, 61
    K-W-L method of, 201
Questions
    for analyzing media messages, 314
    as response to speaker, 310
Quotations
    in book reviews, 166
    direct, 66
Quotation marks, with titles of short works, 217

Radio
    advertisements on, 255
    as information source, 280
Ragged text, 266
Rate (or tempo)
    talking slowly, for audience, 46, 223
    as verbal element in speech presentation, 304
Readers' Guide to Periodical Literature, 278
Reading for enjoyment, 290
Reading for mastery (reading to learn), 290
Reading log, 290
Reading process, xviii–xix
    after reading, xviii–xix
    prereading, xviii–xix
    while reading, xviii–xix
Reading rate, adjusting, 290
Reading script, marking, 308
Reading skills and focuses
    adjusting reading rate, 290
    analyzing text structures, 291–93
    author's point of view, 286
    author's purpose, 188, 194–95, 286
    cause-and-effect relationships, 286
    chronological order, 18, 23–24
    clue words, 287
    comparison-contrast structure, 120, 124–25
    drawing conclusions, 188, 192–93, 287
    fact and opinion, 228, 231–32, 287
    forming generalizations, 18, 21–22, 287–88
    forming mental images, 86, 91
    implied main idea, 288
    inverted pyramid structure, 50, 54–55
    main idea, 50, 53–54
    making inferences, 18, 21–22, 188, 192–93, 288
    making predictions, 86, 87–88
    paraphrasing, 288–89
    persuasive techniques, analyzing, 289
    points of comparison, 120, 123–24
    predicting, 289
    problem-solution relationships, 289–90
    reading log, 290
    reasons and evidence, 228, 232–34
    SQ3R, 290
    stated main idea and supporting details, 291
    summarizing, 291
    using transitional words and phrases, 293
    visuals and graphics interpretation, 293–95
Reading with a focus, 346
Reading-writing connection, xviii–xix
Realism, 333
Real life, photographs compared to, 147
Rearranging (as revision technique), 12, 36, 69, 103, 214
Reason(s)
    for buying product, 254
    in persuasive essay, 228, 232–34, 253
    in persuasive letter, 241–42, 244
Reasonable request, 243
Reasoning or logic questions, 323
Record, writing to. *See* Writing to record.
Reference materials and resources for writing. *See also* Sources.
    bibliographies as, 277
    dictionary, 40, 69
    to edit and revise, 69
    reference sources chart, 281
    sources for research, 202–204
    using library as resource in prewriting, 162
    to verify facts in prewriting, 132
    word-processors thesaurus, 38
Reflecting on writing. *See* Writing to reflect.
Regional dialect, 274
Rehearsing, for oral interpretation, 308
Relevant details, 135
Repetition, in poetry, 178
Report(s). *See also* Research report (writing).
    comparison-contrast in, 151
    database of, 185
    on journalism careers, 83
Reporters, 336. *See also* Newspaper article (writing).
    for television news segment, 80
Request letter, 342
Research presentation, giving and evaluating, 222–24
Research report (writing). *See also* Informative article (reading).
    asking questions, 201
    categorizing ideas, 207
    documenting sources, 202–203, 210
    K-W-L chart (to organize prior knowledge), 201
    main idea statement, 209
    making a source list, 202–203, 210
    oral presentation of, 222–24
    organizing information for, 207

outlining, 207–208
paraphrasing, 206
prewriting, 198–209
proofreading and publishing of, 217–18
purpose and audience for, 200
reviewing outline and revisiting research, 208
revising, 214–16
sources for, 202–203
Student's Model, 213
summarizing information for, 205
taking notes, 205
Writer's Model, 211–12
writing, 210–13
Resolution, of plot, 165
Resources for writing. *See* Reference materials and resources for writing.
Responding to others' writing. *See* Content and Organization Guidelines for Self-Evaluation and Peer Evaluation; Peer evaluation; Peer review.
Restatements, as context clues, 295
Review. *See also* Book review (reading); Book review (writing).
of music recording (writing), 225
Revising (writing). *See also* Content and Organization Guidelines for Self-Evaluation and Peer Evaluation; Style Guidelines; Writing applications.
autobiographical incident, 36–38
of book review, 171–73
of comparison-contrast essay, 139–41
of "how-to" paper, 103–105
of news article, 69–71
of persuasive letter, 248–50
and proofreading symbols, 349
research report, 214–16
Rhyme, 178
Rhythm, 178
Richardson, Lisa, 51–52
Right-aligned text, 265
Road map, as graphic organizer, 28
Roots, 196
definition of, 126, 297
list of, 297
Rosa Parks: My Story (Parks), 19–20
Rules (lines), 267
Run-on sentences, 72

Salutation, of business letter, 341
Sayings, 46, 311
Scanning of text, 290
Science, articles about, 83
Script
for electronic media, 327

for TV news segment, 80–81
Search, computer
on Internet, 283–84
in online card catalog, 280
on World Wide Web, 204
Search engine, 204, 282, 283
Self-expression, documentary for, 146
Selling, in persuasive speech, 256–58, 313
Sensory details, 30, 109
in short story, 177
in storytelling, 46
Sentence(s)
combining sentences, 141
run-on sentences, 72
stringy sentences, 250
transitional words in, 104, 105
varying for interest, 71
Sentence-completion questions, 323–24
Sequence chain. *See* Text structures.
Sequential order. *See* Chronological order; Organization.
Series, commas with, 106
Setting, 162, 163
for novel, 156
for short story, 176
and verbal elements of speech, 304
Shadow style, 269
Short-answer questions, 324
Short stories, 83, 176–77
about research topic, 225
Show and tell, in storytelling, 46
Signature, of business letter, 342
Silliness, in humorous advertisement, 255
Similarities, 129, 131, 145. *See also* Comparing and contrasting.
Simile, 42, 109, 151, 296
Single-spaced text, 269
Skimming, 162, 290
key words in, 207
Slang, 45, 275
Slow motion, creating effects with images, 331
Small capitals, 269
Social situations, speaking in, 306–307
Social studies, letters and forms for field trips, 259
Soft news, 336. *See also* Feature news.
Software. *See* Computer software.
Sound
in film and video, 327–28
in humorous advertisement, 254
Sound effects, in poems, 178, 180
Sources, reference, 281. *See also* Authority; Credibility; Dictionary; Information; Messages; Reference materials and resources for writing; Thesaurus.
books, 277
card catalog, 162
electronic, 276, 278–85

interviews, 61
lists of, 203, 210
media, 336
online catalog, 162
primary and secondary, 202
print and electronic, 276–85
reference sources, 69
for research reports, 202–203
visual and graphic, 293
on World Wide Web, 204

"South American Guanaco, The," 211–12
Spacing, line. *See* Leading.
Spatial order, 110
Speakers
listening to, 309
responding to, 310
as sources, 202
Speaking. *See also* Listening; Speech.
connecting with others, 17, 85, 119, 187, 305–306
demonstration, 117
formal, 301–305
giving a research presentation, 222–24
informal, 305–307
juncture in, 308
oral interpretation, 307–308
oral response to literature, 180
persuasive speech, 259
pronunciation, 304
props, 223
self-evaluation, 308
stress in, 308
supporting ideas in, 222, 303
television advertisements and, 255
in television news segment, 80, 81–82
Specialized dictionary, 262
Specific language
elaboration with, 97, 98
forming mental images and, 86, 91
Speech. *See also* Presentation; Speaking.
evaluating persuasive speech, 256–58
Spellchecker, on computer, 107
Spelling
British *vs.* American, 273
changes in English and, 273
correcting, in final drafts, 40, 73, 107, 175, 218, 252
using resources to correct, 40, 107
SQ3R (Survey, Question, Read, Recite, Review) strategy, 290
studying and, 317
Standard English, 274–75
using in presentation, 305
Stated main idea. *See* Main idea.
Statement. *See* Declarative sentences.
Stereotype, 333
Stevenson, Robert Louis, 179, 180
Still image, 331

Stories. *See also* Short stories.
elements of, 156
Storyboards, 271
for script, 328
Storytelling, 45–46
Stringy sentences, 250
Structure
comparison-contrast structure of essay, 120, 124–25, 134
inverted pyramid, in a news article, 50, 54–55, 63
of texts, 291–93
Student's Model
autobiographical incident, 35
book review, 170
comparison-contrast essay, 138
"how-to" paper, 102
news article, 68
persuasive letter, 247
research report, 213
Study skills, 315–18. *See also* Reading skills and focuses; Tests.
Style. *See also* Style Guidelines; Style (sentence style); Style (word choice).
adapting to audience, 29, 141
adapting to purpose, 29, 250
definition of, 349
revising to improve, 37, 70, 104, 140, 172, 215, 249
Style guidelines
clichés, 172
combining sentences, 140
exact verbs, 37
precise nouns, 215
stringy sentences, 249
transitional words, 104
varying sentences, 70
Style (sentence style)
combining sentences, 141
stringy sentences, 250
transitional words, 105
varying sentences, 71
Style (word choice)
clichés, 173
exact verbs, 38
precise nouns, 216
Subheadings, 266–67
Subtitle, 267
Subtopics
in informal outline, 210
in outline, 207
Suffixes, 126, 196
definition of, 126, 298
list of, 298
Summarizing. *See also* Paraphrasing.
in book review, 164
in captions, 150

in chronological order, 168
definition of, summary, 288, 291, 317
discussions, 306
information from nonprint sources, 116
information gathered in research, 205
in interviews, 61
as note-taking strategy, 116
in persuasive letter, 244
as reading strategy, 291
as study skill, 317–18

Support
for comparison-contrast essay, 132
details, 127
evidence as, 242
logical support, 135, 241
revising to add, 69, 139, 248
stated main idea and supporting details, 291

Suspense, 45
in short story, 177

Symbols, on diagrams, 113

Synonyms, 235
books of, 281
as context clues, 295

Tab, setting, 264
Table of contents, of a book, 277
Tables, 197, 294
using in documents, 271
Taking notes, 205, 207
from authoritative sources, 202
guidelines for, 116
informal outline and, 207–208
about persuasive speech, 258
from relevant sources, 202
for studying, 316–17
Tall tale, writing a, 47
"Ta-Na-E-Ka," 176
Target audience. *See also* Audience.
for media, 336
T-chart, 145
Technology. *See also* Computers; Computer software; Presentation; Television; Videos and videotapes; Web sites.
collaboration in database of reports, 185
e-mail messages, 47
for oral research presentation, 224
technology presentation, 332
Telephones, guidelines for speaking on, 307
Television
advertisements on, 255
comparing with film and literature, 181–84
learning "how-to" from TV and videos 112, 115–16
producing a news segment, 79–82
as source, 202, 280
video and, 115–16
Testimonial, as persuasive technique, in speech, 257
Tests, 319–24. *See also* Study skills.
Test taking. *See* Mini-lesson (test taking).
Text
arranging in document, 265–67
in media message, 336
Text structures, 291–93. *See also* Clue words.
Thank-you letter, 343
Thesaurus, 235
on computer, 38
precise nouns and, 216
Thesis and thesis statement, 133, 209. *See also* Main idea; Main idea statement.
for composition, 338
opinion statement as, 238
Thompson, Stephanie, 102
Tidwell, Amy, 68
Time lines, 31, 96, 208, 221, 271, 295. *See also* Road map.
prewriting and, 348
Tired words, 296
Title page, 218, 277
Titles (personal), **capitalization of,** 39
Titles (works), 267
of books, 168
of books in card catalog, 278
capitalization of, 217
choosing, 143
punctuation of, 217
quotation marks and, 217
underlining (italicizing) of, 217
for visual and graphic, 293
Tone (mood) in speaking
changing, in storytelling, 46
identifying, in oral interpretations, 310
as verbal element, 304
Topics. *See also* Subtopics.
in book review, 168
of "how-to" paper, 94–95
of persuasive letter, 238
for presentation, 301
of research report, 198–99
Topic sentences, in composition, 338
Trading card, for athlete, 225
Transitional words and phrases (transitions), 136, 349
in book review, 166, 168
composition and, 338
revising, in "how-to" paper, 104, 105
identifying, 293
True-false questions, 324
Tuck Everlasting (Babbitt), 169
Typed papers, 264
Typefaces. *See* Fonts (typefaces).

Unabridged dictionary, 262
Underlining (italics), 268
    with titles of works, 217
Understanding
    monitoring, 224, 258
"U.S. Has a Garbage Crisis, The" (Dudley), 229–30
Uppercase letters. *See* Capital letters.
URL, 282
Usage. *See* English language.

VCR, for oral research presentation, 224
Venn diagram, 132
    prewriting and, 348
    tools for writers, TV producers, and filmmakers, 183
Verb(s)
    in essay questions, 320
    exact, 37, 38
Verbal elements, in speech delivery, 304
Vertical file, 281
Videos and videotapes. *See also* Documentaries; Films.
    in electronic media, 328
    "how-to" videos, 112
    producing a television news segment, 79–82
    as sources, 202–203, 280
    for television advertisements, 255
    television and, 115–16
Viewing and listening to learn, about charts and graphics, 112–16
Viewing and representing, 325–36
    analyzing an editorial cartoon, 259
    analyzing visual media, 112–16, 146, 148, 149–50, 183–84
    assessing language, medium, and presentation of TV news segment, 82
    comparing documentaries, 146
    comparing film, TV, and literature, 181–84
    comparing ideas in photographs, 147–50
    creating a graphic showing a process, 117
    creating a humorous advertisement, 254–55
    creating an editorial cartoon, 83
    creating charts comparing folk tales, 185
    creating illustrations, 34, 151
    evaluating how various media influence or inform, 150, 329–30
    giving a multimedia presentation, 151, 225
    interpreting and evaluating visual media, 116, 146, 147, 150, 181–84, 224
    interpreting visuals and graphics, 293–95
    key ideas for critical viewing, 329
    making a trading card, 225
    newspaper production, 76–78
    predicting while viewing, 285
    producing a TV news segment, 79–82
    producing visual media, 34, 76–78, 79–82, 101, 220
    sharing information through visuals, 220–21
    summarizing information, 116
    using visuals to complement meaning, 34, 101, 220
    viewing to learn, 112–16
Visualizing, 91
Visual literacy, 333
Visuals, 221. *See also* Graphic(s); Illustrations; Photographs and photography.
    creating, 220–21
    elements of effective visuals, 293
    in humorous advertisement, 254
    interpreting, 293–95
    types of, 293–95
    using visuals to complement meaning, 34, 101, 220
Vocabulary. *See also* English language; Mini-lesson (vocabulary); Word(s).
    skills and strategies, 295–300
    unfamiliar vocabulary, 160
    word meanings, 296–98
    word origins, 273–74
    word parts, 297–98
    words to learn list, 298–300
Voice (writing)
    adapting to audience, 29, 239
    adapting to purpose, 29, 95, 131, 200
    defined, 349
    for news article, 61
    revealing writer's point of view, 167
Volume
    speaking loudly, for audience, 46, 223
    as verbal element in special presentations, 304

Wakin, Edward, 121–22
Warm colors, in graphics, 270
Webbing. *See* Clustering.
Web pages, 281, 282, 283
Web search, 204
Web sites, 281, 282
    evaluation of, 284–85
    presentation and, 332
"Whale Watch: Kids Use Internet to Track Progress of Newly Freed J. J." (Richardson), 51–52
"What if?" questions, prewriting and, 344
Willis, Patricia, 170
Wilmore, Kathy, 189–91

Index **367**

"Windy Nights" (Stevenson), 179, 180
Word(s). *See also* Compound words; Vocabulary.
    borrowed, 273–74
    clichés, 172–73
    loaded, 297
    location words, 109
    from names, 274
    positive and negative words, 157–58
    tired, 296
    transitional, 293
Word bank, 296
Wordbusting strategy (CSSD), 159
Word choice, revising for. *See also* Style (word choice).
Word meanings, 296–97
Word origins, 274
Word parts
    prefixes, 297–98
    roots, 297
    suffixes, 298
Word pictures, 210
Word processing. *See* Computers.
Word roots. *See* Roots.
Works Cited list, 210. *See also* Sources.
World Wide Web. *See also* Internet; Web pages; Web sites.
    browser and, 282
    databases, 280
    evaluating Web sites on, 284–85
    hyperlink and, 282
    as information source, 281–83
    searching, 204, 283–84
    URL of, 282
Writer's journal or notebook, 346
Writer's Model
    autobiographical incident, 33–34
    book review, 169
    comparison-contrast essay, 137
    "how-to" paper, 99–100
    news article, 67
    persuasive letter, 245–46
    research report, 211–12
Writing (first draft). *See also* Description; Narrative writing; Persuasive writing; Writing applications; Writing to learn.
    autobiographical incident, 32–35
    of book review, 168–70
    comparison-contrast essay, 136–38
    "how-to" paper, 98–102
    news article, 66–68
    persuasive letter, 244–47
    research report, 210–13
Writing portfolio, tall tales, 47
Writing process, xviii–xix. *See also* Writing to learn.
    prewriting. *See* Writing Workshop.
    publishing, 39, 72, 106, 142, 174, 217, 251
    reading-writing connection, xviii–xix
    revising, 36, 69, 103, 139, 171, 214, 248
Writing to develop ideas. *See* Chronological order; Prewriting.
Writing to discover, 318. *See* Expressive writing; Journal; Prewriting.
Writing to express, 17
    documentary for self-expression, 146
Writing to learn
    autobiographies, 318
    diaries, 318
    freewriting, 318
    journals, 318
    learning logs, 318
    studying and, 318
Writing to persuade. *See* Persuasion; *headings beginning with* Persuasive.
Writing to problem solve, 74–75
    in advice column, 74–75
    analyzing problem-solution relationships, 289–90
Writing to record, 107, 116, 175, 218, 252
    details in autobiographical incident, 30
    news article, 73
    note-taking guidelines, 116
Writing to reflect
    on autobiographical incident, 40
    on book review, 175
    comparison-contrast essay, 144
    on "how-to" paper, 107
    on news article, 73
    persuasive letter and, 252
    on research report, 218
Writing Workshop
    autobiographical incident (life experience), 27–41
    book review, 161–75
    comparison-contrast essay, 128–45
    "how-to" paper, 94–108
    newspaper article, 58–73
    persuasive letter, 237–53
    research report, 198–219
Written works. *See* Quotation marks.

ACKNOWLEDGMENTS

For permission to reprint copyrighted material, grateful acknowledgment is made to the following sources:

Neil Armstrong: Quote by Neil Armstrong from Apollo 11 on January 23, 1969.

Ballantine Books, a division of Random House, Inc.: From review of *Catherine, Called Birdy* by Karen Cushman from *Great Books for Girls: More Than 600 Books to Inspire Today's Girls and Tomorrow's Women* by Kathleen Odean. Copyright © 1997 by Kathleen Odean.

Cobblestone Publishing, Inc., 30 Grove Street, Suite C, Peterborough, NH 03458: From "Making a Flying Fish" by Paula Morrow from *Faces: Happy Holidays*, vol. 7, no. 4, December 1990. Copyright © 1990 by Cobblestone Publishing, Inc.

Dial Books for Young Readers, an imprint of Penguin Putnam Books for Young Readers, a division of Penguin Putnam Inc.: From "You're Under Arrest" from *Rosa Parks: My Story* by Rosa Parks with Jim Haskins. Copyright © 1992 by Rosa Parks. All rights reserved.

Tyler Duckworth: From "Let's Clean Up the Planet for Future Generations" by Tyler Duckworth from *Time for Kids Archive*, February 1, 1997. Copyright © 1997 by Tyler Duckworth.

Farrar, Straus and Giroux, LLC: From *Tuck Everlasting* by Natalie Babbitt. Copyright © 1975 by Natalie Babbitt.

Greenhaven Press, Inc.: From "The U.S. has a garbage crisis" from *The Environment: Distinguishing Between Fact and Opinion* by William Dudley. Copyright © 1990 by Greenhaven Press, Inc.

HarperCollins Publishers, Inc.: From "Last Night I Dreamed of Chickens" from *Something Big Has Been Here* by Jack Prelutsky. Copyright © 1990 by Jack Prelutsky. From *How TV Changed America's Mind* by Edward Wakin. Copyright © 1996 by Edward Wakin.

Los Angeles Times Syndicate: From "Whale Watch; Kids Use Internet to Track Progress of Newly Freed J. J." by Lisa Richardson from *Los Angeles Times: Orange County Edition*, April 3, 1998, Metro, p. 1. Copyright © 1998 by Los Angeles Times.

Scholastic Inc.: From "The California Gold Rush" by Kathy Wilmore from *Junior Scholastic*, vol. 100, no. 8, December 1, 1997. Copyright © 1997 by Scholastic Inc. From "Ta-Na-E-Ka" by Mary Whitebird from *Scholastic Voice*, December 13, 1973. Copyright © 1973 by Scholastic Inc.

Weekly Reader Corporation: "Foul Shot" by Edwin A. Hoey from *Read*®. Copyright © 1962 and renewed © 1989 by Weekly Reader Corporation. All rights reserved.

Wiley Publishing, Inc.: Dictionary entry for "cloud" from *Webster's New World™ College Dictionary*, Fourth Edition. Copyright © 2000, 1999 by Wiley Publishing, Inc.

The H. W. Wilson Company: Entry for "Bears" from *Reader's Guide to Periodical Literature*. Copyright © 1999 by The H. W. Wilson Company.

SOURCES CITED:

Screen shot for "Grizzly fate" from *FirstSearch*® database, at http://firstsearch.oclc.org/. FirstSearch and WorldCat are registered trademarks of OCLC Online Computer Library Center, Incorporated.

PHOTO CREDITS

Abbreviations used: (tl)top left, (tc)top center, (tr)top right, (l)left, (cl)center left, (c)center, (cr)center right, (r)right, (bl)bottom left, (bc)bottom center, (br)bottom right.

PART OPENERS: Page 1, 260, 261, Kazu Nitta/The Stock Illustration Source, Inc.

TAKING TESTS: Page 2, Rob Gage/Getty Images/Taxi; 4, Steve Kaufman/CORBIS; 7, Theo Allofs/CORBIS.

CHAPTER 1: Page 23, Peter Baumann/Animals Animals/Earth Scenes; 34, Randal Alhadeff/HRW Photo.

CHAPTER 2: Page 53, Bill Bachmann/Photo Edit.

CHAPTER 3: Page 89, Ron Dahlquit/SuperStock; 115, Richard Drew/AP/Wide World Photos.

CHAPTER 4: Page 130, Robert Pickett/CORBIS; 148 (bl) (br), Peter Van Steen/HRW Photo; 149 (tl) (tr), Peter Van Steen/HRW Photo; 149 (bc), Kennan Ward/CORBIS; 150 (tc), Kennan Ward/CORBIS; 150 (bl) (br), Peter Van Steen/HRW Photo.

CHAPTER 5: Page 158, From *Catherine, Called Birdy* by Karen Cushman/copyright ©1994 by Karen Cushman. Jacket illustration copyright ©1994 by Trina Schart Hyman. Jacket calligraphy by Iskra. Reprinted by permission of Clarion Books/Houghton Mifflin Co.; 181, John Springer Collection/CORBIS.

CHAPTER 6: Page 193, Bettmann/CORBIS; 220, F. Gohier/Photo Researchers, Inc.

CHAPTER 7: Page 230, Tim Davis/Photo Researchers, Inc.; 243, David Young-Wolff/Getty Images/Stone; 254 (c), John Langford/HRW Photo; 254 (br), Sam Dudgeon/HRW Photo.

ILLUSTRATION CREDITS

TABLE OF CONTENTS: Page viii, Tom Voss/Vicki Prentice Associates Inc. NYC; ix (cl), Christin Ranger; x (cl), Susan Sanford; xi (cl), Susan Tolonen/Wilson-Zumbo; xii (tl), Tim Spransy/Wilson-Zumbo; xiii (cl), Fred Lynch; xiv (tl), John Ceballos/Carol Guenzi Agents.

CHAPTER 1: Page 16 (all), Tom Voss/Vicki Prentice Associates Inc. NYC.

CHAPTER 2: Page 48 (all), Christin Ranger.

CHAPTER 3: Page 84 (all), Susan Sanford; 90 (b), Leslie Kell; 91 (bl), 101 (cl), HRW; 113 (cl), Leslie Kell.

CHAPTER 4: Page 118 (all), Susan Tolonen/Wilson-Zumbo.

CHAPTER 5: Page 152 (all), Tim Spransy/Wilson-Zumbo.

CHAPTER 6: Page 186 (all), Fred Lynch; 189 (cl), Ortelius Design; 199 (bl), Leslie Kell; 221 (tr), HRW; (br), Ortelius Design.

CHAPTER 7: Page 226 (all), John Ceballos/Carol Guenzi Agents; 254 (c), HRW.

QRH: Page 270 (br), Precision Graphics; 271 (b), HRW; 283 (tl), Leslie Kell.